The Wild Flowers
of the Isle of Purbeck,
Brownsea and Sandbanks

Where to find them
and help with identification of similar species

The Rev. Edward A. Pratt M.A.

Brambleby Books

The Wild Flowers of the Isle of Purbeck,
Brownsea and Sandbanks
© Edward Andrew Pratt, 2008

ISBN-13: 978 0 9553928 4 9

Published 2008 by
BRAMBLEBY BOOKS
Luton, Bedfordshire, UK
www.bramblebybooks.co.uk

*Cover design and book layout by Creatix
Front and back cover photos by Edward A. Pratt*

Printed in Germany for Brambleby Books by
AZ Druck und Datentechnik GmbH, Kempten

Dedicated to Almighty God.

God saw all that He had made, and it was very good.
(Genesis 1, verse 31)

Great are the works of the Lord; they are pondered by all who delight in them.
(Psalm 111, verse 2)

About the author

Edward A. Pratt was named after Edward A. Wilson, the doctor, biologist and artist on Scott's last expedition to the South Pole, whom his parents both admired. He was encouraged to take an interest in wild flowers as a child in Sussex and Hampshire. Whilst in the Navy at Cambridge University he became a committed Christian. Invalided out of the Navy because of his declining hearing, Ted followed the call he had heard from God to the Anglican ministry. His interest in botany was renewed when he was in country parishes in Derbyshire for seven years, living in a vicarage with a two-acre garden. It continued during nineteen years in an urban parish in Portsmouth, during part of which, on his days off, he looked after a small nature reserve for the Hampshire Wildlife Trust. Whilst in Portsmouth, he founded a charity which led to the creation of National Marriage Week. He retired with his wife Jo to Swanage in 1997. He is a botanical volunteer for the National Trust, Durlston Country Park and the RSPB, and leads wildflower walks for several organisations.

Photographs, sketch maps and drawings are by the author.

Although this book gives locations of some plants on cliffs, bogs and road verges, neither the author nor anyone involved in the publication of this book accept any responsibility for people's safety there or at any other location.

Every effort has been made to ensure that all plant locations given are on, or can be seen from, land to which the public has access, so no responsibility is accepted for anyone who leaves public land without permission.

Contents

Foreword

As I began to learn the native flora of England as a child, local floras were always very useful. I still have my very battered copy of The Rev. H. J. Riddelsdelle's *Flora of Gloucestershire*. I remember looking up the localities for many plants and then going to find them in the field. The species I found were then duly noted in my diary of the Wild Flower Society. This early exploration was certainly something that set me along the way to my career as a botanist. Many of my botanical colleagues also started out with an interest in the plants around the area where they grew up. Anything to stimulate this interest is most valuable, especially in these days of so much urbanisation. The Isle of Purbeck and Brownsea and Sandbanks are very special places with a rich flora of both native and introduced plants. I am glad to see that the non-flowering plants such as Marsh Clubmoss, Spring Quillwort, horsetails and ferns are included in this book. This new flora of such a botanically interesting area will surely provide a lot of interest for young and old alike.

In the tradition of Gilbert White and many other 19th century clergymen and of H. J. Riddelsdell, The Rev. Edward Pratt has produced a most useful, well-researched and well-illustrated account of the plants of one of the botanical treasures of Dorset. This is obviously a thorough work to which the author has dedicated much time. I hope that it will encourage many people to take a greater interest in this flora and to fight for its protection. The problem today is the destruction of habitat in so many parts of England. Alas, many of the Cotswold limestone localities where I saw some of the rarest plants, such as the Pasque Flower (*Pulsatilla vulgaris*) have now been destroyed. I am glad to see in this book that photographs of the habitats of many of the plants are provided. To protect the species for the enjoyment of future generations, it is the conservation of habitat that is so vital. This makes the relatively well-conserved Isle of Purbeck even more important. A good knowledge of the flora is often the key to conservation initiatives.

The localities of where to find many plants are given here with useful sketch maps provided, and so it is important for us to remember that we leave all these plants growing in their habitat and help to protect them rather than pick them or dig them up. Collect only memories, sketches and photographs of rare plants and when you find even the commonest of species be careful not to pull them up if you are collecting a sample for identification. I know that I will enjoy using this book. It will take me east of Lyme Regis where I live and it will bring back many childhood memories of the happy time I had studying the flora of Gloucestershire. My hope is that this book will stimulate both interest in and conservation of the wild flowers of a botanically important part of England.

Professor Sir Ghillean Prance FRS, VMH
Director of the Royal Botanic Gardens, Kew 1988-1999

Preface – One day in Purbeck

It was a sunny afternoon towards the end of my first May in Swanage when I set off along the cliff-top path towards Ballard Down. One of the grass fields on my left had just been cut for silage, and I noticed a dark object on the far side. Training my binoculars on it, I saw a fox. After a while it saw me, and sat down facing me, curling its tail around it, peacefully returning my gaze. I was too far away to be a problem, but I needed watching.

Reaching the Down I turned left along the path at its foot, away from the sea. I wanted to examine the seedcases of the small pink plants of a species of Cornsalad, which I had found in flower three weeks earlier. There are five similar species, and the seedcases are the chief point of difference between them. To my delight this was the one that I had not seen before – Hairy-fruited Cornsalad – a little species with a long name. It had already been recorded on Purbeck Limestone in several places, but not previously on Chalk in Dorset.

Next I climbed up the steep slope of the Down, looking for Early Gentians, which I had been told grew somewhere in the area. They do, chiefly near the Purbeck Way across the Down further up. I did not find them that day; but the Down was a mosaic of colour: yellow Horseshoe Vetch, blue and purple Common Milkwort, yellow Rockrose, blue Speedwell species and much more.

Earlier, I had seen gorgeous Small Copper butterflies, also a Common Blue and a Speckled Wood. But there before me, flitting among the flowers, was one that outshone them all. It was my first sight in Purbeck of a dazzling male Adonis Blue. I had seen them in some previous years on the Isle of Wight, but I had not realised that their season began quite so early. The Downs a mile to the west, either side of Ulwell, have the largest population of this species in Britain. It is the butterfly equivalent of the electric blue Kingfisher.

I turned right along the top of the down, enjoying one of the best views in southern England. To the south, Swanage is spread out at the foot of the Down, the Wealden valley runs inland to the west, and the Purbeck Limestone ridge rises beyond them both. To the east, the downland ridge leads beyond Ballard Head to 16 miles of sea, with the chalk cliffs of the Isle of Wight shining in the distance. To their right, the southern tip of the island can often be seen; to their left, the view is past Hurst Castle and up The Solent. Swinging the eyes left, one sees Hengistbury Head, Bournemouth, Sandbanks with its ferry, Poole Harbour with its islands like Brownsea, beyond them Poole itself in the north-west, and behind Poole some gentle hills. In the foreground, to the north is Studland village, and beyond it the long sands of its bay, backed by dunes and Little Sea lake, with the wonderful expanse of the National Nature Reserves of Studland and Godlingston Heaths, the latter so little visited. Riches indeed.

I walked east along the ridge, and passing the trig point, went a little south to the cliff edge, still looking for the Gentians. But what I saw put all thoughts of them out of my mind. Parts of that south-facing cliff are at an angle of 60 to 70 degrees, rather than vertical. Here and there from the cliff-top are glimpses of one of the most amazing wild rock gardens to be seen in Britain. Sheets of white Ox-eye Daisies, yellow Horseshoe Vetch, Red Valerian in three colours – red, pink and white – and pale yellow Rockroses cascade downwards to the waves breaking at the bottom. The best and safest place to view is immediately below the trig point, where the configuration of the cliffs gives a view along them eastwards. Timing is important; the colour is going by mid-June.

Continuing eastwards, now back from the cliff edge in the long grass, I came across clumps of Nottingham Catchfly, a Nationally Scarce plant, which I had heard was here in one of its very few Dorset sites. There was also plenty of Wild Cabbage, the yellow-flowered ancestor of cultivated Cabbages, Brussel Sprouts, Cauliflower and Broccoli; no-one can be sure whether Wild Cabbage is a native or introduced plant.

Turning north-east along the cliff-top, there was a place where the cliff-nesting colony of Cormorants could be seen safely with care. Inland from the path there was a long and colourful hay meadow. Further down the path, I moved right to peep over the cliff edge again. Forty metres away there was a dark object on a spur of the cliff. Training my binoculars on it, I had an excellent sight of a Peregrine Falcon. It sat there watching me for a while, twisting its head one way and another. Eventually it flew off, but without any urgency. I followed its flight with my glasses, and then suddenly there was another, flying the other way. I had seen Peregrines before, but never so close, nor had I ever seen one do its renowned power dive stooping on to prey. Perhaps one day I would ...

It was time to head for home, and I made my way back up the path and turned west at the corner. Then I saw one of the Peregrines again – stooping! It was not aiming at prey, but at a Buzzard, which had entered its territory. Down it came in a flash, but as it neared the Buzzard, the latter rolled to present its beak and talons to the challenger. Probably the Peregrine never intended to touch the larger bird, but was just warning it off. Bottoming out many feet below, the Peregrine swept up again to make another challenge. But now the Buzzard was close to the cliff, and the Peregrine, realising the danger of trying again, broke off the assault. I went on my way rejoicing.

Yes, all that really did happen on one afternoon. Yet there is much more than the chalk downs and cliffs in Purbeck, Brownsea and Sandbanks. There are Limestone hills, slopes and old quarries, ancient woods, modern forest, salt-marshes, dunes, shores, fields, hedgerows, paths, bridleways, lanes, roadsides, an abandoned village, and especially the almost deserted heaths.

Months before, someone who had heard that my wife and I were going to retire to Purbeck wrote to me of his longing to do so. 'It's my idea of heaven', he said. I hope you too enjoy this beautiful area, and that this book will add to your appreciation of it.

Introduction

Purpose and Content

The aim of this book is to encourage people of all ages, including the young, to increase their interest in wild flowers. It will enable them to discover the pleasure of finding and identifying flowers; there are no better parts of the country in which to see so many.

There is, however, much in the book which will be of interest to those who are already involved in botany, including much more precise detail of sites than in *The Flora of Dorset* by Humphry Bowen (2000), and discoveries since it was published.

The introduction provides background information on the area, ideas on how to use the book and advice on equipment, maps, plant identification and the reporting of finds. A section on flower-rich locations follows to encourage exploration of the wide range of habitats that make the area so special. The Calendar will help with enjoying outstanding displays as the year progresses, whilst there is also a list of suggested walks.

The major part of the book is the Plant List, preceded by an explanation of its layout. This list provides information on the habitats where each species may be found, time of flowering and specific public sites for less frequent species, all occasional species and almost all rare species. There is also advice on distinguishing similar species with some line drawings, all made from living or dried material, to augment illustrations in identification books.

Photographs of species have been included either to illustrate some of the special species of the area, or to show some species or hybrids not illustrated in the most-used books, or for their beauty. Sketch maps add to the information on the other maps needed.

The Area

The 'Isle of Purbeck', together with Brownsea, is part of a designated Area of Outstanding Natural Beauty. It is a privilege to live in it, especially for nature-lovers, and its natural riches need to be shared. Parts get crowded in the height of the summer, but most do not. It is an excellent area in which to get away from the pressures of life.

For the purposes of this book, the Isle of Purbeck is bounded by the River Frome in the north-west as far upstream as Holme Bridge and West Holme Manor, and by the Army Ranges to the west. It also includes roads and paths through those Ranges as far west as the Coast Path at Arish Mell, because those routes are open to the public at most weekends and holiday times. (The traditional western boundary of the Isle of Purbeck is the stream called Luckford Lake, but most of that stream's course is now within the Army Ranges.) The book also covers Brownsea Island, Sandbanks, Canford Cliffs, some of Branksome and Branksome Dene Chines, and some of Lilliput.

The sketch maps cover much of the area. They include village road names, reserves, path and bridleway numbers, parking places, a few field names and buildings used as points of reference in the Plant List, and other tracks open to the public. Open access areas increased in December 2004, when the Countryside and Rights of Way (CROW) Act (2000) came into force. They are marked in pale yellow on the Ordnance Survey (O.S.) Outdoor Leisure map and on the sketch maps. Other areas regarded as open by their owners, such as the National Trust, Natural England, the Royal Society for the Protection of Birds (RSPB) and the Dorset Wildlife Trust, have also been shaded yellow in the sketch maps; however as these are not covered by the CROW Act they may be closed at any time. Yellow shading does not mean that it is practical to access the whole of these areas; in places they may have impenetrable scrub, dangerous bog or be too steep for walking.

Richest area in Britain

Although Purbeck has only a few nationally rare species, it is the richest area for its size for native and anciently introduced species in the British Isles. During the survey for *The New Atlas of the British and Irish Flora* (Preston, Pearman & Dines, 2002), the 10km National Grid square (a hectad) SY98, which includes Wareham and Corfe Castle, was shown to have the highest total of such species of any hectad in the British Isles. The three adjoining hectads have many of those species and others besides.

Each hectad contains 25 2km squares, called tetrads. The tetrad SZ0280 (Ballard Down and North Swanage) was found in surveying for *The Flora of Dorset* (Bowen, 2000) to be the richest tetrad in Dorset, and three tetrads near it (Swanage, Studland and Durlston) were also in the top six in the county, out of 739. The main reason for this variety is the underlying geology with several widely-differing geological formations reaching the surface in a small area.

Geology and soils

Many plant species can only be found on suitable types of soil. A soil is usually described as calcareous (alkaline), neutral, or acid, though in fact there is a continuous spectrum between the most calcareous and most acid. The number of species preferring calcareous soils is greatest, those preferring acid soils least.

Soils overlying limestone, of which chalk is the purest form, are often calcareous because of the lime. However, if the limestone is not present at the surface itself, over time alkalinity diminishes, because rainwater, which is slightly acid, absorbs the lime, a process called leaching. Occasionally, a layer of acid clay above the lime produces a quite different range of flowers, as on parts of Ballard Down. Clays vary in their make-up, some being alkaline. Sandy soils will usually be the most acid, as on heaths.

All the underlying geological layers in the area are sedimentary, and were originally laid down by a gradual process of deposition of sand, mud or shells, usually under water. Some layers have been tilted towards the north by later

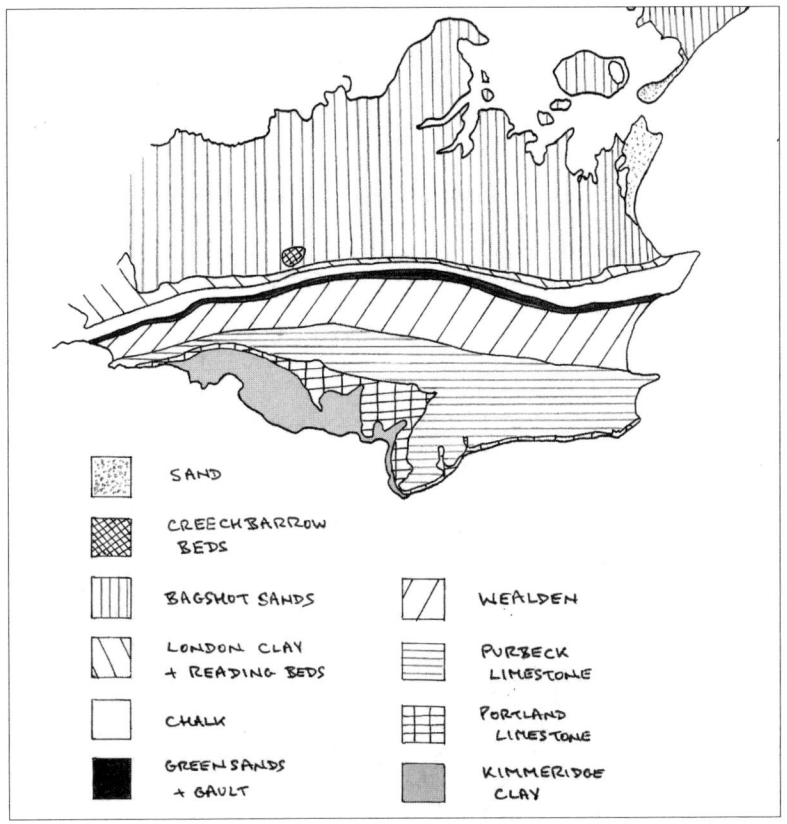

SAND

CREECHBARROW BEDS

BAGSHOT SANDS

LONDON CLAY + READING BEDS

CHALK

GREEN SANDS + GAULT

WEALDEN

PURBECK LIMESTONE

PORTLAND LIMESTONE

KIMMERIDGE CLAY

movements of the Earth's surface. This can best be seen from a boat trip north and south of Swanage Bay. Some of the chalk has been tilted right on end.

The lowest geological formation is **Kimmeridge Clay,** though it contains thin layers of rock and plenty of black shale, as seen in the cliffs of Kimmeridge Bay. It extends along the coast from under Gad Cliff to St. Aldhelm's Head, and inland between them until the higher ground is reached. Though not acid, it is botanically poor.

Above that are the **Portland and Purbeck Limestones.** These add considerably to the variety of species wherever the rock is close to the surface, which happens particularly on slopes, such as those in Durlston Country Park and The Wares, the slopes west of that Park. Being more resistant to erosion, much of these layers are higher ground, ending in cliffs. They stretch from Worbarrow Tout in the west to Peveril Point in the east. Flushes between Winspit and Belle Vue add to the interest. Woods overlying Purbeck Limestone have a rich variety of spring flowers, as in Langton West Wood and Talbot's Wood.

North of these limestones are the **Wealden** beds. These are mostly clay and some are fairly alkaline, but they also have harder bands, as seen at their west and east ends in the cliffs of Worbarrow and Swanage Bays. Most of this land is ploughable farmland, so it is very good that one area has not been cultivated but has been continuously grazed – Corfe Common. Three parts of it, West, Middle and Little East Commons, are one of the jewels in Purbeck's crown, as will be seen later.

Moving north, the layers of **Upper Greensand, Gault (clay) and Lower Greensand are** all thin in Purbeck. They do not have much influence on the flora, except for the springs, which occur at the junction of the first two of these layers. Some of these make the paths and bridleways under the south side of the downs very muddy.

Next comes the **Chalk,** which, being harder than the strata north and south of it, provides a narrow line of downs from Flower's Barrow in the west to Ballard Head in the east. The south-facing slopes are one of the richest areas for flowers, provided they are well grazed. When that ceases they get smothered with Gorse. Ballard Down is the best area, with the downs from Ulwell westwards to Knitson, and Steeple Down not far behind.

Many species are the same as on the steeper parts of the limestones to the south, but there are interesting contrasts. The following are on Purbeck and Portland Limestones but not on Chalk: Grass and Yellow Vetchlings, Italian Lords-and-ladies, Green-winged Orchid. Others are more frequent on those limestones than on Chalk: Dwarf Mouse-ear, Stars-in-grass, Chalk Milkwort, Hairy-fruited Cornsalad, Woolly Thistle, Early Spider Orchid. However, Nottingham Catchfly and Calamint are only on the Chalk, whilst Rockrose, Long-stalked Cranesbill and Marjoram are much more frequent on Chalk.

On the north-facing slopes of the Chalk are three outstanding ancient woods open to the public: the Stonehill Down group, King's Wood and Studland Wood. The displays of Ramsons in them are particularly magnificent.

Continuing north, the **Reading Beds and London Clay** are the next two formations; they are narrow and are not of great interest botanically, but clay mining has left valuable watery habitats to the north of them, west of Corfe – on the south of Creech Heath, at Kilnwood, at the Blue Pool and at Norden Heath. These decline in plant diversity if they get covered with scrub when left ungrazed and unattended.

The final principal layer is the infertile **Bagshot Sands** (also called the Poole Formation), which give rise to the large areas of heath and some acid grassland across the north of the Isle and on Brownsea. Pines have been planted over considerable areas, and north of Poole Harbour most such land is now covered by houses or gardens, except for the cliffs and chines. However, there is a gradual felling programme in the forests of Wytch, Rempstone and Newton Heaths, after which only 30% of the area will be replanted. The other 70% will revert to heathland and will form an almost continuous band of heath between Stoborough Heath in the west and Studland Heaths in the east.

Dry heath contains very few plant species; Heather, Bell Heather, Gorse, Dwarf Gorse and Bristle Bent (a grass) dominate large areas. In high summer, the plant enthusiast heads for the wet areas and is richly rewarded with Bog Asphodel, Sundews, Beak-sedges, Cross-leaved Heath, Dorset Heath (the county flower) and their hybrid Dorset Hybrid Heath and much more, especially Marsh Gentian later in the season.

The sandy grassland may be seen both by the bridleway south-eastwards from Game Copse and in the fields north of Godlingston Heath. May to early June is the best time for the small annual species which like the habitat.

There is a small area of younger age – Creech Barrow Hill. It gives its name to the **Creechbarrow Beds** of which it is composed. These are mostly infertile but do include a **Bembridge Limestone** cap.

Two recent types of accretion need to be mentioned. Firstly, soil has been carried down valleys by water which flowed more strongly at times in the past. The meadows north of Corfe either side of the Corfe River (now only a stream) lie on this **Alluvium,** and there are smaller amounts in valleys elsewhere. These are not marked on the geology map. The wettest meadows have the greatest plant diversity; some are beautiful when covered with Cuckooflower in early May.

Secondly, there are areas of **Sand** which have built up either side of the mouth of Poole Harbour. These support deep-rooted plants like Heather and Marram, which are able to survive with little surface moisture in summer, and shallow-rooted annuals, especially some members of the pea and grass families, which flower earlier.

Those who wish to read more about geology will enjoy the chapter in *The Flora of Dorset* (Bowen, 2000) and Ensom's *Geology* (1998) in the *Discover Dorset* series and Chaffey's *Purbeck Landscapes* (2006).

Flowers covered by this book

It covers 'higher' species – herbs, shrubs, trees, ferns, clubmosses and horsetails. It does not include lower plants – mosses, liverworts, algae and lichens. However, the microspecies of bramble and dandelion have been omitted; it is presumed that they will not be of interest to the large majority of readers.

The book includes species if they are visible in the wild from places, roads and paths where the public have access. Ornamental species known or thought to have been planted in wild situations are included, but not those planted in streets, public gardens, town parks, churchyards, cemeteries, caravan and car parks or by paths down Poole cliffs; however, native species occurring in all such public places are included, together with species introduced to Britain before AD1500 (early introductions).

How to use this book

Here are a few suggestions:
Visit a flower-rich location described in this book: in mid-summer you will find many more species there than are listed in the description of the location.
Make notes in your diary of the special sights listed that you would like to see from the Calendar.

Go on a suggested walk, or plan your own.

Choose a general area – for example Church Knowle. Make your own sketch map based on the one in this book, or copy the map. Go through the Plant List and mark on your map all species you would like to see, provided they are in flower at the time. Plan your route and enjoy walking it. If you find that any points of reference in the Plant List are not completely clear, when you get near them they should become so.

Choose particular species you would like to see – and visit sites for them. Do not forget that due to mowing, shading, etc. some may not be at the first chosen site.

Decide to get to grips with a particular group of species – for example, white umbellifers. Plan a tour to visit sites for different species.

Equipment

Basic
The basic equipment for finding and identifying flowers is very simple: **a map, pencils, paper, a small plastic bag and at least one identification book**. Red or yellow pencils show up well in the herbage. Some people use a notebook to make dated lists.

The plastic bag is for preserving small pieces of a plant until you have time to consult an identification book at greater leisure. If you do not have time soon, put the specimens in water or press them as described below.

Maps
The 2 1/2 inch to the mile **O. S. Explorer Outdoor Leisure map (OL15 Purbeck and South Dorset)** shows field boundaries and where public paths run in relation to them. The 2004 and later editions also show the areas open to the public under the CROW Act in pale yellow, and some alterations to public paths; it is **important** to have one of these later editions. Also the sketch maps in this book do not cover Tyneham and Holme. You will need street plans of **Swanage** (published by Amberwood Graphics) and of **Poole** (any recent edition) if looking for plants in Swanage (including most of Herston) or north of the ferry. The Philips Street Atlas of Dorset covers both.

Identification Books
It is a good idea to get to know your books to become familiar with the plant shapes and families, so you will not have to search the whole book for a plant too often. Introductions describe the parts of a flower, and may include keys to recognition. Access to more than one book has the advantage of giving you additional descriptions and illustrations.

It is important to get books which cover most of the British flowers, not just the most common species. Some may wish to begin with a book in which flowers are arranged by colour. Soon you will want to know about their arrangement in families, therefore it might be a better idea to start with a book which does that.

Opinions about the correct order in which to place families change from time to time. However, it is unusual for any one species to be moved from one family to another.

The best book, I believe, with which to start is *The Wild Flower Key* (Rose & O'Reilly, 2006). It introduces one to the fun of working through keys to identify plants. The ID Tips boxes are particularly helpful.

Many identification books do not include Clubmosses, Horsetails, Ferns, Rushes, Sedges and Grasses with other flowers. Francis Rose's beautifully produced *Colour Identification Guide to the Grasses, Sedges, Rushes and Ferns of the British Isles and North-western Europe* (1989) covers these, but it is not pocket-sized. A cheaper pocket-sized book is by Fitter, Fitter and Farrer (1984) – *Grasses, Sedges, Rushes and Ferns of Britain and Northern Europe*. The latter has a different type of key – which is equally enjoyable. Most people do not start on groups like grasses until they have had a season or two on colourful flowering plants which are more easy to identify.

The widely available book, *Wild Flowers of Britain and Ireland* by Blamey, Fitter and Fitter (2003), includes short descriptions of grasses etc., but the illustrations of them are not that good. It does have helpful small-scale distribution maps and covers many more recently introduced species than *The Wild Flower Key*. Regrettably, as The Wild Flower Society say, although *Wild Flowers of Britain and Ireland* is a useful book, there are mistakes in it, and they strongly recommend that it 'must not be relied upon alone'.

The best book for illustrations, the magnificent *Wild Flowers of Britain and Northern Europe* by Blamey and Grey-Wilson (2003), is well worth getting, but it is too heavy for use in the field.

Another outstanding book for illustrations is *The Concise British Flora in Colour* by Keble Martin (1965). Though out of print, it is usually obtainable second-hand. The original 1965 edition, has the best colour; in some later editions the colour paled.

Common trees, including all native species, are often covered by flower books. For more details, also on introduced species planted in parks, etc., consult *Tree Guide* by Johnson and More (2004), which has replaced the *Field Guide to the Trees of Britain and Northern Europe* (Mitchell, 1978), though the latter remains valuable, not least for its keys which *Tree Guide* lacks. One new feature in *Tree Guide* is the portrayal of winter twigs.

Later, with more experience, you may wish to obtain Stace's *New Flora of the British Isles* (1997), which has descriptions of all the native flowers and also of the vast majority of the introduced species found in the wild in Britain. It does not have coloured illustrations, but has drawings and photographs to help discriminate between similar species. The *Field Flora of The British Isles* (Stace, 1999) is the pocket edition, entirely arranged in keys, with fewer illustrations.

The Wild Flower Society published in 1990 *A Guide to Some Difficult Plants.* The articles are on bird seed aliens, Willows, Dandelion-like species, Rushes and Woodrushes, St. John's Worts, Heathers and Yellow Crucifers.

Beyond that there are the **Handbooks** published by the Botanical Society of the British Isles (BSBI) for particular groups of plants – **Umbellifers** (Tutin, 1980), **Docks and Knotweeds** (Lousley & Kent, 1981), **Willows and Poplars** (Meikle,

1984), **Crucifers** (Rich, 1991), **Roses** (Graham & Primavesi, 2005), **Pondweeds** (Preston, 1995), **Dandelions** (Dudman & Richards, 1997), **Sedges** (Jermy *et al.*, 2007). *Grasses* by Hubbard (1992) gives similar helpful details. A BSBI handbook on grasses is nearing completion.

Dorset Flower Books

The principal book is *The Flora of Dorset* by Bowen (2000), County Botanical Recorder for Dorset for 40 years. It opens with a chapter on geology, climate, rivers and marine erosion and continues with a chapter on the vegetation of old woodlands, grasslands, fens, heaths and bogs, and the coast. Chapter three covers the effects of man on flower distribution, including forestry, agriculture, gardening, quarrying, hedges, roads and railways. David Allen contributes a chapter on earlier Dorset botanists.

The Plant List in this Flora covers both the Higher Plants and the Lower Plants – Liverworts, Mosses, Lichens, Fungi and Algae, including Stoneworts and Seaweeds. Entries under each plant sometimes contain additional information, such as the important chemicals in them, or that they are the foodplant of a particular insect, or even that the early 19th-century Dorset poet William Barnes wrote a poem about them. Many species have a dot map showing their distribution in Dorset on a 2km-square basis.

This was Humphry Bowen's *magnum opus*. He only lived a few months after it was published. It is a book to which anyone studying flowers in the whole county needs to have access, whether in a local library, at the Visitor Centre at Durlston Country Park, or on their own shelves. It remains a most valuable and enduring monument to its author.

Earlier Floras had been written by Mansel-Pleydell (1874, 1895) and Good, who produced in 1948 the *Geographical Handbook to the Flora of Dorset*. He was particularly interested in the factors influencing the distribution of plants, using dot maps in a Flora for the first time. *A Concise Flora of Dorset* (1984) is a summary of the first part of his earlier Flora and an update of the records by Bowen. These Floras can be consulted in public libraries. Most of the plant records in them are not precise; some plant names, particularly the scientific ones, have changed since.

In 2004, Edwards and Pearman compiled the *Dorset Rare Plant Register* – 'An account of the rare, scarce and declining plants of Dorset'. This gives six- or eight-figure National Grid references for 1990 to 2003 sites for almost all such plants in Dorset (a very few sensitive sites are not so closely defined). The '*Register*' thus gives sites to within 100m or sometimes 10m, whereas Bowen's '*Flora*' gives them only to the nearest 2000m. However, some of the sites in the '*Register*' are on private land, so permission is needed from the relevant owner and/or tenant to visit them, such as those in the Isle of Purbeck which are not included in this book.

Smaller books about Dorset's flowers include *Wild Flowers of the Dorset Coast Path* (2003) and their *Wild Flower Walks in Dorset* (2006) by Peter and Margaret Cramb. Both books are pocket-sized and excellent accompaniment to a walk. *Wild Orchids of Dorset* (Jenkinson, 1991) contains colour photographs, distribution maps and interesting information for the county's 28 species.

Sedges and their Allies in Dorset (Pearman, 1994) has identification tips, 1km-square distribution maps and also a section on sedge habitats in its introduction. The *Flora of the Christchurch Area* by Woodhead (1994) has 1km-square maps, not only for Christchurch but also for some distance inland. See also the Bibliography.

Optional Extras

A **transparent ruler** makes recording map references in the field or back home easier (see below). Coloured labels on the ruler make it easier to find when dropped.

Some identification depends on the use of magnification. Binoculars can be used when turned around, although a 10x **lens** is much better and best attached to a cord around the neck. A pair of lenses can be obtained mounted together (10x and 20x is better than 8x and 15x). Hold the lens close to your eye, and move the specimen in front of the lens until it comes into focus. **Binoculars** can also be of help for seeing flowers out of reach, or for locating the next stile.

From spring to early summer it is necessary to get down on one's knees to see small species. A pair of **knee-pads** from a gardening shop may help.

For walks away from roads, you may wish to carry some basic **safety items**: first aid equipment, whistle, mobile phone, glucose tablets, torch, very thin emergency blanket.

A **stick** is helpful for testing the ground in a bog and has other uses. Straight sticks are better for wrists than ones with curved handles.

On a steep hillside a pair of Four-point Instep **Crampons**, worn with boots, can be a great help in moving about with confidence and keeping on one's feet. They can be obtained from e.g. Trailwise (see Appendix). The buckles need to go on the outside of each foot, so not to tread on any loose strap end. The straps go over the foot, then round the heel, then over the top again and finally back over the top to the buckle. Any surplus length can be cut off.

On really steep and scrubby ground, a pair of thick gardening **gloves** allows grasping of prickly plants like gorse bushes.

For plants in water, a **grapple** (waterplant drag) is helpful for collecting pieces of plant out of reach (e.g. a section of a wire clotheshanger, a length of string, and something to wind the string around when not in use will do).

Finally, although not essential to botany, a pair of small **secateurs** enables cutting of brambles, shoots and other vegetation impeding or threatening to impede paths, for which others will be grateful.

Picking

If there is a good quantity of the same plant there is rarely any harm in picking small pieces off for the purpose of identification – a flower on a short piece of stalk, an upper and a lower leaf, a ground-level runner if any and, if available, a seed head/pod/capsule. There are usually enough grasses, sedges and rushes to pick a whole stem. Do not pick orchids or Marsh Gentians though.

Under the terms of the Wildlife & Countryside Act (1981), it is illegal to dig up a plant without the permission of the landowner and even to pick certain rare or endangered plant species, although currently only three of these occur in Purbeck – Early Gentian, Early Spider Orchid and Vipersgrass.

Pressing and Drying

To preserve pieces of flowers for identification longer than they can be preserved in water, or to send them away for identification, they need to be dried. This is easiest with grasses, sedges and rushes, which can be hung upside down to dry until they stiffen. Later they make a pleasant decoration in a dry vase, and can be used for revision!

Other pieces of plant are dried by pressing them between blotting paper (best, and still available from some stationers), or tissue paper, or failing all else, paper handkerchiefs. The sheets are then placed between newspaper with a weight on top. The newspaper should be changed after a day, with a possible further change if there is a great deal of moisture in the plant. Do not apply heat or the specimen will shrivel.

For identification, a flower on its stalk is needed, together with any appendage at the base of the stalk, leaf-like or otherwise, one developed seedpod if available on its stalk, a piece of upper stem, leaves from the top and bottom of the stem, and one sideways shoot from the base of the stem if there are any. If it is an umbellifer, press an umbel. In the case of grasses, sedges, rushes and horsetails, cut off a whole stem at ground level. Really fleshy plants are not suited to drying, so take photographs of them from different angles.

Photography

Flowers often move in the slightest breeze; thus experience is needed to judge the correct shutter speed. Attention to depth of focus is also important. Sometimes you need the background out of focus, so that the flower shows up well rather than getting lost in the background vegetation. At other times the background needs to be in focus so as to show the flower in its habitat. **Do watch your feet and knees.** Many a flower in bud or in seed has been crushed by a photographer concentrating on the perfect specimen nearby.

Help with Identification

If uncertain, advice can be sought. The plant will need to be seen on site, or a few pieces of it provided as listed above. Identification from photographs is sometimes, but not always, possible. Most flowers change their colours on drying, but other features such as shapes and hairs remain, although they will shrink a little.

More knowledge can be gained by taking advantage of **organised walks**. The Dorset Flora Group was formed in 2007, and welcomes beginners on its field trips. Durlston Country Park include some flower walks in their summer programme, as does The Dorset Wildlife Trust. See Appendix for these organisations.

Another source of help are collections of dried flowers (**herbaria**) in museums, such as the Dorset County Museum and the Bournemouth Natural Science Society (see Appendix).

Reporting Finds

Please report interesting finds. There is always more to be found, both because no flower enthusiast may have been at a particular spot at that time of year before, and because seeds or roots of new species may be brought in by wind, birds or other means. More records are needed of species in this book classed as 'rare', and also of those classed as 'occasional' which have less than 10 sites given here.

Before making reports from sites beyond the area covered in this book, *The Flora of Dorset* (Bowen, 2000) is best consulted to see whether a species has been found there before.

Records of 'Dorset Scarce' or 'Dorset Rare' and 'Nationally Scarce' or 'Nationally Rare' species as in the Plant List of this book, or in the *Dorset Rare Plant Register,* are most welcome, whether or not they have been recorded previously. This will provide information on individual species distribution and persistence.

Instructions on how to make a grid reference are found on every O.S. map. Unless on a heath, it should not usually be difficult to make an accurate six-figure grid reference for one's finds using the Outdoor Leisure map. Very few hedges have been removed since the map was made. If a six-figure reference is given, it locates plants to within 100m. It is important always to follow the botanical convention of using the **lower** numbers for a reference. In the example drawn below, the easting of the plant at X is just over 947, as you will find if you measure it, so 947 is its easting. However, the northing is just under 828, so it should be recorded as 827, not 828. The map reference is therefore 947827.

An eight-figure reference if possible is even better as it locates a plant to the nearest 10m, but that is only possible if one is close to a feature on the map, or using a Global Positioning System Navigator. Please also describe the position, or make a sketch map, which will locate your find more closely, especially if your map reference does not clarify on which side of a road or field boundary your plant is.

Records should only be made of plants found 'in the wild'. Garden

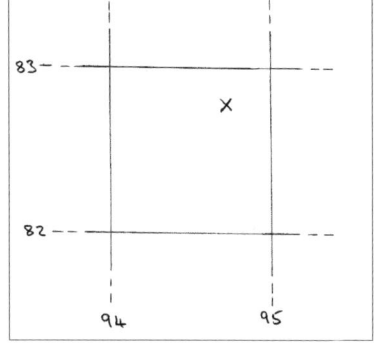

plants found in gardens, even former garden plants now growing in a garden as weeds, should not be recorded. Likewise omit trees and shrubs planted in town parks, roadsides, car and caravan parks, golf courses, churchyards, and cemeteries; do record plants, shrubs and trees planted in wild situations though. Wild native and anciently introduced plants in gardens, provided they have not been deliberately introduced, are also worth recording, as are garden plants which have escaped into pavement cracks and road gutters. Ignore those growing at the foot of a low garden wall or coming through a garden hedge.

Please send your Isle of Purbeck, Brownsea and Sandbanks records to the author (see Appendix). If the record is of a plant which might be confused with another, please also enclose one flower, upper leaf and lower leaf, and a seedpod if possible. The author will note and map records, unless they are already frequent in the immediate area, and will send them on to the County Botanical Recorders, who are appointed by the Botanical Society of the British Isles. They will note them and pass them to the Dorset Environmental Records Centre at Dorchester. If your records were obtained when you were on private land with permission, you must ask the landowner (not just the tenant) before sending them in.

Warnings

Whilst botanising is fun, there are a few hazards and other matters of which to be aware.

Cliffs are of course dangerous places. Do not go close to the edge; also do take great care on slopes above them, which should be avoided on windy days.

Chapman's Pool is best visited in a dry spell of weather. The steep clay paths to it get very slippery.

Bogs are another obvious hazard. Regarding cliffs and bogs – **look where you are putting your feet.** The author has yet to lose a boot in many happy hours by bogs; others say that if you do begin to sink it is important to forget your dignity and fall backwards so as to distribute your weight as soon as possible. Then you have to turn over and pull yourself out by holding on to tussocks until you get to firmer ground. It is best to visit bogs with a companion; it would also be sensible if each carry a mobile phone.

Road Verges are another danger area. Face the oncoming traffic whenever possible, and do not walk on roads in dull clothing at times of poor visibility.

Gates. Only climb a locked or jammed gate if there is no other way on to open access land. If you have to do so, climb over at the end nearest the hinges, so as to put less strain on them.

The RSPB and **Natural England** have both put, at some of their reserve entrances, notices which begin with words like 'This reserve is open at all times...access is by public rights of way and permissive paths.' This wording has been designed to encourage walkers to keep to the paths, if they are happy to do so. However, if the area is marked as open access on the O.S. map, there is **no** obligation to stay on paths, for example on Grange and Stoborough Heaths. You may go anywhere to look for flowers. If you accidentally flush a nesting bird, move away quickly.

Opening Hours. Tyneham and the Army Range Walks paths are only open at weekends (except for six weekends a year when the Territorial Army train) and at holiday periods. The Blue Pool, Little Pool and their Exit Road south of the railway are open from March to October. Brownsea is open from mid-March (dates vary) to October.

Hay Meadows. In a few parts of Purbeck some hay meadows are open to the public to walk around, though they are not official open access land. Three examples of the latter are meadows south of Ridge, Corfe Charity's Meadows and on Durlston Country Park. They should **not** be walked across in summer since, apart from trampling wild flowers, nesting birds may be disturbed. There is often an animal track around the edges, which can be followed, but at Durlston one is asked to use designated paths only, which are shown on the relevant sketch map in this book.

Dogs. The Kennel Club and Natural England have produced a useful leaflet *You and your dog in the countryside* which is available from visitor centres. It gives helpful advice and guidance on many different points. Dog-owners should not allow dogs to run over heaths and hay meadows from March to July, disturbing nesting birds and trampling wild flowers. Under the Countryside and Rights Of Way Act, it is a condition of access that dogs are only walked on open access areas if on a short (max. 2m) lead during those months; that should also protect them from Adder bites. Dogs should always be on short leads when passing through any area which might contain livestock.

Deer. It is best to avoid male deer in the rutting season (July to August for Roe Bucks, September to December for Sika Stags), though there will usually be no problem if they see you coming some distance away. The danger is surprising them at close quarters, especially if they are used to humans and have little fear of them. Even a Sika hind with young may charge when surprised. Back away slowly.

Parking. In unfenced areas where stock graze (for example Hartland Moor), parking is at your own risk.

Poisonous plant species. A few species have been marked as poisonous, chiefly those with poisonous berries. In addition, most members of the Buttercup and Spurge Families are poisonous, including Caper Spurge.

Digging. It is an offence to dig up a plant without the permission of the landowner. In any case removal of a wild plant to a garden often results either in it dying, or in it rapidly increasing and becoming a pest. If anyone sees wild plants like Cowslips, which they believe have been dug up, being sold at a market or car boot sale, they should take appropriate action.

Ticks and Lyme Disease. It is best to botanise in long trousers tucked into socks, especially on heaths to avoid picking up a tick. Use of insect repellent may deter them. A tick should not be confused with other bites; it can be seen as a dark spot in the middle of the mildly irritating bite. A lens will reveal its details.

If you should get one, cover it with TCP, methylated spirit, alcohol or nail varnish to encourage it to lose its grasp; after 10 min remove it gently with forceps. Disinfect the site. If you develop flu-like symptoms and a circular rash around the tick site, contact a doctor **immediately** or go to Accident and Emergency because you probably have Lyme disease; it is very important to get treatment early. The author has had several ticks but never Lyme disease; it is a greater risk in the New Forest, though it has been known to occur in Purbeck.

Enjoy yourself

Many people limit the types of flower which they try to identify when making a start, omitting in their first year the more difficult groups like white umbellifers, yellow dandelion-like plants, and families with brown or green flowers like docks and goosefoots. Grasses, sedges and rushes, too, are best left for a second or third season, apart from a few easy ones. It is good to take identification in stages and enjoy what you are doing.

Finding, identifying and recording flowers is not all there is to enjoy about them. Step back and marvel at their beauty. Then take a closer look. Discover the pale lines on the white petals of Wood Sorrel, or the wonderful spots inside a Foxglove flower.

Some Flower-rich Locations

These are given in sequence generally from west to east, with National Grid map references, denoting the centre of each area and the sketch map in this book on which each occurs. See the Plant List for precise directions to the occasional and rare species mentioned.

Steeple Down (west) – SY909816 Map 4 See Plate 1.
A splendid bank of Primroses at the south-west foot of the Down marks the start of the flowering season; Hairy Violet is out at the same time further up. Later there are many colourful downland species on view, including Rockrose, Wild Thyme, Horseshoe Vetch, Mouse-ear Hawkweed, Common Milkwort, Squinancywort, Lady's and Hedge Bedstraws, Long-stalked Cranesbill, Fairy Flax, Wild Basil, Small Scabious, Yellow-wort, Ploughman's Spikenard, a few Pyramidal Orchids and the best populations of Stars-in-grass and Meadow Fescue (a grass) in this area. In July, Harebell, Betony and Common Toadflax appear too. Park at the viewpoint to the north-west and enter from bridleway 3. Some way over a stile at the east end there are patches of Narrow-leaved Everlasting Pea growing up through low scrub near the bottom of Steeple Down (east) – see p.142. The old name for the Down, still used by some, is North Hill, but to provide a clearer location and also to avoid confusion with another North Hill this name has not been used.

Road through Great Wood (Grange Hill, Creech Hill) – SY910819 Map 3
Great Wood itself is private, but the south side of the road going through it is a good place for less common plants of ancient woods. Though fairly narrow, the road is almost straight; but bright clothing is recommended, especially in dull weather. Park at the viewpoint at the top. Mid-May is best. Sanicle, Yellow

Archangel, Woodruff, Wood Spurge and Red Currant can all be found without difficulty, and there are masses of the beautiful grass Wood Melick, as well as commoner species.

East Holme Meadows

These grazing meadows are private, but both the owner and the farmer of some have kindly agreed to the author leading an occasional walk for a small number of people, probably on a Saturday in July (to contact the author see Appendix). Flowering Rush, Tubular Water-dropwort, Yellow Water-lily, Yellow, Lake and Purple Loosestrifes, Water Forget-me-not, Marsh Woundwort, Blue Water Speedwell, Arrowhead, Marsh Ragwort, Sneezewort, Nodding Bur-marigold and Tasteless Water Pepper are among species that can usually be seen. The last named is nationally scarce. This area is one of very few British sites for Lake Loosestrife, an introduced species.

River Frome – SY920868 Map 2 See Plate 2.

An open motorboat trip on the Frome from Wareham Quay is a very pleasant experience, and at different seasons conspicuous species like Marsh-marigold, Yellow Water-lily, Water Dock and Purple Loosestrife can be enjoyed from it. However, hiring a rowing boat from the west side of South Bridge will give you more time to recognise species. Shining and Fennel Pondweeds are frequent in the water, and towards the bypass bridge (the boating limit) both Perfoliate Pondweed and Willow-leaved Pondweed (the wavy-leaved hybrid of Perfoliate and Shining Pondweeds) can be seen. Blue Water Speedwell, Common Valerian and Water Forget-me-not are on the south bank towards the bypass bridge, and there is a good population of Purple Willows nearer South Bridge and a group of Fine Osiers further upstream. Rowing is difficult when the tide is going out strongly, so if in doubt contact the boatman (see Appendix).

Priory Meadow Reserve, Wareham (Wareham and District Development Trust) – SY924871 Map 2

This small meadow just south-east of South Bridge is a good place to see some commoner plants of wet ground, together with a diverse assemblage of species on the dry bank along the north side. Fat, Greater, Least and Ivy-leaved Duckweed have been seen under the wooden bridge at the east end, and Spear-leaved Willowherb near the south-west corner. Visitors are asked to keep to the track that runs around the reserve.

Creech Heath Herpetological Conservation Trust Reserve – SY925838 Map 3 See Plate 2.

Creech Heath is an open access reserve managed for reptiles and amphibians. Much of the western and southern parts are former clay workings, with plenty of mounds and large ponds. The latter are particularly interesting for flowers. Some of them have introduced species. Water Soldier fills the large south-east pond, pink Cultivated Water-lilies are in five ponds, being particularly outstanding in Icen Barrow Pond when the sun is out, and the native White Water-lilies are in two ponds. The grass-like fern Pillwort and the buttercup-like Lesser Water-plantain are on the edge of at least two ponds. In the north-west, Marsh Gentians may be seen in two areas, and Brown Beak-sedge in one. Marsh St. John's Wort is plentiful, as is Trailing Tormentil on a track. The old clay workings and scrub make for demanding walking at times, and the edges of some ponds are soft.

The Heath is divided in two by the lorries track from Furzebrook to Creech. The north part can be entered via three paths or a track from Grange Road starting west of Icen Barrow Pond. The south part can be entered from either end of path 34, but entrance from the west is not advised because the path is undefined when it reaches the Heath.

Stonehill Down Dorset Wildlife Trust Reserve – SY926823 Map 3

The wood north of the Down was originally three: Caldecott's Wood west of the public path, Creech Wood east of that path, and Furlong's Coppice the long narrow extension to the east. Together with the Down, they are a Dorset Wildlife Trust reserve, and the woods are open access as well as the Down. Much of the ground of the woods is carpeted with Ramsons, making a wonderful sight in early May; but the leaves make slippery walking, so keep to tracks as much as possible. The woods are important for the best population of Toothwort in Purbeck, growing parasitically on Hazel roots. Most of it appears in clusters near the top edge of the woods, where Ramsons is thinner or absent.

There is usually room for one car to park on the roadside at the start of the short path into the middle of the wood (there is more room by the road at the top of the hill to the west). Entering the woods by that short path, firstly there is a good colony of Snowdrops, escaped from the cottage garden. Under 20m from the stile there are a few Goldilocks Buttercups just on the left of the path. Wood Dog Violets occur there and in other places. Further on there is Wood Melick, and halfway up small amounts of Sanicle, Woodruff and Yellow Archangel on or over the bank to the right. Golden Saxifrage is by the stream to the west. Wood Anemones are widespread, and Pignut here and there.

There are several stiles across the fence, separating the woods from the Down. Some way beyond the third stile to the east of the public path stile there are good colonies of Sanicle and Woodruff on the upper side of the wood, and a few albino Wood Dog Violets have been seen. A small part at the west end of the woods is private and not part of the reserve; the boundary is marked by posts.

The Down itself is also part of the Nature Reserve. However, the farmer has had a full agricultural tenancy dating from before the Wildlife Trust's ownership, which gives the Trust no control over the grazing. At times it is grazed too hard, so a visitor may be disappointed, but sometimes there is a good display of flowers. Despite grazing pressure there is a good colony of Autumn Gentian towards the east end on top of the Down, and earlier a good colony of Hairy Rockcress on a steep slope at the extreme east end.

Kilnwood (Kilwood) Dorset Wildlife Trust Reserve – SY937826 Map 6

This also is a Dorset Wildlife Trust reserve, and has open access. There is room for a few parked cars by the entrance at the west end. Much of the area is long-abandoned clay workings, and there are few paths, but one can get around with care, though it is also possible to get lost, at least temporarily!

The Trust is clearing vegetation from around most of the ponds gradually, and as that happens their interest increases. Lesser Water-plantain, Tufted Forget-me-not, Grey Clubrush and Rigid Hornwort are in the pond just west of the field. The reserve takes its name from Kilnwoods field, where there was once a cottage, and from Kilnwood Copse in the north, which is an area of ancient woodland; that has Early Purple Orchid, Wood Anemone, Pignut, Wood Speedwell, Hairy Woodrush and Wood Melick, some of which occur in other areas. South of that a very wet piece of wood supports the best colony of Opposite-leaved Golden Saxifrage on public access land in this area. Elsewhere there is plenty of Wood Sorrel. The central field has Heath Spotted Orchids and Common Spotted Orchids, and also Devilsbit Scabious, Betony, Ragged Robin and Meadow Thistle. More areas have just been purchased and have been added to the sketch map.

Stoborough Heath RSPB Reserve – SY928848 Map 2

This reserve chiefly consists of the two parts of Stoborough Heath between the A351, the railway and Grange Road. It is the western part between Grange Road and Furzebrook Road which is of much interest. The sketch map shows the actual paths and tracks, which differ from the O.S. map. This area can be entered by various paths and at the south end of the houses on the west side of Furzebrook Road. Path 7 in the south-west is easy to miss on the map, being so close to the railway. The low centre of the heath is the best place in this area to find the tiny pimpernel Chaffweed, along with plenty of more easily noticed Allseed, and some tiny Yellow Centaury, though these may not be found in a dry summer. Pale Dog Violet also has its largest population not far away, but flowers earlier. There is some Brown Beak-sedge in the south-west, and various garden escapes along path 5. See the Plant List for directions to all of these. The whole heath is open access, not just the paths.

Stoborough Heath National Nature Reserve (Natural England) – SY937853 Map 2

Bounded by Stoborough Green and New Road on the west, Arne Road on the north, the north part of Soldiers Road and farmland on the east, and the A351 on the south, this is partly heath and partly farmland reverting to heath. It can be entered from either end of the Dismantled Tramway (described separately below) and there is a car park east of the north end of the tramway; other entrances are from New Road and Soldiers Road. The constraint on the width of the sketch maps in this book has made it necessary, in the Plant List, to enter sites on the west side of the north end of Soldiers Road under Hartland Moor, though they are strictly Stoborough Heath.

The reserve is the best place in the area for the nationally scarce Brown Beak-sedge. There are good patches of it near the track in the north-west of the reserve south-east of the entrance from New Road; see the Plant List for other sites. Southern Marsh Orchid is found in Sandlings field. Yellow Bartsia is scattered around the north half of the reserve, especially near Soldiers Road.

Marsh Valerian and Opposite-leaved Golden Saxifrage are near the stream east of the south end of the tramway. Allseed is on the heath west of Hartland Stud. Bog Orchid has been found in the past in various places in the north-east. Meadow Thistle and Marsh Gentian are features of some of the wet areas, the latter especially west of the tramway towards its south end.

Hartland Moor National Nature Reserve (Natural England and National Trust) – SY950850 Map 5 See Plate 3.
This was the first area in England to be declared a National Nature Reserve. It includes the areas marked Middlebere Heath and South Middlebere on the O.S. map. (In this book the name South Middlebere has been used, according to National Trust practice, for the area east of Slepe Road, as marked on the sketch map. It is described separately below.)

As with all heathland, most of the interesting parts for flowers are the wet ones. On Hartland Moor there is a marked contrast between the area with more alkaline water which begins in the south-west, and the area with more acid water which begins in the north-west. The flow of both is generally eastwards and they meet in the middle.

The wet area, which begins in the south-west, is of fen vegetation. Over the whole length of the fen, Meadow Thistle and Creeping Willow occur often, and Ragged Robin, Marsh Willowherb, Tufted Forget-me-not, Oval and Flea Sedges are here and there. Certain areas have Marsh Valerian, Water-purslane, Blunt-flowered Rush, Bog Hair-grass, Early Marsh Orchid, Southern Marsh Orchid, Heath Spotted Orchid and Orchid hybrids, and Royal and Lady Ferns. Narrow-leaved Buckler Fern is in a few places, and Brown Bent is along the whole of the south side of Middle Fen.

Pillwort Pond, by the track, which crosses the middle of the fen, is particularly worth a visit. Petty Whin, Marsh Speedwell and other species of interest occur west of the track. Small-flowered Sweet Briar, Lesser Water-plantain, Blue Water-speedwell, Marsh and Fen Bedstraws, Bristle Club-rush and Pillwort are among those on or near the pond edges. Beyond the pond there are splendid bushes of Burnet Rose.

The interesting species of the area beginning in the north-west, with more acid water, can mostly be found near Soldiers Road. Sites of Bog and Dioecious Sedges, and of Nordic Bladderwort, are given in the Plant List. Brown Beak-sedge can be found in the small open area of Slepe Heath to the north. A longer walk is needed to find Bottle Sedge, another to the site for Great Sundew and its hybrid with Round-leaved Sundew, north of Great Knoll, and another later in the year to the best site for Marsh Gentian. Bog Asphodel shines brightly in most wet areas in late June and early July.

A drier area of interest is the track near and parallel to Soldiers Road, which has Allseed and Chaffweed – see p.118 and 158.

Arne Road verges – SY950864 Map 5
Several road verges, marked by coloured posts at their ends, are protected from early cutting by an agreement between Dorset Wildlife Trust and Dorset County Council. They vary in botanical value, but those of Arne Road between the north

ends of Soldiers Road and Slepe Road are the best in this area.

Limestone was used in construction, providing a contrast between the flowers of the verges and those of the heaths just beyond. The road is used by clay lorries from Arne on weekdays, but they can be heard a long way off.

The south side is best, and includes Southern Marsh Orchid, Heath Spotted Orchid, hybrids between them, which take various forms, and also Common Spotted Orchid, Twayblade, Meadow Thistle, Yellow Rattle, Fairy Flax, Creeping Willow, Zigzag Clover (towards the west end), Marsh and a few Fen Bedstraws and a clump of Royal Fern. Sedges include Common, Brown, Oval and Flea, and grasses include Quaking Grass, much Brown Bent, Downy Oat-grass and Heath Grass.

The north side has Fragrant Agrimony and Pale Flax, and grasses include Wood Melick, Meadow Fescue, Yellow Oat-grass and much Upright Brome.

The Moors RSPB Reserve (Arne Moors)
This is a large area of wet meadows south of the River Frome between Ridge and Arne, much but not all of which is managed by the RSPB as a closed reserve to protect breeding birds. There is usually a guided walk in July to see the interesting plants, including Vipersgrass, Whorled Caraway, Tubular Water-dropwort, Unbranched Bur-reed, Least Bur-reed (some years), Opposite-leaved Pondweed, Great Fen-sedge, Cyperus Sedge and Long-stalked Yellow Sedge. For walk details contact the RSPB (see Appendix). Permission and directions to see Vipersgrass is given to individuals on request in June. Wellington boots are essential in all weathers.

South Middlebere (National Trust) – SY965853 Map 5
This is an open area **east** of Slepe Road opposite the words 'South Middlebere' printed to the west of the road on the O.S. map. It is a very successful area of heathland restoration, and particularly good for small clovers in early summer. Rough Clover and Slender Trefoil are near the gate by the road at the south-west end; the latter is widespread further north. Subterranean Clover has one of its sites 30m north where the bridleway meets the heath, and the clovers' relative Birdsfoot is there too. It is also plentiful on some other parts of the area. Clustered Clover is about 20m further along the bridleway. Lesser Trefoil and Hop Trefoil are widespread on the heath. Little Mouse-ear is another species that may be found near tracks. As the bridleway approaches White House Wood, look out for the tiny Mossy Stonecrop, which turns red in May. Just beyond the north-west corner of the wood, opposite a field gate, Suffocated, Subterranean and Clustered Clovers and Slender Trefoil grow close together. Further north on the south-west facing slopes Haresfoot Clover is here and there.

Meadows west of Corfe River – SY966841 Map 5A(large scale) See Plate 4.
These meadows stretch from Sharford Bridge in the north to two south of Scotland Barn. They belong either to The National Trust or to Corfe Charity, and are all managed by The Trust. Path 80 and bridleway 3 run through the meadows. The Trust and the Charity kindly allow people to walk around the edges of those meadows with names on Map 5A, to look for flowers and shrub

entirely at their own risk. The meadow south-west of Sharford Bridge has a splendid display of flowers: Cuckooflower in late spring, and the broad-headed form of Common Knapweed in July, and there is much else. Along the north side of this field Greater and Lesser Pond Sedges grow together by bridleway 4, affording the opportunity for comparison of these two species. Following bridleway 3 southwards, there is a patch of Yellow Loosestrife at the north end of the next field. Alternatively, following the bank of the Corfe River southwards, there are patches of Smooth Brome (grass) near it, and Almond Willows and Osiers here and there. Corky-fruited Water-dropwort is a feature of most of the meadows. At the south end, the last meadow, Paddle Dock, is wet in places, with a range of marsh species.

Corfe Castle (National Trust) – SY959823 Map 11
The castle mound outside the walls is freely open for exploration, though many may be put off by its steepness. Four-point crampons are useful. Paths made by livestock make it easier to get around in some places. The mound provides interesting examples of plant preferences. Wild Clary and Leer's Sedge dominate large areas of the warmest slope on the south-west side or nearby inside the castle. Also Borage can sometimes be found. Early in the year, Alexanders is a feature of that area. These last two species may be descendents of plants in cultivation in medieval times. Downy Oat-grass is found scattered all round the mound, just as Pellitory-of-the-wall grows all round the walls. Pignut is only frequent on the north side, and Early Purple Orchid and Common Spotted Orchid occur on both the north side and the west end of the north-west side. The colony of Hairy-fruited Cornsalad faces east, as does Pale St. John's Wort and most of the Hairy Tare. Marjoram takes advantage of areas of thin soil, particularly on the south-west.

Inside the castle there is plenty of Calamint, some Ivy Broomrape beyond the gateway to the West Bailey on the left, also usually a few plants of Great Prickly Lettuce on and/or under the bridge just before that gateway, and the best Isle of Purbeck colony of Hairy Rockcress on ruins north of the keep.

Corfe Common (National Trust) – SY960810 Map 11 See Plate 4.
This is a wonderful area of neutral grassland, presumably continuously grazed for centuries, and so has a rich diversity of flowers, particularly in the wetter parts (Wellingtons needed). It is divided into four by roads and railway – West, Middle, Little East and Big East Commons. 'Corfe Common' refers to the whole. Big East Common was agriculturally improved in the past and so became of less interest for wild flowers, however it is now gradually regaining species.

Many of the wetter areas have Southern Marsh Orchid, some have Early Marsh Orchid, and Heath Spotted Orchid is very widespread; hybrids of various forms between any two of these three can be found. Marsh Ragwort appears later in the same areas and hybridises with Common Ragwort. Some of the wettest areas have Ragged Robin, and later Marsh St. John's Wort. Slightly damp parts are beautified by Lousewort in May.

Sedges are a feature; at least 19 species can be found: Lesser Pond, Green-ribbed, Spring, Grey, Star, Glaucous, Hairy, Tawny, Common, False Fox, Oval, Carnation, Greater Tussock, Flea, Remote, Bottle, Pendulous, Wood and Common Yellow Sedges. It is not always easy to describe plant sites on the Commons for lack of reference points; there are many more than in the Plant List.

West Common. The higher and drier parts have a splendid spread of Bluebells, and later Pignut, and also Heath Speedwell and Bitter Vetch here and there in early summer. There are large areas of English Sticky Eyebright between First and Second Valleys and on the opposite side of the unclassified road. Heath Grass is plentiful by dry tracks. Later in summer, there are patches of Slender St. John's Wort and Harebells, with much Betony, and later still Saw-wort. Before the last three are over, large amounts of Devilsbit Scabious begin to bloom in August. Chamomile is a particular treasure of the Common; most of Dorset's population of this declining species is here, particularly along and near bridleway 36 on West Common, though some of its flowers are grazed.

The north-west wet edges of West Common are rich in species. Greater Tussock Sedge has made its home there, together with Yellow Iris, Common Valerian (not common generally), Marsh Valerian, Purple Loosestrife, Bog Asphodel, Bogbean, Water Horsetail, Marsh Lousewort (probably the best place in Dorset for it) and much else.

Middle Common has a higher and drier part with similarities to those on West Common, including a small amount of English Sticky Eyebright. The north-facing wet lower slope south of the pond is an excellent area for learning to identify plants of wet ground without risk of sinking into it. Do not miss the plants by the little stream which runs down the middle. The pond itself has been plagued by the invasive aliens New Zealand Pigmyweed and Parrot's Feather, which The National Trust have been controlling, but Water Plantain competes well with them. Recently, Water Whorl-grass and small amounts of Thread-leaved Water-crowfoot and Opposite-leaved Pondweed have (re)appeared. The area surrounding the pond holds plenty of interest. There is an area of Chamomile to the east of it.

South-west valley has good amounts of Pale Butterwort and Bog Pimpernel, also Fine-leaved Sheep's Fescue, Bristle Club-rush and Common Yellow and Tawny Sedges, and the hybrid between the last two. (Rather more of that hybrid can be found in the south-east valley of West Common.)

Little East Common. Another good area is between the streams and south-east of the bridleway on the north-east side of Little East Common, which has plenty of Yellow Iris, some Marsh Cinquefoil, various sedges, and a great deal more. The shallow northern stream is a particular delight. On the way to it on the bridleway, under the hedge on its north side, four umbellifers flower in late June in close proximity, allowing comparison: Hogweed, Upright Hedge Parsley, Ground Elder and Corky-fruited Water-dropwort.

Byle Copse (National Trust) – SY966816 Map 11

This narrow strip of woodland between the railway and the east side of Corfe village is part of Little East Common. It is divided in two by a small open area; the south part of woodland is the longer one. The stream running along its west side is called the Byle Brook. This woodland apparently has no name. For future reference in the book, the author has called it Byle Copse.

For its size it has a remarkable variety of woodland species. Few species which clearly indicate that it is ancient are present, but nor does it look recent. Wood Anemone, Moschatel, Bluebell, Common Valerian, Wood Speedwell, Tutsan, Trailing St. John's Wort, Three-nerved Sandwort, Common Dog Violet, Raspberry, Gooseberry, Red and Black Currants are all there, some in small quantity. Woodruff is the clearest indication of antiquity. There are also garden escapes by the stream adjacent to the gardens on the other side of it. The path through the copse is narrow – carrying secateurs can be helpful.

East Hill Steps – SY961822, and Purbeck Way SY968821 Map 11
Over 300 steps take you to the top of East Hill from Sandy Hill Lane, beginning just east of the rail bridge. The first fifty steps through scrub are old, and, at the time of writing, in need of some repair; the rest are through more open hillside and are recent. Ascending them in early July there is a wealth of species to be seen: white ones: Daisy, Ox-eye Daisy, Wild Carrot, White Clover, Bramble, Burnet-saxifrage; yellow ones: Lady's Bedstraw, Pale and Perforate St. John's Worts, Birdsfoot Trefoil, Catsear, Smooth Hawksbeard, Hop and Lesser Trefoils, Black Medick, Fennel, Common Toadflax; blue ones: Small Scabious, Common Milkwort, Selfheal; purple ones: Spear and Musk Thistles; pink ones: Field Convolvulus, Marjoram, Red Clover. Nit Grass may be seen near the top and there are many other grasses. The view from the top is magnificent. There is parking for a few cars in the lane, and a free car park at Challow.

For the less energetic, the gradual ascent up the Purbeck Way from Sandy Hill Lane near Challow car park to the radio mast is nearly as good for flowers, particularly in its east half.

Bridleway 14 from Brenscombe Hill to B3351 – SY985820 Maps 13 and 14
This is a route of considerable antiquity. It is part of the old route from Corfe to Rempstone, dating from before the B3351. It is sometimes called Forest Lane, though that name is now often reserved for its continuation as a metalled lane to the north.

The sides of the south-west half, in some places cut deeply out of the Down, are beautiful sites for species characteristic of ancient woodlands. Wood Anemones and Wood Spurge flower here in March. In late March and the first half of April this and the northern, lower half of the bridleway are one of the best sites in Purbeck for Wood Dog Violet. In late April and early May, displays of Bluebells and Ramsons can be seen by both parts of the bridleway and also Wood Sorrel and Three-nerved Sandwort near the top. Vast sheets of Bluebells can be seen from the bridleway in Brenscombe Wood, but their contrasting display on the downland off bridleway 15, which branches off to the south-east, is even more dramatic.

In May, the pretty grass Wood Melick flowers on the banks of bridleway 14, as do Wood Sanicle and Woodruff. Later in May, in one place by the bridleway, the tall stately Wood Millet can be seen, and in another Twayblades. Later in summer, Wall Lettuce, Hairy St. John's-wort and Nettle-leaved Bellflower add to the riches. This is a place to allow your imagination to slip back in time to the 18th century or earlier, and expect a donkey-cart to come round the next bend, rumbling over the worn chalk surface.

Brenscombe Heath (South) – SY986828 Map 10
This is south of Bushey Lane and west of Rempstone Farm; it is entered at its north-east corner. The chief feature is the larger artificial pond, with good populations of Hybrid Reedmace, Grey Bulrush and Curled Pondweed, and of the attractive introductions Pickerelweed and a pink Water-lily. Many usual plants of wet heath are elsewhere on this heath; the north-west corner is good for Marsh Gentian.

Langton West Wood – SY998794 and Talbot's Wood – SY991794 (National Trust) Map 14
The National Trust does not manage these woods for public access, but the public may visit them to view flowers, shrubs and trees **entirely at their own risk.** Langton West Wood is one of the best ancient woods in the area, with a splendidly colourful display of spring flowers, notably Bluebells, Primroses, Wood Anemones, Lesser Celandines, Early Purple Orchids, Common and Wood Dog Violets, Barren Strawberry and Greater Stitchwort. Spurge Laurel plants are near the west end of the valley. Later, a good range of woodland grasses is in flower, and six species of St. John's Wort have been found flowering within or close to the outside of the wood on the same day. Most of these can be seen from the rides, which are wet in places. By the east ride there is an unusual hybrid Crab x Domestic Apple. The easiest way to get into the wood is through one of the two gates on the south side from the path which runs outside of it. The part north of the main west-east stream is not ancient.

There is an interesting shrubby area east of the wood through which path 44 runs diagonally. It is shown as wood on the O.S. map. It has the best population of False Oxlip, and Great Burdock and a few of both Pale and Square-stalked St. John's Worts are found there later in the year.

At first, Talbot's Wood appears to be ancient. It has Wood Anemone and Wood Sedge scattered throughout, Thin-spiked Wood Sedge along the damper north side, and Wood Millet and Wood Vetch (the latter not appearing recently), all of which are among the most reliable Ancient Woodland Indicator Species. It also has Bluebell, Ramsons, Moschatel, Dog's Mercury, Early Dog Violet and Primrose, all of which are associated with ancient woodland, but which are also found in other habitats. The well-grown oaks also give it a feeling of antiquity. However, it does not appear as a wood on the 1840s Tithe Map, apart from the small piece south of Wilkswood Farm. Measuring the oaks reveals that, apart from those on the boundaries, only one is over 160 years old. The wood is sited on old quarries, as is soon evident from the ground. It must have grown naturally during the second half of the 19th century when quarrying had ceased. The proximity of Langton West Wood upstream and to windward provided a good source of seeds. There is also a hybrid Crab x

Domestic Apple in this wood – see p.134. Entrance is from Crack Lane, by the cemetery vehicular entrance.

The (Purbeck) Wares (almost all National Trust) – SZ000770 Maps 15 and 16 See Plate 5.

Ware is a Saxon word for an area of rough grazing. Some of the rough slopes from Seacombe eastwards are called Wares or Wears on the 1840s Tithe Maps (see the sketch maps), and so The Wares is now used to describe the area from Seacombe to Belle Vue. The slope west of Dancing Ledge Ware, Scratch Arse Ware, was named after one of the abandoned cliff quarries below it, which the quarrymen used to enter on their backsides. For consistency the word Ware has been added to some areas in the east which lacked it. In the west, the areas of Hedbury Rough Ground and Hedbury Bottom now lack delineation, so they have been combined as Hedbury Ware.

The Wares' slopes are similar to the slopes of Durlston Country Park (below), but they have two extra features. Firstly, there are several accessible cliff quarries with Wild Cabbage, Brookweed, and Greater Sea-spurrey, which are difficult to see on Durlston, and Distant Sedge in two quarries. Secondly, in the sloping fields there are a number of places where water emerges from the ground and creates small wet areas (flushes); these have distinctive flowers. Brookweed, Hoary Willowherb, Square-stalked St. John's Wort and Hairy Sedge occur in many of them, in too many sites to list separately in the Plant List. Wild Celery and Bog Pimpernel are in some flushes.

In common with Durlston many dry areas with thin soil support Bee Orchids, Lesser Centaury, Small Scabious and Autumn Lady's-tresses. Stars-in-grass occurs here and there, and good colonies of Green-winged Orchid and Early Gentian. Autumn Gentian occurs at five sites. But the most important feature of these areas are the nine sites for the little Hairy-fruited Cornsalad, a national rarity, flowering in the first half of May.

Well over 10,000 of the nationally scarce Early Spider Orchid flower in the Wares every year, at their best in late April and early May; this is one of the largest population in Britain. The best areas are the Wares either side of Dancing Ledge Ware.

The third most important species on the Wares, on a national basis, is Nit Grass, one of our smallest grasses, which is visible in a few places from July. However, botanists who divide Rock Sea-lavenders into microspecies will tell you that the rarest species here is a Rock Sea-lavender, *Limonium dodartiforme*, which is found in the world only in Dorset, between Portland and Durlston. There may even be a second microspecies totally confined to this area, if the larger-leaved plants present are judged to be a separate one.

Other nationally scarce plants present are Wild Cabbage, Dwarf Mouse-ear (in the east half), Golden Samphire, Carrot Broomrape, Curved Hard-grass (on some cliff quarry floors), and Slender Tare (in the west half). Colonies of Italian Lords-and-ladies nestle under the east side of half the north-south stone walls and elsewhere, but produce few flowers. All these, apart from the Cornsalad, can also be seen at Durlston.

Wasp Orchids, which are a variety of Bee Orchid, may be found with some of the Bee Orchid colonies, especially in the west half of The Wares, in mid-June. This is the best area for Wasp Orchids in Britain.

If ever an area deserved, but has not yet been given, National Nature Reserve status it is this one.

Access to the Wares involves a good walk, either from Worth Matravers, or from the small car park at the end of Durnford Drove in Langton Matravers, through Durlston Country Park, or by one of several other paths running south in between these.

King's Wood (National Trust) – SZ001816 Map 18

For a visit in the first week in May, you can park your car with care on the verge of the B3351 nearly opposite the start of bridleway 16 (not path 16). Enjoy the view of Bluebells in the private plantation of Western Hemlock conifers on your right as you start up the bridleway. Carry on up the slope for 125m and bear left (ignoring the private track to the right). Soon you will come to the National Trust sign at the entrance to King's Wood. You are unlikely to forget the sight you will see on your left in another 20m.

But that is not all King's Wood and its approach has to offer. You may have already noticed Wood Sorrel, Sanicle, Hairy Woodrush, Wood Dog Violet and the little white Three-nerved Sandwort by the first part of the bridleway. A little further on you will find Wood Spurge. There is a good display of Bluebells at the top of the wood. See the Plant List for directions to Small-leaved Lime, Yellow Archangel and Opposite-leaved Golden Saxifrage. The triangular section of wood south-west of the west bridleway is not old, but ancient woodland indicator species have spread to it from the main area of the wood.

Kingswood Bog – SZ004826 Map 18

This area west of the golf course can be entered from the forest track on its north side, though it needs a good walk to get there. Along with other bog species, it has Heath Spotted Orchids, Early Marsh Orchids and hybrids between them, and much Dioecious Sedge. Directions to those are found in the Plant List. Other species include Dorset Heath, Dorset Hybrid Heath, Pale Butterwort, Meadow Thistle, Bog Pimpernel, Lesser Skullcap, Bogbean, Bog Stitchwort, Water Forget-me-not, and Common Sedge (not common). Being remote and also soft underfoot in places, it is advisable to go with company.

Newton Heath (Rempstone Forest) bridleway 34 – SZ002845 Map 13 See Plate 5.

Bridleway 34 was once part of a clay tramway, and a quantity of limestone was used in the construction. Its strengthening as part of the BP access road, or 'oil road' as it is called in the Plant List, presumably involved bringing in yet more limestone, and certainly there is plenty of interest on its verges. One of the best colonies of Southern Marsh Orchid occurs on both sides of the bridleway south-east of Claywell (800 plants one year), and further north-east among other species Blue Fleabane is plentiful and the native Golden Rod extends over more than 100m of verge, Lesser Centuary is here and there, and Leafy Rush,

Dotted Sedge and Black Spleenwort occur in small quantities – see the Plant List for sites.

Townsend Dorset Wildlife Trust Reserve – SZ024781 Map 21A

Easy to reach on the south edge of Swanage, this is at its best in May when four nationally rare or scarce species can be seen: Hairy-fruited Cornsalad on a couple of anthills and a nearby bank, Early Spider Orchid, Dwarf Mouse-ear and Early Gentian, together with tiny Early Forget-me-not and Rue-leaved Saxifrage, Hairy Violet and Early Purple Orchid, some within a splendid display of Cowslip.

Later in the summer, the grazing leaves it rather untidy, but there is still plenty of colour, except in a dry period, and plenty to see, not least the hybrid between Burnet Rose and Dog Rose. A rather different feature are the escaped Cotoneasters; five species are represented near the north edge, presumably bird-sown. Townsend is a maze of paths and scrub, and it takes several visits to learn the ways around; the sketch map will help.

King George's Field (north side) (Swanage Town Council) – SZ024791 Swanage Street Map

A small part of the area marked Playing Fields on the Swanage Map is good to visit for summer flowers. Starting from the main car park, go past both the skate park and the children's play area. You come first to an area of reeds through which a walkway has been made. Some way beyond that, there is an area where the grass is left unmown during summer months, apart from paths, which enable you to get close to a splendid display of wild flowers. Do keep to the paths. The old cemetery south of the car park is also left partly unmown in the summer, with frequent mown paths and is worth a visit.

Durlston Country Park (Dorset County Council) – SZ028773 Map 21 See Plate 6.

Durlston has over 500 species in a relatively small area, and so is a very good place to begin finding flowers at any time from spring to early autumn. The two types of habitat that are outstanding are the rough grassy slopes down to the Coast Path and the flat meadows above the slopes.

Most of the nationally scarce species present are listed in the description of The Purbeck Wares above, but Durlston is much more easily accessible. It also has much more Yellow Vetchling around meadow edges, and has Toothed Medick in the grass outside the present site of The Lookout café. Lists of species present can be purchased cheaply from the Visitor Centre; there are also separate ones for grasses/sedges/ rushes/ferns and for trees/shrubs. The Centre has maps that can be copied showing where the less common interesting species can be found. The car park fee is money well spent, but the area can be reached from Swanage on foot, though that will leave less time to explore.

Early Spider Orchid is the first of nine species of orchid to flower. Nit Grass appears regularly in July (ask at the Centre for directions). In May, it is a good place to see Early Gentian; an easy spot is on the bank between the two tall nautical mile markers. The meadows should be visited at intervals in the summer to see their various glorious displays (see the Calendar); keep to the designated paths in them. Visit one morning in early June to see the beautiful Pale Flax before it begins to drop its petals around midday.

When visiting the Johnston Pond keep a look out for adders. Note that Lighthouse Road is the north-south road from Durlston Road to the car parks, not the tarmac road from the car parks to the lighthouse, which is not open to public motor traffic but is a public footpath with designated path number.

Much of the Country Park may soon become a National Nature Reserve.

Godlingston Heath and Studland Heath National Nature Reserves (National Trust) – SZ023836 Maps 17 and 19 See Plate 6 and back cover.

In 1948, Good wrote '… during a biological study of the South Haven Peninsular (Studland Heath) made before the late war some 450 species of vascular plants…were noted for this area of something under one-and-a-half square miles.' Studland Heath is not quite so rich today, as birch, sallow and rhododendron have shaded out a number of species, but this area and its neighbouring Godlingston Heath are deservedly National Nature Reserves, for their reptiles, birds and dragonflies at least as much as for their flowers. The dune system is the second largest in England, only Braunton Burrows in Devon is larger.

'Studland Heath' is **printed at the wrong place** on many maps, including the O.S. map. It is the area north of Pipley Bridge and east of Ferry Road, and the area west of Ferry Road, east of Brand's Bay, and north of the east end of the bridleway to Greenland. The area south-west of that and west of Ferry Road, where 'Studland Heath' is printed, is part of Godlingston Heath.

As with all heaths it is the wet areas on both heaths which provide the greatest diversity of plants. The dry areas are a marvellous spectacle when Bell Heather and Heather bloom in July and August, with Dwarf Gorse and a few Western Gorse providing a contrast, but the total of species is small. The wet areas are marked by pink Cross-leaved Heath, and sometimes by Dorset Heath, though the latter is much less frequent than in the Hartland Moor area. Brilliant golden patches of Bog Asphodel show up in early July, and closer examination will reveal all three species of Sundew in some places, and infrequently the tiny Pale Butterwort, another insect-eating plant. Heath Spotted Orchid is in a few areas, and in late August and September the beautiful blue of Marsh Gentian can be seen above the edges of bogs.

Note that there is a nudists' area along one section of Studland Bay and in the dunes behind it, marked by green-topped posts. The dry area around Black Down in the south-east of Godlingston Heath is best avoided as it is covered with small trenches hidden under the heather, probably made by the Home Guard in the Second World War.

Despite the yellow shading on the O.S. map, the areas of the Golf Course used for golf are **not** open access. However, areas north of the bridleways along the north side of the course to Kingswood Heath in the north-west and to the Agglestone in the north-east are not used for golf, except for the Greenkeepers' Depot and the track leading to it.

Six parts of the Heaths are singled out for special mention as below. See also several references in the Calendar of special sights.

North end of Godlingston Heath (National Trust) – SZ022845 Map 17

Several different kinds of habitat within a small area make this well worth a visit. Park on the west side of the road, just south of bridleway 36. Not far from Ferry Road Short-haired Eyebright is on the north-east verge of the bridleway to Greenland, and there is a hybrid Dog Rose/Sweet Briar near them on the opposite side.

The rushy corner of Brands Bay to the north can be negotiated with care, and includes Brookweed, Sea Arrow-grass, Sea Plantain, Slender Spike-rush, Slender Club-rush, Parsley Water-dropwort, and much Blunt-flowered Rush.

Further along the bridleway there is a gate leading to fields on the north side. The National Trust does not manage these fields for public access, but one may enter those east of the north-south fence shown on the sketch map **entirely at one's own risk.** The best site is in the middle of a fenced square area 150m north of the gate. Where the ground is disturbed by rabbits there is Annual Knawel, Smooth Catsear, Hairy Birdsfoot Trefoil, Birdsfoot, and Clustered, Knotted, Haresfoot and Subterranean Clovers. Hoary Cinquefoil appears some years. Blinks, Slender Trefoil and Strawberry Clover may be found in fields nearer the bridleway.

Lying south of the bridleway, Brand's Bog (public open access) is best approached through the heath gate by the parking place. The best area is roughly north-south just before the field fence to the west. As well as the usual bog species, Lesser Bladderwort can be seen there in August. There is a small amount of Brown Beak-sedge in one very small pool (see Plant List), and a much larger amount of Dorset Hybrid Heath.

Spur Bog (National Trust) – SZ027843 Map 19

This is on the east side of Ferry Road and is one of the richest and certainly the most accessible bog in the area. It is entered from the north-west corner after parking just south of bridleway 36. Dorset Heath is close to the 'entrance', about 25m east of the road. Bog Asphodel makes a dazzling display in early July on the west side. Round-leaved Sundew, Oblong-leaved Sundew, Great Sundew and its hybrid with Round-leaved Sundew are all down the middle of the bog. Marsh Gentian occurs around the edges, sometimes with an albino or semi-albino towards the south-east. A patch of Brown Beak-sedge is halfway along the north side; a small amount more is at the west of two sites for Marsh Clubmoss. Heath Spotted Orchids and Early Marsh Orchids and their hybrids are plentiful, and a few Common Spotted Orchids are by the entrance.

Primrose Way (National Trust) – SZ029842 Map 19 See Plate 7.

As shown on the sketch map, this is a circular walk, wet in places. It begins on the east side of Ferry Road at the gate, which is a black bar. Follow the path in for about 100m until there is a metal sheet on the ground about 20m to your left. Turn right for the shorter walk to the Primroses, going up a bank after 15m and then keeping left of a pile of logs. The Primroses begin about 125m further on, after the path has taken a left turn, and continue for 200m. If you miss the path and find yourself approaching Little Sea, continue on the path which bears right and carry on for about 100m to the other end of the Primroses.

Little Sea Beaches (National Trust) – SZ031843 Map 19

Most of the edges of Little Sea are banks, but along the southern half of the east side a few years ago the National Trust recreated six short sandy beaches for study (not for bathing or sandcastles). Six-stamened Waterwort, an uncommon plant, is the most interesting species here; it has been found in two different forms, one on the beach, when the water level is low, the other floating; a lens is needed for viewing its tiny red flowers. Other species on several beaches include Bog Pimpernel, Lesser Skullcap, Gypsywort, Marsh St. John's Wort and Birdsfoot. Many leaves of Shoreweed are washed up on the beaches, along with some strands of Perfoliate and Blunt-leaved Pondweeds, Alternate-leaved Water-milfoil and Nuttall's Waterweed. However, the beaches are getting covered with rushes.

War Hill (National Trust) – SZ032845 Map 19

This blown-up wartime defensive position on Studland Heath consisting at first sight just of pieces of concrete and wire on a mound, with an outlying site 50m north-west, is a botanical treasure store. It is not marked on the O.S. map. It is about 1km north of Knoll car park and is reached by a track through the dunes, which at some point skirts the east shore of Little Sea. Its value is in the limestone provided by the concrete in the midst of acid sandy heathland. During the past 60 or more years, seeds blown by the wind or carried by fauna have led to the establishment in a very limited area of numerous species not found nearby. There are several other intact or destroyed defensive positions on Studland and Godlingston Heaths, but none with such rich assemblages of plants.

Several of the flowers are small, so hands-and-knees botany is needed. They include Thyme-leaved Sandwort, Changing Forget-me-not, Wall Speedwell, Little Mouse-ear, Sea Mouse-ear, and Small Cudweed. Common Cudweed (not common) is also there. There are two Dorset Scarce species, Bearded Fescue and Smooth Catsear, on the north-west outlier, together with Blue Fleabane. The species especially dependent on limestone are Ploughman's Spikenard and Carline, Dwarf and Musk Thistles, which are easy to see.

War Hill is best visited in spring or early summer, but not after dry weather because the small plants perish quickly.

Knoll Beach Dunes (National Trust) – SZ033838 Map 19 See Plate 7.

Several areas from the Knoll Beach café and shop northwards have been fenced off to prevent erosion and to preserve plants and Sand Lizards. In the first one, between the café and the sea, Prickly Saltwort, a species which was on the decline not long ago, has appeared in recent years. By tracks immediately north of the car park the little English Stonecrop and the small grasses Dune Fescue and Bearded Fescue grow. By the 'Heather Walk' track about 300m further north the tiny plants Mossy Stonecrop and Allseed can also be found. Crossing to the fore-dunes to the east, Sea Bindweed is a more conspicuous plant, extending for a length of 200m, with more further north. Returning to the car parks, Hairy Birdsfoot Trefoil can be found on the south edge of the little triangular area between the upper north car park entrance and the small area for coaches. All these eight species qualify for inclusion in the *Dorset Rare Plant Register*.

Ballard Down (National Trust) – SZ034813 Map 20 See Plate 7.

This comprises all the downland from the Swanage to Studland road at the west end to Ballard Head (Point), and includes the area marked Studland Hill on the O.S. map. In 1966, Good wrote 'Nowhere else in the whole county is there a view so fine as that looking north ...' and east and south as well! It is also the richest piece of chalk down in Purbeck for wild flowers. The open parts of the south slopes are a glory to see in summer with a host of colourful species. Rockrose is a particular feature. Here and there are less common ones in their season, including Early Purple Orchid, Early and Autumn Gentians, Autumn Lady's-tresses, Long-stalked Cranesbill, Milk Thistle, Hairy-fruited Cornsalad, Small Scabious, Nit Grass, Wild Basil, Common Calamint and Common Gromwell (both uncommon species). On the top of the Down there is a layer of acid soil in a few places, giving rise to a different range of plants: Bell Heather in three areas, Western Gorse in two, and also Bristle Bent, Heath Milkwort, Sheep's Sorrel and Heath Bedstraw. The largest of these areas is about 175m south-east of the obelisk.

At the eastern end of the Down, south of the fence, Nottingham Catchfly and Wild Cabbage occur here and there in the long grass. A careful look down the cliff slopes in late May or early June is commended.

Clayton Meadow (National Trust) – SZ036817 Map 20

This small meadow in the Glebeland Estate was given to the National Trust as an example of unploughed downland vegetation. The Estate Committee kindly allow the public to walk to it from the bridleway on the east side of the Estate on the private roads (but not to drive on them). Please follow a beaten path near the edge of the meadow, or if there is none make one.

Over 100 species have been recorded in this small area, including Common Spotted and Pyramidal Orchids, Twayblade, Dwarf Thistle, Rough Hawkbit, Yellow Rattle, Sweet, Hairy and Common Dog Violets, Field Scabious, Hedge and Lady's Bedstraws, Spring and Glaucous Sedges. There are also remnants of garden species around the edges.

Brownsea (National Trust) – SZ020880 Map 22 See Plate 8.

The island is chiefly visited for its birds and Red Squirrels, but it is a good place to learn to identify native and introduced trees, particularly south of the church, and in Venetia Park west of The Villa. Sea Storksbill is another feature, occurring near several shores and by several paths which are not close to the shore; it has not been seen elsewhere in the area recently. Changing Forget-me-not is here and there in grassy areas. The low wall north-west of the Visitor Centre is host to interesting small species, as is both the grassland south-east of the churchyard and the café lawn near the Landing Pier. Heath Speedwell often appears in open areas in the south half of the island. Bog Pimpernel can be found in places by the track west of The Villa.

Along the south-west shore and the western end of the south shore Skullcap and English Stonecrop are plentiful, and small plants of Balm-leaved Figwort and Heath Pearlwort may be found. Sticky Groundsel is at its most plentiful around the west shores.

Brownsea is open from around April or Easter to the end of October, by boat from Sandbanks or Poole Quay. In addition to the boat fare and the National Trust landing charge, a small fee is payable to the Dorset Wildlife Trust for entering the Nature Reserve in the north-east of the island. If you visit the latter be sure to go into The Villa to see the interesting wildlife displays and the 1856 painting of Brownsea, with Sandbanks undeveloped in the foreground.

Sandbanks – SZ043876 O.S. Map See Plate 8.

Despite all the 'developments' there are areas of interest near the main car park. Early in the year Early Meadow-grass can be found sometimes in the lawn west of the café. In spring and early summer the lawns between the road and the car park have plenty of Lesser Chickweed and several small clovers, including Suffocated Clover. The necessary hands-and-knees botany may attract some attention, so be prepared to answer questions!

Small areas of fenced dunes north of the car park and at the top of the beach south and north of the car park are also worth examining. Large-flowered and Fragrant Evening-primroses are plentiful, and Small-flowered Evening-primrose is in small quantity beyond the south end of the beach dunes. The beach dunes flora also includes Sea Spurge, Sea Bindweed and Sea Rocket. The last named can be found beyond the south end of the beach dunes too. Four-leaved Allseed is easiest to find along part of the south-east side of the main car park. Great Brome (grass) can be found around that car park and the dunes to the north of it. In late summer, Bermuda Grass flowers in the verge between the road and Poole Harbour here and there, all the way from the car park to Evening Hill. Earlier, at the end of June, Hard Grass shows its strange flowers in the first 500m of the verge north-east of the roundabout.

Luscombe Valley Local Nature Reserve (Borough of Poole) – SZ047892 O.S. Map

The entrances are at the south end and there is, currently, free parking in Brudenell Avenue and Road. This reserve is wet underfoot, which is why it is a good place for learning how to identify sedges. Black, Brown, Carnation, Dotted, False Fox, Hairy, Lesser Pond, Oval, Pendulous, Sand, Spiked and Star Sedges can all be found here in June in what is a relatively small reserve. Most are northwards from the small pond, or just over the metal bridge, but Sand Sedge is towards the south-west corner, and Star and Pendulous Sedge are towards the north end. Dotted Sedge, a nationally scarce species, is frequent. There are many other more colourful species too.

Calendar of special sights

The times given below are for the average season.

January to early March – When there is frost on the grasses and other plants and shrubs; its beauty is greatest on the plants of the heaths.

Late January to early February – Best display of Snowdrops is in the ruined village of Tyneham in the Army Ranges, especially behind the main group of houses. (Tyneham is open most weekends, but not during the last in January.) Next best display is in the valley south of Steeple crossed by path 10.

Late March – Wild Daffodils on the east edge of Rempstone Forest, where bridleway 33 enters it – probably introduced but well worth seeing.

Late March to mid-April – Two contrasting Primrose Ways – (1) in the wood west of the south end of Little Sea, Studland Heath (see the sketch map and the description in Some Flower-rich Locations), (2) 600-900m west of the north-east corner of West Hill, Corfe, along the Purbeck Way – it is worth doing both walks. They are muddy in places.

Mid-April to early May – Cowslips are outstanding in some meadows at Durlston and in two meadows to the south of Langton to Kingston road just west of the junction with the road to Worth near Acton – Broad Meadow has path 9 going through it.

Late April to early May – Early Spider Orchids on slopes above sea, especially in the fields east and west of Dancing Ledge Ware. Cuckooflowers in the field south-west of Sharford Bridge (Map 5A) and also visible from that field in the field to the north. A display of flowers of ancient woodland in Langton West Wood, particularly by the rides. Bluebells and Ramsons (Wild Garlic) by the path through Quarry Wood, Kingston.

May Day bank holiday weekend – Ramsons in the wood south-west of Tyneham car park – one narrow track goes through it; keep to tracks (Tyneham is usually closed the following weekend).

Early to mid-May – Ramsons in King's Wood and in Studland Wood. Green-winged Orchids in east side of White Ware (east of Dancing Ledge Ware).

Mid-May – Ramsons in Stonehill Down Wood, East Creech. Bluebells west of car park on Povington Hill on the weekend when Army Ranges open (usually closed the weekend after bank holiday), on the Central Ridge of West Common, Corfe (especially near Monkey's Hump) from both bridleways 14 and 15 at Brenscombe and in a field south of Godllingston Heath – see p.267 (Bluebells flower later in fields than in woods).

Mid- to end of May – Thrift on cliff-top near south-east end of Worbarrow Bay, Tyneham and in Durlston Country Park from south-west to south-east of lighthouse.

Mid-May to early June – See Pale Flax in some of Durlston Country Park meadows in the mornings, before petals begin to drop around midday.

Mid-May to mid-June – Kidney Vetch in Old Nick's Ground, Studland.

Late May – Ox-eye Daisies, Horseshoe Vetch and Red Valerian (red, pink and white) on the east half of the sloping chalk cliffs on the north side of Swanage Bay (the best view is from cliff-top below the trig point looking east; take care).

Early June – Ox-eye Daisies and Rough Hawkbit in Ox-eye Daisy Field and Centenary Meadow at Durlston and in Northbrook Road Cemetery, Swanage.

Early to mid-June – Heath Spotted Orchids, with some Southern Marsh Orchids and hybrids, west of path leading north from St.Michael's Garage, Harman's Cross at south end of second field. Orchids in damp areas of Corfe Common.

Mid-June – Sheepsbit's sapphires in the sand dunes at Studland. Foxgloves near the west end of Harmony Farm, Studland and in several places by tracks at Arne.

Late June to July – Bell Heather on dry areas of Studland Heath either side of Ferry Road and on dry areas of Hartland Moor. Dorset Heath and Cross-leaved Heath on damp areas of and near Hartland Moor. Water-lilies in Icen Barrow Pond best viewed from the north side. Lesser Hawkbit and Catsear on Stoborough and Norden roundabouts from morning to mid-afternoon, when not recently mown (these continue to look good until August).

Early July – Bog Asphodel around the edge of Spur Bog, Studland.

Mid-July – Nettle-leaved Bellflower at sides of roads east and south-east of East Creech.

Mid- to late July – Betony and Harebells on drier parts of Corfe Common and many colourful flowers on wetter parts. Visit Middle Field, some distance south-east of Spyway Barn on The Wares, if ungrazed, for a splendid display of Field Scabious, Greater Knapweed, Lesser Hawkbit and Hedge and Lady's Bedstraws.

Late July – large-flowered form of Common Knapweed in north end of field west of Sharford Bridge and in the triangular field beyond the junction of the roads to Kingston and Worth from Langton (view from road).

August – Heather (Ling) on the heaths.

Early September – Marsh Gentians near entrance to Spur Bog and a larger number across the bog before the wood.

October – Autumn colours on the heaths as well as in hedges and trees. (Some shrubs and trees are easier to spot when turning, for example Dogwood, Field Maple).

December – As for January.

Suggestions for walks

These are listed roughly west to east. This list needs to be used in conjunction with the O.S. map and the sketch maps, the numbers of which are given. There are many more possible walks, but here are a few with which to start, mostly circular ones. Use of maps will show the lengths and also ways of shortening or lengthening some of them. They can also be walked in reverse, or started at a different point, but are probably best begun and walked as described. These routes are usually passable, but expect mud in some places when it has been raining. Access from a bus route is given where possible, as is the possibility of mountain-biking the few which are entirely on bridleways, though you will see more flowers if you walk. (If you are on a bike do not approach any horse rider ahead of you too quietly, or you may scare the horse when it suddenly finds you behind.)
UCR = unclassified road = route with public access (marked with green dots)

South of Tyneham (O.S. map only)   Walk from village southwards to Coast Path (the first part of the route is a zigzag up the hill, not straight as wrongly shown on the O.S. map; when you walk it the route becomes clear) – east to Tyneham Cap for the very best of many excellent views in Purbeck – then turn round and follow Coast Path to Worbarrow Bay – (climb Worbarrow Tout as an extra) – back up valley to Tyneham – taking signed woodland path on left (not on O.S. map) when approaching village.

Stoborough and Ridge (Map 2)   Proceed from Stoborough to Wareham along B3075 – visit Priory Meadow – follow Purbeck Way to Redcliffe Farm and on to New Road – path 11 to Stoborough.

Stoborough Heath (West) (Maps 2 and 3)   From Grange Road take path 9 – take track to the right past the pond and on to a very short piece of Purbeck Way – take track down middle of heath to meet path 6 by pond – follow path 6 to railway – cross railway onto Creech Heath – continue on path 37 to Purbeck Way – follow Purbeck Way north-west to another rail crossing – continue on Purbeck Way to rejoin track used at start. (This walk could equally well be started off Grange Road via paths 7 or 19, or off Furzebrook Road via a short track to path 6, or via path 37.)

Stoborough Heath (East) (Map 2) From car park off Arne Road walk nearly the length of the Dismantled Tramway (it has muddy patches near south end) – take the track north-westwards across the heath to New Road – then the track north-eastwards through fields back to Arne Road. If using the bus, start at south end of tramway.

Kimmeridge (Maps 4 and 8, which do not quite meet) (long walk) Start by the church and take path through the farm – turn left on to path 15, which takes you through withybed – continue on path 15 to join path 16 – which becomes path 7 – reach bay – take Coast Path to south-east up steps to Clavell Tower – on to Rope Lake Head – turn left on to Permissive Path up to Swyre Head viewpoint (highest point in the Isle of Purbeck) – follow ridge north-west first on bridleway 26 – which becomes a UCR – then bridleway 18 – to road – use path 1 to return to church.

Ridgeway and Knowle Hills (Maps 7 and 3) From the road at top of the Down north-west of Cocknowle take UCR along top of Ridgeway Hill – turn right at end of Stonehill Down – and right again near north-west corner of Down (no path, but open access) – proceed along the top of the Down to path 32 – follow this down to the hairpin road bend – proceed along the road to path 6 – take that path up to Knowle Hill – go along UCR eastwards – turn right and descend the Hill using bridleway 39 – follow path 3 along the foot of the Hill to Cocknowle – go up the road to the start.

Swyre Head (Map 8) Walk along West Street, Kingston, or drive to the car park near west end – take bridleway 46 there and back to Swyre Head viewpoint. Route can be cycled.
Hartland Way (Maps 5 and 5A) From the corner by Scotland Barn take Slepe Road to south-west – then bridleway 77 – turn right onto the old tramway – follow it past Langton Wallis to Hartland Moor and continue on it all the way back to Slepe Road – go south down the road – turn left across the Heath to join bridleway 4 along edge of White House Wood – turn right early in next field on to bridleway 3 – which takes you through meadows back to Scotland Barn.

Slepe Road to Thrasher's Lane and back (Maps 5, 10 and 5A) Take bridleway 4 from Slepe Road to Thrasher's Lane (passing over medieval Sharford Bridge en route) – return to Slepe Road by path 80.

West Common (Map 11) West Street (or West Street car park) – south-westwards to the end of West Street – then continue south-westwards to the top of the hill on UCR – left along central ridge of the Common – near Monkey's Hump descend north-eastwards to Purbeck Way – then bridleway 36 back to the end of West Street.

Rollington Hill and East Hill (Map 11)   Start from Corfe or from car park off Sandy Hill Lane at Challow – take Purbeck Way eastwards to the radio mast on Rollington Hill – return westwards along the top edge of the hill – descend East Hill by over 300 steps.

Worth (Map12)   From car park south of Renscombe Farm take path 18 westwards to Coast Path – follow Coast Path south to St. Aldhelm's Head (n.b. many steps down and up en route) – continue on Coast Path to Winspit – take path 13 up Winspit Bottom – fork left on to path 14 (or continue on path 13 for refreshments in Worth) – take road to Weston Farm – path 18 back to start.

Brenscombe (Maps 10 and 14)   From small car park south of B3351 take bridleway 14 up to Brenscombe Hill – then go westwards along Purbeck Way to the radio mast on Rollington Hill – path 13 back to B3351 near start. **Alternatively,** at Brenscombe Hill go east to the barrows on Ailwood Down – turn around and go back to the end of bridleway 15 – take that bridleway back to bridleway 14 – return to start. This latter route can be cycled, but it is best to walk (push) up the south-west half of bridleway 14 or you will miss some of its treasures.

Langton West Wood (Map 14)   Start at the car park on south side of B3069 near Acton – path 37 to Castle View – path 39 to south-west corner of wood – path 3 to the first gate into the wood – follow rides around the wood clockwise at own risk – return by paths 3, 39 and 37.

Dancing Ledge (Maps 14, 15 and 16)   Take the bus to Langton and walk down Durnford Drove, or use the car park at south end of Drove – take path 25 to Priest's Way – go eastwards along Priest's Way to path 22 – go south to White Ware – take Coast Path westwards to Dancing Ledge – visit quarry – use path 27 north-westwards and then northwards to Priest's Way – go west a short distance to visit pond south of Way – return to path 27 – go northwards to path 28 – take path 28 back to Durnford Drove.

Godlingston Heath (Map 17)   Park on north side of B3351 west of Harmony Farm Fields – take bridleway 25 to bridleway 27 – after a short length take bridleway 26 northwards across the heath – turn left onto bridleway 33 to visit the edge of the forest and pond – back eastwards on bridleway 33 to take bridleway 23 – take path 24 to Agglestone – then bridleway 25 back to start. Alternative for bus-users: access the Heath bridleways from Wadmore Lane. Cyclists can do much the same round but use bridleway 17 instead of path 24 and bridleway 25.

West of Studland (Map 20, and Map 17 for longer route)   Start from Heath Green Road northwards along bridleway 23 – turn left onto path 20 – then along Agglestone Road – take short path to bridleway 17 – turn right onto that bridleway – right again when you reach bridleway 23 – back to start. Longer version: go south-west on bridleway 17 to bridleway 25 – visit

Agglestone – take path 24 and bridleway 23 back to start.

The Warren Wood (Map 20)   Take the Coast Path eastwards from Studland (n.b. there is a path error on the O.S. map) – turn right into The Warren Wood – a track leads southwards down the east side – at the south end follow it westwards – then northwards through the centre of the wood – eastwards at the north end to bring you back to the Wood entrance.

Old Harry Rocks and Ballard Head (Map 20)   Follow the Coast Path from Studland (n.b. there is a path error on the O.S. map) to Handfast Point to view Old Harry Rocks – follow Coast Path up the Down to near Ballard Head – take either the Coast Path or the Purbeck Way westwards – after passing through a gate continue along the top of Ballard Down to bridleway 12 – then turn more than half right following that bridleway down to the top of the Glebeland Estate – either follow it on down the east side of the estate or divert to visit Clayton Meadow and then return to the bridleway – continue back into Studland. This route can be cycled, except to Clayton Meadow.

Ballard Down (Swanage street map and Map 20)   From the bus stop on Ulwell Road at Whitecliff Road proceed up the latter – join bridleway 14 passing a stone cottage on your right – after reaching the Down take the middle of the three paths to your right (the Purbeck Way) which gradually ascends the hill – near the top of the Down turn right down the Coast Path – follow that downhill (steps lower down) and along the cliff-top to Shep's Hollow – go down and up the steps there – through Ballard Estate back to Ulwell Road.

Durlston (Map 21)   From the north side of the Visitor Centre take the path that leads to South Field – go half right and cross it diagonally – through the gateway turn left to look around the area of the shallow quarry – return to the path that goes westwards along the boundary of Fields 13 and 14 – through the gate at the west end – **either** turn left there to go down the east side of Ox-eye Daisy Field, then right along its south side and the south side of Centenary Meadow – **or** proceed on and take the next gate on the left to go down the west side of Centenary Meadow (**both routes**) go into Johnston Meadow and look around its south end – climb the stile into Field 6 – use path 56 to head half right down and then up to the top of the slope overlooking the sea – turn left along the top on path 55 into Field 10A – down the slope and into the next field to the lighthouse – **either** return to the car park up the tarmac road (paths 48, 52 and 50) – **or** leave the lighthouse on your left and take the Coast Path to descend into the gully – ascend the steps the other side – **either** take the Diagonal Path back to the start – **or** continue along the Coast Path for refreshments at the castle.

PLANT LIST

Almost all the species listed have been seen by the author in the wild at the sites given in the four years up to 2007, most of them in 2006 or 2007. Species are listed in the order of plant families in the most recent books on identification. However, some books omit Clubmosses, Horsetails and Ferns, which come at the beginning of the Plant List, and Rushes, Sedges and Grasses which are listed towards the end.

In most families it is not difficult to recognise common characteristics shared by all species in them; for example all British members of the pea family have flowers of similar form, though of widely different sizes and shapes. However, some families contain species with little apparent likeness to each other, e.g. the Buttercup, Rose and Figwort families.

Each entry is given as follows:
Name
Status, frequency, habitats and flowering months
Official frequency classification of scarce species in italics
Sites
Notes and drawings

Names

The entries begin with the **English name** followed by the **scientific name** (Latin or latinised international name) of each species.

English names were standardised in the mid-20th century. As differing English names were being used for the same species in different parts of Britain, and sometimes even in the same area, the standardisation of them has been very helpful, except for one feature – they were reduced to not more than two words. This could only be done by excessive and inconsistent use of hyphens, a practice which has not been followed below. Most English names used in this book are as in the *New Flora of the British Isles* by Stace (1997). A second English name has been added very occasionally. Old Dorset names can be found in *Names of Wild Flowers in Dorset* (Horsfall, 1991).

Scientific names were reduced from several words to two words (the genus and species) in the mid-18th century by the Swedish botanist Carl Linnaeus (1707-78). However, these names have changed from time to time as a result of research on species relationships, or when it has been discovered that another name has been used earlier in another country. When there has been a recent change, the old name has been added in brackets if there is likely to be confusion.

As with English names, scientific names in this book conform to those used by Stace (1997), except in the case of Brome and Couch Grasses, where it follows the BSBI referee Thomas Cope (pers. com.), and for a few species where there have been changes since Stace.

The first word, the generic name, indicates similarity to other species which are placed in the same genus, e.g. all the clovers are in the genus *Trifolium*. The second word, the specific name, is more clear-cut. It defines plants that are usually incapable of interbreeding with another species, though if they do, the hybrid offspring will usually be partially or totally infertile.

Abbreviations

agg. – aggregate; used in a very few cases when it is difficult to distinguish between the species of a genus, e.g. *Taraxacum* agg. is used for all dandelions.
x – used when two species have interbred and produced a hybrid e.g. *Typha angustifolia* x *latifolia* for the Reedmace hybrid. It is also given a shorter name of its own with an x in the middle – *Typha* x *glauca*.
subsp. – subspecies; used when there is more than one type of a species with several significant differences; the originally named type is given a subspecific name the same as its specific name, e.g. *Orobanche minor* subsp. *minor* (Common Broomrape), and the other type, which in this case is usually found by the sea, is named *Orobanche minor* subsp. *maritima* (Carrot Broomrape).
var. – variety; used for plants similar to the species as originally described, but with one, two or three fairly trivial differences. However, the scientific definition of the terms 'subspecies' and 'variety' are still debated.
cv. – cultivated variety

Status

Native – means that the species is believed to have arrived in Britain without intervention by man. If, however, a native plant is thought to have been introduced into this area, rather than being in its native range, that is stated in its entry.
Early Introduction (Archeophyte) – a species believed to have been deliberately or accidentally introduced by man before 1500 AD. Most crop weeds fall into this category, as well as most ancient cooking and medicinal herbs.
Introduction (Neophyte) – a species introduced since about 1500 A.D. when gardening took off.

This book usually gives the status as given in *The New Atlas of the British and Irish Flora* (Preston, Pearman & Dines, 2002). However, in a few cases in which uncertainty has been expressed since, it follows *The Vascular Plant Red Data List for Great Britain* (Cheffings & Farrell, 2005), in which case the status is given as e.g., 'native or introduced'.

Frequency

Abundant, Frequent, Occasional, Rare – are terms in common use in biological studies, and are self-explanatory. In this book they refer to occurrence within the <u>usual</u> habitat of the species. For example Daisy is abundant in short grass, and so is described as abundant, but it is not abundant in woods or marshes.

The terms refer to how often a plant can be found in the wild in <u>this</u> area. For example our County Flower, Dorset Heath, is nationally rare, but in this area it is frequent on some heaths. Also some species listed are frequent in gardens, but if they do not often escape they are occasional or rare in the wild.

Sometimes a frequent, occasional or rare species is abundant at a site. In that case it will be described as 'plentiful' there. If a species occurs more thinly in several places, it will be described as 'scattered' or 'here and there'.

It is difficult to give sites for common arable weeds and other plants of disturbed ground because they depend upon a field being used for an arable crop rather than as grassland. Species like Common Fumitory have therefore been described as occasional without sites being given.

For **abundant** or very **frequent** species no sites are given unless for outstanding populations. Sample sites for less frequent ones are given.

For an **occasional** species, up to 10 or 11 sites across the area are given, unless, like an arable weed, it is ephemeral. More sites are given for local specialities – Dwarf Mouse-ear, Glabrous Whitlowgrass, Dorset Heath, Dorset Hybrid Heath, Mossy Stonecrop, Small-flowered Sweet Briar and its hybrid with Dog Rose, Yellow Vetchling, Stars-in-grass, Early Gentian, Marsh Gentian, Carrot Broomrape, Hairy-fruited Cornsalad, Italian Lords-and-ladies, Brown Beak-sedge, Dotted Sedge and Nit Grass. More sites are also given for some inconspicuous species – Hairy Rockcress, Birdsfoot Clover, Clustered Clover, Slender Trefoil, Allseed, Autumn Gentian, Early and Changing Forget-me-nots, Spring Sedge, and also for the commoner Orchids.

A **rare** species is one that has only three or less public sites in this area, and all those where it has occurred recently and may continue are given, except in a very small number of cases when that would be unwise. The general consensus now is that it is better that the sites of most rarities are known to prevent accidental damage.

National and county organisations have given the scarce species an official frequency classification: **Nationally Rare, Nationally Scarce, Dorset Rare,** or **Dorset Scarce** which has been added in italics on the next line.

Nationally Rare are species which have occurred in only 1 to 15 hectads (out of about 2500) in Great Britain and the Isle of Man since 1987.

Nationally Scarce are species which have only occurred in between 16 to 100 hectads nationally since 1987.

Dorset Rare are species which have been found in 3 or fewer sites in the county since 1st January 1990 and are not in the previous two categories.

Dorset Scarce are species which have been found in 4 to 10 sites in Dorset since the same date, and are not nationally rare or scarce.

Some species have a national classification in *The Vascular Plant Red Data List for Great Britain* (Cheffings & Farrell, 2005) in descending order of conservation concern: **Critically Endangered, Endangered, Vulnerable,** or **Near Threatened.** These have been added when applicable.

Habitats

Woods, grassland, hedges, marshes, beaches are examples of habitats, areas where the species in question grows of its own accord, though it may sometimes be found in other habitats, especially outside this area. Sometimes there will be a qualification, e.g. old woods. 'Verges' includes any type of verge – road, bridleway, path, field. 'Walls' refers to mortared rather than drystone walls. Habitat is not given when a species is only found planted, and not always for escapes from cultivation.

The term '**casual**' describes the appearance of plants in places where they are only likely to occur for one or a few years e.g. in a pavement, in dumped soil, or on a building site. There would be no point in including such sites, unless the same species might occur in later years nearby. Some species are regular in some sites, but casual in other areas, so 'casual' is added to the other habitats given for them. Garden plants which have only been found as escapes once recently have been omitted.

Flowering months

The main flowering period is given for most species, but not for those chiefly identified by their leaves, e.g. most trees, pondweeds. If a plant has been cut, e.g. on a verge, it may flower late. For those plants which do not flower (clubmosses, horsetails and ferns), months are given when their foliage is identifiable.

'June to July' does not necessarily mean that the species will be in flower throughout the whole of these months. Sometimes, especially when the flowering period is short, the words early, mid or late have been added.

Docks, many rushes and most sedges are best identified by their fruits. These are usually retained on the plant for several months after flowering, except for sedges of the genus *Carex* which may fall a month after flowering. Grasses are also identifiable from their seed heads, which persist for a month or more after flowering.

Sites

Sites follow on the next lines and are usually given from **west to east;** they start with a general area, e.g.**Church Knowle.** The names of Corfe Castle, Langton Matravers and Worth Matravers have been shortened to Corfe, Langton and Worth, as is done locally. The sites continue with more detailed reference points. These are shown either on a sketch map, on a recent O. S. map or on the street maps of Swanage and Poole. All references in the text to 'O.S. map' are to the editions of O.S. Outdoor Leisure map 15 published in or since December 2004.

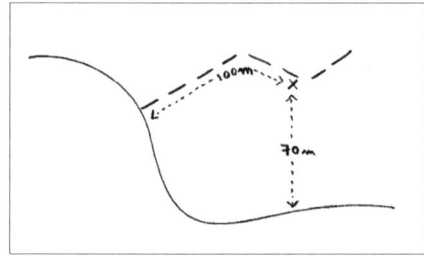

When there are two or more sites within a general area, a semi-colon is used to separate them.

Distances and points of the compass have usually been used rather than National Grid map references, because most people are more at home with the former. However, map references have been used in a very few cases, usually in the middle of heaths, where other reference points are lacking.

Distances are often given to the nearest 10m (metres), but sometimes to the nearest 25, 50 or 100m. Figures like 30m or 160m are accurate to within 10m; but figures like 125m, 350m, and 600m indicate more approximate distances. To convert to yards add 10%, for example 400m is 440 yards. Unless stated otherwise the distance between two places is measured along the route between them, rather than the shortest distance. So the plants located at X (right) are described as south of bridleway 100m from road, not 70m.

If you are not used to compass points you will soon pick them up. It is quite easy to work out sites in this book with a map in front of you.

Bearings are approximate. N indicates anything bearing about 345 to 015 degrees ($^\circ$), NE anything from 015 to 075°, E anything from 075 to 105°, SE anything from 105 to 165°, and so on.

NNE has occasionally been used, when greater accuracy is necessary, to indicate a bearing of between 015 to 030°, when otherwise NE would have been used. Likewise ENE has occasionally been used to indicate a bearing of between 060 to 075°, and so on clockwise with ESE, SSE, SSW, WSW, WNW, and NNW (below).

'Path' and **'bridleway'** and the abbreviation **'UCR'** are used respectively to refer to a public footpath, public bridleway or unclassified road (route with public

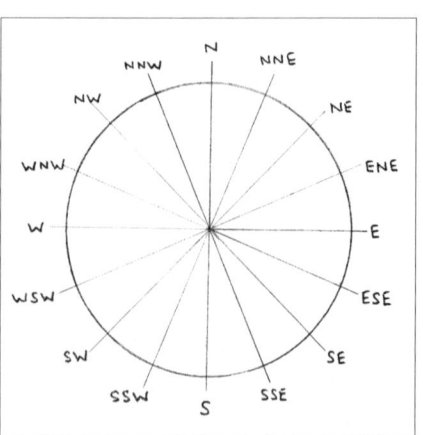

access) marked as such on O.S. maps. A path or bridleway may be as wide as a metalled private road, or only just wide enough for one person.

'Track' is used for a track or path which is not marked on a map as a public bridleway or public path, but which is open to the public. Occasionally the start of a private track is used as a reference point, in which case it is described in the Plant List as 'private track' and marked on a sketch map with a couple of short black dashes. A very few private paths have been opened to the public; those are marked as permissive paths (PP) or permissive bridleways (PB) on the sketch maps.

In an open access wood, '**ride**' is used to describe an open strip between trees which includes a path which can be used by the public, whether or not it is marked on the O.S. map as a public footpath or bridleway.

When a path, bridleway or road has **a particular name**, that is given. Examples are Coast Path, Purbeck Way (each marked on O.S. map with diamonds), Diagonal Path (at Durlston), Sunnyside (a road at Ridge village), A351, B3351.

Public bridleways and paths have numbers which are on the sketch maps. Each civil parish has its paths and bridleways numbered separately and so has its own paths or bridleways 1, 2, 3 etc. Numbers change at parish boundaries.

There are some places where the **public paths and bridleways,** marked in green on the O.S. map, differ from reality. The County Council, who are responsible for supplying details of them to the O.S., have been informed. Some of those can be seen; the correct path is marked less conspicuously in black nearby, as in several places on Godlingston Heath. But in some places these discrepancies will only become apparent when the path is walked. The bridleway from Holme Lane to New Hall Farm is one which is inaccurate in parts, and indeed it has recently been officially re-routed at its north end because of quarrying; but the green marks have been improved from the previous edition, on which it was marked as going across the rifle range!

The County Council and The National Trust have both embarked upon a helpful policy of replacing **stiles** with kissing gates. So be prepared for a 'stile' to be a gate.

The sites given are those where there is a reasonable expectation that the species will continue to be seen for years to come. However, trees fall, scrub is cut, sites get overgrown, or for some other reason a species disappears – though sometimes it will reappear later. Sometimes plants may be cut down or grazed, and you will have to come back earlier next year. In some places cutting is necessary for safety purposes, but sometimes zealous tidying is to blame. Ditches, and some streams and ponds, have to be cleared out from time to time, but plants usually reappear in a year or two. When you go to look for a species and fail to find it, you are likely to find other plants of interest.

There may be **other public sites** unknown to the author for a species rare in the area. Please tell him (see Appendix) of any. Likewise please write about any site where it is certain that a plant, rare or otherwise, no longer grows.

Notes and Drawings

Finally, in a species entry there may be **notes** to help distinguish it from similar species, or other items of interest. Botanical terms have been kept to a minimum; for example sepals joined into a tube are really a calyx, but in this book the easier words 'sepals' or 'sepal-tube' have been used. The sexual parts of a flower need to be used occasionally in the notes; parts of a flower are described in the introduction in identification books. With rushes, sedges and grasses use of the terms panicle, spikelet, bract, ligule, auricle, glume, lemma, and awn cannot be avoided; they are explained in identification books. Points of description are underlined very occasionally when there are mistakes in some identification books.

Drawings have been included when key points of difference are not illustrated in one or more of the commonly used books. There is a **1cm scale bar** by each drawing or set of drawings.

Omissions

The Flora of Dorset (Bowen, 2000) contains records for some species which are probable or possible mistakes. Bowen did not often question records sent to him. Records for public land in our area for the following species may be wrong: Hard Shield Fern, Luccombe Oak, Sessile Oak, Marsh Violet, Narrow-fruited Watercress, Spring Vetch, Buckthorn, Boston-ivy, Sticky Storksbill, Large Thyme, Purple Mullein, Welted Thistle, Rough Hawksbeard, Autumn Hawkweed (*Hieracium sabaudum*), Flattened and Wood Meadow-grasses, Ripgut Brome, Field Garlic.

Errors

Any book with so much information will probably contain a few author's errors, despite much checking. If you think you have found one, please let the author know.

Half-day closing

A few species are best sought in the morning, because they close up in the afternoon. Goatsbeard (Jack-go-to-bed-at-noon) is the best known for this, though its seed-clocks are visible all day. But the little Yellow Centaury, Lesser Centaury, Yellow-wort, Scarlet Pimpernel, the three Sundews and their hybrids, and Nymphaea species of Water-lily all often close in the afternoon. That matters little for the Sundews, since it is the leaves which are the key to recognition; but seeing the Yellow Centaury is difficult anyway, as there are always many bolder yellow flowers in its vicinity. Dandelion-like flowers close later in the afternoon. Pale Flax begins to drop its petals at midday, so it looks better in the morning.

Albinos

Many species occasionally occur with white flowers rather than in their usual colours. A few, like Marsh Thistle, frequently do. Yellow flowers rarely do so. However, albinos often do not reappear in the same place year by year, so their sites have only occasionally been included in this book.

Plant List

CLUBMOSSES

CLUBMOSS FAMILY
Marsh Clubmoss
Lycopodiella inundata
Native. Occasional. Damp bare sand or peat. June to October.
Nationally Scarce. Endangered.
Godlingston Heath: in area 3 x 1m 30m NE of point on bridleway23 itself 180m SE of where stream flows through pipe under bridleway E of grass field; few at map reference SZ02648325 2m S of prominent population of Round-leaved x Oblong-leaved Sundew hybrid; few 8m W of that. **Studland Heath:** 70m ESE of entrance to Spur Bog just before lower level of bog (25m NE of low trees) (with small amount of Brown Beak-sedge); 60m ESE of that along 4m S-N of N-seeping bog at map reference SZ02718429; small group on peat near N end of Fifth Beach on SE edge of Little Sea. **Shell Bay:** much 450m SSE of NE end of boardwalk in large circular depression 80m behind fore-dunes (easiest place). (Regrettably this very first species grows at sites difficult to describe!)

QUILLWORT FAMILY
Spring Quillwort *Isoetes echinospora*
Native. Rare. On lake bottom under acidic fresh water at depths up to 2m. Visible June to October.
Dorset Rare.
Studland Heath: various sites in Little Sea – easiest to see in SE by wading on sandy bottom in shallow water 2m off N end of Fourth Beach (between Reeds and shore); likewise 2m off shore 40-80m N of Fifth

Beach (there may be still some unexploded bombs and shells in Little Sea, but it is unlikely that they are close to shore). This is the most easterly Spring Quillwort locality in Britain.

Spring Quillwort has leaves which arch over towards horizontal, around 1mm wide with four hollows (lens), whereas Shoreweed (p.186) has 2mm wide pithy leaves, mostly fairly vertical. Pieces of Spring Quillwort are occasionally found on SE beaches of Little Sea – however, there is far more Shoreweed found, because Shoreweed is much more plentiful and is not so firmly rooted.

HORSETAILS

HORSETAIL FAMILY
Horsetails are sometimes called Marestail, as is in some areas in the past, but the name Marestail is now reserved for the superficially similar but quite unrelated species *Hippuris vulgaris.*

Water Horsetail *Equisetum fluviatile*
Native. Occasional. Acidic marshes, ditches and water. Visible May to November.
Stoborough: 100m SE of NW end of path13 on E side of path (Marsh Horsetail nearby). **Creech Heath:** plentiful (with varying thickness and amounts of branching) in pond S of W-E track which crosses path34 midway along that path. **The Moors:** see p.27. **Corfe:** scattered in places in W and NW parts of West Common especially all down Second Valley; S of Middle Common Pond; in tiny E

stream in Little East Common 10m SE of bridleway30; in East Valley in Big East Common 150m from railway fence. **Corfe Charity's Meadows:** much down NW side of Paddle Dock meadow (with some Marsh Horsetail). **Harman's Cross:** by path26 between woods in S end of second field N of A351.

About four-fifths of the stem is hollow.

Field Horsetail *Equisetum arvense*
Native. Frequent. Verges, hedges, ditches, arable fields, gardens. Visible late April to November.

The main stem has about 12 shallow ridges, and the teeth of the sheaths are entirely black. As it can be found in shallow water, it could also be mistaken there for either the previous or next species. Specimens with many branches have been mistaken for Wood Horsetail (which has branched branches), which does not occur in the area.

Marsh Horsetail *Equisetum palustre*
Native. Occasional. Wet places. Visible May to November.
Stoborough: by Cobbs Lake watercourse at NW end of path13; E of same path50 and 100m SE of Cobbs Lake (Water Horsetail near latter site). **Creech Heath:** bottom of former clay mining depression 250m SE of Icen Barrow Pond. **Furzebrook:** much in valley 450m SE of E end of Blue Pool. **Stoborough Heath:** valley SW of A351 250m NW of Halfway Inn. **Corfe Charity's Meadows:** much down NW side of Paddle Dock meadow (with rather more Water Horsetail). **Harman's Cross:** by path26 in third field N of A351. **Ower:** on NW side of bridleway8 150m SW of where bridleways7 and 8

cross. **Godlingston Heath:** pond where bridleway33 enters forest S of Greenland; S side of bridleway36 S of SE corner of Brand's Creek (with Field Horsetail).

Main stem usually has 6-8 pronounced ridges, and sheath teeth are black edged with white.

Great Horsetail *Equisetum telmateia*
Native. Frequent. Verges, waterlogged soil above clay, including places where water emerges from the ground, for example at the bottom of a layer of Upper Greensand, because the water cannot penetrate the layer of Gault clay beneath. Visible April to December.
Kimmeridge: grows to nearly 2m high by path through withybed.
Church Knowle: plenty on parts of E side of bridleway16. **Corfe:** N end of Byle Copse. **Woolgarston:** S side of road at Ailwood Farm. **Swanage Railway:** plentiful in several places by railway especially SE of Corfe station. **Woolgarston:** S side of road 400m SE of Ailwood Farm for 75m. **Langton:** S side of A351 just E of junction with B3069. **Swanage:** W side of N end of Cowlease (road); NE side of E part of Court Road; near Peveril Point. **Luscombe Valley:** 55-65m N of W side of metal bridge in centre of reserve.

FERNS

Many ferns remain green in winter, as noted below, and so can still be enjoyed then.

ADDERSTONGUE FAMILY
Adderstongue
Ophioglossum vulgatum
Native. Occasional. Grassland uncul-

tivated for many years, banks. Late April to June.

Corfe: several places on NW side of UCR across West Common (mostly on bank – largest colony 350m SW of end of West Street); SE side of same route 250m from West Street below bank for 25m; large colony by E edge of West Common 45-55m NE of Purbeck Way 15m wide. **Wares (east):** very small amount on track across Sherwood's Wear 12m N of S wall 12m W of bottom of slope halfway across field. **Durlston:** near N edge of Field13 50m from E edge; in SE of same field beginning 15m W of gateway from Tasker's Meadow and extending N and W from that point; in Tasker's Meadow both 15 and 40m NE of SW corner; SE corner of Smith Field 20m from S hedge 40m from E wall; 70m NE of SW corner of Skipworth Meadow just NW of diagonal track; largest population in our area in NE of Long Meadow especially to 70m S of N edge and to 25m across meadow from E edge (but extending to 100m and 40m, respectively).

ROYAL FERN FAMILY
Royal Fern *Osmunda regalis*
Native. Occasional. Wet open woods, ditches, watersides on heath – always on acid soil. Not wintergreen, but nevertheless recognisable all the year around whether alive or dead.
Stoborough Heath: W end of pond 120m SE of NW corner of heath (SE of hotel). **Hartland Moor:** several clumps for 125m N-S in Upper Fen NE of Isolation Cottages. **Norden:** SW and NW sides of Michael's Pond. **Wytch:** 200m S of NE corner of Wytch Moor. **Kingswood:** by stream where bridleway29 enters forest. **Godlingston Heath:** 20m N of where

bridleway33 enters forest. **Studland:** E side of Ferry Road 10m S of E end of bridleway38 on opposite side. **Studland Heath:** used to be plentiful but now very much reduced by deer – however they do not eat it on edges of Little Sea – especially vast clump opposite Egret Hide (binoculars). **Brownsea:** beside track W of The Villa. **Branksome Dene Chine:** sea cliff 80m NE.

Deer in west of Purbeck and on Brownsea have not developed a taste for it like those in the Studland area.

PILLWORT FAMILY
Pillwort *Pilularia globulifera*
Native. Rare. Edge of ponds, flooded in winter. Visible June to October, depending on water level.
Nationally Scarce. Near Threatened.
Creech Heath: towards W end of S edge of second pond W of Furzebrook Road N of path34; between logs laid to walk on at NW corner of pond in SE corner of open access area of Heath (may get overgrown at both sites soon, as it has at other past sites on that heath).
Hartland Moor: W side of Pillwort Pond.

POLYPODY FAMILY
Common Polypody
Polypodium vulgare
Native. Occasional. Acid ground, mostly banks. All year – wintergreen.
Creech: on SW side of bridleway2 – here and there 25-125m beyond gate after passing cricket ground; on S side of bridleway35 40m W of Grange Road. **Stoborough:** E side of Grange Road 200-350m N of railway bridge (with next species – where leaf shapes can be compared – see below); same side 15m N of path9. **Furzebrook:** S side of path13 NW of Blue Pool; S

side of Purbeck Way 200m E of Furzebrook Road. **Stoborough Heath:** SE side of bridleway23 – 145-160m from A351 (next species is 50-70m from A351). **Norden:** N side of bridleway77 200m E of A351; E side of Slepe Road nearly opposite path78. **Bushey:** W side of Thrasher's Lane 80m S of private track on other side to Lower Bushey Farm. **Godlingston Heath:** close to bridleway27 where it passes through small wood 450m W of junction with bridleway26. **Studland:** halfway down both sides of Coast Path from car park to Middle Beach. **Sandbanks:** near W end of footpath between and parallel to Grasmere Road and Seacombe Road.

This and the next species are difficult to separate. All accessible sites for this species are north of the chalk ridge. This species produces new fronds in early summer; the next one produces them in late summer and autumn. Fronds of this species, when well grown, are mostly parallel-sided, but not always, whereas those of the next species are slightly oval in outline. 'Side-leaves' (pinnae) which are very sharply pointed in outline show that it is the next species. If in doubt, especially when plants are small, use the microscope to examine sporangia in which spores develop (see drawing). Collect pinnae when the spore-cases have turned from cream to brown but have not yet reduced to darker brown dots; September and October are the best months for identification. If still in doubt, record them as *Polypody* agg. Hybrids between this and the next species seem to occur frequently in some parts of Britain, but have only once been found in this area despite examinination of many specimens; spores of mature hybrids are mostly colourless rather than golden.

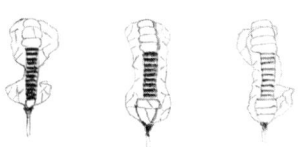

Polypody sporangia – Common (left), Intermediate and Southern; about x100 magnification. These are idealised drawings. Under the microscope most sporangia that have opened will be seen lying on their sides; some will have been torn in two when scraped off the pinna; they will be jumbled with spores and other sporangia; upper and lower edges, which have torn apart from each other to release spores, will be irregular in outline as shown.

Common x Intermediate Polypody-hybrid *Polypodium* x *mantoniae* (*P. vulgare* x *interjectum*)
Native. Rare. Bank. All year – wintergreen.
Shell Bay: SE side of Ferry Road 250m SW of roundabout at highest point of bank.

Intermediate Polypody
Polypodium interjectum
Native. Frequent. Walls, trees, roofs, rocks, verges. All year – wintergreen. All polypodies growing on walls, trees and roofs in this area appear to be this species.

(Southern Polypody
Polypodium cambricum
Native. Limestone rocks, walls, trees. Not yet recorded but may be present.)

BRACKEN FAMILY
Bracken *Pteridium aquilinum*
Native. Abundant. Anywhere where the ground is undisturbed and not too wet. Not wintergreen, but visible all year.

MARSH FERN FAMILY

Marsh Fern *Thelypteris palustris*
Native. Rare. Wet woods. Not winter-
green.
The Moors: see p.27.

SPLEENWORT FAMILY

Hartstongue *Phyllitis scolopendrium*
Native. Frequent. Shady, somewhat
damp places, including walls. All year
– wintergreen.

Black Spleenwort

Asplenium adiantum-nigrum
Native. Occasional. Walls, rocks,
banks. All year – wintergreen.
Holme: on ha-ha NE of East Holme
church (approach via Holme Priory
drive). **Norden:** Norden Farm Pets
Corner S-facing wall; E side of Slepe
Road 5m S of path78 opposite.
Hartland Moor: on N side of path80
5-15m E of Slepe Road. **Arne:** plentiful on churchyard wall; some on E
end of church. **Wares (west):** W end
of S wall of low building at N end of
Spyway Meadow. **Rempstone:** NW
side of bridleway34 (Oil Road) 50m
SW of where bridleway31 crosses it.
Studland: N side of Rectory Lane 30-
80m from W end (with three more
common species of Fern). **Brownsea:**
left of church porch; inner wall of
café courtyard.

Sea Spleenwort *Asplenium marinum*

Native. Occasional. Limestone rock
by sea, usually cliff quarry faces. All
year – wintergreen.
Worth: by entrances to cliff quarry
caves on E side of Winspit 200 and
275m NE of SW corner. **Wares
(west):** cliffs at W end of W half of
main Hedbury Quarry; cliffs at E end
of E half of same quarry; both at W
and near E ends of Dancing Ledge
Quarry; **(east)** W end of middle level

of White Ware Quarry. **Durlston:**
easily seen at closed steps to Tilly
Whim Quarry on Coast Path – stand
on block of stone midway along foot
of wall of entrance and look down
over wall. (Completely natural sites
known are on the roof of Blackers
Hole cave and in the sea cave at the
foot of Ballard Head; both sites are
very difficult to inspect.)

Maidenhair Spleenwort

Asplenium trichomanes
Native. Occasional. Mortared walls.
All year – wintergeen.
Holme: ha-ha N of East Holme
church (approach via Holme Priory
drive). **Steeple:** N wall of churchyard.
Kimmeridge: W side of wall on E
side of playground. **Church Knowle:**
churchyard wall W of church.
Kingston: N side of B3069 just E of
Scott Arms. **Corfe:** NE Wall of
churchyard. **Hartland Moor:** side of
Sharford Bridge. **Langton:** S side of
B3069 W of entrance to Putlake
Adventure Farm. **Swanage:** both ends
of Kings Road East; in several other
roads. **Brownsea:** low wall NW of
Visitor Centre.

Wall Rue *Asplenium ruta-muraria*

Native. Frequent. Mortared walls,
rocks. All year – wintergeen.
Holme: old bridge. **Steeple:** N wall of
churchyard. **Creech:** Grange Arch.
Kimmeridge: E face of quarry car
park at junction of road to Bradle
over halfway up just N of steep narrow track (binoculars) (see note
below). **Corfe:** walls in centre of
village. **Hartland Moor:** by path80
on buttresses on W and S sides of
Scotland Barn. **Harman's Cross:** W
side of railway bridge at station.
Wares (east): few plants near W end
of low vertical rock face 35m S of gate

from Hay Brimble to Balston Wear (see note below). **Langton:** S side of B3069 W of Putlake Adventure Farm entrance (with other species). **Swanage:** several walls in centre of town. **Studland:** church porch.

Sites at Kimmeridge and The Wares are two of only four areas in Dorset where this fern is found other than on man-made walls. Small ferns like this, the other Spleenworts above and Rustyback below, do not harm walls, so there is no need to clean them off.

Rustyback *Ceterach officinarum*
Native. Occasional. Mortared walls. All year – wintergreen.
Church Knowle: plentiful on S facing roadside wall at Bradle; S side of road 100m SW of church. **Kingston:** N side of West Street 30m E of path50. **Corfe:** W side of East Street especially opposite Corfe Castle School (on British Legion wall); E side of East Street N of Colletts Close. **Swanage:** W side of Bell Street near S end; W side of Bon Accord Road 40-50m S of Atlantic Road. **Durlston:** by steps S of main entrance to Castle.

LADY FERN FAMILY
Lady Fern *Athyrium filix-femina*
Native. Occasional. Banks of streams and ditches, fens. Not wintergreen.
Stoborough: S side of New Road 50m from B3075. **Stoborough Heath:** here and there along valley in area about 250m W of Halfway Inn. **Ridge:** S side of Arne Road by stream 400m E of Sunnyside. **Hartland Moor:** here and there in Upper Fen; E boundary ditch of heath 50m SW of Scotland. **Bushey:** streambank in S of Brenscombe Heath by slight bend in Bushey Lane. **Langton:** by stream in NW corner of West Wood S of marshy pond. **Godlingston Heath:**

where bridleway33 crosses stream at E edge of forest. **Studland:** plentiful by stream which is crossed by bridleway23. **Studland Heath:** stream bank just beyond S end of Knoll Beach car park. **Brownsea:** S of Middle Street 100m E of E end of Vinery ruins.

Soft Shield Fern
Polystichum setiferum
Native. Abundant. Woods, hedgebanks. All year – wintergreen. May be confused with Hard Shield Fern.

BUCKLER FERN FAMILY
Male Fern *Dryopteris filix-mas*
Native. Frequent. Woods, hedgebanks. Remains green until early winter.

Can be fairly scaly most of the way up the stem, especially when young (see next species).

Scaly Male Fern *Dryopteris affinis*
Native. Occasional. Woods. All year – wintergreen.
Stoborough: 10m W of SW corner of Stoborough Heath SW of path7. **Furzebrook:** N of track in Kilnwood reserve 400m from road. **Stoborough Heath:** valley SW of A351 250m NW of Halfway Inn. **Furzebrook:** few by short NW-SE stretch of Purbeck Way compass bearing SE from Blue Pool. **Hartland Moor:** SE side of Arne Road opposite Bank Gate Cottages. **Wytch:** by bridleway4 starting 200m NW of Thrasher's Lane onwards to private Oil Road. **Durlston:** W side of top end of Diagonal Path. **Studland Heath:** plentiful by Woodland Nature Trail in S end of wood. **Studland:** W of N half of N-S ride through centre of The Warren Wood. **Brownsea:** NE of church by stream.

Usually found with Male Fern,

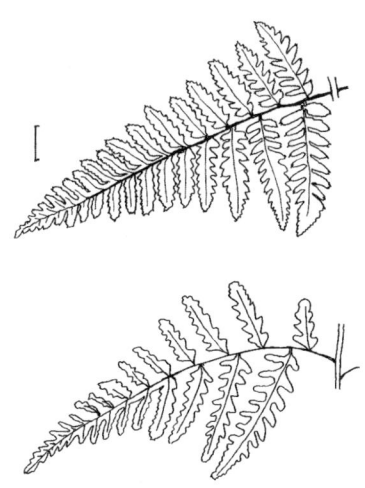

Lowest Pinna of Buckler Ferns – Narrow (above) and Broad.

sometimes abundantly, but at only a few of Male Fern's sites.

Remains <u>green</u> over winter. Brown scales remain all the way up the central stem when fully grown. Side branches have dark bases. This species shows variations which have led to attempts to divide it into subspecies; further research is in progress.

Narrow Buckler Fern
Dryopteris carthusiana
Native. Occasional. Marshes, wet woods, with other ferns. All year – wintergreen.
Hartland Moor: in Upper Fen 300m NE of Isolation Cottages; in Middle Fen 10m W of exclosure fence; 40m ENE of same exclosure; N side of Snag Valley 200m W of Slepe Road; along S edge of Snag Valley 125m W of Slepe Road; in shallow wet valley 225 and 350m NNE of Scotland.
Corfe Charity's Meadows: in wet strip of woodland W of Long

Meadow 150m N of Close Next The Barn. **Corfe:** among Greater Tussock Sedge in NW of West Common (with Broad Buckler Fern). **Wytch:** 200m S of NE corner of Wytch Moor. **Studland Heath:** very small amount 35m E of Ferry Road 150m N of Knoll Beach Road.

Scales on base of stems are pale brown, in contrast to pale edges and dark centres of scales of Broad Buckler Fern with which it sometimes grows. Upper and lower innermost pinnules (branchlets) of lowest pinnas are not so different in size, and pinnules are not so divided – see drawing.

Broad Buckler Fern
Dryopteris dilatata
Native. Frequent. Woods, verges, marshes. All year – wintergreen.

HARD FERN FAMILY
Hard Fern *Blechnum spicant*
Native. Occasional. Acid woods and shaded ditch-banks. All year – wintergreen.
Stoborough Heath: E side of path5 100m NW of small fenced field; in valley 250m W of Halfway Inn; stream banks S of Hartland Stud 300m N of A351. **Creech Heath:** by small pond 75m ENE of crossing of path34 by W-E track (site best approached from track). **Furzebrook:** N of Purbeck Way 350m E of Furzebrook Road.
Hartland Moor: several on streambank on SE side of Langton Wallis Heath 125m SW of Langton Wallis; E boundary ditch of heath 50m SW of Scotland. **Godlingston Heath:** banks of stream crossed by bridleway33 where it enters forest; stream banks 50-175m S of that; wood W of Ferry Road 100m S of Sewage Works. **Studland:** plentiful on banks of stream crossed by bridleway23.

CONIFERS

As with many ferns, conifer identification can be done in winter.

PINE FAMILY
Silver Fir *Abies alba*
Introduction. Occasional. Planted and self-seeding.
Creech Heath: 225m W of Furzebrook Road 40m N of path34.
Furzebrook: E side of Blue Pool Exit Road 65m N of car park (open March to October). **Arne:** by track which runs E from steps N of car park S of SE corner of fields. **Rempstone:** E end of Breaches Lane 500m E of Forest Lane.

Firs of the genus *Abies* are difficult to tell apart. Cones are only formed at the tops of mature trees, and they disintegrate on trees rather than fall. Leaves of some species look very similar.

Giant Fir *Abies grandis*
Introduction. Rare. Planted.
Holme: S side of Holme Lane 275m W of W end of Holme Lane Plantation.

Douglas Fir *Pseudotsuga menziesii*
Introduction. Occasional. Planted.
Holme: N side of Holme Lane 700m E of B3070. **Rempstone:** N side of B3351 100m NW of bridleway16 on opposite side. **Brownsea:** W of Visitor Centre (var. *glauca*).

Some trees produce many of their easily-recognised cones, but some produce few or none. In winter, the buds at the ends of the shoots have a characteristic neatly pointed appearance.

Western Hemlock-spruce
Tsuga heterophylla
Introduction. Occasional. Planted and self-seeding.
Stoborough: by path7 at SW corner of Stoborough Heath. **Rempstone:** both sides of bridleway8 under Black Pines from 100-250m from SW end of bridleway; on NW side of bridleway9 150-375m N of Burnbake Plantation; SE corner of Nelson Plantation on N side of B3351; another private plantation of this species on S side of B3351 opposite previous site. **Branksome Chine:** in wooded strip S of Pinecliff Road almost opposite end of Beach Road.

Top shoot of the tree bends over.

Sitka Spruce *Picea sitchensis*
Introduction. Occasional. Planted.
Kimmeridge: N of path14 in E-most of three private largely coniferous copses. **Kingston:** by path44 at S end of Quarry Wood. **Wytch:** N of bridleway4 – both just W of private Oil Road and 100m further NW. **Arne:** plenty on S side of Big Wood 300m N of bridleway1. **Godlingston Heath:** near N and W corners of Sewage Works (visible from outside fence).

Serbian Spruce *Picea omorika*
Introduction. Rare. Planted.
Wytch: small group visible (especially with binoculars) 60-100m E of Thrasher's Lane 250m N of crossing of bridleway4 (view from just N of lone pine on W verge of Lane).

Very narrow conical trees with light undersides of needles showing on upturned upper branches, and weeping twigs showing lower down.

Norway Spruce *Picea abies*
Introduction. Occasional. Planted.
Creech Heath: 10m S of path34 180m W of Furzebrook Road. **Church Knowle:** on W side of path18 180m S of road. **Kingston:** plenty along NW side of path44 S of West Street. **Arne:** by track which runs E from N of car

park S of SE corner of fields. **Remp-stone:** by bridleway16 through E end of Rempstone Wood. **Studland:** by path2 25m E of Ferry Road. **Brownsea:** several on both sides of Middle Street W of Vinery ruins; in NW part of Venetia Park.

Blue Spruce *Picea pungens* cv. *glauca*
Introduction. Rare. Planted.
Studland: in wood 100m S of Knoll Beach car park 100m W of shore.

European Larch *Larix decidua*
Introduction. Occasional. Planted.
Creech: large trees on SE side of road halfway up hill through Great Wood.
Arne: by track which runs E from N of car park S of SE corner of fields. **Studland:** Warren Wood W of central ride.
Cone scales are straight.

Hybrid Larch *Larix* x *marschlinsii*
Introduction. Occasional. Planted.
Arne: by track which runs E from N of car park S of SE corner of fields.
Rempstone: scattered on SW side of bridleway16 along 125-175m from N end (with Japanese Larch).
Cone scales turn slightly outward at the tips.

Japanese Larch *Larix kaempferi*
Introduction. Occasional. Planted.
Rempstone: SW side of bridleway9 at Churchill's Green; scattered along SW side of bridleway16 along 125-175m from N end (with Hybrid Larch).
Kingswood: by path30 on NE side of private Foxground Plantation 125-175m from NE corner of plantation; at NE corner itself.
Cone scales bent outward at right angles or more.

Deodar *Cedrus deodara*
Introduction. Rare. Planted.

Brownsea: in NE of Venetia Park; 100m SE of church.
Branch tips usually droop (D for Deodar and for droop); leaves 30mm or more long.

Cedar of Lebanon *Cedrus libani*
Introduction. Rare. Planted.
Holme: in private field visible N of Holme Lane 200m W of Holme Lane Plantation. **Studland:** triangle of land between Ferry Road and SE end of Wadmore Lane (young tree, with next species). **Brownsea:** small tree 100m SW of church.
Branch tips are usually level (L for Lebanon and for level); leaves *c.*25mm long.

Atlas Cedar *Cedrus atlantica*
Introduction. Rare. Planted.
Studland: triangle of land between Ferry Road and SE end of Wadmore Lane (young tree, with previous species).
Branch tips usually ascend (A for Atlas and for ascend); leaves 20mm long or less.

Scots Pine *Pinus sylvestris*
Native in Scotland, but reintroduction here (present here after Ice Age).
Abundant. Woods, heaths, hedges.
Needles in pairs.

Corsican Pine
Pinus nigra subsp. *laricio*
Introduction. Abundant. Planted and self-seeding.
Stoborough: Grange Road E side by railway bridge. **Wytch:** most pines in Wytch Heath plantation. **Rempstone:** most pines on Rempstone and Newton Heaths. **Durlston:** all pines in Country Park. **Ulwell:** above and near Water Works.
Needles in pairs.

Lodgepole Pine *Pinus contorta*
Introduction. Rare. Planted and self-seeding.
Rempstone: here and there in forest by bridleway27.
Cones are 2-6cm long, with long prickles on scales; needles in pairs.

Maritime Pine *Pinus pinaster*
Introduction. Occasional. Planted and self-seeding.
Stoborough: Grange Road E side 400m S of hotel. **Stoborough Heath:** SW corner of Stoborough Heath by path7. **Creech:** W side of Purbeck Way 50m S of railway crossing. **Corfe:** by path72. **Langton:** planted on E side of young National Trust wood S of junction of B3069 and the E road to Worth. **Godlingston Heath:** lone tree in bog 275m E of junction of bridleway27 and path32 with half-size needles and cones; loose group in middle of heath 300m W of bridleway26. **Wares (east):** by path61 250m S of California Farm. **Studland:** Woodhouse Wood SW corner. **Brownsea:** St. Michael's Mount. **Canford Cliffs:** low on cliffs 250-400m NE of Canford Cliffs Chine.
Like next species, its large cones are retained on trees for years, unless stripped off by squirrels which like them; needles in pairs.

Monterey Pine *Pinus radiata*
Introduction. Occasional. Planted and self-seeding.
Creech: N side of road 250m E of road junction at Creech Grange. **Church Knowle:** N side of road 300m E of church. **Wytch:** 400m W of Wytch Farm along 100m of path5. **Rempstone:** planted and self-seeding on N side of B3351 100m W of Forest Lane; planted by bridleway16

through E end of Rempstone Wood. **Kingswood:** along 25m of W side of bridleway29 just after it enters forest. **Godlingston:** planted W of cemetery. **Studland:** self-sown 160m S of Knoll Beach car park behind beach huts. **Brownsea:** W end of Daffodil Field; S of Public Hide. **Branksome Chine:** S of Pinecliff Road 50m E of Library.
Large cones are retained on trees for many years. Needles in threes.

Weymouth Pine *Pinus strobus*
Introduction. Rare. Planted.
Brownsea: 375m WNW of Vinery ruins 20m N of Middle Street (pick it out from Scots Pines by its smoother trunk, use binoculars to see the large curved cones).

REDWOOD FAMILY
Wellingtonia, Giant Redwood
Sequoiadendron giganteum
Introduction. Rare. Planted.
Rempstone: two tall trees can be seen from B3351 in W end of Rempstone Wood nearly opposite Rempstone Hall. **Brownsea:** young tree 100m SW of church.

CYPRESS/JUNIPER FAMILY
Monterey Cypress
Cupressus macrocarpa
Introduction. Occasional. Planted and self-seeding.
Tyneham: W of ruined cottages in village. **Creech Heath:** on S side of path34 160m W of Furzebrook Road. **Church Knowle:** old quarry N of Cocknowle. **Furzebrook:** S side of new bridleway41 just S of railway bridge. **Durlston:** SE corner of Large Copse; large tree in NE woods S of main glade; large tree visible from Zigzag Path. **Brownsea:** N of Vinery ruins wall; NW of churchyard.

Leyland Cypress X *Cupressocyparis leylandii* (*Cupressus macrocarpa* x *Chamaecyparis nootkatensis*)
(X in front of the name signifies that it is a hybrid between species of two different genera, though their hybridisation casts doubt on whether these species should be classified in different genera.)
Introduction. Occasional. Planted.
Rempstone: at NE end of large passing place on SE side of bridleway34 (Oil Road) 425m SW of crossing of bridleways31 and 34. **Brownsea:** group halfway along N side of Portland Avenue.

Much planted elsewhere but usually near buildings or in semi-natural situations like a golf course.

Can be confused with next species, but the ends of Leyland Cypress shoots point in different directions and its cones are larger.

Lawson's Cypress *Chamaecyparis lawsoniana* (originally, perhaps better, *Cupressus lawsoniana*, see Leyland Cyprus above)
Introduction. Frequent. Planted and self-seeding.
Creech: two very large trees on SE side of road halfway up hill through Great Wood. **Stoborough:** Grange Road E side by railway bridge.
Furzebrook: by Purbeck Way 50m W of Furzebrook Road. **Church Knowle:** old quarry N of Cocknowle. **Kingston:** plenty on S side of bridleway48 near its SE end. **Corfe:** B3351 NW side 100m NE of rail viaduct.
Bushey: on E side of bridleway10 250m N of Bushey Lane. **Rempstone:** W of bridleway9 600m N of Burnbake Plantation; self-seeding on NW side of Dismantled Tramway (bridleway10) near previous site.
Brownsea: N of Vinery ruins wall.

Ends of shoots are all in one plane. Top shoot of tree bends over. There are over 200 cultivated varieties of this species, with a range of shapes and colours. Those in the wild are usually, but not always, similar. When a variety with foliage hanging well down (pendulous) is found next to a normal tree, they may be mistakenly thought to be two different species.

Sawara Cypress
Chamaecyparis pisifera
Introduction. Rare. Planted.
Luscombe Valley: E side of stream 25m S of bridge at N end of reserve.
Like the pendulous form of the previous species, but the leaf-tips spread outwards and the cones are much smaller.

Common Juniper
Juniperus communis
Native, but planted here. Rare.
Rempstone: visible from N side of B3351 140m NW of bridleway16 on opposite side of road.

MONKEY PUZZLE FAMILY
Monkey Puzzle
Araucaria araucana
Introduction. Rare. Planted.
Herston (north): one tree can be seen from and between paths1 and 2 200m from their S ends (on private site of former caravan park now partially flooded). **Brownsea:** NW part of Venetia Park.

YEW FAMILY
Yew *Taxus baccata*
Native, also planted. Frequent. Woods, hedges, verges.
Studland: there is one tree probably at least 500 years old W of church.
Poisonous.

FLOWERING PLANTS

LAUREL FAMILY
Bay *Laurus nobilis*
Introduction. Occasional. Planted and self-seeding in woods and hedges. April to May.
Durlston: scattered in woods at E of Country Park especially at S end. **Swanage:** middle of N side of the green E of Ballard Estate (can be seen from path). **Studland:** E side of Ferry Road 40m N of village crossroads.

This is the true Laurel, used for victors' crowns in ancient times, hence its scientific name. Cherry Laurel and Portuguese Laurel (Rose Family), Spotted Laurel (Dogwood Family) and Spurge-laurel (Daphne Family) have similar leaves but are not true Laurels.

WATER-LILY FAMILY
White Water-lily *Nymphaea alba*
Native. Occasional. Freshwater (usually still water), sometimes planted. June to September.
Holme: East Holme Meadows – see p.23. **Creech Heath:** second pond W of Furzebrook Road N of path34 (with next species); largest pond N of W-E track which crosses path34 midway. **The Moors:** see p.27. **Hartland Moor:** E end of Fen Pool. **Norden:** Michael's Pond. **Corfe:** private pond E of road NE of Afflington Farm (view from road). **Arne:** pond N of track from viewpoint towards hide 125m W of bridleway1. **Studland Heath:** East Lake. **Brownsea:** Lily Pond (SW of Vinery ruins).

No tinge of pink on the petals.

Cultivated Water-lilies *Nymphaea* cvs.
Introduction. Occasional. Planted or escape, in still freshwater. June to September.
Creech Heath: pink plants in Icen Barrow Pond; in pond 200m S of it; in second pond W of Furzebrook Road N of path34 (with previous species; in small pond 125m NNW of latter pond; in largest pond S of W-E track which crosses path34 midway. **Furzebrook:** pink plants in both ends of E-most of three ponds in S of Kilnwood Reserve; pink plants in Little Pool S of Blue Pool. **Norden:** pink plants in Michael's Pond. **Bushey:** pale yellow plants in larger pond on Brenscombe South Heath. **Godlingston Heath:** pale yellow plants in Lily Pond. **Durlston:** pink plants in Johnston Pond. **Studland Heath:** pale yellow plants in Little Sea E of Spur Bog. **Brownsea:** pink and pinky-white plants in one of the ponds in SW of island.

There are over 100 cultivars. No attempt to separate them has been made by the author; likewise none was made in *The Flora of Dorset*. Anyone interested in doing so should begin by visiting Bennett's Water Gardens; the display there will delight. (See Appendix).

Yellow Water-lily *Nuphar lutea*
Native. Rare. Flowing freshwater. June to August.
Holme: East Holme Meadows – see p.23. **Stoborough:** in Cobbs Lake watercourse at NW end of path13. **Wareham:** SE side of River Frome here and there from bypass bridge to South Bridge (boat).

HORNWORT FAMILY
Rigid Hornwort
Ceratophyllum demersum
Native. Occasional. Ponds, broad ditches.

Tyneham: ponds E of ruined Rectory. **Wareham:** edge of creek (reached by short paths made by fishermen) 10m S of Purbeck Way 170-250m E of South Bridge. **Furzebrook:** E-most of three ponds in S of Kilnwood Reserve. **Norden:** Michael's Pond.

BUTTERCUP FAMILY
Marsh-marigold *Caltha palustris*
Native. Occasional. Watersides, wet ground in fields, commons and woods (often too shaded to flower in woods). March to May.
Stoborough: along 100m ditch W of W part of path13. **Wareham:** just W of South Bridge; here and there further W (boat trip); also for 250m E of bridge. **Ridge:** by river at Redcliffe Farm; by Purbeck Way for 200-250m NW of Redcliffe Farm. **Hartland Moor:** SE corner of White House Wood by bridleway4. **Corfe:** near NW end of First Valley on West Common; towards E corner of West Common near B3069; on Little East Common 10m S of bridleway30 150m from A351. **Durlston:** Visitor Centre Pond (view from hide)(introduced). **Studland:** Village Pond.

Stinking Hellebore
Helleborus foetidus
Native, but introduced in this area and self-seeding. Occasional. Woods, verges, waste ground. January to March.
Nationally Scarce as a Native.
Stoborough: E side Grange Road 400m N of railway bridge; on SW side of path7 10 and 70m SE of Grange Road. **Arne:** NW of Arne Road 20 and 30m SW of car park. **Swanage:** beside path between Northbrook Road and Cauldron Crescent. **Durlston:** S side of Solent Road 35m from Lighthouse Road.

Love-in-a-mist *Nigella damascena*
Introduction. Occasional. Casual. June to August.
Ulwell: usually on NE side of Ulwell Road within 75m SE of path15.

Wood Anemone
Anemone nemorosa
Native. Occasional. Ancient woods and hedge-banks. March to April.
East Creech: here and there in woods N of Stonehill Down.
Furzebrook: plentiful in NW part of Kilnwood Reserve S of Purbeck Way 350m E of Furzebrook Road.
Corfe: few by or visible from first 600m of Purbeck Way W of path72; good patches on bank W of stream N of West Mill ruins; W bank of Byle Brook near S end of Byle Copse. **Harman's Cross:** E side of Haycrafts Lane 250m N of reservoir. **Langton:** plentiful in drier parts of West Wood. **Harman's Cross:** by N end of path44 through The Wilderness. **Kingswood:** here and there on S side of B3351 for 350-500m W of Kingswood Farm. **Studland:** by Coast Path in N end of Studland Wood.

Peacock Anemone
Anemone pavonina
Recent Introduction. Rare. Planted and self-seeding. May.
Studland: planted and spread at Clayton Meadow.

Japanese Anemone *Anemone* x *hybrida* (*A. hupehensis* x *vitifolia*)
Introduction. Rare. Escape. July to September.
Swanage: SE side of Victoria Avenue opposite Triangle Garage (pink flowers). **Canford Cliffs:** by path from Nairn Road to Brudenell Road 50m from former (gets cut down).

Traveller's Joy, Old Man's Beard
Clematis vitalba
Native. Abundant. Woods, hedges, mostly on calcareous soil. July to September.

Virgin's Bower *Clematis flammula*
Introduction. Rare. Planted or escape.
Corfe: above N side of Sandy Hill Lane 30-55m E of railway bridge. July to August.

Meadow Buttercup *Ranunculus acris*
Native. Abundant. Meadows on calcareous and neutral soil. May to July.
Flower stalks are not furrowed. Sepals are not reflexed.

Creeping Buttercup
Ranunculus repens
Native. Abundant. Anywhere but sand, salt-marsh and most acid soil. May to September.
Flower stalks are furrowed. Sepals are not reflexed.

Bulbous Buttercup
Ranunculus bulbous
Native. Abundant. Calcareous or neutral soils, not in shade. March to June.
Sepals are reflexed (turned back down stem).

Hairy Buttercup *Ranunculus sardous*
Native. Occasional. Arable fields, other disturbed or thinly vegetated ground. May to October.
Kimmeridge: by Coast Path between Oil Well and Gaulter Cottages (with other buttercups, distinctive capsule bumps difficult to see in this population). **Holme:** few near entrance to open access part of Battle Plain at Doreys Farm; East Holme Meadows – see p.23. **Stoborough Heath:** 40m SW of NE corner of Sandlings field (with other buttercups). **Corfe:** on N edge of West Common by wooden fence posts E of cattle grid (other species of buttercup nearby).
Harman's Cross: by path6 150, 400 and 450m NE of stile E of New Barn.
Ulwell: by path15 in first field E of Ulwell Road (with other buttercups).
Swanage: on N side of Kings Road on small raised lawn on S side of Co-op supermarket.
Look with lens for a row of bumps inside the margin at the edge of the developed seed capsule, although they are not always present. It has reflexed sepals like the previous species but starts flowering later and has smaller, slightly paler petals.

Corn Buttercup *Ranunculus arvensis*
Early Introduction. Rare. Arable fields. June to August.
Dorset Rare. Critically Endangered.
Wares (east): may be visible from gate at NE corner of Golter in field to E (short-range binoculars). See plate 9.

Small-flowered Buttercup
Ranunculus parviflorus
Native. Frequent. On bare ground and in short grass over calcareous soil or sand. April to May.
Steeple: here and there on Steeple Down (west). **Kimmeridge:** N of bridleway12 along S side of large field N of village (when crop is Rape – some plants over 25cm high). **Church Knowle:** plentiful on E end of Ridgeway Hill. **Worth:** on valley sides N of Renscombe Farm. **Wares (west):** flat top of Long Close S of Eastington Farm; along N edge of E half of Taylor's Ware; along N edge of Dancing Ledge Ware; **(east)** in N parts of wares from Verney Ware to Belle Vue East Ware. **Durlston:** E of

Visitor Centre. **Ballard Down:** here and there along S side near bottom. Plentiful at all those sites.

In this area it grows close to the ground and usually has only one or two narrow petals, unlike illustrations in books. Foliage is green, not greyish. See Plate 9.

Goldilocks Buttercup *Ranunculus auricomus*

Native. Occasional. Old woods and hedge-banks. April to May.
Stoborough: can be seen on private land by looking over disused iron gate on private land on N side of Holme Lane 70m from E end. **East Creech:** several 20 and 40m S of N edge of Woods N of Stonehill Down on E edge of path32 (best site). **Langton:** one plant seen on NW side of path5 through Talbot's Wood 18m NE of bottom of steps; (also worth watching in Langton West Wood where it has been seen at some unrecorded site in past). **Studland:** very small amount by track at SE corner of Studland Wood.

Typical flowers only have few (if any) petals and look imperfect.

Celery-leaved Buttercup
Ranunculus sceleratus
Native. Rare. Mud. June to July.
The Moors: see page 27.

Greater Spearwort
Ranunculus lingua
Native, but also planted. Rare. Ponds, ditches. June to August.
Dorset Rare as a native. (Can spread naturally; sometimes difficult to know whether planted.)
Norden: Michael's Pond. **Worth:** pond on NE side of Renscombe Road. **Durlston:** Johnston Pond (planted).

Lesser Spearwort
Ranunculus flammula
Native. Frequent. Marshes, ponds, wet places in woods and fields. May to October.

Lesser Celandine   *Ranunculus ficaria*
Native. Abundant. Verges, woods, fields, marshes, gardens. February to May.
Corfe: two growing unusually in holes about 1m up trees on N side of Purbeck Way 200 and 240m W of foot of NE corner of West Hill.

Separate records of subspecies have not been kept.

Crowfoots and Water-crowfoots
See *The Wild Flower Key* (Rose & O'Reilly, 2006) for help with identification on pages 108-9.

Ivy-leaved Crowfoot
Ranunculus hederaceus
Native. Occasional. Bare mud or very shallow water, sometimes near springs. March to May.
Corfe: N side of Second Valley 40m NW of UCR; S of path65 50m SW of car park; W of UCR 120m SW of end of West Street; near N corner of Middle Common close to drinking trough; plentiful S of Middle Common Pond; in East Valley in Big East Common 30m from railway fence.
Wytch: by path5 through S corner of triangular field NW of Wytch Moor.
Wares (east): plentiful in Y-shaped flush in middle of Verney Ware; in flush in SW of Belle Vue West Ware.
Studland: by path13 150m S of B3351.

Round-leaved Crowfoot
Ranunculus omiophyllus
Native. Occasional. Still or slow-moving shallow acid water, mud. April to June.

Holme: towards E side of open access woodland SW of East Holme E of conspicuous area of Bog Myrtle in middle of wood. **Corfe Charity's Meadows:** ditch on NW side of Paddle Dock meadow 175m SW of gateway from Home Mead (W). **Corfe:** in East Valley in Big East Common 250m from railway fence. **Studland Heath:** on soft and dangerous mud under willows W of Woodland Nature Trail – recently easiest to see 12m W of point on trail 20m before (N of) post 6 (but sites move); few in depression 30m N of centre of main N car park at Knoll Beach.

Brackish Water-crowfoot
Ranunculus baudotii
Native. Rare. Ponds near sea.
Studland: Westwood Pond. May to June.

Sepal tips are usually dull grey-blue. Nectary shape varies, as with similar species.

Thread-leaved Water-crowfoot
Ranunculus trichophyllus
Native. Occasional. Ponds. May to June, but sporadic.
Corfe: W end of Middle Common Pond. **Wares (west):** pond S of Priest's Way 250m E of path30 (best site); **(east)** pond at junction of bridleways18 and 20. **Durlston:** pond of N edge of Field 3 (but only seen when cattle have not been in that field in spring).

Stream Water-crowfoot
Ranunculus pencillatus
Native. Rare. Rivers, streams. May to June.
Holme: River Frome at Holme Bridge. **Swanage:** Swan Brook S of Health Centre.

Columbine *Aquilegia vulgaris*
Native elsewhere but escaped cultivar in this area; usually short-lived (slugs and snails like it).
Rare. May to June.
Hartland Moor: both pink and white 40m E of Jubilee Bridge.

Common Meadow-rue
Thalictrum flavum
Native. Occasional. Ditches. Mid-June to early July.
Holme: East Holme Meadows – see p.23. **Stoborough:** W side of B3075 N of village in several places. **Wareham:** N of Purbeck Way in four places between 175 and 400m E of South Bridge each along several m. **Ridge:** NE side of Purbeck Way 250m NW of Redcliffe Farm. **Furzebrook:** along 15m of E side of Furzebrook Road opposite road to East Creech. **Norden:** SW side of A351 700m NW of railway bridge; on S side of bridleway77 70m from A351; along 20m of N side of same bridleway 90m from A351. **Rempstone:** S side of Breaches Lane 130m E of new farm buildings.

Not common.

Lesser Meadow-rue
Thalictrum minus
Native, but introduced here. Rare. Verge. June to July.
Studland: N side of Heath Green Road by South Lea Wood.

BARBERRY FAMILY
Barberry *Berberis vulgaris*
Native. Rare. Hedges. May.
Corfe: along 2m of W side of minor road 60m N of N end of stone wall in front of Afflington Farmhouse.

Thunberg's Barberry
Berberis thunbergii
Introduction. Rare. Planted, and self-seeding. May.
Stoborough Heath: SE of Purbeck Way on bend ENE of railway crossing (green leaves). However, in gardens and parks it has purple leaves more often than green.

Darwin's Barberry *Berberis darwinii*
Introduction. Rare. Planted and self-seeding. March to May.
Studland: by path21 150m from W end; on right of entrance to Middle Beach car park.

Oregon-grape *Mahonia aquifolium*
Introduction. Rare. Planted. April to May.
Kingston: S side of West Street 150m E of W edge of The Plantation; SE side of B3069 10m SW of N end of path40.

POPPY FAMILY
The appearance of species of Papaver genus below is impossible to predict with accuracy, since they depend upon bare ground, which varies from year to year.

Opium Poppy *Papaver somniferum*
Early Introduction. Frequent. Arable fields, other disturbed ground. June to July.

Common Poppy *Papaver rhoeas*
Early Introduction. Frequent. Arable fields, other disturbed ground. June to early October.

Long-headed Poppy *Papaver dubium*
Early Introduction. Occasional. Arable fields, other disturbed ground. June to July.

Scrape the stem to see white juice.

Yellow-juiced Poppy
Papaver dubium subsp. *lecoqii*
Early Introduction. Occasional. Arable fields, other disturbed ground. June to July.
Kingston: some seen near NE corner of churchyard S of E Horse Chestnut.
Scrape the stem to see yellow juice.

Welsh Poppy *Meconopsis cambrica*
Native, but introduced here. Rare. Casual. June to July.

Yellow-horned Poppy
Glaucium flavum
Native. Occasional. Cliffs and cliff-tops. June to July.
Kimmeridge: visible from Coast Path 400m E of Rope Lake Head.
Kingston: by Coast Path 400m E of South Gwyle. **Ballard Down:** scattered along W end of bottom of chalk cliffs for over 100m; top edge of cliff 130m SE of trig point (view from distance).

Greater Celandine
Chelidonium majus
Early Introduction. Occasional. Verges. April to August.
Holme: S side of Holme Lane 80m SW of bend near NE part of open access woodland. **Stoborough:** S of path13 20m W of West Lane. **East Creech:** near N end of path32. **Ridge:** NE side of Purbeck Way 50m NW of Redcliffe Farm. **Kingston:** several on S side of The Lane E of path49. **Corfe:** near SE corner of old cemetery on East Street. **Hartland Moor:** W side of track to Middlebere Farm 100m N of cattle grid on track. **Swanage:** Sentry Road. **Studland:** by path21 by Village Hall; in Church Road; near entrance to Middle Beach car park; in several other places in village.

Californian Poppy
Eschscholzia californica
Introduction. Occasional. Casual.
June to September.

FUMITORY FAMILY
Yellow Corydalis
Pseudofumaria lutea
Introduction. Occasional. Walls. May
to October.
Kingston: wall on W side of South
Street SE of church; wall 100m S of
there. **Langton:** W side of N end of
Durnford Drove.

Climbing Corydalis
Ceratocapnos claviculata
Native. Occasional. Woods, hedges,
verges. April to July.
The Moors: see p.27. **Hartland
Moor:** NE side of Slepe Road – NW
of entrance to Slepe Farm (Natural
England offices) for 100m and again
from 200-300m; here and there for
100-400m SE of same entrance.
Kingston: along 30m of E side of
track on W edge of open access land
125m NE of 'y' in 'Encombe Dairy'
on O.S. map (approach along track
from SSE keeping to open access
land). **Wytch:** on both sides of bridle-
way4 50m SE of private Oil Road.

Fumitories
There are helpful drawings of
Fumitory sepals and fruits in *The
Wild Flower Key* (Rose & O'Reilly,
2006) on page 117.

Common Ramping-fumitory
Fumaria muralis
Native. Occasional. Verges. May to
August.
Creech: on W side of Purbeck Way
just S of railway crossing. **Hartland
Moor:** N side of path80 for 30m E of
Slepe Road. **Harman's Cross:** N side

of A351 just E of path41. **Ower:** N
side of where bridleways7 and 8 cross.
Swanage: N corner of junction of
Northbrook Road and Beach
Gardens road; E side of Redcliffe
Road NE of All Saints church hall.
Studland: corner of School Lane and
Church Road. **Lilliput:** inside fence
halfway along bottom of Evening
Hill. **Luscombe Valley:** outside fence
along S edge of Reserve. **Sandbanks:**
in/by bushes either side of main car
park exit. **Canford Cliffs:** here and
there by stepped path from Cliff
Drive to beach.
  Can be transient.

Common Fumitory
Fumaria officinalis
Early Introduction. Occasional.
Arable fields, other disturbed ground.
June to July.
  A smaller version of this species is
subsp. *wirtgenii* – the flat apex of
seedcase shows that it is a variety of
Common Fumitory. This has
occurred at the N side of entrance to
caravan field at **East Creech**.

PLANE FAMILY
London Plane *Platanus* x *hispanica*
(*P. occidentalis* x *orientalis*)
Introduction. Occasional. Planted.
Godlingston: N side of Washpond
Lane by path2. **Durlston:** two trees
in wood in NE corner of Park – one
tall tree 35m N of Coast Path and
25m W of the stream bridge which is
NE of main glade; one tree 25m
beyond same bridge 5m E of track.
Ballard Down: between Coast Path
and cliff-top 350m NE of Shep's
Hollow. **Brownsea:** NE of Visitor
Centre; SW of track 100m SE of
church.
  Leaves are similar to Sycamore but
the fruits are very different.

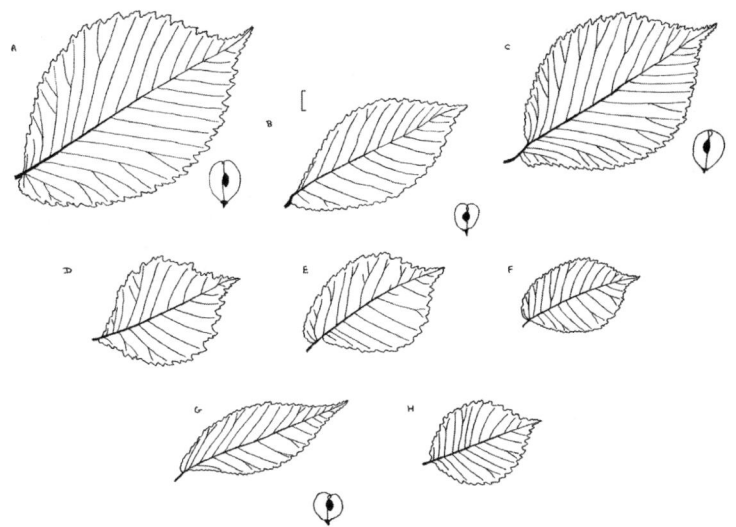

Leaves and fruit of Elms: A - Wych, B - Huntingdon's, C - Dutch, D - English, E, F, G - forms of Small-leaved, H - Cornish.

ELM FAMILY

Opinions vary about how many Elm species and subspecies there are. All agree about Wych Elm, but otherwise, the literature differs as to how many species are described, and various scientific names are used. Leaves are the most important feature for identification. The usual advice is to examine leaves of side shoots from branches, rather than leaves of leading twigs; definitely avoid leaves of suckers. See drawings. Most elms carry the Dutch Elm fungus and die back to ground level every 20-40 years, regenerating from suckers from the roots.

Wych Elm *Ulmus glabra*
Native. Occasional. Some planted. Woods, hedges. April to May.
Creech: both sides of Grange Road 175m S of path19. **Kingston:** around N half of car park 250m W of church. **Harman's Cross:** seen from path44 along 60m of S edge of The Wilderness either side of path (including large trees). **Langton:** by E end of path28; W side of old cemetery N of B3069 near road; where paths14 and 21 cross. **Godlingston:** across road from SW corner of Marsh Copse. **Durlston:** W side of road N of car parks opposite the 'No overnight parking' sign. **Swanage:** 70m NE of gate at SW corner of The Downs; S side of Washpond Lane 25m W of Ulwell Road. **Studland:** at junction of path20 and bridleway23; by path3 50m NE of Manor Road.

Huntingdon Elm *Ulmus* x *vegeta* (*U. glabra* x *minor*) (*U.* x *hollandica* var. *vegeta*, *U.* x *hollandica* 'Vegeta') Native. Rare. Planted. April to May.
Durlston: just W of N end of Diagonal Path.

Leaves are more or less smooth on the upperside, usually over 7cm long, and nearly twice as long as wide; rust-coloured hairs on buds.

Dutch Elm *Ulmus* x *hollandica*
(*U. glabra* x *minor*)
(*U.* x *hollandica* 'Hollandica')
Native, but planted here. Occasional.
Wood edges, hedges. April to May.
Tyneham: planted in several places by path from Tyneham Farm to Worbarrow; also in village. **Steeple:** opposite side of road to Blackmanston Farm. **Stoborough Heath:** 100m NW of Halfway Inn by gate to heath SW of A351. **Norden:** on S side of bridleway77 opposite start of permissive path running NNE from near New Line Farm. **Worth:** several on N side of Coast Path 50m and more W of Hill Bottom hamlet. **Knitson:** S side of bridleway8 in three places – 50, 200 and 450m W of bridleway12. **Durlston:** E side of bend of unmade part of Durlston Road; between roads at entrance to car park.

Leaves and buds are like Huntingdon Elm, but leaves are not nearly twice as long as wide.

English Elm
Ulmus procera (*U. minor* var. *vulgaris*).
Native. Frequent. Hedges. Not seen in flower now.

Due to the Dutch Elm fungus, they grow into young trees and then die down again to their roots.

Small-leaved Elm
Ulmus minor subsp. *minor*
(*U. minor* var. *minor*) (*U. carpinifolia*)
Native. Occasional. Wood edges, hedges. April to May.
Tyneham: N side of path to Worbarrow 325m W of Tyneham Farm. **Ridge:** SE side of New Road both 200 and 225m SW of Arne Road. **Norden:** by permissive bridle-

way SE of A351 roundabout.
Swanage: halfway down W edge of Pitch and Putt course (players only) with other elms; E end of copse W of D'Urberville Drive. **Durlston:** between one-way roads between two sides of car park. **Brownsea:** several S of Middle Street E of Vinery ruins.

Some main branches are horizontal or drooping; leaf-bases are strongly asymmetric.

Cornish Elm *Ulmus minor* subsp.
angustifolia (*U. minor* var.
angustifolia, U. minor var. *cornubensis,*
U. angustifolia, U. stricta)
Native. Occasional. Woods, hedges. April to May.
Creech: along bridleway2 here and there on SW side 400-450m NW of Grange Road. **Ridge:** S side of Arne Road 300m E of Sunnyside (road). **Langton:** W side of A351 along 40m N of junction with Crack Lane (may die soon). **Durlston:** along N part of wood in NE of Country Park; also W of castle.

Main branches ascend; leaf-bases are weakly asymmetric. The scientific name is confusing as leaves are broader than on Small-leaved Elm.

HEMP FAMILY
Hop *Humulus lupulus*
Native. Occasional. Hedges, wood edges. July to August.
Stoborough: NW side of West Lane at junction with B3075. **Kingston:** 60-90m N of Scott Arms on W side of B3069. **Church Knowle:** both sides of road 175-225m S of sharp bend near Puddle Mill Farm. **Corfe:** W side of minor road 100m N of Afflington Farm. **Worth:** 100m S of London Row 30m E of path13 on N side of field. **Bushey:** S side of Thrasher's Lane 800m N of B3351

along 40m. **Woolgarston:** three
places on roadside between Higher
Grove Wood and Ailwood Farm.
Ulwell: SW side of Ulwell Road
100m SE of road to Ulwell Cottage
Caravan Park. **Studland:** N side
Watery Lane 20m W of path7.
Brownsea: NW of track where it
emerges from buildings W of Landing
Pier. **Sandbanks:** towards E end of
path from Chaddesley Glen to the
beach.

MULBERRY FAMILY
Mulberry *Morus nigra*
Introduction. Rare. Planted.
Brownsea: in SE of Venetia Park; also
S of church.

Fig *Ficus carica*
Introduction. Rare. Escape.
Swanage: few inaccessible on cliff
70m N of N end of promenade
(binoculars from beach). **Canford
Cliffs:** on cliff 150m SW of Flaghead
Chine (view from promenade).

NETTLE FAMILY
Nettle *Urtica dioica*
Native. Abundant. Enriched ground
almost anywhere. May to September.

Stingless Nettle *Urtica dioica* subsp.
galeopsifolia
Native. Rare. With Nettle. May to
September.
Wareham: small amount S side of
Purbeck Way 170m E of South
Bridge. **Kingston:** by path22 on E
side of Newfoundland (wood) 20m N
of S end of wood.

It may sting but it is less than 10%
as effective as Nettle. Longer narrower
lower leaves – see drawing.

Small Nettle *Urtica urens*
Early Introduction. Occasional.

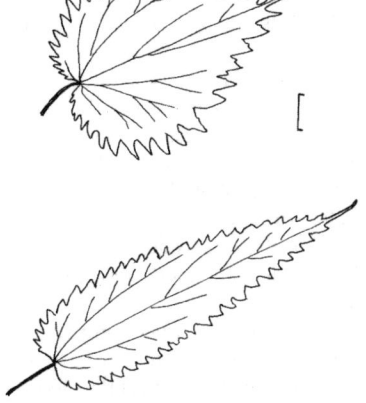

Lower leaves of Nettle (above) and Stingless Nettle

Arable fields, other disturbed
ground. April to September.
Hartland Moor: NE side of permissive bridleway on Langton Wallis
Heath 375m NW of SE end at bridleway77. **Kingston:** 800m S of S
end of South Street on both sides of
path41 (with Nettle). **Ower:** 110m
W of W edge of Game Copse on
both sides of bridleway8. **Knitson:**
on SW side of bridleway9 70m from
SE end of bridleway. **Ulwell:** near
SW corner of Round Down.
Godlingston Heath: 20m NE of
barn by bridleway33 in fields SE of
Greenland; by bridleway35 S of
height mark 7 on O.S. map.
Swanage: may be seen from path
through allotments W of Cauldron
Barn Road. **Brownsea:** 30m N of
Visitor Centre. **Branksome Chine:**
seen in flowerbed at SE end of chine
NW of road.

It is not at all of these sites every
year. The Godlingston Heath sites
are the most reliable.

Pellitory-of-the-wall *Parietaria judaica*
Native. Occasional at native sites –
rocks, cliffs; frequent on walls. March
to October.
Corfe: plentiful on castle walls.
Durlston: rocks near Coast Path S of
castle. **Swanage:** various walls and
buildings in town. **Ballard Down:** foot
of chalk cliffs 500m E of W end of
chalk. **Studland:** plentiful out of reach
on chalk cliffs on S side of Studland
Bay (visible with binoculars at low
tide).

As this species is usually only seen on
man-made walls, it is interesting to see
it here also on rocks and cliffs – its original habitat. Similarly, the vast majority
of House Martins now nest on man-
made buildings, but here some nest on
chalk cliffs between Ballard Head and
Old Harry Rocks. Interestingly,
Pellitory-of-the-wall is also across the
sea on the chalk cliffs of the Isle of
Wight (Pope *et al.*, 2003).

Mind-your-own-business
Soleirolia soleirolii
Introduction. Frequent. Gardens, pave-
ments, bottom of walls, stone river and
stream banks. May to October.
Kimmeridge: E side of road 30m S of
path9. **Wareham:** on S riverbank stones
20m E of South Bridge. **Corfe:** S side of
West Street W of right-angled bend.
Church Knowle: SE side of road 30m
W of path20. **Ulwell:** SW side of
Ulwell Road 25m NW of road to
Ulwell Cottage caravan park. **Swanage:**
in council flowerbeds W of Shore Road
between Victoria Avenue and Walrond
Road; near top of steps on N side of
Peveril Point Road bearing S from outer
end of pier. **Branksome Chine:** SE end
of chine especially on walls of stream.

If you find a small piece of this plant
in your garden remove it without delay,
or you will regret it.

BOG MYRTLE FAMILY
Bog Myrtle *Myrica gale*
Native. Frequent. Firmer parts of bogs.
April to May.

BEECH FAMILY
Beech *Fagus sylvatica*
Native in SE England, but planted and
self-seeding here. Frequent. Woods,
hedges, fields.

Sweet Chestnut *Castanea sativa*
Early Introduction. Frequent. Planted
and self-seeding.

Turkey Oak *Quercus cerris*
Introduction. Occasional. Planted
and self-seeding. Woods, hedges.
Kingston: by path22 on E side of
Newfoundland (wood) 15m N of S
end of wood. **Arne:** SE side of Arne

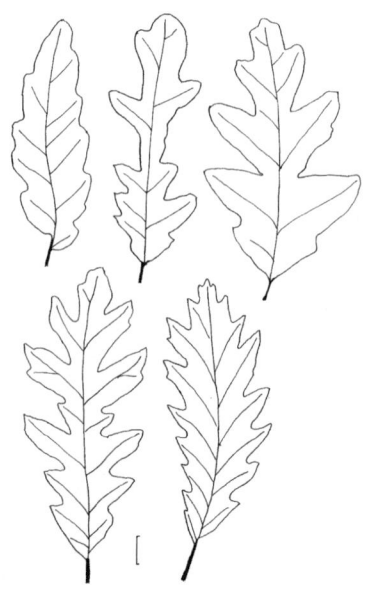

Leaves of Turkey Oak showing range of variation

Road here and there 100-700m NE of Bank Gate Cottages. **Wytch:** W side of Thrasher's Lane 25m S of SE corner of Thrasher's Heath; 25m further S on E side of Lane. **Bushey:** several along E side of N end of Meadus' Lane; by bridleway10 where it joins Dismantled Tramway E of Bushey; large one 200m S of B3351 on E side of bridleway14. **Kingswood:** N side of B3351 100m W of bridleway16 on S side; also on N side opposite that bridleway. **Brownsea:** N side of Portland Avenue 300m SW of Visitor Centre.

Leaves vary considerably in shape (see drawing) Can be mistaken for Sessile Oak.

Evergreen Oak, Holm Oak
Quercus ilex
Introduction. Frequent. Planted in woods and self-seeding in open ground.

Far too frequent, in author's view. Multiplies on calcareous soils; when full grown its dense shade kills off all vegetation beneath it, as can be seen SW of **Durlston** Castle.

Pedunculate Oak, English Oak
Quercus robur
Native. Abundant. Woods, hedges, fields; not often on calcareous soil; planted and self-seeding.

Red Oak *Quercus rubra*
Introduction. Occasional. Planted. **Tyneham:** several planted in village. **Holme:** N side Holme Lane 225m E of road to East Holme. **Rempstone:** visible on S side of Bushey Lane 100m NW of Forest Lane; small plantation SW of crossing of bridleways9 and 10 (Dismantled Tramway). **Brownsea:** several places around Church Field.

In this area leaves of most trees turn

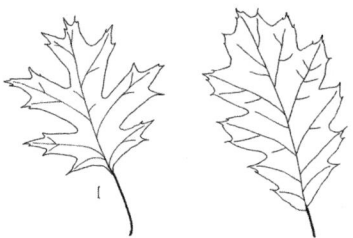

Leaves of Red Oak showing range of variation.

mid-brown rather than red in autumn, but some foliage is reddish when emerging. See drawing.

BIRCH FAMILY
Silver Birch *Betula pendula*
Native. Abundant. Woods, heaths, hedges, chiefly on acid soils. Planted but not self-seeding on other soils.

Twig surface is smooth (lens). Primary leaf-teeth are prominent. Trunk colour is often misleading; in shade, it can be as little silver as Downy Birch.

Downy Birch *Betula pubescens*
Native. Abundant. Woods, heaths, hedges, chiefly on wet acid soils.

Twigs are downy. Leaf-teeth are even in length. Trunk may have some silver, but less than most Silver Birch above.

Alder *Alnus glutinosa*
Native. Frequent. By still or running freshwater, wet copses, sometimes planted elsewhere.

Leaf apex not pointed, often indented, leaf-base not heart-shaped. 'Cones' 3 to 8 on common stalk; see drawing p.76.

Grey Alder *Alnus incana*
Introduction. Rare. Planted.

Corfe: few W side of path72 just N of Purbeck Way. **Wytch:** by new route of path5 (Oil Road) at NW corner of Wytch Moor (SE of oil well).

Leaf apex is pointed, leaf base not heart-shaped; 3 to 8 'Cones' on common stalk; see drawing.

Italian Alder *Alnus cordata*
Introduction. Rare. Planted.
Swanage: in several places by Swan Brook where it passes through Pitch

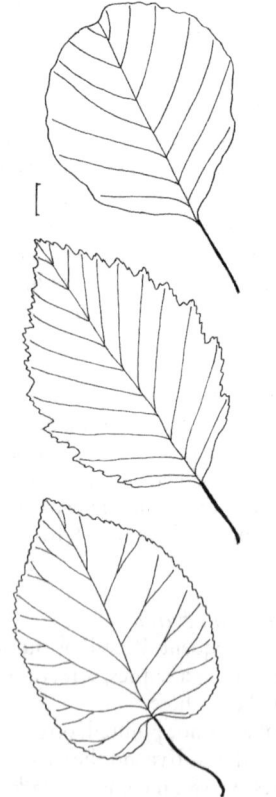

Leaves of Alders – Alder (above), Grey Alder (middle), Italian Alder (below).

and Putt course – for example S and W of 5th green (players only) (planted when farmland).

Leaf is heart-shaped; 'Cones' larger, 1 to 3 on common stalk; see drawing.

Hornbeam *Carpinus betulus*
Native in SE Britain, including E Dorset, but mostly planted here. Occasional. Woods, hedges.
Stoborough Heath: E side of Dismantled Tramway 75m from N end. **Hartland Moor:** few on E side of Slepe Road at Slepe Copse. **Arne:** 50m N of car park on E side of Arne Road. **Bushey:** E side Meadus' Lane 250 and 350m N of B3351.
Rempstone: along 20m on N side of Bushey Lane beginning 60m NW of Forest Lane; along N side of B3351 from 125-375m W of bridleway16 on opposite side. **Knitson:** hedge of it along N side of road 75-325m SE of Knitson Farm. **Durlston:** young trees in Hingston Copse. **Studland:** W of village pond. **Brownsea:** several E of Vinery ruins either side of Middle Street.

Leaves are similar to Beech but toothed, somewhat pleated and more pointed; trunk with criss-cross pattern in places except when young.

Hazel *Corylus avellana*
Native. Abundant. Woods, hedges.

MESEMBRYANTHEMUM FAMILY
Hottentot-fig *Carpobrotus edulis*
Introduction. Rare. Escape on cliffs. April to August.
Branksome Chine: small amount by seafront 525m SW of chine (20m SW of end of beach chalets).
Branksome Dene Chine: large amount at foot of sea cliffs to NE.

GOOSEFOOT FAMILY

Goosefoots and oraches can be difficult to tell apart. Examine with lens whether male and female flowers are separate on the same plant (Oraches).

Strawberry-blite
Chenopodium capitatum
Introduction. Rare. Casual. July to September.

Red Goosefoot
Chenopodium rubrum
Native. Occasional. Arable fields, other disturbed ground, manure heaps, pondsides. July to September.
Leaves are similar to Nettle-leaved Goosefoot but parts of the plant are usually reddish.

Many-seeded Goosefoot
Chenopodium polyspermum
Early Introduction. Occasional. Arable fields, other disturbed ground, manure heaps. July to October.

Nettle-leaved Goosefoot
Chenopodium murale
Early Introduction. Occasional. Arable fields, other disturbed ground. July to October.
Vulnerable.
Godlingston Heath: 20m NE of barn by bridleway33 (sometimes with Red Goosefoot). **Swanage:** by path through allotments W of Cauldron Barn Road. **Studland:** W side of N end of bridleway12 along short narrow verge S of gate to Manor Farm old farmyard.
Brownsea: behind one section of wooden sea defence fence halfway along S shore 50m W of 'easy way down'; sometimes in flowerbed W of Landing Pier (with Red Goosefoot).

Leaves are similar to Red Goosefoot but parts of the plant are usually mealy, not reddish. Tiny rounded teeth on edge of sepals are best seen after the flower has been fertilized and the ovary is beginning to swell beneath sepals.

Maple-leaved Goosefoot
Chenopodium hybridum
Early Introduction. Rare. Arable fields, other disturbed ground. August to October.

Fig-leaved Goosefoot
Chenopodium ficifolium
Early Introduction. Occasional. Arable fields, other disturbed ground, manure heaps. July to September.

Fat Hen *Chenopodium album*
Native. Frequent. Arable fields, other disturbed ground. July to October.
Highly nutritious: the leaves can be cooked like Spinach.

Spear-leaved Orache
Atriplex prostrata
Native. Frequent. Beaches (often with next species), arable fields, other disturbed ground. July to September.

Babington's Orache
Atriplex glabriuscula
Native. Occasional. Beaches (often with previous species). July to September.
Worth: S end of W side of Chapman's Pool. **Studland:** on South Beach here and there towards SE end. **Studland Heath:** Bramble Bush Bay. **Sandbanks:** on shore opposite W end of Chaddesley Glen.

Plants are purple-tinged; fruits are usually warty, unlike some illustrations.

Grass-leaved Orache
Atriplex littoralis
Native. Occasional. Tops of shores.
July to September.
Studland Heath: neck of Redhorn
Quay; tip of Sandy Point. **Lilliput:**
by seawall at SE end of Evening Hill.
Luscombe Valley: just outside SE
corner. **Sandbanks:** sandbank 80m
W of junction of Shore Road and
Banks Road; along sand for 40m N
of that; here and there W of Banks
Road for 100m S of junction with
Shore Road.

Inland, any narrow-leaved oraches
are almost always a form of the next
species. Branches of this species do
sometimes spread widely like next
species. Examine fruit cases to tell
them apart.

Common Orache *Atriplex patula*
Native. Frequent. Arable fields, other
disturbed ground; occasional on
beaches. July to October.

The translucent nature of leaf veins
is not easy to see.

Frosted Orache *Atriplex laciniata*
Native. Occasional. Sandy beaches –
comes and goes. July to September.
Dorset Scarce.
Kimmeridge: occurred once recently
on beach E of Charnel (accessible
when Army Range Walks are open).
Studland: found twice on South
Beach (once towards N end and once
towards S end). **Shell Bay:** rare in
small quantity on Shell Bay (position
varies yearly, sometimes none).
Sandbanks: seen recently on sandbank 80m W of junction of Shore
Road and Banks Road.

Shrubby Orache *Atriplex halimus*
Introduction. Rare. Planted near sea.
Sandbanks: SE side of Banks Road S

of roundabout. **Canford Cliffs:**
stepped path from Cliff Drive to
beach; near foot of cliff 300m NE of
Canford Cliffs Chine.

Sea-purslane *Atriplex portulacoides*
Native. Frequent. Salt Marshes. July
to October.

Sea Beet *Beta vulgaris*
Native. Frequent. Tops of shores,
cliffs. May to September.
Kimmeridge: here and there near sea.
Wares: White Ware cliff quarries.
Durlston: SW of lighthouse.
Swanage: on cliff 50m N of end of
path from Burlington Road. **Lilliput:**
scattered along bottom of Evening
Hill. **Luscombe Valley:** several in
SW corner. **Sandbanks:** near shrubs
by harbour shore opposite main car
park entrance.

Perennial Glasswort
Sarcocornia perennis
Native. Occasional. High on firm
sandy or muddy shores. July to
September.
Nationally Scarce.
Godlingston Heath: on Brand's
Point; also on spit 40-70m to SE.
Studland Heath: several 275m N of
Brand's Bay Hide; few on N-facing
shore 75m E of tip of Redhorn Quay;
several 175m NW of S corner of
Bramble Bush Bay from 10-20m W
of shingle bank. **Sandbanks:** salt-
marsh W of junction of Shore Road
and Banks Road.

Sprawling grey-green plant; some
branches are without flowers.

One-flowered Glasswort
Salicornia pusilla
Native. Rare. Tops of salt-marshes.
July to September.
Nationally Scarce.

Studland Heath: from inner corner to one-third way along inner side of Sandy Point spit.

Plants are 3-6cm long, fairly prostrate and short-branched. Best seen in September when flowers of all species are fully out, and these plants remain greenish when many Diploid Glassworts have changed to reddy-purple. See drawing.

Hybrid Glasswort
Salicornia pusilla x *europaea*
Native. Rare. Tops of salt-marshes, with parents. July to September.
Studland Heath: from inner corner to one-third way along inner side of Sandy Point spit

Plants are 5-8cm long, somewhat less prostrate than parent above. Mature plants have some single and some triple flowers; may be mistaken for immature plants of next species in which pairs of smaller side flowers have not emerged from sheaths. See drawing. Plants are green with tinges of reddy-purple in September.

Diploid Glassworts, Marsh Samphire *Salicornia europaea* agg., including *S. ramosissima*
Native. Frequent. Tops of shores, upper to middle salt-marshes. July to September.
Arne: very plentiful in area S of RSPB beach noticeboard. **Wytch:** plentiful 50m S of NW corner of Wytch Moor. **Studland Heath:** N-facing shores of Plateau Bay and Dyke Bay. **Sandbanks:** upper shore opposite W end of Chaddesley Glen.

Central flowers are conspicuously larger than side flowers. Plants are mostly upright, beaded and reddy-purple in September. See drawing. There are no clear-cut divisions within this aggregate.

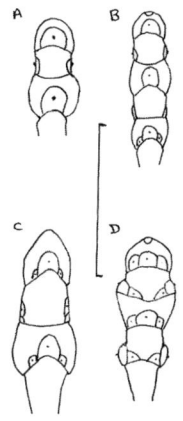

Upper flower spike of Glassworts:
A - One-flowered, B - Hybrid, C - Diploid,
D - Tetraploid.

Tetraploid Glassworts, Marsh Samphire *Salicornia procumbens* agg., including *S. dolichostachya*
Native. Rare. Middle to lower salt-marshes, with previous species. July to September.
Dorset Rare.
Arne: plentiful in area S of RSPB beach noticeboard. **Godlingston Heath:** on Brand's Point, and for 25m to SE on spit. **Studland Heath:** along shore 200-300m N of Brand's Bay Hide; few by N-facing shore 75m E of tip of Redhorn Quay; many scattered along S shore of Dyke Bay.

Central flowers are the same size as the side ones, or only slightly larger. Plants are upright, hardly beaded, with a longer terminal spike than the previous species and go yellowy-green in September. See drawing. There are no clear-cut divisions within this aggregate.

Shrubby Sea-blite *Suaeda vera*
Native. Occasional. Tops of shores. July to October.

Nationally Scarce.
Studland Heath: neck of Redhorn Quay; NW-facing shore of Plateau Bay; plentiful on Sandy Point spit itself.

Annual Sea-blite *Suaeda maritima*
Native. Frequent. Sand by sea, salt-marshes. July to October.

Prickly Saltwort *Salsola kali* subsp. *kali*
Native. Occasional. Sandy beaches. July to September.
Dorset Scarce. Vulnerable.
Studland Heath: in fenced area E of Knoll Beach café. **Shell Bay:** very plentiful from middle to SE end of bay. **Brownsea:** found near W end of S shore. **Sandbanks:** 80m W of junction of Shore Road and Banks Road; along sand for 60m N of that.

Sites vary from year to year. Increasing in numbers after a low point a few years ago.

AMARANTH FAMILY
Common Amaranth
Amaranthus retroflexus
Introduction. Rare. Arable fields, other disturbed ground. July to October.
Norden: W side of S end of Slepe Road in field gateway. **Shell Bay:** near toll-booths.

PURSLANE FAMILY
Spring Beauty *Claytonia perfoliata*
Introduction. Rare. Escape on stable sand. April to June.
Sandbanks: plentiful on SE side of Banks Road between E end of Panorama Road and roundabout; along SE side of main car park.

Blinks *Montia fontana*
Native. Occasional. Short winter-damp acid grassland and tracks. March to June.
Stoborough: few on The Green.
Stoborough Heath: near Nature Reserve notice 50m N of S cattle grid on Soldiers Road. **Hartland Moor:** scattered throughout much of large unfenced field E of Soldiers Road 300-700m N of A351; W side of Slepe Road 200 and 700m N of bend at Scotland. **Corfe:** scattered on NW part of West Common NW of cattle grid; on N part of Little East Common 70-110m NNW of bridle-way30 bridge across railway.
Godlingston Heath: scattered on E side of bridleway25 for 10m S of junction with bridleway27. **Studland:** by path19 crossing field E of bridle-way23. **Luscombe Valley:** centre of S end 20m N of fence. **Sandbanks:** in triangular lawn between Banks Road and Shore Road at their junction.

Divided into four subspecies with different sculpturing on the surface of the seeds, which are less than 1mm wide (microscope). Blinks seen in this area are the subsp. *chondrosperma*.

PINK OR CAMPION FAMILY
Thyme-leaved Sandwort
Arenaria serpyllifolia
Native. Frequent. Short calcareous grassland including verges and anthills. May to July.

This was once divided into two species, later that division was dropped and later still it was divided into two subspecies; the author has not kept separate records.

Three-nerved Sandwort
Moehringia trinervia
Native. Occasional. Verges, woods. April to July.
Holme: SW corner of East Holme churchyard (approach via Holme

Priory drive). **Furzebrook:** S side of grazed woodland E of central field in Kilnwood Reserve. **Norden:** N side of bridleway77 by gate 190m from A351. **Corfe:** near N end of Byle Copse. **Rempstone:** on E side of bridleway16 30m S of B3351. **Kingswood:** by bridleway87 50m from B3351. **Godlingston:** E side of Burnham's Lane just N of SW corner of Marsh Copse. **Ballard Down:** 50m N of cottage NW of Whitecliff Farm on E side of bridleway14. **Studland:** N side of Watery Lane 40m E of junction with Manor Road. **Studland Heath:** by Woodland Nature Trail just NW of trail 'crossroads'.

Sea Sandwort *Honckenya* (not Honkenya) *peploides*
Native. Occasional. Stable sandy beaches and dunes. May to July. *Dorset Scarce.*
Kimmeridge: very small amount on upper shore at Charnel (bay) 100m around corner W of Kimmeridge Bay (accessible when Army Range Walks are open). **Studland Heath:** behind fore-dunes scattered through S half of nudists' area (some may prefer to visit when it is raining steadily). **Sandbanks:** scattered along 20m of grass verge W of Banks Road 300m S of junction with Shore Road.

Its presence on beaches varies.

Common Chickweed *Stellaria media*
Native. Abundant. Woods, verges, arable fields, other disturbed ground. All year.

See below for differences from the next species.

Lesser Chickweed *Stellaria pallida*
Native. Occasional. Bare sandy soils, especially near coast. February to April.

Tyneham: plenty on Tyneham Cap summit. **Arne:** tiny plants at top of shore by RSPB noticeboard. **Durlston:** plentiful in grass around W side car park. **Swanage:** on grass bank S of Health Centre. **Studland Heath:** by south wall of shop at Knoll Beach. **Studland:** between car park rows N and S of rise in middle of Middle Beach car park. **Shell Bay:** on both sides of Ferry Road plentiful through 200m S from roundabout. **Sandbanks:** plentiful in lawns around N part of main car park especially either side of its entrance. **Canford Cliffs:** here and there between Cliff Drive and cliff-top. **Branksome Dene Chine:** E of café near sea.

Larger plants can be mistaken for the previous species; some plants are tiny. This species is often yellowish. Its petal-less flowers only open briefly, usually in the sun; they have 1 to 3 stamens; they remain upright when in fruit and all or most of its small leaves have short stalks. However, the Common Chickweed usually has petals, 3 to 8 stamens, its flowers turn downwards in fruit and its upper leaves are stalkless.

Greater Stitchwort *Stellaria holostea*
Native. Frequent. Woods, hedge-banks. April to June. See Plate 9.

Lesser Stitchwort *Stellaria graminea*
Native. Frequent. Rough open grassland, verges. May to October.
Steeple: here and there on NE side of N half of bridleway3. **Stoborough Heath:** near junction of paths5 and 6. **Hartland Moor:** plentiful in grassland 250m N of Langton Wallis; here and there by bridleway3 from 150-500m E of Slepe Road. **Church Knowle:** much above quarry just N of Lime Kiln. **Corfe:** by tiny E stream in

Little East Common 20m S of bridle-way30. **Arne:** N side of bridleway1 250m from W end for 5m.
Woolgarston: here and there on top of Ailwood Down. **Langton:** N side of bridleway42 160-200m W of private track to Wilkswood Farm.
Luscombe: much in Reserve.

Bog Stitchwort *Stellaria uliginosa*
Native. Occasional. Marshes. May to June.
Holme: on open access part of Battle Plain 100m NW of entrance at Doreys Farm. **Hartland Moor:** in rushy ground 400m N of Langton Wallis (plentiful); here and there along S side of Snag Valley W of Slepe Road; E of copse E of Slepe Road 400m N of corner by Scotland.
Corfe: near SW corner of Middle Common Pond; in East Valley in Big East Common 60 and 150m from railway fence. **Corfe Charity's Meadows:** W side of Great Close opposite E-most point of Five Acres hedge. **Kingswood:** by path30 outside NE corner of Foxground Plantation. **Godlingston Heath:** 40m E of junction of bridleways23, 26 and 33. **Studland Heath:** by Woodland Nature Trail 50m along track to Woodland Hide from 'crossroads'.
It occurs usually in low numbers; it is only visible when you are looking down at it.

Snow-in-summer
Cerastium tomentosum
Introduction. Occasional. Planted or escaped. May to June.
Stoborough: E side of Furzebrook Road from path24 S-wards for 150m.
Furzebrook: E side of Furzebrook Road 100m S of railway bridge.
Langton: old spoil heap N of Bower's Quarry entrances. **Swanage:** W side

of Panorama Road 175m S of E of two right-angled bends; on S side of E end of path through copse W of D'Urberville Drive; above promenade S of Grand Hotel. **Canford Cliffs:** near top of stepped path from Cliff Drive to beach. **Branksome Dene Chine:** in sea-front grass SW of chine.

Common Mouse-ear
Cerastium fontanum
Native. Abundant. Grassland. May to September.
No glands on hairs, unlike next four species.

Sticky Mouse-ear
Cerastium glomeratum
Native. Abundant. Grassland, anthills. April to May.
Stems are often sticky from the glands, but sometimes they are only on the sepals.

Sea Mouse-ear *Cerastium diffusum*
Native. Frequent. Sand, anthills, cliff-tops, short grass (including some not near the sea). March to June.
Tyneham: on Tyneham Cap summit.
Durlston: here and there along S edge (brow) of Fields 3 and 6 (with patches of Dwarf Mouse-ear nearby); near base of Visitor Centre flagpole.
Studland: on South Beach in front of beach huts 70m S of Watery Lane.
Shell Bay: both sides of road S of roundabout (with patches of Little Mouse-ear nearby); here and there in car park. **Branksome Chine:** in lawn on NW side of road at SE end of chine.
Usually only four divided petals which are shorter than, or of same length as, the sepals; but it sometimes has 5-petalled flowers on the same or nearby plants.

Dwarf Mouse-ear
Cerastium pumilum
Native. Occasional. Thin soil over limestone (but very little on chalk), anthills. April to May.
Nationally Scarce. Near Threatened.
Wares (west): in Hedbury Ware near SE corner of Cliff Middle Field; **(east)** on rise in NE corner of Middle Field; in Golter on W side 75m S of gateway to Middle Field; also 100m SE of same gateway below brow of slope; in NE of Verney Ware 50 and 130m SW of corner; 30m SE of NW corner of Western Mile Posts Ware; in Belle Vue Middle Ware 25m S track across middle 50m from W wall, and several places along old quarry banks near top of Belle Vue East Ware.
Knitson: one plant once found on Down 175m ENE of N end of bridleway12. **Durlston:** here and there along S edge (brow) of Fields 3, 6 and 10 (with patches of Sea Mouse-ear nearby); on anthill 90m from W wall of Lighthouse Field 5m S of path50. **Townsend Reserve:** at least twelve places including W side of path59 25m S of Twayblade Bank; W side of path59 25m S of permissive bridleway; 10m E of Burry's Road 40m S of Burry's Circle; two sides each of Orchid and SE Bastions.

It always has 5 petals, which are usually slightly longer than the sepals; comes into flower slightly later than Sea Mouse-ear (p.82), which sometimes grows nearby; often few.

Little Mouse-ear
Cerastium semidecandrum
Native. Occasional. Sandy soil; ground where builders' sand has been (two sites*). March to June.
Hartland Moor: here and there by Slepe Road from corner by Scotland N-wards for 450m; scattered near bridleway4 and tracks across South Middlebere E of Slepe Road. **Wares (west):** Seacombe Quarry floor*. **Durlston:** near base of Visitor Centre flagpole*. **Godlingston Heath:** 50-100m SW of W end of bridleway36 on NW side of bridleway33. **Shell Bay:** both sides of road along 200m S of roundabout; here and there behind dunes in Shell Bay (with Sea Mouse-ear in both sites). **Sandbanks:** lawn between main car park and café. **Canford Cliffs:** much between Cliff Drive and cliff-top NE of start of steps down cliff. **Branksome Chine:** path along cliff-top 200m SW of chine.

Petals are irregularly toothed rather than divided and shorter than or equal to the sepals. Leaf-like bracts under flowerheads are diagnostic. The plant is very small (5-20mm high).

Water Chickweed
Myosoton aquaticum
Native. Occasional. By rivers, streams; in ditches, ponds, verges. July to August.
Holme: by ford in East Holme hamlet; in East Holme Meadows – see p.23 **Wareham:** 10m SE of gate into Priory Meadow; by Purbeck Way 80m E of South Bridge. **Norden:** in vegetation on N side of bridleway77 at W cattle grid; NW side of Slepe Road 5-10m S of bridleway77. **Corfe:** by stream along E end of S edge of West Common; by same stream along S edge of Middle Common from B3069 to E of Purbeck Way footbridge. **Corfe Charity's Meadows:** on Sharford Bridge; on banks of Corfe River (stream) 10m S of path80 bridge (old sluice).

Upright Chickweed *Moenchia erecta*
Native. Rare. Open vegetation on acid

sandy soil. April to May.
Dorset Scarce.
Godlingston Heath: on bridleway27 very small amounts 170 and 230m SE of junction with path32; larger amount 200m N of B3351 along 10m on E side of bridleway25.

Flowers open <u>only slightly</u> in the sun. See Plate 9.

Knotted Pearlwort *Sagina nodosa*
Native. Verges. July to September.
Holme: plentiful on NW side of B3070 125-575m NE of bridge over Luckford Lake stream; plentiful on SE side of same road 400-525m NE of same bridge.

Heath Pearlwort *Sagina subulata*
Native. Rare. Open sandy soil. June to August.
Brownsea: upper part of broad section of beach near SW corner of island; on track in NW of W low-fenced area in SW part of island. Difficult to pinpoint and not always in same places.

Procumbent Pearlwort
Sagina procumbens
Native. Abundant. Anywhere on bare ground, including pavement cracks. May to September.

Stems grow sideways at first and tend to root.

Annual Pearlwort *Sagina apetela*
Native. Occasional. Dry, bare soil. May to June.
Ower: by bridleway8 S of Game Copse. **Swanage:** 40m N of S end of W side of De Moulham Road.
Studland Heath: N end of S car park at Knoll Beach; NW side of Ferry Road 50 and 320m NE of track to Jerry's Point; SE side 275m SW of toll roundabout; NW side 130m SW of

roundabout. **Shell Bay:** plentiful in car park. **Brownsea:** low wall opposite Visitor Centre. **Canford Cliffs:** W side of path in Flaghead Chine 30m from S end; 10m W of top of steps from Cliff Drive to beach.
Branksome Chine: by cliff-top path 80m SW of chine.

It <u>does</u> have a small central rosette when young, but not nearly as leafy as that of the previous species. Stems grow generally upward and do not root.

Sagina ciliata, previously considered a distinct species, is a sub-species of *S. apetala* – subsp. e*recta.* As in *The Flora of Dorset,* separate records have not been made.

Sea Pearlwort *Sagina maritima*
Native. Occasional. Bare places near sea, including pavements, and salted road edges inland. May to September.
Stoborough: NE edge of A351 just above kerb from S end of Dismantled Tramway NW-wards for 125m (see note below). **Wares (west):** plentiful on floor of main Seacombe Quarry near sea; **(east)** S of lower Western Mile Post. **Durlston:** near Coast Path where it passes lighthouse and gully.
Swanage: plentiful under promenade railing along N half of Shore Road; between stones near Stone Quay; by railings on inner (stone) part of pier.
Sandbanks: surface cracks near ferry hut; seafront near SE end of Shore Road. **Branksome Chine** and **Branksome Dene Chine:** here and there in cracks near sea-front.

The Stoborough site benefits from salt treatment of the roads. This species may be widespread in such places, but they are risky and noisy places to search. Unlike Early Scurvy-grass, Sea Pearlwort cannot be spotted from moving vehicles. Leaves may have very short end bristles (lens), but they are not nearly as long as those on leaves of the previous two species.

Annual Knawel *Scleranthus annuus*
Native. Rare. Dry, open ground including tracks. June to August.
Dorset Scarce. Endangered.
Godlingston Heath: by rabbit holes in rectangular fenced area 150m N of field gate on N side of bridleway36.

Four-leaved Allseed
Polycarpon tetraphyllum
Native, but introduced here. Rare. Dry ground near sea. June to October.
Nationally Rare.
Sandbanks: by SE edge of main car park 20-25m SW of hedge which divides car park in two; scattered further SW along same edge; sometimes in dunes at top of beach just S of car park. **Canford Cliffs:** by kerb of Cliff Drive for 10m SW of tarmac path to top of steps to beach.

Corn Spurrey *Spergula arvensis*
Early Introduction. Occasional. Arable fields, other disturbed ground. June to October.
Vulnerable.
Holme: few at entrance to open access part of Battle Plain at Doreys Farm. **Ridge:** on path12 125m from NE end. **Stoborough Heath:** much in NE corner of Sandlings field 10-25m SW of gate. **Rempstone:** 500m W of Oil Road on S side of path5 W of Green Pond. **Harman's Cross:** here and there by path6 from 300-425m NE of stile E of New Barn.
Godlingston Heath: by rabbit holes in middle of rectangular fenced area 150m N of field gate on N side of bridleway36. **Studland:** in wide area of grass between Coast Path and cliff-top beginning near The Warren

Wood and finishing near Studland Wood – disturbance provided by moles. **Sandbanks:** mound SW of café E of main car park.

Rock Sea-spurrey
Spergularia rupicola
Native. Occasional. Sea cliffs, walls near sea, or just below either. June to August.
Tyneham: foot of Worbarrow Bay cliffs here and there N of end of path from Tyneham (with small amount of Lesser Sea-spurrey). **Wares (west):** on ground below cliff at W end of W half of main Hedbury Quarry 30m from drop to sea; low on quarry face halfway along E half of Hedbury Quarry (with next species on adjacent quarry floor; near E end of Dancing Ledge quarry face. **Durlston:** S side of Coast Path just W of steps from The Globe.
Stems are very glandular (lens).

Greater Sea-spurrey
Spergularia media
Native. Occasional. Salt-marshes, wet cliffs, sea quarry floors. May to September.
Worth: good patch in Winspit E quarries 150m NE of SW corner 3m from drop to sea (take care). **Arne:** plentiful along edge of salt-marsh S of RSPB noticeboard. **Wares (west):** on floor of E half of main Hedbury Quarry halfway along under quarry face (with previous species on face adjacent), and **(east)** S of lower Western Mile Post. **Studland Heath:** on S shore of Plateau Bay (albino halfway along); E of Sandy Point; in SW corner of Bramble Bush Bay. **Sandbanks:** salt-marsh W of junction of Shore Road and Banks Road.
Stems are only glandular close to the flowers (lens). Petals are some-

times only as long as the sepals, but usually longer. Flowers are mostly 10-12mm across.

Lesser Sea-spurrey
Spergularia marina
Native. Occasional. Near sea; may appear on salted roadsides in future. May to August.
Tyneham: foot of Worbarrow Bay cliff 300m N of end of path from Tyneham (rather more Rock Sea-spurrey nearby). **Wytch:** plentiful 120m S of NW corner of Wytch Moor. **Godlingston Heath:** Brand's Point; in Brand's Creek 200m SE of Point. **Swanage:** cracks in ground level stones, concrete and brickwork at Stone Quay; near railings on inner (stone) part of pier. **Sandbanks:** near end of grass verge W of Banks Road N of roundabout. **Lilliput:** by seawall at SE end of Evening Hill; at edge of path above seawall 50m NW of that.

Stems are only glandular close to the flowers (lens). Petals are shorter than the sepals. Flowers are mostly 6-8 mm across; seeds 0.6mm or more in diameter (lens: x15 or x20 best).

Sand Spurrey *Spergularia rubra*
Native. Occasional. Heath tracks and bare places – not salty sites. May to July.
Holme: on open access part of Battle Plain 20m W of entrance at Doreys Farm. **Stoborough Heath:** 20m NE of cairn on track up hill from S cattle grid on Soldiers Road. **Hartland Moor:** on track 10m SE of Soldiers Road parallel to it 125, 150 and 225m NE of S cattle grid; on N side of bridleway3 175m E of Slepe Road. **Arne:** small amount in triangular field S of car park 10m from kissing-gate. **Godlingston Heath:** scattered either side of track for 600m SSW of true E

junction of bridleways35 and 36.
Studland: on Coast Path 320m E of The Warren Wood. **Lilliput:** near seats SW of road on centre of Evening Hill. **Canford Cliffs:** SE side of Cliff Drive 125m NE of top of steps to beach.

It is difficult to find except when the flowers open in the sun; stems are only glandular close to the flowers (lens); flower 3-5mm across; seeds 0.5mm or less in diameter (lens: x15 or x20 best).

Rose Campion *Lychnis coronaria*
Introduction. Rare. Escape. June to August.
Studland: behind beach huts 40m NNE of footbridge at Middle Beach.

Ragged Robin *Lychnis flos-cuculi*
Native. Occasional. Marshes. May to July.
Creech: rushy areas in NW and SE of S RSPB field W of Grange Road (enter from RSPB field to N).
Hartland Moor: here and there in Upper and Middle Fens (albino seen in S-most part bordered by trees); by N end of short boardwalk on path79 SW of Scotland. **Corfe Charity's Meadows:** scattered by bridleway3 through W half of meadow SW of Sharford Bridge. **Corfe:** scattered in most of wettest areas of West, Middle and Little East Commons; in East Valley in Big East Common 150m from railway fence. **Wytch:** E side of Thrasher's Lane 100m N of bridle-way4. **Swanage:** by track from 15th green to 16th hole of Pitch and Putt course (players only). **Brownsea:** in Orchid Meadow between boardwalk and church.

Nottingham Catchfly *Silene nutans*
Native. Rare. Calcareous cliff-tops.

May to June.
Nationally Scarce. Near Threatened.
Ballard Down: from trig point –
250m WSW in rough grassland;
150m SW near cliff edge; here and
there from 200-350m E-wards in
rough grassland (safest site); near or
on cliff-top from 100-600m NE of
Ballard Head here and there.

Bladder Campion *Silene vulgaris*
Native. Occasional. Calcareous verges
and rough grassland. May to July.
Corfe: NW side of B3069 350m SW
of A351. **Woolgarston:** on W side of
bridleway23 125m N of road. **Wares
(west):** S side of Priest's Way 50m E
of path32; **(east)** 80m ESE of NW
corner of Golter; on W side of
path46 110m S of Priest's Way.
Kingswood: 40 and 150m E of viewpoint on N side of B3351. **Ulwell:**
near crossing of path4 by Purbeck
Way. **Durlston:** in SW part of
Skipworth Meadow. **Studland:** on E
side of bridleway12 5m N of end of
middle E-W road of Glebeland
Estate. **Ballard Down:** here and
there in ungrazed grass between trig
point and Ballard Head. **Sandbanks:**
SE side of Banks Road between NE
end of Panorama Road and roundabout.

Sea Campion *Silene uniflora*
Native. Frequent. Shores, cliffs. April
to July.
Kimmeridge: plentiful near way
from main car park to beach; near
Coast Path: and on banks at SE end
of bay. **Wares (west and east):** here
and there by sea, including White
Ware cliff quarries. **Studland Heath:**
shore SE of Redhorn Quay; along
60m of shore S of Brand's Bay Hide;
scattered elsewhere on shore of
Redhorn Bay.

White Campion *Silene latifolia*
Early Introduction. Frequent.
Grassland, verges. May to September.
   Do not confuse with albino Red
Campion.

Hybrid Campion *Silene* x *hampeana*
(*S. latifolia* x *dioica*)
Native. Occasional. Verges, grassland.
May to July.
Norden: 325m NW of roundabout on
NE side of A351. **Arne:** 210m N of
bridleway1 W of track to Big Wood
from SW. **Studland:** by E end of path3
down cliff to South Beach; sporadic in
grassland N of Coast Path 400-600m
E of The Warren Wood. **Ballard
Down:** near SW corner of Old Nick's
Ground. **Lilliput:** towards SE end of
fenced area of Evening Hill.
   Often occurs with both parents
nearby.

Red Campion *Silene dioica*
Native. Frequent. Woods, verges. May
to September.
   Male plants far outnumber females.
See Plate 29.

Small-flowered Catchfly *Silene gallica*
Native. Rare. Disturbed verges. May to
June.
Nationally Scarce. Endangered.

Soapwort *Saponaria officinalis*
Early Introduction, but cultivated
variety here with 'double' flowers
(**Bouncing Bett**). Rare. Escape. July to
October.
Holme: NW side of B3070 800m SW
of Holme Lane. **Wareham:** W of road
at S end of South Bridge; rather more
on side of inlet just W of that.

Pink *Dianthus plumarius* cv.
Introduction. Rare. Planted. June.
Stoborough: E side of Furzebrook

Road 30m S of track on to heath S of roundabout.

Pink petals have deep red central sections.

DOCK FAMILY

A new edition of the helpful BSBI handbook on docks and knotweeds is in preparation.

Red Bistort *Persicaria amplexicaulis*
Introduction. Rare. Verges. July to November.
Swanage: S side of Victoria Avenue just W of W end of Prospect Crescent opposite (may be cut in August, but will grow again); W side of Townsend Road 100m S of S end of pavement kerbs.

Amphibious Bistort
Persicaria amphibia
Native. Rare. Still water, or ground near water. June to September.
Holme: East Holme Meadows – see p.23. **Wareham:** 10m E of gate into Priory Meadow (terrestrial form).
Corfe: by stream under trees in NW of West Common 100m S of Copper Bridge (terrestrial form).
Luscombe Valley: 100m N of metal bridge in centre of Reserve W of stream (terrestrial form).

The terrestrial form looks quite different from the water form (not illustrated in most books). It is up to 1m tall, has spear-shaped leaves and rarely flowers, but the sheaths on the stems above the leaf-bases are like those of a Knotweed.

Pink-headed Knotweed
Persicaria capitata
Introduction. Rare. Escape on pavements. July to October.
Corfe: pavement on N side of The Square; down street to NE.

It has short heads of pink flowers, pointed oval leaves with brown marks and lobes at the base and glandular-hairy stems (lens).

Redshank *Persicaria maculosa*
Native. Frequent. Arable fields, other disturbed ground. June to October.
Compare with next species.
Sometimes it has whitish flowers but it has either no or, occasionally, a few glands on the flower-stalks.

Pale Persicaria *Persicaria lapathifolia*
Native. Frequent. Arable fields, other disturbed ground. June to October.
Sometimes it has pink flowers and/or spotted leaves, so it can be confused with the previous species, but it has many glands on the flower-stalks (lens).

Water Pepper *Persicaria hydropiper*
Native. Frequent. Wet places on commons, by tracks and by watercourses, and wet field corners. July to September.
Stoborough: much by path13 125m W of bypass. **Stoborough Heath:** gaps in boundary of Rushy Hollow field and Sandlings field. **Hartland Moor:** SE side of Soldiers Road 250m NE of S cattle grid; along S side of Snag Valley 50-250m W of Slepe Road; on South Middlebere 10m W of White House Wood.
Corfe: W end of First Valley on West Common; SW corner of Middle Common; just S of bridleway30 W of tiny E stream on Little East Common. **Corfe Charity's Meadows:** gateway at N of Paddle Dock; halfway along S side of Cowleaze. **Woolgarston:** 50m S of road at Ailwood Farm on E side of path26. **Godlingston Heath:** by Lily Pond.

Tasteless Water Pepper
Persicaria mitis (*P. laxiflora*)
Native. Rare. Water-meadow ditch
edges. June to August.
Holme: East Holme Meadows – see
p.23.

Equal-leaved Knotgrass
Polygonum arenastrum
Early Introduction. Frequent. Arable
fields, other disturbed ground especially
gateways, tracks and roadsides. July to
October.

It can be confused with small plants
of the next species, but latter has leaves
of various lengths.

Knotgrass *Polygonum aviculare*
Native. Frequent. Arable fields, other
disturbed ground. July to October.
Worth: robust form (with leaves about
1.5 x normal maximum) by path18 in
field E of steps down to Chapman's
Pool.

Japanese Knotweed *Fallopia japonica*
Introduction. Frequent. Waste places,
roadsides. August to September.
Stoborough: on SW side of B3075 30-
70m SE of path7. **Norden:** on NE side
of A351 150m NW of entrance to
Norden Farm on opposite side.
Kingston: NW edge of churchyard.
Langton: N side of Priest's Way by
path32. **Durlston:** 50m NW of Visitor
Centre. **Swanage:** plentiful by path
down the cliff from Burlington Road.
Studland: plentiful near NE end of
Watery Lane. **Canford Cliffs:** E side of
Flaghead Chine 70m from N end.
Branksome Chine: 400m up chine
from road at SE end.

See hybrid below regarding identification. The need to eradicate this invasive alien is nowadays widely discussed,
but few attempt to do so. The herbicide
'Roundup' mixed with oil (e.g. paraffin)
and poured down cut hollow stems is
said to kill it (e.g. Ford, 2004).

Japanese x Giant Knotweed – hybrid
Fallopia x *bohemica*
(*F. japonica* x *sachalinensis*)
Introduction. Rare. Verges. September.
Norden: female along 20m on NE side
of A351 200m SE of roundabout by
car park capacities sign and beyond it
in scrub.

Shapes of the bases of the leaves of
this and its parent above vary and can
be misleading during identification.
The size of the largest leaves is a better
guide; also leaf tips are drawn out to a
point. See drawing. Tiny sparse stubby
hairs on the leaf undersides (lens) con-
firm hybridisation. The flowers are
greeny-cream like the parent below,
which has larger leaves (not drawn out
to point) and sparse longer hairs on leaf
undersides.

Giant Knotweed *Fallopia sachalinensis*
Introduction. Rare. Waste ground.
September.
Corfe: S of Challow Farm SW of

*Knotweed leaf-tips – Hybrid (above) and
Giant*

path18 (which runs along field edge – not across field) – mostly eradicated in 2007.

Russian-vine *Fallopia baldschuanica*
Introduction. Occasional. Escape.
June to October.
Kimmeridge: N side of Coast Path 50m W of Gaulter Cottages.
Godlingston: by path80 SE of lake.
Swanage: plentiful on cliff N of E end of path down cliff from Burlington Road; plentiful on cliff below S end of green E of Ballard Estate (view from beach). **Studland:** N side Agglestone Road W of bend.
Canford Cliffs: plentiful on cliff 150-250m SW of Flaghead Chine.
Branksome Dene Chine: on sea cliff to NE.

Black Bindweed *Fallopia convolvulus*
Early Introduction. Occasional.
Arable fields, other disturbed ground.
June to October.
Kingston: by path22 on E side of Newfoundland (wood) 30m S of N end of wood. **Sandbanks:** on newly-disturbed (2007) ground E of main car park S of café.

Wireplant *Muehlenbeckia complexa*
Introduction. Rare. Escape on cliffs.
Late September to October.
Canford Cliffs: plenty at foot of cliff 200m SW of Flaghead Chine behind block of single-storey beach chalets (with Russian-vine). **Branksome Dene Chine:** just above beach chalets 125m SW of chine.
    Small flowers with 5 green sepals and 8 cream stamens.

Sheep's Sorrel *Rumex acetosella*
Native. Abundant. Acid grassland, heaths. May to August.
    In May/June, its flowers turn some acid grassland on heaths and in fields rusty-red. See Plate 10.

Common Sorrel *Rumex acetosa*
Native. Frequent. Grassland, verges.
May to June.
    Its flowers are never so dominant in colour as those of the previous species, but it does give a red sheen to some fields, for example – **Worth:** field N of Chapman's Pool through which path42 passes; **Wares (west):** part of Dancing Ledge North Ware.

Docks
Flowering periods are given, but most Docks are much easier to identify when in fruit, which they retain for several months after flowering.

Water Dock *Rumex hydrolapathum*
Native. Occasional. Watersides, ditches, reedbeds. July to August.
Holme: East Holme Meadows – see p.23. **Stoborough:** NW end of path13 (take care on bank).
Wareham: SE side of River Frome here and there from bypass bridge to South Bridge (boat). **Studland Heath:** around East Lake. **Shell Bay:** in reedbed crossed by boardwalk from car park (easiest site).

Curled Dock *Rumex crispus*
Native. Frequent. Grassland, verges, waste ground, beaches. June to October.
    The subspecies *littoreus* is the most common form by the sea, also frequent.

Curled x Broad-leaved Dock – hybrid *Rumex x pratensis*
(*R. crispus* x *obtusifolius*)
Native. Rare. Verges. Casual. July to October.
Kingston: occurred on E side of

South Street S of The Plantation. **Langton:** 125m W of Durnford Drove by path15. **Swanage:** E side of path24 on road to Sludge Works opposite stile on W side.

This is the most common dock hybrid. Leaves have somewhat wavy margins and squarish bases.

Clustered Dock
Rumex conglomeratus
Native. Frequent. Wet verges, fields, other wet ground; often with other docks. July to October
Stoborough Heath: one plant on W of path5 in S of small field through which path passes. **Corfe:** near E side of Copper Bridge. **Worth:** plentiful in NE part of Worth Mead. **Wares (west):** W arm of Y of Seacombe Bottom; S half of Bottom (with other docks in both places). **Harman's Cross:** W side of path4 10m S of cattle grid S of railway crossing; E side of same path 25m S of grid (other docks nearby both sites). **Langton:** by path7 50m SW of bridleway5. **Durlston:** one plant E-facing under hedge on W side of Long Meadow near where road divides by Reservoir gate. **Brownsea:** in S end of Orchid Meadow.

It has swellings on all three sides of its fruits. Branches of some plants spread more widely than other docks, except for Fiddle Dock.

Wood Dock *Rumex sanguineus*
Native. Frequent. Woods, verges. June to August.

Occasionally, it has three swellings rather than one on some of its fruit, causing confusion with Clustered Dock (see above), though one swelling is bigger than the other two. Wood Dock fruits are longer and branches ascend (at narrow angle to stem) rather than spread.

Fiddle Dock *Rumex pulcher*
Native. Occasional. Permanent grassland. June to July.
Kimmeridge: on bridleway12 500m from E end. **Church Knowle:** by path29 on field N of playing field. **Kingston:** on grassy track leading steeply downhill to SW from bridleway46 S of E end of Polar Wood (with Broad-leaved and Curled Docks); by path41 160m S of gate at S end of South Street. **Corfe:** by path64 20m S of Church Knowle Road; 25m N of Purbeck Way just E of gate at junction with Sandy Hill Lane. **Worth:** here and there near UCR from Renscombe Farm to Hill Bottom hamlet. **Wares (west):** plentiful along N side (top) of Dancing Ledge Ware; **(east)** by kissing-gate in NE corner of Balston Wear. **Ulwell:** extreme SE corner of Round Down near path83.

Branches spread almost at right angles to zigzag stem.

Broad-leaved Dock
Rumex obtusifolius
Native. Abundant. Grassland, verges. May to October.

SEA-LAVENDER FAMILY
Common Sea-lavender
Limonium vulgare
Native. Frequent. Salt-marshes. July to August.

A Rock Sea-lavender
Limonium dodartiforme
Native. Occasional. Sea cliffs – **take great care.** July to August.
Nationally Rare.
Worth: visible (binoculars) from Coast Path 500m SW of W end of Winspit Quarries. **Wares (east):** down the slope on cliff-top just W of entrance to White Ware Quarries; on

sloping cliff S of lower Western Mile Post (easiest place to see it); several places on cliff edge in W half of Belle Vue West Ware; plentiful near climbers' track on cliff-top SW of Belle Vue East Ware. **Durlston:** S of Coast Path just W of gully.

Rock Sea-lavender is divided into microspecies (Stace, 1997). This one is only currently found in the world on the Dorset coast between Portland and Durlston, but another yet unaccepted species (*Limonium 'obesifolium'*) may also be present. See Plate 10.

Thrift *Armeria maritima*
Native. Frequent. Cliffs, sea quarries, salt-marshes. April to June.
Tyneham: much between Coast Path and cliff-top 200 and 250m NW of S end of Worbarrow Bay. **Wares (west):** plentiful at Dancing Ledge Quarry W side. **Durlston:** very plentiful SW to SE of lighthouse. **Branksome Dene Chine:** albinos by sea-front 300m NE of chine.

WATERWORT FAMILY
Six-stamened Waterwort
Elatine hexandra
Native. Rare. Lake-edge and shore. July to September.
Dorset Rare.
Studland Heath: off two beaches of Western Arm of Little Sea; off Second, Third, Fourth and Fifth Beaches at SE of Little Sea; plentiful submerged off many other parts of Little Sea shores (it appears on beaches in years when the water level is low; the leaves are then smaller than when growing underwater).

ST. JOHN'S WORT FAMILY
Rose of Sharon *Hypericum calycinum*
Introduction. Occasional. Planted and spreading. July to September.

Stoborough: SE side of West Lane SW of The Green. **Langton:** spoil heap opposite entrances to Bower's Quarry. **Swanage:** W side of Townsend Road 110m S of end of pavement. **Studland Heath:** ruins of Curlew Cottage. **Lilliput:** near NW end of Evening Hill. **Sandbanks:** S of upper steps at E end of path from Chaddesley Glen to sea beach.

Olympic St. John's Wort
Hypericum olympicum
Recent Introduction. Rare. Pavements. June to October.
Swanage: W side near S end of D'Urberville Drive (often too small to flower).

Tutsan
Hypericum androsaemum
Native. Occasional. Woods, scrub. June to August.
Creech: W side of Grange Road 30m S of bridleway35. **Ridge:** S side of Barnhill Road 50m W of Sunnyside (road). **Kingston:** W side of path44 130m NE of S end of Quarry Wood. **Corfe:** 10m N of S end of Byle Copse. **Langton:** in E-W ride in S of West Wood 80m from SE corner of wood. **Swanage:** here and there by path through copse W of D'Urberville Drive. **Durlston:** small number near Coast Path S of main glade in NE woods of Country Park. **Ulwell:** E side of path4 40m from S end. **Brownsea:** few by stream NE of church. **Branksome Chine:** 300m up chine from road at SE end.

Usually few, sometimes only singletons.

Perforate St. John's Wort
Hypericum perforatum
Native. Frequent. Woods, verges, dry grassland. June to August.

Des Etang's St. John's Wort
Hypericum x *desetangsii*
(*H. perforatum* x *maculatum* subsp.
obtusiusculum)
Native. Rare. Verges. July to August.
Hartland Moor: on N side of Arne
Road 375m E of Soldiers Road
halfway between E side of gate and
road (backcross with Perforate St.
John's Wort so closer to that in
appearance).

Leaves with a small number of
translucent dots; petals with some
black lines and black dots; parts of the
stem with a trace of a second pair of
raised lines. Most importantly it has
some sepals with tips intermediate
between those of its parents: they are
broader like Imperforate St.John's
Wort sepals, but with a central tooth
which is as sharp like the tip of
Perforate St. John's Wort sepals
(N.K.B. Robson, pers. com.).

Square-stalked St. John's Wort
Hypericum tetrapterum
Native. Frequent. Wet places, but not
acid ones. June to September.
Furzebrook: on track in Kilnwood
Reserve 325m E of Furzebrook Road.
Hartland Moor: plentiful in N half
of Upper Fen. **Corfe:** by path53 plank
bridge in First Valley; by NW corner
of Middle Common Pond. **Wytch:** E
side of Thrasher's Lane 40m N of bri-
dleway4. **Worth:** top of flush in S end
of Fields 23/27. **Wares (west and
east):** most flushes, especially plentiful in top of flush in SE of Long
Close. **Langton:** on track leading W
from Crack Lane cemetery vehicular
entrance 25m W of second gate for
15m (other St. John's Worts in area).
Studland: SE side of junction of bri-
dleways23 and 38. **Brownsea:** here
and there by boardwalk through
Orchid Meadow.

Trailing St. John's Wort
Hypericum humifusum
Native. Occasional. Open places in
woods, heaths including tracks. June
to August.
Hartland Moor: on heath track just
E of Soldiers Road S of cattle grid;
on track just W of Slepe Road 400m
N of corner near Scotland. **Wytch:**
thinly scattered along path80 for
450m from E end. **Rempstone:** W
side of bridleway31 400m S of crossing of bridleways31 and 34 along
25m; scattered along E side of bri-
dleway31 425m S of same crossing
for 100m S-wards. **Godlingston
Heath:** where bridleway33 enters
forest crossing stream. **Swanage:**
small raised lawn on N side of
King's Road on S side of Co-op
supermarket. **Studland:** near stream
in W side of Harmony Farm NW
Field; 20m S of NE gateway from
bridleway17 to Harmony Farm NE
Field. **Brownsea:** very scattered in
open areas on S side of island.

Both, Marsh St. John's Wort and
Perforate St. John's Wort have trailing stems when young.

Slender St. John's Wort
Hypericum pulchrum
Native. Occasional. Rough grass-
land, verges. June to August.
Stoborough Heath: along
Dismantled Tramway from 150m N
of A351 for 200m. **Hartland Moor:**
S side of Arne Road 300m E of
Soldiers Road. **Corfe:** here and
there on West and Middle
Commons. **Durlston:** unusual site
in Field 3 120 NE of gate into Belle
Vue East Ware to S of track for 10m
E-wards. (**Ballard Down:** will re-
appear on N-facing slopes above
Glebeland Estate when Gorse is
cleared.)

Hairy St. John's Wort
Hypericum hirsutum
Native. Occasional. Open areas in woods, scrub or verges on calcareous soil. June to August.
East Creech: coppiced area near S edge of Caldecot's Wood 50m W of path32. **Kingston:** N side of car park S of West Street in The Plantation. **Swanage Railway:** N end of NE side of Corfe cutting. **Langton:** scattered in rides in West Wood; N and W of Crack Lane cemetery near path5. **Kingswood:** on N side of B3351 100m W of road that passes Currendon Farm (Perforate St. John's Wort nearby).

Pale St. John's Wort
Hypericum montanum
Native. Occasional. On calcareous soils where vegetation is not short. June to August.
Dorset Scarce. Near Threatened.
Corfe: E side of castle mound below path2 (if not grazed); E of 75th to 85th steps up East Hill; few both S of Purbeck Way 50m E of junction with bridleway20; few N of Purbeck Way 125m E of same junction; more on both sides 175m E of same junction along 20m. **Langton:** few near path44 running NW – SE across scrubby area between West Wood and Talbot's Wood (marked as wood on latest Outdoor Leisure map) (with other St. John's Wort species). See Plate 10.

Marsh St. John's Wort
Hypericum elodes
Native. Frequent. Bogs, marshes, lakesides, clay-pits, ponds, streamlets. June to September.
Creech Heath: here and there in old clay workings. **Furzebrook:** in Little Pool S of Blue Pool; in pond midway between paths8, 10 and 11 and

Purbeck Way. **Corfe:** here and there in very wet areas of Common. **Studland Heath:** plentiful at low area N of main N car park at Knoll Beach; here and there near edges of Little Sea; near edges of swamps to N of it.

LIME FAMILY
Large-leaved Lime *Tilia platyphyllos*
Native, but planted here. Rare.
Ulwell: S of gate to waterworks by Ulwell Road.
   Sometimes it has many shoots at the base of the trunk like Common Lime. Leaves are hairy all over underneath (lens); usually 2 to 4 flowers; fruit strongly ribbed.

Lime *Tilia* x *europea* (*T. platyphyllos* x *cordata*) (*T.* x *vulgaris*)
Native, but planted here. Occasional.
Steeple: on S side of no through UCR 110m W of sharp bend in road N of Steeple Leaze Farm. **Creech:** W side of Grange Road N of bridleway35. **Church Knowle:** on E side of path18 10m S of road. **Knitson:** two on E side of bridleway12 near its N end; NE side of road just NW of Marsh Copse. **Durlston:** in wood in NE of Country Park 100m E of pedestrian entrance. **Ulwell:** halfway along path15 at field boundary. **Ballard Down:** between Coast Path and cliff-top 350m NE of Shep's Hollow. **Studland:** W side of W end of Heath Green Road 40 and 100m N of B3351. **Brownsea:** W of entrance to Nature Reserve.
   Leaves can be as big as the previous species; leaves have tufts of hairs only at the vein junctions underneath (lens); usually 4 to 10 flowers; fruit weakly ribbed.

Small-leaved Lime *Tilia cordata*
Native. Occasional. Woods and

hedges. Difficult to say whether or not planted.

King's Wood: plentiful N of 'Wood' in name King's Wood on O.S. map. **Durlston:** young trees planted in Hingston Copse. **Studland:** field edge NW of Westwood Pond; 50m SW of junction bridleways23 and 38 W of pond on W side of bridleway23.

MALLOW FAMILY

Musk Mallow *Malva moschata*
Native. Occasional. Wood rides, verges. Late June to September.
Wareham: one on inside of bend in track at SW of Priory Meadow. **Hartland Moor:** albino 5m W of S cattle grid on Slepe Road. **Swanage Railway:** behind Norden station platform 7m NW of Waiting Room. **Wytch:** one on NE side of bridleway4 220m NW of Thrasher's Lane (gets cut so flowers late); on both sides of path5 by SE corner of oil well NW of Wytch Moor. **Langton:** in SW corner of recently planted National Trust wood S of junction of B3069 and E road to Worth, (may reappear in rides of Langton West Wood when they are next cleared).

Simple hairs only on plant (lens); can easily be confused with the next species.

Greater Musk Mallow *Malva alcea*
Introduction. Rare. Escape. July to August.
Harman's Cross: albino on W side of Haycraft's Lane 100m S of path8 on opposite side of Lane. **Langton:** inside gate at vehicular entrance to Crack Lane cemetery. **Durlston:** on W side of path43 65m N of junction with path42.

Has hairs which divide in two or more at their base (lens) (see species above).

Common Mallow *Malva sylvestris*
Early Introduction. Frequent. Verges, near cliffs. June to September.

Large specimens are sometimes mistaken for Tree Mallow.

Dwarf Mallow *Malva neglecta*
Early Introduction. Occasional. Verges. June to September.
Worth: by bridleway19 300m NE of Chapman's Pool 5m W of small building. **Harman's Cross:** by bridleway6 70m S of Quarr Farm. **Studland:** W side of bridleway12 just S of gateway to Manor Farm old farmyard.

Tree Mallow *Lavatera arborea*
Native. Occasional. Verges, and sea-cliffs. May to September.
Kimmeridge: by information displays at W end of main car park; plenty by adjacent steps to beach. **Kingston:** S side of West Street just E of South Street. **Langton:** untended garden on W side of Durnford Drove. **Swanage:** E side of Victoria Avenue 25m N of railway bridge; cliff behind beach huts 70 and 120m N of N end of Shore Road; by Taunton Road 20m S of Queens Road. **Ulwell:** both sides of road somewhere between W end of path15 and Ulwell Cottage Caravan Park exit (positions vary). **Studland:** near N end of Church Road. **Sandbanks:** on paths between Grasmere Road and Seacombe Road; N side of E end of Shore Road between buildings.

Its flowers look like small Hollyhock flowers, but Tree Mallows are shorter and broader. It is biennial (sometimes short-lived perennial), so sites can vary.

Garden Tree Mallow *Lavatera* x
clementii (*L. olbia* x *thuringiaca*)
Introduction. Rare. Planted. July to
September.
Swanage: temporarily on cliff 90m N
of N end of promenade (inaccessible
but visible from beach). **Lilliput:** NW
end of Evening Hill.

Short-lived perennial.

Hollyhock *Alcea rosea*
Introduction. Occasional. Casual.
June to September.
Swanage: on cliff above three levels of
beach chalets 40m N of end of path
from Burlington Road.

SUNDEW FAMILY

There are few reference points on the
middle of heaths, so map references
are often given. See drawing of leaves.

Round-leaved Sundew
Drosera rotundifolia
Native. Frequent. Bogs, wet heath.
June to August (leaves from May).

**Godlingston Sundew, Round-leaved
x Oblong-leaved Sundew – hybrid**
Drosera x *belezeana* (*D. rotundifolia* x
intermedia)
Native. Occasional. Bogs, wet heath.

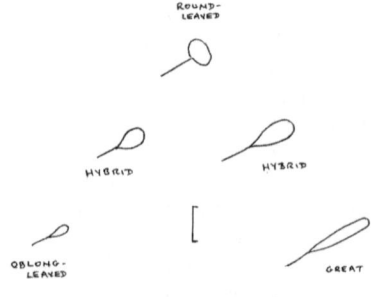

*Outlines of leaves of Sundew species and
hybrids*

July to August (leaves from June).
Vulnerable.
Godlingston Heath: well up W side
of Western Valley at map reference
SZ01068316; 175m W of junction of
bridleway 26 and track going NW
towards small area of Maritime Pines;
N of those pines at SZ01438274
(unusually inconspicuous, all five
Sundews in this area); patches near S
end of Central Valley at map reference
SZ01898270; on S side of Lily Pond;
175m NW of Agglestone at map
reference SZ02188287; much 60m W
of Agglestone (best place); 250m NE
of Agglestone 50m SE of path 24;
50m NE of bridleway 23 at map reference SZ02648324; at five sites spread
along and above S side of Knoll Bog
for 100m W-E; one site in Knoll Bog
at map reference SZ02728341.

Usually easily recognisable by
masses of leaves pointing upwards.
Discovered in 1999 by David
Pearman. All earlier records of this
hybrid in Britain are now assumed to
be errors and many of those from
Europe are also doubted. In fact,
Godlingston Heath is possibly the
only area in Europe where this hybrid
can currently be seen (Pearman &
Rumsey, 2004). See photo on back
cover.

**Round-leaved x Great Sundew –
hybrid** *Drosera* x *obovata*
(*D. rotundifolia* x *anglica*)
Native. Occasional. Bogs, with parents, usually few. July to August
(leaves from June).
Dorset Scarce.
Hartland Moor: in area 95-105m N
of track N of Great Knoll due N of
largest group of trees on NE side of
Knoll. **Godlingston Heath:** N of
small area of Maritime Pines marked
in green on O.S. map at map reference

SZ01438273 (all five Sundews in this area); on E side of bog (which has bridleway26 on W side) at map reference SZ01728348; in Brand's Bog Extension both in area SZ023836 and SZ02428362; on N side of Knoll Bog at SZ02768345. **Studland Heath:** good number down centre of Spur Bog in area 80m W-E for 40m N-S.

Leaves can vary in shape on the same plant. Flowers 8-10mm across when open in the morning sun.

Great Sundew
Drosera anglica (*D. longifolia*)
Native. Occasional. Bogs. July to August (leaves from June onwards).
Dorset Scarce. Near Threatened.
Hartland Moor: in area 20m W-E 75-115m N of track N of Great Knoll due N of largest group of trees on NE side of Knoll. **Godlingston Heath:** N of small area of Maritime Pines marked in green on O.S. map at map reference SZ01438273 (all five Sundews are in this area); on E side of bog (which has bridleway26 on W side) at map reference SZ01728348 for 25m N-wards; in Brand's Bog Extension very large numbers both in areas SZ023836 for 45m E-W 35m N-S and SZ024836 for 15m E-W 30m N-S; N side of Knoll Bog at SZ02768345. **Studland Heath:** plentiful in centre of Spur Bog in area 90m W-E 50m N-S.

Flowers are 10-13mm across when open in the morning sun.

Oblong-leaved Sundew
Drosera intermedia
Native. Frequent. Bogs. June to August (leaves from May).

It usually likes wetter ground than Round-leaved Sundew, but not so wet as Great Sundew, though all three species overlap in places.

ROCK-ROSE FAMILY
Common Rock-rose
Helianthemum nummularium
Native. Occasional. Downs. May to September.
Steeple: plentiful on Steeple Down (west). **Church Knowle:** plentiful on lower slope of Down through which bridleway39 runs NE-wards. **Corfe:** plentiful on W part of long SW slope of castle mound outside walls; much by upper half of steps up East Hill; between Purbeck Way and bridleway20 on both sides of UCR N of Sandyhills Farm. **Swanage Railway:** plenty on NE side of N end of Corfe cutting. **Knitson:** plentiful on Down between bridleways8 and 9. **Wares (east):** plentiful 30-35m S of gate from Hay Brimble to Balston Wear. **Durlston:** 40m ENE of NE corner of lighthouse enclosure. **Ballard Down:** plentiful on S-facing slope especially near foot.

VIOLET FAMILY
Sweet Violet *Viola odorata*
Doubtful if native nationally. Occasional. Verges; always near buildings or former buildings in this area. February to April.
East Creech: partial albinos on E side of E access track to NW corner of Stonehill Down Reserve 40m S of road. **Stoborough:** albinos on N side of Nutcrack Lane 150m E of B3075. **Church Knowle:** by postbox at N end of path18. **Kingston:** W side of South Street opposite house Aeolia. **Corfe:** NW side of road NW of castle 100m SW of A351. **Hartland Moor:** by path80 on S side of Scotland Barn. **Worth:** E side of Kingston Road opposite car park. **Swanage:** E side of Northbrook Road opposite cemetery. **Ulwell:** albinos on W side of road to Studland 225m N of junction with

road towards Currendon Farm. **Studland:** by old thatched cart shed at W end of Watery Lane. **Sandbanks:** three sites by paths between Grasmere Road and Seacombe Road.

Hairs on leaf stems inconspicuous; leaves mid-green; some shoots grow sideways from base; petals usually dark purple (see next species).

Hairy Violet *Viola hirta*
Native. Occasional. Downs (usually thinly spread), calcareous verges. April to May.
Steeple: here and there along Steeple Down (west). **East Creech:** along lower part of SE-facing slope of Stonehill Down for 300m SW of hair-pin bend in road (especially 125-200m from hairpin). **Hartland Moor:** E side of track to Middlebere Farm from 100-300m from road. **Langton:** near gate on path5 at S side of Talbot's Wood (N not W of cemetery). **Godlingston Heath:** 100m N of B3351 on heath E of bridleway25 (with Common Dog Violet; limestone was used as founda-tions there in World War II).
Durlston: Downs – 20m S of Small Copse for example; around shallow quarry in NE of Field 14; (sometimes with Common Dog Violet).
Townsend Reserve: widespread.
Ballard Down: three-quarters of way up S side of Down 100m NNW of gate on bridleway14; here and there in short grass N of fence above Ballard Cliff.

Hairs on leaf stems conspicuous; leaves pale green; shoots do not grow sideways from base; petals not dark purple (see species above).

Common Dog Violet *Viola riviniana*
Native. Frequent. Woods, downs (sometimes with Hairy Violet), heaths (can be mistaken for Marsh Violet),

verges. April to June; occasionally August to October.

Petals mid-purple not dark purple. Spur is lighter in colour than the rest of the petals; its thickness varies, it is notched at the end (see next species). Leaves about as long as wide.

Early Dog Violet
Viola reichenbachiana
Native. Occasional. Woods, verges; not on acid soils. March to April, flower two weeks earlier than previous species.
Creech: SE side of road passing through Great Wood halfway up the hill. **East Creech:** here and there in woods N of Stonehill Down, with albinos 30 and 80m from E end. **Norden** and **Corfe:** scattered along Purbeck Way N of West Hill. **Bushey:** many here and there by bridleway14 (best site). **Harman's Cross:** near bend in path44 on N side of The Wilderness. **Knitson:** N of bridle-way8 just E of wet area due N of Knaveswell Farm. **King's Wood:** SE of bridleway87 30m SW of E corner of wood. **Ulwell:** along 30m of SW side of Road N of Godlingston Hill 300m SE of Currendon Farm.
Durlston: W side of Diagonal Path 30m from N end; towards S end of Caravan Terrace (previous species is near N end).

Spur is darker or has the same colour as the rest of petals, sometimes narrow and notched at end but less notched than Common Dog Violet. Leaves about as long as wide.

Heath Dog Violet *Viola canina*
Native. Rare. Heathy verges. Late April to May.
Near Threatened.
Stoborough Heath: E side of Dismantled Tramway 70 and 240m N

of A351. **Hartland Moor:** E side of Soldiers Road 200m N of track to Isolation Cottages. **Studland:** scattered in Harmony Farm NE Field – few 20m SE of N gate from bridleway17; more 40 to over 50m SE of gate in area 25m wide. (Some records of this species in *The Flora of Dorset* should be Common Dog Violet, as Bowen (2000) hints.)

Petals are bluer than previous four species, but still <u>mauve</u>. Spur off-white with tinge of cream at first two sites, clear pale yellow in Studland. Leaves at least 1.25 times as long as wide. Some leaf-bases heart shaped; some meet stalk at right-angles. (Lack of basal rosette is difficult to discern).

Pale Dog Violet *Viola lactea*
Native. Rare. Heaths. May to June. *Nationally Scarce. Vulnerable.*
Stoborough Heath: in area 25m square SE of plank bridge on true route of Purbeck Way (marked with black dashes on O.S. map) about halfway from rail crossing to Wareham bypass. **Hartland Moor:** one plant seen each side of Jubilee Bridge. **Godlingston Heath:** on S side of bridleway27 35m W of track to greenkeepers' private depot.

Petals mauvey-white. Some leaf-bases taper into stalk, others meet it at right angles, none have heart-shaped bases.

Field Pansy *Viola arvensis*
Early Introduction. Occasional. Arable fields, other disturbed ground. April to October.

TAMARISK FAMILY
Tamarisk *Tamarix gallica*
Introduction. Occasional. Planted near the sea.
Durlston: by Coast Path around Durlston Head; SW of lighthouse.
Swanage: above promenade 55-70m N of path to beach from Burlington Road. **Sandbanks:** raised dune SW of main car park. **Canford Cliffs:** cliff near stepped path from Cliff Drive to beach; behind beach chalets 100-175m NE of Canford Cliffs Chine.

GOURD FAMILY
White Bryony *Bryonia dioica*
Native. Occasional. Hedges, verges, cliff-tops. May to September.
Kimmeridge: W of path15 at N end of withybed. **Steeple:** near S edge of Steeple Down (east) 250 and 300m E of W fence. **East Creech:** S side of road 30m W of W end of large chalk quarry opposite. **Stoborough:** W side of West Lane N of E end of path13; W side of Furzebrook Road 225m N of path24 on opposite side. **Corfe:** on SW side of path79 40m NW of rail crossing. **Norden:** both sides of Slepe Road 150m N of railway bridge (with unrelated Black Bryony and Hedge Bindweed nearby for comparison). **Worth:** near small building by bridleway19 NE of Chapman's Pool. **Ridge:** S side of Nutcrack Lane 80m from E end. **Bushey:** E side of UCR 80m S of gate S of Rollington Farm.

Poisonous. Surprisingly absent from E part of this area.

WILLOW FAMILY
Willows and Poplars of Great Britain and Ireland (Meikle, 1984) is helpful for species and hybrids. Chapter 2 of *A Guide to Some Difficult Plants* (Wild Flower Society, 1990) is also helpful for willows, as is *Willows of The British Isles* (Brendell, 1985), which has a tabular key on page 15.

Except for Weeping Willow, male and female flowers of willows and poplars are borne on separate trees/shrubs; for added interest, sexes are given below when there are few examples of a species. Catkins are not much use for identification in most cases. Mature leaves are the best guide, from about mid-June onwards. Ignore leaves on suckers and most vigorous shoots. Leaves in drawings are full-grown late summer and autumn ones; all trees/shrubs will also have smaller leaves.

White Poplar *Populus alba*
Introduction. Occasional. Planted and suckering.
Kimmeridge: 50m N of toilet building by Coast Path at SE end of Kimmeridge Bay. **Knitson:** N side of road at Knaveswell Farm. **Durlston:** NE corner of Smith Field; S of E side car park. **Swanage:** S side of Washpond Lane 50m W of Ulwell Road; on cliff N of E end of path to beach from Burlington Road. **Studland:** N side of B3351 400m E of W end of Heath Green Road; E side of Ferry Road 40m N of village crossroads. **Shell Bay:** several N of restaurant. **Sandbanks:** raised dune SW of main car park.

Medium height (15-20m) when full-grown. Leaves are white underneath – see drawing.

Grey Poplar *Populus* x *canescens* (*P. alba* x *tremula*)
Introduction. Occasional. Planted and suckering.
Holme: along S side of Holme Lane 200-250m W of B3070 (with next species). **Norden:** SW side of permissive bridleway which runs NW from New Line Farm 150m from S end. **Hartland Moor:** W side of permissive path just SW of Langton Wallis. **Wytch:** 300m W of Wytch Farm along 75m of S side of path5. **Woolgarston:** on E side of bridleway23 150m N of road; few 40m S of road in centre of Higher Grove Wood (view from road). **Studland:** above shore on South Beach 150m SE of Joe's Café (with Aspen). **Brownsea:** several on both sides of Middle Street N of Vinery ruins; several along Nature Reserve track on W side of Lagoon.

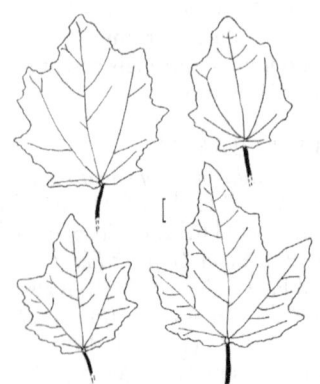

Variation in White Poplar leaves.

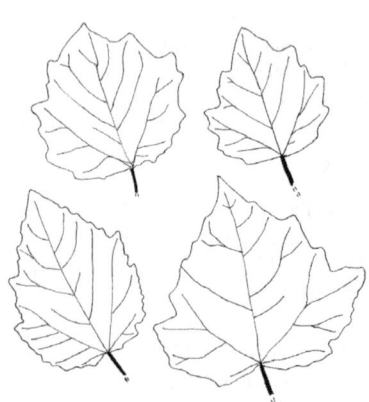

Variation in Grey Poplar leaves.

Tall (30-35m) when full-grown. Leaves pale grey underneath – see drawing.

Aspen *Populus tremula*
Native. Occasional. Woods, verges, suckering, some planted.
Holme: along S side of Holme Lane 200-250m W of B3070 (with Grey Poplar). **Furzebrook:** NW edge of Kilnwood Reserve from 50m S of Purbeck Way for 40m S-wards. **Ridge:** E side of Dismantled Tramway 120-130m S of Arne Road. **Corfe Charity's Meadows:** by bridleway3 at S end of meadow SW of Sharford Bridge. **Norden:** several for 50m on N side of bridleway77 around 350m from A351. **Wytch:** along 25m of E side of path5 100m S of Wytch Farm. **Harman's Cross:** NE side A351 70m NW of railway bridge E of village. **Studland Heath:** several by SE part of Woodland Nature Trail; small group W of fixed dunes 125m N of Knoll Beach main N car park. **Studland:** above shore on South Beach 150m SE of Joe's Café (with Grey Poplar). **Brownsea:** several on W side of Nature Reserve track W of Lagoon.

Suckers have leaves like Grey Poplar.

Black Poplar
Populus nigra subsp. *betulifolia*
Native. Occasional. Hedges; difficult to know whether planted.
Holme: several on SE side of Holme Bridge. **Swanage:** S side of junction of Darkie Lane and Washpond Lane; N side of Washpond Lane 90m W of Ulwell Road; NE corner of Cricket Ground. **Durlston:** planted – NW edge of Reservoir Copse; N of Coast Path NW of castle.

No glands at base of leaves; (see Hybrid Black Poplar).

Lombardy Poplar
Populus nigra var. *italica* cv.
Introduction. Occasional. Planted.
Swanage Railway: S side of track just E of Herston Halt. **Durlston:** NE corner of Large Copse. **Swanage:** two on S side of railway just W of Northbrook Road bridge. **Luscombe Valley:** 100m N of SE corner of reserve.

Hybrid Black Poplar *Populus* x *canadensis* (*P. nigra* x *deltoides*)
Cultivated. Occasional. Planted.
Wareham: along SE side of Priory Meadow. **Stoborough:** W side of

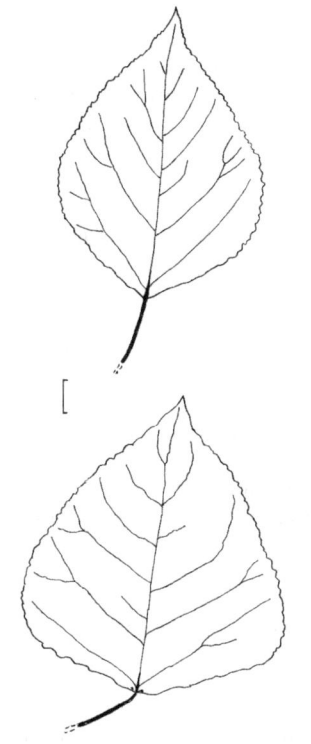

[

Leaves of Poplars – Hybrid Black (below) and Marilandica

Furzebrook Road 125m SW of A351
roundabout. **Church Knowle:** N side
of road 200m W of crossroads W of
village. **Bushey:** S side of Bushey Lane
in several places. **Rempstone:** row on
W side of Forest Lane between B3351
and Bushey Lane. **Langton:** 140m N
of B3069 by path1. **Knitson:** row
150m NW of NW corner of Marsh
Copse. **Swanage:** S side of long
Playing Field W of cemetery towards
W end of field; N of Court Road E of
railway bridge (female). **Durlston:** 5m
E of Coast Path 30m S of NE corner
of Long Meadow. **Branksome Chine:**
near foot of steps up cliff 250m SW
of chine.

Distinguished from Black Poplar
(p.101) by having a pair of glands at or
near the leaf base (lens). See drawing.

Males are usually planted because
females produce copious amounts of
fluffy seed.

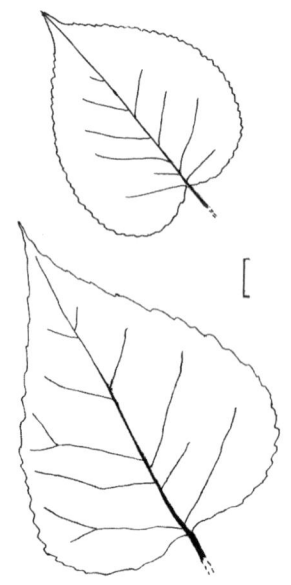

Leaves of Balm-of-Gilead showing variation.

Marilandica
Populus x *canadensis* cv. Marilandica
(*P. nigra* x *P.* x *canadensis* cv. Serotina)
Cultivated. Rare. Planted.
Church Knowle: few on W side of
path18 125m S of road (with larger
Balm-of-Gileads). See drawing.

Western Balsam Poplar
Populus trichocarpa
Introduction. Rare. Planted.
Bushey: SE side of Meadus' Lane
300m NE of B3351 (male).

Balm-of-Gilead *Populus* x *jackii*
(*P. deltoides* x *balsamifera*)
Introduction. Rare. Escape.
Church Knowle: several on W side of
path18 within 200m S of road (with
few small Marilandicas). **Durlston:**
visible on cliffs at short range (binoculars help) – looking N from N end
of Caravan Terrace (originally wrong-

ly reported by this author as being
previous species, and is listed in error
in *The Flora of Dorset*).

Always female. Not variegated here.
Most leaves have heart-shaped bases,
but some on leading shoots have flat
bases. See drawing. Conspicuous in its
autumn colours in October.

Crack Willow *Salix fragilis*
Early Introduction. Occasional. Wet
woods, verges, watersides, some
planted.
Tyneham: NE of pond near tele-
phone box (with White Willow).
Kimmeridge: several in withybed.
Wareham: W side of B3075 40m S of
South Bridge. **Stoborough Heath:** by
both gates where path5 passes
through small fenced field.
Furzebrook: two in Kilnwood
Reserve near NW edge 30 and 50m
NE of access track. **Church Knowle:**

N side road to Corfe 200m E of path16 (with Golden Willow). **Woolgarston:** S side of road 225m SE of Ailwood Farm. **Swanage:** young ones S of hedge 225m W of car and coach park. **Durlston:** W of castle entrance (with other willows). **Brownsea:** near start of boardwalk through Orchid Meadow.

Hybrid Crack Willow *Salix* x *rubens*
(*S. fragilis* x *alba* var. *vitellina*)
Early Introduction. Occasional. Planted.
Hartland Moor: female on E side of Slepe Road 100m SE of Slepe Copse. **Kingston:** SW side of B3069 50m NW of bend at Kingston Barn. **Corfe:** S side of Purbeck Way 25m E of junction with Sandy Hill Lane. **Woolgarston:** N side of road 250m SE of Ailwood Farm (cut along with hedge). **Swanage Railway:** female by bamboo on S side of track just E of Herston Halt. **Swanage:** females in small young copse on SW side of S end of Benlease Way; male at E end of N side of copse W of D'Urberville Drive. **Brownsea:** males N of track W of Landing Pier (with other willows). **Sandbanks:** several females on dunes 175m NE of main car park. **Luscombe Valley:** males W and NW of houses near SE corner of reserve.

Conspicuous orange-yellow twigs are diagnostic, especially noticeable in winter.

White Willow *Salix alba*
Early Introduction. Frequent. Wet woods, watersides, planted on verges. **Kimmeridge:** several in withybed. **Wareham:** SW of South Bridge. **Ridge:** several by River Frome NW of Redcliffe Farm. **Norden:** young tree E of roundabout. **Rempstone:** W side of Thrasher's Lane 150m N of

entrance to Oil Gathering Station. **Durlston:** W of castle entrance (with other willows). **Swanage:** S side of Washpond Lane 25m W of Ulwell Road. **Shell Bay:** E of car park. **Brownsea:** N of track W of Landing Pier (with other willows). **Luscombe Valley:** 40 and 80m N of SE corner of reserve.

Golden Willow
Salix alba var. *vitellina*
Cultivated. Occasional. Planted. **Steeple:** male by private entrance to Whiteway Farm (view from road). **Norden:** females along here and there on NE side of A351 SE of railway bridge. **Church Knowle:** female N side road to Corfe 200m E of path16 (with Crack Willow). **Corfe:** female N end of S half of Byle Copse. **Worth:** by pond on NE side of Renscombe Road (pollarded). **Wares (west):** four males on W edge of Long Close 120m S of NW corner. **Ballard Down:** one tree about halfway between Whitecliff Farm and sea can be seen from Down.

Orange twigs, conspicuous in winter.

Weeping Willow
Salix x *sepulcralis* nothovar.
(= variety of hybrid) *chrysocoma*
(*S. alba* var. *vitellina* x *babylonica*)
Introduction. Rare. Planted. **Church Knowle:** W of path18 at junction with path17. **Bushey:** 100m from Meadus' Lane on SE side of UCR running NE from near N end of Lane.

Corkscrew Willow *Salix babylonica*
var. *pekinensis* cv. Tortuosa
Introduction. Rare. Planted. **Studland:** female E side of Ferry Road at low point 180m N of Beach Road.

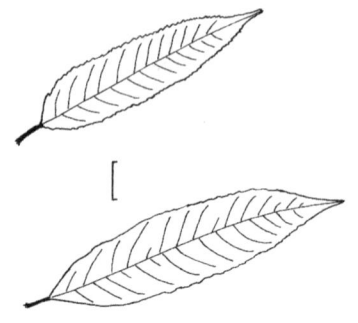

Leaves of Almond Willow (above) and Broad-leaved Osier.

Almond Willow *Salix triandra*
Early Introduction. Occasional. By
fresh water; may have been planted.
Corfe Charity's Meadows: SE corner
of Five Acres (female); four trees on E
side of Great Close; SW side of
Bankes Mead; three sites on E side of
Long Meadow; two trees on E side of
meadow SW of Sharford Bridge.

Usually male. Leaves are variable –
some have ears at the leaf-base (like
Eared Willow and some Grey
Willows), but all have long drawn out
leaf-tip (see drawing). Distinctive and
attractive smooth, flaking, cinnamon
bark visible on some. Best willow
species for basketwork, because it
bends without breaking.

Purple Willow *Salix purpurea*
Native. Occasional. By river and
ditches.
Wareham: several on SE side of River
Frome 275-425m upstream from
South Bridge (boat). **Ridge:** by
Purbeck Way 75m NW of Redcliffe
Farm along length of 10m; also by
Purbeck Way 350m NW of same
farm along 30m. **Swanage:** looking
right from gate on S side of E end of

Washpond Lane two trees can be seen
in a small private field (binoculars).
Brownsea: several N of track W of
Landing Pier (with other willows).

Fine Osier *Salix* x *forbyana*
(*S. purpurea* x *viminalis* x cinerea?)
Introduction. Rare. Planted.
Only current Dorset site.
Wareham: females on E side of River
Frome 600m upstream from South
Bridge along 25m (boat).

May be a triple hybrid. Formerly
highly-valued for finer kinds of basketwork.

European Violet Willow
Salix daphnoides
Introduction. Rare. Planted.
Wares (east): male on W side of
path64 200m N of private track to
California Farm.

Osier *Salix viminalis*
Early Introduction. Occasional.
Hedges, wet places, often planted.
Kimmeridge: females in Withybed.
Stoborough: NE side of bypass 50m
NW of path13. **Wareham** and **Ridge:**
male and few female trees here and
there by Purbeck Way from 250m SE
of South Bridge to Redcliffe Farm.
Church Knowle: females on W side
of road at Puddle Mill Farm. **Corfe
Charity's Meadows:** female W side of
Home Mead (W) 70m S of Scotland
Barn; female halfway along S side of
Home Mead (E); male on S side of
Great Close; two females on E side.
Bushey: female on E side of bridle-
way10 200m N of Bushey Lane.
Wares (east): females on E side of
path64 30m S of private track to
California Farm. **Herston (north):** N
of stile 100m NW of SE end of path1.
Durlston: female W of castle
entrance (with other willows).

Studland: females by village pond.
Used for straight supports in basketwork, e.g. corner pieces.

Broad-leaved Osier
Salix x *sericans* (*S. viminalis* x *caprea*)
Native, but probably planted here.
Rare. Hedges.
Church Knowle: females on W side of
road at Puddle Mill Farm. **Wares
(east):** females along S side of path64
on short E-W section of path (see Map
16) NW of quarry. **Godlingston:**
females on N side Washpond Lane
20m E of Brickyard Lane
Formerly planted for use in rough
basketwork; this species is easily overlooked and there may indeed be more
present locally. See drawing.

Goat Willow *Salix caprea*
Native. Occasional. Woods, hedges;
some planted.
Norden: both sides of S end of Slepe
Road. **Kingston:** on SE side of
path44 275m from West Street.
Bushey: Thrasher's Lane at S end on
E side. **Harman's Cross:** E side of
Haycraft's Lane 10m NW of bridle-
way6. **Langton:** near gate on path5 at
S side of Talbot's Wood (N not W of
cemetery). **Knitson:** N of bridleway8
60m W of bridleway12. **Wares (east):**
on E side of path64 30m S of private
track to California Farm. **Swanage:**
near SE corner of Pitch and Putt
course (players only). **Durlston:** W
side of Long Meadow 100m S of NW
corner. **Brownsea:** near start of boardwalk through Orchid Meadow.

Grey Willow
Salix cinerea subsp. *oleifolia*
Native. Abundant. Hedges, wet
woods, cliffs.
Leaf shape varies considerably (see
drawing); ears are often present on

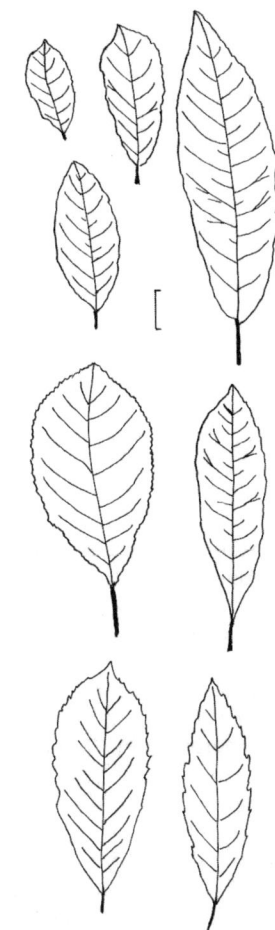

Variation in Grey Willow leaves.

the stem; broad-leaved forms may be
misidentified as Goat Willow; small-
leaved forms can be mistaken for
Eared Willow or its hybrid (see
below).

Grey x Eared Willow Hybrid *Salix* x *multinervis* (*S. cinerea* x *aurita*)
Native. Occasional. Marshes; often
with small specimens of Grey Willow.

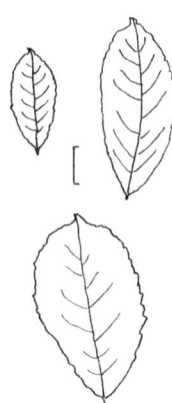

Variation in Grey x Eared Willow Hybrid leaves.

Hartland Moor: in Upper Fen around 325 and 350m NE of Isolation Cottages at map references SY94328255 and 94338458; in Middle Fen 110m SW of Fen Pool at S end of area of low trees/scrub at map references SY95148501 and 95188501 (approach from W and E, respectively); on island of scrub in Tramway Bog 75m SE of Post Pool. Corfe: several in large low wet area halfway up W side of West Common (especially near S end of area); several in First Valley SE of UCR; several at head of South-west Valley on Middle Common; several near tiny E stream in Little East Common 10-125m SE of bridleway30. Ulwell: two by SW side of Ulwell Road in private withybed 50m NW of road to Ulwell Cottage Caravan Park (view from pavement).

From *A Guide to Some Difficult Plants* (Wild Flower Society, 1990) – 'When you think you have (found) Eared Willow in lowland England, the chances are you have not. You have found the hybrid (with Grey Willow).'

It is fertile and interbreeds with its parents, producing bushes with differing proportions of its parents characteristics. Look for twist at apex of most leaves, slight wrinkling of leaf edges; fairly downy mature leaf undersides (mature Grey Willow leaf undersides have few hairs). See drawing.

Creeping Willow *Salix repens*
Native. Frequent. Dunes and heaths where wet in winter.
Stoborough Heath: plentiful on heath NW of Hartland Stud. **Hartland Moor:** here and there in Upper and Middle Fens; S side of Arne Road W of Arne Triangle. **Corfe:** wetter areas of Common. **Wytch:** on path80 along S of Wytch Heath plantation. **Bushey:** in SW of Brenscombe Heath including 100m N of slight bend in Bushey Lane. **Rempstone:** on both sides of bridleway9 120m N of crossing of bridleways9 and 10. **Studland Heath:** by Heather Walk 250m N of Knoll Beach main N car park. **Shell Bay:** 450m SSE of NE end of boardwalk in large circular depression 80m behind fore-dunes. **Luscombe Valley:** near N end on E side 20m S of wooden bridge.
Leaf size varies considerably.

CRUCIFER OR CABBAGE FAMILY
Eastern Rocket *Sisymbrium orientale*
Introduction. Rare. Verges. June to October.
Sandbanks: on short path from Panorama Road to N shore (W of The Horseshoe); SE side of main car park near S end.

Hedge Mustard
Sisymbrium officinale
Early Introduction. Frequent. Verges, arable fields, other disturbed ground. June to October.

Garlic Mustard *Alliaria petiolata*
Native. Frequent. Verges, hedge-banks. April to June.

Thale Cress *Arabidopsis thaliana*
Native. Occasional. Pavements, verges, arable fields, gardens, other disturbed ground. March to August.
Ridge: NW side of Barnhill Road near SW end. **Langton:** W side of path27 just S of B3069. **Swanage Railway:** Herston Halt. **Swanage:** area including W end of Court Road and N end of Argyle Road; roadsides on Ballard Estate. **Studland:** near entrance to Village Hall. **Shell Bay:** sides of Ferry Road. **Lilliput:** S end of short path between Lilliput Road and Greenwood Avenue (see street map for road names and O.S. map for path). **Sandbanks:** SE side of Banks Road between NE end of Panorama Road and roundabout. **Branksome Chine:** flowerbed weed at SE end of chine just NW of road.

Wallflower *Erysimum cheiri*
Early Introduction. Rare. Escape on cliffs and walls. March to June.
Kimmeridge: wall on W side of road S of church. **Corfe:** E side of railway cutting S of railway viaduct (view from train). **Swanage:** here and there on cliffs above promenade (binoculars); by path down the cliff from Burlington Road.

Dame's-violet *Hesperis matronalis*
Introduction. Occasional. Escape. May to July.
Kingston: wild in churchyard 25m E of NW gate; plentiful on W side of B3069 150m N of N end of path40 on opposite side (including albino). **Corfe:** on E side of A351 30m N of Sandy Hill Lane. **Godlingston Heath:** on Harmony Farm West

Fields just outside private garden at map reference SZ01928195.
Swanage: near Swan Brook on Pitch and Putt course S of course entrance (players only).

Virginia Stock *Malcolmia maritima*
Introduction. Rare. Casual. June to August.

Hoary Stock *Matthiola incana*
Introduction. Rare. Escape on cliffs. May to July.
Swanage: albinos here and there high on cliffs between N end of Shore Road and path down cliff from Burlington Road (binoculars).
Branksome Dene Chine: albino at foot of cliffs 80m NE of Chine.

Wintercress *Barbarea vulgaris*
Native. Occasional. Verges, arable fields, other disturbed ground, water-sides. April to June.
Steeple: just over fence on N side of road opposite hill-top viewpoint NW of Steeple. **Wareham:** wall of inlet on S side of River Frome just W of South Bridge; few scattered in Priory Meadow. **East Creech:** S side of road to East Creech 50m W of Furzebrook Road. **Corfe Charity's Meadows:** SE corner of Home Mead (E). **Worth:** by path17 going from Weston Farm S-wards. **Knitson:** S side of road at top of rise W of Knaveswell Farm; N side of road near Farm (position varies). **Herston (north):** NW side of first right-angled bend in Washpond Land N of Herston Halt. **Swanage:** on W side of car and coach park near N bridge over stream.

May not occur at the same sites each year; Wareham and Worth (Weston Farm) sites are probably the best. Upper leaves have on average one pair of lobes at the base.

Medium-flowered Wintercress
Barbarea intermedia
Introduction. Rare. Casual. May to June.
Wares (east): in Golter 50m from W wall by diagonal band of Gorse which crosses field.

Upper leaves with several lobes; lowest leaves usually with 2 to 6 pairs of side lobes; petals 4-6.3mm long; seed capsules under 35mm long.

American Wintercress
Barbarea verna
Introduction. Rare. Casual. May to June.

Upper leaves with several lobes; lowest leaves with usually 4 to 10 pairs of side lobes; petals 5.6-8.4mm long; most developed seed capsules over 35mm long.

Watercress
Rorippa nasturtium-aquaticum
Native. Frequent. Streams, ponds, ditches, flushes. May to October.
Tyneham: in pond by telephone box. **Creech:** 300m NW of Grange Road at low point by bridleway1. **Norden:** vigorous plants by permissive path leading NNE from near New Line Farm for 120m from S end.
Kingston: Coast Path by South Gwyle. **Corfe:** plentiful in Challow Pond. **Worth:** in stream in NE of Worth Mead. **Bushey:** N side of Bushey Lane 150m E of Higher Bushey Farm. **Wares (west and east):** most flushes. **Langton:** stream in N of West Wood 30m E of path44.
Swanage: in Swan Brook near bridge at SW corner of car and coach park. **Studland:** stream by E half of Watery Lane. See Plate 10.

Marsh Yellowcress *Rorippa palustris*
Native. Rare. Watersides and wet verges. June to September.
Wareham: by inlet just W of South Bridge. **Studland:** NW side of bridleway23 40m SE of junction with Wadmore Lane.

Creeping Yellowcress
Rorippa sylvestris
Native. Rare. Muddy ditch edges.
Holme: East Holme Meadows – see p.23.

Horseradish *Armoracia rusticana*
Early Introduction. Occasional.
Escape on verges, waste ground. May to June.
Kimmeridge: on N side of path14 10m E of gate at Kimmeridge Farm (gets cut). **Langton:** 15m E of path27 just S of Playing Field.

Cuckooflower, Lady's Smock
Cardamine pratensis
Native. Frequent. Marshes, wet fields and lawns. April to May.
Stoborough: plenty visible E of B3075 in field N of King's Arms car park. **Corfe Charity's Meadows:** much especially in Bankes Mead; in meadow SW of Sharford Bridge; many more visible from latter field in field to N. **Worth:** many in SE part of churchyard (helpfully left unmown). **Swanage:** good number visible from Washpond Lane in field N of bend N of railway.

Wavy Bittercress *Cardamine flexuosa*
Native. Frequent. Wet places in woods; gardens. April to September.
'Wavy' refers to the stem. The hairiness of stems is the easiest way to distinguish it from the next species, which has hairless slightly wavy stems. Flowers have 6 stamens (lens). Young seedpods overtop flowers slightly in this species and much more in next.

Hairy Bittercress *Cardamine hirsuta*
Native. Abundant. Thin soils, anthills, gardens, pavements. February to June.

The English and scientific names are both misleading. Hairs, which are on the leaves, are few (lens), whereas the short hairs on the stems of Wavy Bittercress above can be seen unaided. Flowers have 4 stamens (lens).

Hairy Rockcress *Arabis hirsuta*
Native. Occasional. Sloping calcareous grassland. May to June.
East Creech: scattered along NW side of bridleway31; E end of Stonehill Down 40m SW of gate from road in NE corner extending 15m W-wards up slope N of old quarry. **Church Knowle:** 25m E of gate where UCR from Knowle Hill meets road on top of Down. **Corfe:** several areas in castle N of keep (easiest site). **Worth:** W side of bridleway15 just N of St. Aldhelm's Head (working) Quarry; near top of SE-facing slope above Hill Bottom for nearly 300m SW-NE (SW end is just above a small lone Hawthorn). **Woolgarston:** NE side of bridleway21 60m from junction with bridleway17; on Ailwood Down near E end of top of Long Barrow (which is near E end of main E-W line of round tumuli and S of them). **Wares (east):** on slight mound near top of slope in S part of Golter 110m SE of Middle Field gate. **Knitson:** 10m below upper half of zigzag track 50m SW of Purbeck Way.

Often few.

Aubrieta *Aubrieta deltoidea*
Introduction. Rare. Escape. March to May.
Swanage: wall of Swan Brook just SW of W end of Kings Road East.

Honesty *Lunaria annua*
Introduction. Frequent. Escape on verges, usually near houses. April to May.
Corfe: plentiful on NE side of A351 N of Sandy Hill Lane. **Herston (north):** sides of Washpond Lane 75m N of A351. **Studland:** NW side of B3351 175m SW of village crossroads. Albinos frequent.

Golden Alyssum *Alyssum saxatile*
Introduction. Rare. Escape. April to May.

Sweet Alison *Lobularia maritima*
Introduction. Frequent. Escape on pavements, stable dunes. March to December.

Common Whitlowgrass
Erophila verna
Native. Frequent. Thin soils, sand, pavements, paths. February to May. (See below).

Glabrous Whitlowgrass
Erophila glabrescens
Native. Occasional. Thin calcareous soil, anthills, sand. February to May.
Kimmeridge: S side of entrance to car park by road junction NE of village. **Norden:** on path3 100m E of railway crossing. **Wares (west):** below wire fence in Seacombe Quarry 25m W of fence's SE corner; on anthill 10m from NW fence of Taylor's Ware; **(east)** on anthills on bank in NE corner of Middle Field; two places along old quarry banks near middle of top of Belle Vue East Ware. **Townsend Reserve:** S of SE Bastion; also just W of SW corner of Manwell Field. **Durlston:** here and there near path55 along brow of Down in fields 3, 6 and 10; just N of NW corner of lighthouse enclosure; by Visitor Centre

flagpole. **Studland Heath:** War Hill. **Studland:** here and there on S and E sides of Middle Beach car park. **Shell Bay:** S of roundabout sign both sides of road. **Sandbanks:** raised lawn of café E of main car park.

Similar in appearance to Common Whitlowgrass, with which it usually grows, but stalks are hairless when in flower (lens) or perhaps just 1 or 2 hairs at the base of the stalk; petals are divided to no more than half their length (petal division is greater on some but on by no means all plants of Common Whitlowgrass). Leaf hairiness varies. NB. Hairs may drop off mature stalks, so ignore stalks which have only fruits and no young flowers. From its outward appearance in this area it looks like a variety of Common Whitlowgrass, but laboratory work could show otherwise.

English Scurvygrass
Cochlearia anglica
Native. Occasional. Tops of salt-marshes, in gaps in rushes or in grass above them. April to June.
Studland Heath: groups of plants below Brand's Bay Hide; 450m S of it; halfway along inner shore of Sandy Point spit; on SW shore of Bramble Bush Bay 150m NW of Ferry Road; small amounts in about 20 other places on shore W of Heath. **Sandbanks:** in salt-marsh around head of inlet (not shown on maps) in sandy area S of W end of Chaddesley Glen.

Danish Scurvygrass
Cochlearia danica
Native. Occasional. Cliff-tops, sea-walls, pavements, roadsides (benefitting either from road salt, or from absence of species that cannot tolerate salt). February to May.

Stoborough: scattered along NE side of A351 both SE of River Frome bridge; NW of S end of Dismantled Tramway. **Norden:** NE side of A351 40m SE of bridleway77. **Wares (west):** Seacombe Quarry. **Harman's Cross:** on NE side of A351 5 and 40m E of path41. **Durlston:** plenty near cliff-top SW of lighthouse. **Godlingston Heath:** smaller of two traffic islands where road from Swanage meets B3351. **Shell Bay:** E side of road 20m N of toll-booth. **Sandbanks:** near shrubs by harbour shore opposite main car park entrance. **Branksome Chine:** plentiful on steps above promenade 150m SW of chine.

Upper leaves are stalked.

Shepherd's Purse
Capsella bursa-pastoris
Early Introduction. Frequent. Arable fields, other disturbed ground. All year.

Field Pennycress *Thlaspi arvense*
Early Introduction. Occasional. Arable fields, other disturbed ground. May to July.
Worth: field edge by path S of St. Aldhelm's Chapel.

Garden Candytuft *Iberis umbellata*
Introduction. Rare. Escape. March to May.

Field Pepperwort
Lepidium campestre
Early Introduction. Rare. Dry bare ground. May to June.
Corfe: plentiful just W of scrub 120m W of radio mast at top of Rollington Hill; plentiful on SW side of UCR 110m SE of same mast.

Main stems are upright, anthers pale yellow, most styles not protruding above notch in seedcase.

Smith's Pepperwort
Lepidium heterophyllum
Native. Rare. Dry banks. May to July.
Lilliput: few inside bottom of fenced
area of Evening Hill 70-100m from
NW end.

Main stems often at angle to ground,
anthers browny-purple, styles protrude
well above notch of seedcase, <u>which is</u>
<u>covered with tiny warts that are smaller</u>
<u>than those on the seedcases of the pre-</u>
<u>vious species.</u>

Hoary Cress
Lepidium (Cardaria) draba
Introduction. Occasional. Cliffs,
beach, verges. May to June.
Kimmeridge: cliff-top 100-150m SE
of steps to beach (take care); on beach
either side of slipway in SE of bay.
Swanage: close to A351 on W side of
N end of path (not bridleway) going S
to Verney Farm (see O.S. map).
Studland: in front of Middle Beach
shop.

Swine-cress, Wart-cress
Coronopus squamatus
Early Introduction. Frequent. Arable
fields, other disturbed ground, espe-
cially near gateways. June to
September.

Lesser Swine-cress *Coronopus didymus*
Introduction. Frequent. Arable fields,
other disturbed ground, especially near
gateways. May to September.

Annual Wall Rocket
Diplotaxis muralis
Native. Occasional. Pavements, verges.
April to October.
East Creech: E end of Stonehill Down
8m downhill from Entire-leaved.
Cotoneaster. **Harman's Cross:** NE side
of A351 for 50m SE of path41 (gets
cut). **Swanage:** car and coach park;

here and there between E end of railway station and S end of De Moulham
Road (but weedkiller is used).
Durlston: various places within 50m
of castle. **Shell Bay:** has occurred
around N end of car park. **Luscombe
Valley:** plentiful between bushes on N
side of Sandbanks Road. **Sandbanks:**
SE side of main car park especially near
S end; SW side of Shore Road opposite W end of Chaddesley Glen.
Canford Cliffs: scattered near beach
chalets below Cliff Drive. **Branksome
Chine:** cliff-top near top of steps
125m SW of chine.

Wild Cabbage *Brassica oleracea*
Native or Early Introduction.
Frequent. On and near cliff-tops; cul-
tivars are found rarely as casuals
inland. May to July.
Nationally Scarce.
Wares (west): Seacombe Quarry to
(east) White Ware Quarry. **Ballard
Down:** Ballard Head to Handfast
Point.

Rape *Brassica napus*
Introduction. Occasional. Casual.
April to June.
Buds overtop flowers and most
petals are 13-18mm long – compare
with next species.

Turnip, including **Turnip-rape, Wild
Turnip** *Brassica rapa*
Early Introduction. Occasional.
Casual on verges. May to June.
Flowers overtop buds and most
petals are 6-13mm long – compare
with previous species; the scientific
name can cause confusion.

Black Mustard *Brassica nigra*
Native or introduced. Abundant. Cliff-
tops, verges, field-edges, banks of
streams and dredged ditches; may be

Seed capsules of Black Mustard (left) and Hoary Mustard.

escape from cultivation at all sites. May to September.

Kimmeridge: plentiful by road from village to Kimmeridge Bay; in Bay; by Coast Path E of Bay for long distance. **Corfe Charity's Meadows:** various places by Corfe River (stream). **Worth:** very plentiful in arable field edges both near Renscombe; by bridleway15 near St. Aldhelm's Head. **Swanage Railway:** plentiful both 800m W of Herston Halt; E of Victoria Avenue bridge. **Swanage:** W-E part of Panorama Road; near Peveril Point. **Durlston:** 10m NW of Visitor Centre; many S of stone chart on plinth S of castle (with few look-alike Hoary Mustard).

Up to 2m high – the tallest of similar yellow-flowered species. Bright yellow petals are mostly 9-13mm long. No seed in narrow upper end of seed capsule (compare with Hoary Mustard below, see drawing).

Charlock *Sinapis arvensis*
Early Introduction. Frequent. Arable fields, other disturbed ground. March to September.

White Mustard *Sinapis alba*
Early Introduction. Rare. Disturbed calcareous ground. June to August.
Studland: may reoccur at SE corner of Glebeland Estate E of bridleway12; usually somewhere S of Coast Path 300-500m E of The Warren Wood.

Garden Rocket *Eruca vesicaria*
Introduction. Rare. Casual. June to August.

Hoary Mustard *Hirschfeldia incana*
Introduction. Rare. Waste ground, verges. June to August.
Durlston: few by path S of stone chart on plinth S of castle (with many look-alike Black Mustard). **Shell Bay:** W side of Ferry Road N of toll-booth.

Pale yellow petals are 5-10mm long. One seed in narrow upper end of the seed capsule (compare with Black Mustard p.111). See drawing.

Sea Rocket *Cakile maritima*
Native. Occasional. Top of sandy beaches. June to October.
Kimmeridge: on beach E of Charnel (only open when Army Range Walks open). **Swanage:** sometimes at base of cliffs within 200m N of N end of promenade (position varies). **Studland Heath:** dunes E of Knoll Beach café. **Studland:** near Joe's Café; further NW on South Beach. **Shell Bay:** near Ferry. **Sandbanks:** below Shell Bay Ferry hut; here and there along shore from NE of Haven Hotel to SE of main car park (positions vary year to year); on small sandbank surrounded by salt-marsh opposite W end of Chaddesley Glen; 70m W of junction of Shore Road and Banks Road; in and beyond narrow dunes 550-600m NE of main car park. Irregular in appearance at some sites.

Sea Kale *Crambe maritima*
Native. Rare. Casual high on shingle beaches. June to July.

Wild Radish *Raphanus raphanistrum* subsp. *raphanistrum*
Early Introduction. Occasional. Arable fields, other disturbed ground. May to September.

East Creech: N side of entrance to campsite. **Studland:** visible from gateway S of Coast Path 325m E of NE corner of The Warren Wood; seen from Old Nick's Ground in NE corner of field W of S half of Old Nick's Ground (with albinos and Corn Marigold).

Needs ground disturbance. Fruit case is weakly ribbed; narrow top end up to 5 times as long as next swollen section; breaks apart easily at joints (see subspecies below).

Sea Radish *Raphanus raphanistrum* subsp. *maritumus*
Native. Rare. Near the sea. April to August.
Lilliput: plentiful in fenced area of Evening Hill. **Canford Cliffs:** by first left turn on stepped path from Cliff Drive to beach.

Fruit case strongly ribbed; narrow top end up to twice as long as next swollen section; does not break apart easily at joints (see subspecies above).

MIGNONETTE FAMILY
Weld *Reseda luteola*
Early Introduction. Occasional. Arable fields, other disturbed ground. June to July.
Hartland Moor: in old field corner on E side of Soldiers Road 275m N of A351 (ground disturbed by rabbits).
Knitson: in area W of junction of bridleways8 and 9. **Ulwell:** sporadic near and up to 50m above Purbeck Way above lower lay-by. **Townsend Reserve:** on large area cleared of scrub NE of gate on path56 on S edge of Reserve. **Ballard Down:** plentiful along bottom of chalk cliffs especially 350-400m from W end of chalk. **Studland:** N of Coast Path 250m W of Studland Wood (ground disturbed by moles).

White Mignonette *Reseda alba*
Introduction. Rare. Escape.
Ulwell: NE side of Ulwell Road 5m SE of path15.

Wild Mignonette *Reseda lutea*
Native. Rare. Dry bare calcareous soil. May to June.
Corfe: S of Purbeck Way 500m E of junction with Sandy Hill Lane.

HEATH FAMILY
Rhododendron
Rhododendron ponticum
Introduction. Abundant. Woods on acid soils (woods N of chalk ridge) and heaths. June, but one plant on NE of bridleway2 N at W corner of Breach Plantation at **Creech** flowers in September, as do several on wooded SE side of path34 near its W end at **Creech;** one almost opposite car park entrance at **Arne** flowers in October.

This is a pest species as it spreads and blankets out all other vegetation beneath it. It is difficult but not impossible to control. If planted on calcareous soil, as by summer-dry stream in N end of woods above cliffs at **Durlston,** it survives but does not flower and spread.

Other Rhododendron species
Difficult to identify which species they are.
Introduction. Rare. Planted. April to June.
Brownsea: just W of Vinery ruins wall; also in Venetia Park.

Strawberry Tree *Arbutus unedo*
Native in Ireland, but planted and self-seeding here. Occasional. September to December.
Brownsea: by shore S of Daffodil Field; W side of Venetia Park; E and

NE of The Villa. **Lilliput:** NW end of Evening Hill. **Branksome Chine:** S of Pinecliff Road 120m E of Library. **Branksome Dene Chine:** few behind beach chalets W of café (growing again after cutting).

Trees still carry fruit from previous year at flowering time.

Heather, Ling *Calluna vulgaris*
Native. Abundant. Dry and wet heaths. Mid-July to mid-September.

Dorset Heath *Erica ciliaris*
Native. Frequent. Wet heaths (but not on all), wet acid verges. Mid-July to October.
Nationally Rare.
Stoborough Heath: especially plentiful in area SE of A351 roundabout SW of A351 (approach from SE). **Hartland Moor:** plentiful by and to W of N end of Soldiers Road on Stoborough Heath; very plentiful on Moor itself; very plentiful on Arne Triangle. **Arne:** plentiful on W end of Coombe Heath 100m SE of Arne Road. **Bushey:** Brenscombe Heath South. **Godlingston Heath:** Brand's Bog. **Studland Heath:** S of entrance to Spur Bog. Always present with Dorset Hybrid Heath (see below for further sites).
Flowers are usually spread out down one side of the stem, as shown in books or, like Cross-leaved Heath, are occasionally grouped close together at the top. See photos on front cover and Plate 11.

Chapman (1975) thought population had been gradually expanding. This was backed by Haskins' work (1978) on seed and leaf fossils buried in peat, which showed that it may have spread outwards from Wytch Heath, arriving next at Hartland Moor (and at

Morden Bog, north of Wareham, outside this area) in the Early or Middle Bronze Age. The spread continued outwards gradually, but it only reached Godlingston Heath within the last 300 years.

Dorset Hybrid Heath *Erica* x *watsonii* (*E. ciliaris* x *tetralix*)
Native. Frequent. With parents on wet heaths, but not in every place where they are present. Late June to September.
Stoborough Heath: plentiful for 150m N-wards from near scrub at S end of A351 lay-by (access from road by stile 75m SE of lay-by); plentiful 30m NNE of gateway which is 125m N of A351 on E side of Dismantled Tramway. **Hartland Moor:** near N end of Soldiers Road plentiful in large area to W on Stoborough Heath; on E side Soldiers Road 40m from N end; here and there in wide area between Little Knoll and Great Knoll; hundreds of large plants along N side of Moor; plenty of large plants NE and SE of Tramway Bog; wet heath 100 and 150m S of Scotland E of path79; shallow wet valley 300 and 400m NNE of Scotland. **Arne:** scattered on W end of Coombe Heath 100m SE of Arne Road. **Wytch:** by new route of path5 to E of Wytch Moor 375 and 450m from N tip of Moor. **Bushey:** SW quarter of Brenscombe Heath South. **Ower:** 250m SW of crossing of bridleways7 and 8 on side of bridleway8. **Godlingston Heath:** N side of bridleway27 near gate at NW of golf course; plentiful on SE side of Brand's Bog from 150m SW of bridleway36 for 220m; scattered for 150m W of point on path24 which is 175m NE of Agglestone.

Starts to flower in late June, later than Cross-leaved Heath but earlier than Dorset Heath, both of which can look intermediate, as if they are hybrids. Flowerheads are similar in shape to Cross-leaved Heath, but the flowers are larger and deeper pink. However, a hybrid with a flower-spike like Dorset Heath and the same flower colour as Cross-leaved Heath has also been seen.

To identify this hybrid correctly, look at the anthers (lens). Cross-leaved Heath anthers have back-ward-pointing appendages, nearly as long as the anthers themselves; Dorset Heath anthers have no appendages; hybrid anthers have appendages less than half as long as anthers. These can be seen on fresh flowers in late June right through winter to the following May, when they are shrivelled. (Examination of nine possible signs of hybridisation (Chapman, 1975) concluded that appendage presence and size were much the most reliable ones.) However, first check the flower shape and how much stigma is pro-truding .

When plants are mature they form domed humps, which can be picked out at some distance with experience. See Plate 11.

Data by Rose (2007) suggest that Cross-leaved Heath is usually the female parent of the hybrid – there are many more seeds of the hybrid in the ground under that species.

Cross-leaved Heath *Erica tetralix*
Native. Abundant. Wet heaths. June to September.

Flowers are usually pale pink, but sometimes as deep as Dorset Heath and its hybrid; foliage is greyish (see above for other points).

Bell Heather *Erica cinerea*
Native. Abundant. Dry heaths; unusually on acid grassland on downs. July to October.
Downland sites – **Knitson:** small amount at map reference SZ00178121. **Ulwell:** large area on top of Down 175m SE of Obelisk. **Ballard Down:** two sites under Gorse – 70m SW of SW corner of Glebeland Estate 40m N of bridle-way12; N of Purbeck Way 150m W of path11.

Portuguese Heath *Erica lusitanica*
Introduction. Rare. Escape on cliffs. January to April.
Branksome Dene Chine: sea cliff 75m NE of Chine (binoculars).

Darley Dale Heath
Erica x darleyensis
Introduction. Rare. Planted. February to May.
Godlingston Heath: one large plant 120m W along bridleway27 from track to greenkeepers' private depot 25m N of bridleway (not visible from bridleway).

Bilberry *Vaccinium myrtillus*
Native. Rare. Heaths. June to July.
East Creech: scattered plentifully under Bracken over wide area 100m SW of summit of Creech Barrow Hill (at least 100m N-S 50m W-E).
Godlingston Heath: under Gorse and Bracken on slope just N of Agglestone; (more comfortably) on SE side of path24 down steps 35m NE of Agglestone in small quantity.

PRIMROSE FAMILY
Primrose *Primula vulgaris*
Native. Frequent. Woods, verges, field edges; sometimes planted elsewhere. February to May.

Steeple: plentiful along unusual site of foot of Steeple Down (west) 130m E of S end of bridleway3 for 60m (where later shielded from summer sun by Bracken). **Furzebrook:** good at S end of Blue Pool exit road (open March to October). **Corfe:** plenty S of Purbeck Way N of West Hill especially between 600 and 900m W of NE corner of foot of hill; Sandy Hill Lane between Challow Farm and Sandyhills Farm. **Kingston:** steep N open access half of Swyre Wood. **Arne:** churchyard. **Swanage Railway:** plentiful in several places alongside track especially between Harman's Cross and Herston Halt. **Langton:** first 50m of road from A351 to Wilkswood Farm. **Studland:** plentiful on E side of Ferry Road 75m S of bridleway38 on opposite side. **Studland Heath:** outstanding around Primrose Way.

Pink-flowered plants, some of which are escapes from cultivation, occur in the wild, for example – **Tyneham:** SE corner of ruined cottages W of telephone box; **Ridge:** S side of Arne Road 160m E of crossroads (deep pink); **Furzebrook:** 25m E of Furzebrook Road on N side of path13; **Corfe:** 5m N of Purbeck Way 325m W of NE corner of foot of West Hill; **Arne:** churchyard (various shades); **Durlston:** 30m down Diagonal Path on W side (with pink False Oxlip); on Caravan Terrace near S end (deep pink); **Studland:** S side of W and E ends of Beach Road (two shades of pink at latter). See Plates 1 and 11.

False Oxlip *Primula* x *polyantha* (*P. vulgaris* x *veris*)
Native, and also cultivated hybrid (garden Polyanthus). Occasional. Grass, scrub, wood rides, verges; sometimes with one or both parents. April to May.
Kimmeridge: S side of beginning of road to Bradle. **East Creech:** SW of access tracks to NW corner of Stonehill Down Reserve 10m from gate; in S edge of Furlong's Coppice 350m E of path32. **Creech Heath:** reddish cultivar 2m N of path34 125m W of Furzebrook Road (10m W of corrugated hut). **Norden:** 50m from A351 on S side of bridleway77. **Arne:** 20m E of road on N side of bridleway1. **Wytch:** E side of Thrasher's Lane 40m N of bridleway4. **Harman's Cross:** large plant visible from train on S side of railway 200m W of path4 crossing. **Langton:** in W half of scrubby area between Langton West Wood and Talbot's Wood through which path44 runs NW-SE (area marked as woodland on O.S. map) – best site. **Durlston:** in wood in NE of Country Park on bank SW of main glade; 30m down Diagonal Path on W side (pink, with pink Primrose). **Townsend Reserve:** S of path in small patch of Burnet Rose 70m along track SE of NW entrance to Reserve. **Studland:** deep pink cultivar S of Coast Path towards Fort Henry 20m from Beach Road.

When yellow, it can be confused with the umbelled form of Primrose, but False Oxlip has slightly smaller flowers of deeper yellow colour; also Primrose has long wispy hairs, Cowslip has short hairs, and False Oxlip has hairs of intermediate length (lens). False Oxlip, the flowers of which point in all directions, can be confused with Cowslips with large flowers, but those all hang in the same direction. (True Oxlip occurs only in East Anglia in Britain.) See Plates 11 and 12.

Cowslip *Primula veris*
Native. Frequent. Downs, verges, wood rides, grassland. April to May.
Langton: magnificent display in NW fenced part of Broad Meadow through which path9 runs. **Durlston:** magnificent displays in SW of Field 3, in Ox-eye Daisy Field (introduced), in Field 14 and in Tasker's Meadow. **Townsend Reserve:** plentiful in S end. See Plate 12.

Yunnan Cowslip
Primula helodoxa Balf. f.
Introduction. Rare. Escape in stream. May to July.
Studland Heath: sides of small stream S of Knoll Beach car park.

Not in any recommended identification book, so full scientific name is given here. Thought to be the first time that it has escaped in Britain. Stem can be over 1m high, with yellow primrose-sized cowslip-coloured flowers, in up to 8 whorls each of up to 22 flowers each around the stem, which arises from a rosette of pale green leaves.

Yellow Pimpernel
Lysimachia nemorum
Native. Occasional. Fairly damp usually ancient woods, verges. May to July.
Langton: few sites in rides in West Wood. **Harman's Cross:** near bend in path44 on N side of The Wilderness. **Ower:** on NW side of bridleway8 175m SW of crossing of bridleways7 and 8. **King's Wood:** S of upside-down '150' contour figure on O.S. map. **Studland Heath:** SW of Study Centre near Knoll Beach.

Flowers star-shaped; leaves are oval.

Creeping Jenny
Lysimachia nummularia
Native, but introduced here. Rare.

Damp woods; escape on pavements. June to July.
Godlingston Heath: 5m E of stream at forest edge on S side of bridleway33 along 15m E-wards; E of stream 50m S of that; (a caravan used to be near those two sites).

Flowers are cup-shaped, leaves nearly round.

Yellow Loosestrife
Lysimachia vulgaris
Native. Occasional. Wet but not acid places. July to August.
Holme: East Holme Meadows – see p.23. **Hartland Moor:** by path79 200m S of N end. **Corfe Charity's Meadows:** W of bridleway3 40m from N end of second meadow SW of Sharford Bridge. **Harman's Cross:** by path26 in second field N of A351 (between woods). **Luscombe Valley:** just W of metal bridge in centre of Reserve; 25m SW of that. See Plate 12.

Lake Loosestrife *Lysimachia terrestris*
Introduction. Rare. Escape on ditch-sides. Late July to August.
Holme: East Holme Meadows – see p.23.
Few stems flower. Multiplies from bulbils which grow at base of leaves against stem. See Plate 12.

Bog Pimpernel *Anagallis tenella*
Native. Frequent. Wet places, even wet lawns. June to August.
Stoborough Heath: 750m N of A351 along permissive bridleway 10m E of and parallel to Dismantled Tramway. **Hartland Moor:** here and there in Upper Fen; E side of Slepe Road 50m S of centre of Snag Valley. **Corfe Common:** here and there in some of wettest areas including Second Valley on West Common; S of Middle Common Pond. **Rempstone:** along

30m of both sides of bridleway8 from 350m NE of end of bridleway9 (Oil Road). **Wares (west):** halfway down W-running flush in SE corner of Long Close; **(east):** plentiful 90m E of W wall in Verney Ware 20m N of S fence; in some other flushes. **Studland Heath:** in depression 150m N of main N car park at Knoll Beach. **Brownsea:** along bottom of low wall at S end of Venetia Park.

Flowers repay close examination. See Plate 13.

Scarlet Pimpernel *Anagallis arvensis*
Native. Frequent. Arable fields, other disturbed ground, tracks, dunes, tops of beaches. April to early October.

Chaffweed *Anagallis minima*
Native. Rare. Tracks on heaths which are wet in winter, usually with Allseed. June to July.
Dorset Scarce. Near Threatened.
Stoborough Heath: on Purbeck Way 250m S of A351 there is double junction of tracks – plants are both on SW side of track which runs NW from those junctions 20-30m from SE end; 400m S of those junctions both by and 10m E of track running S. **Hartland Moor:** sometimes plentiful along 20m of ruts in track 10m SE of and parallel to Soldiers Road 150m NE of S cattle grid.

Silvery petals are inconspicuous and short-lived, but seed-cases persist. Amounts vary greatly year to year according to weather and openness of ground. When found, look also for Yellow Centaury which is occasionally nearby.

Sea-milkwort *Glaux maritima*
Native. Frequent. Upper salt-marshes. May to August.
Arne: by salt-marsh S of RSPB notice-board. **Studland Heath:** 20m SE of bow of rusting ship wreck at Redhorn Quay; scattered along E side of Redhorn Bay especially both 250m S of Brand's Bay Hide and 125m NE of it; sides of Bramble Bush Bay. **Brownsea:** beside screened track to MacDonald Hide.

Brookweed *Samolus valerandi*
Native. Occasional. Wet places on cliffs and in cliff quarries, flushes, marshes, upper salt-marshes. June to August.
Tyneham: just N of anti-invasion blocks at Pondfield beach. **Arne:** by Telegraph Cable notice. **Wares (west and east):** in most flushes; plentiful at bottom of quarry face towards E end of Dancing Ledge. **Studland Heath:** here and there at upper edge of salt-marsh in Brand's Creek; in salt-marsh in SE corner of same creek; on shore 350m S of Brand's Bay Hide. **Brownsea:** along bottom of low wall S of Venetia Park; N of track 50m W of The Villa; plentiful N of track under trees E of Public Hide.

PITTOSPORUM FAMILY
Kohuhu *Pittosporum tenuifolium*
Introduction. Rare. Planted or self-sown.
Evening Hill: NW corner.

HYDRANGEA FAMILY
Mock-orange
Philadelphus coronarius
Introduction. Rare. Planted. June.
Herston (north): 200m N of stile at S end of path2 in hedge 50m W of path (binoculars).
Flowers open wide.

Mock-orange cv. *Philadelphus* cv.
Introduction. Rare. Planted. June.
Durlston: 40m N of Long Meadow

on W side of N-S track running between and roughly parallel to Durlston Road and Coast Path; E side of same track behind bamboo 70m N of Long Meadow; W of castle entrance; N of Coast Path NW of castle.

Leaves sparsely hairy underneath; flowers at latter two sites only.

Hairy Mock-orange *Philadelphus* x *virginalis* (parentage uncertain) Introduction. Rare. Planted. June. **Church Knowle:** S side of old quarry N of Cocknowle. **Swanage:** on cliff N of E end of path from Burlington Road to beach (binoculars help).

Leaves densely hairy underneath; flowers cup-shaped.

Deutzia *Deutzia scabra* Introduction. Rare. Planted. June. **Tyneham:** double form behind cottages SW of school.

CURRANT FAMILY
Escallonia *Escallonia macrantha* Introduction. Rare. Planted or escape. June.
Swanage: on cliff N of E end of path from Burlington Road to beach (binoculars). **Canford Cliffs:** two plants SW of bottom of Flaghead Chine; cliff near stepped path from Cliff Drive to beach.

Red Currant *Ribes rubrum* Native. Frequent. Woods, verges. April to May.
Holme: NE side of Holme Lane 800-900m W of B3070. **Creech:** towards bottom of hill on both sides of road passing through Great Wood. **Stoborough:** N side of Holme Lane 100m from E end. **Kingston:** by path44 – 100 and 225m NE of S edge of Quarry Wood. **Corfe:**

between ruins of West Mill and stream; here and there in Byle Copse (with Black Currant). **Langton:** plentiful in lower part of West Wood. **Durlston:** 10m E of Durlston Road on N bank of summer-dry stream N of Coast Path. **Studland:** by track N of SE corner of The Warren Wood.

Leaves can look like next species, but lack glands.

Black Currant *Ribes nigrum* Introduction. Occasional. Escaped into wet woods, marshes, verges. April to May.
Holme: under SW corner of new Holme Bridge. **Stoborough Heath:** plentiful 250m W of Halfway Inn in valley along 50m N-S (one plant 2.5m high); here and there in wood in same valley N of A351 (with some Red Currant). **Norden:** S side of bridleway77 near junction with path78. **Hartland Moor:** clumps in narrow wet wooded valley on E side of Langton Wallis Heath especially 350m NNE of Langton Wallis; visible in wood from S edge of heath SW of Scotland 200m E of Slepe Road. **Corfe:** middle of S half of Byle Copse. **Studland Heath:** N of short E-W track leading to Woodland Nature Trail. **Studland:** sloping wooded cliff at S end of South Beach 140m SE of permissive path up cliff (Red Currant nearby). **Shell Bay:** E side of Ferry Road on dune near bus stop.

Leaves have widely spaced glands underneath (see species above) (lens) which give a characteristic smell.

Flowering Currant *Ribes sanguineum* Introduction. Occasional. Planted and self-seeding. March to May. **Worth:** by wall at W end of E-W road at Renscombe Farm. **Rempstone:**

150m from B3351 on E side of bridle-way16. **Swanage:** W side Victoria Avenue N of Triangle Garage. **Townsend Reserve:** W of Grand-father's Knap. **Brownsea:** W of hut on S side of track 200m W of Daffodil Field.

Fruits are either purple with whitish bloom or glossy black.

Gooseberry *Ribes uva-crispa*
Introduction. Occasional. Woods, verges. March to May.
East Creech: N side of Caldecot's Wood 40m W of path32; by path32. **Church Knowle:** on W side of path18 170m S of road. **Corfe:** 50m S of N end of Byle Copse by brook. **Worth:** scattered near S end of path13. **Langton:** few in N side of Talbot's Wood. **Durlston:** small plant 40m N of Long Meadow on W edge of N-S track running between and roughly parallel to Durlston Road and Coast Path. **Studland:** N side Watery Lane just E of path7; in mid-dle of NW quarter of The Warren Wood. **Studland Heath:** W side of Ferry Road 70m N of E end of bridle-way36.

It may disappear under scrub in the summer. Most do not produce fruits.

STONECROP FAMILY
Mossy Stonecrop *Crassula tillaea*
Native. Occasional. Sandy soil. April to June.
Nationally Scarce.
Hartland Moor: on bridleway4 80-150m SW of White House Wood; on track running NE from W end of same wood 125-300m from NW cor-ner of wood. **Arne:** 8m N of bridle-way1 beside track running NW towards hide; 5m S of same bridleway N of viewpoint; on E part of view-point itself. **Ower:** on bridleway8

140-200m E of where bridleways7 and 8 cross; both sides of bridleway8 S of Game Copse. **Studland Heath:** plentiful E of Heather Walk 250-330m N of Knoll Beach main N car park. **Shell Bay:** level bank above shore 50, 150 and 175m SW of Gravel Point; NW side of Ferry Road 90m NE of roundabout sign; SE side opposite roundabout sign. **Brownsea:** near small brick kiln above shore SW of W low-fenced area; here and there for 70m on N side of Back Break 200m NE of Baden-Powell Centre; E of Vinery ruins; also café lawn. **Lilliput:** near seats SW of road on centre of Evening Hill. **Sandbanks:** just SW of entrance to main car park. **Canford Cliffs:** between Cliff Drive and cliff-top NE of top of steps down cliff. **Branksome Chine:** here and there by path along cliff-top SW of chine for over 200m. **Branksome Dene Chine:** lawn SW of café.

Foliage starts green, not greyish, and turns bright red in May. See Plate 13.

New Zealand Pigmyweed
Crassula helmsii
Introduction. Occasional. Escape in ponds, lakesides, wet ground. June to September.
Corfe: Middle Common Pond. **Durlston:** Johnston Pond. **Studland Heath:** reedbed E of Shell Bay car park; East Lake; swamp nearby; few places on middle of W shore of Little Sea.

Efforts should be made to control this very invasive species wherever it is seen. It spreads rapidly and smothers pond surface, killing off other plants and pond fauna. Please tell the landowner or tenant if you find it elsewhere. **Make sure that you do not carry even small pieces off on your boots.**

Navelwort, Wall Pennywort
Umbilicus rupestris
Native. Occasional. Walls, shady
banks. May to July.
Steeple: plentiful on roadside wall S
of Blackmanston Farm. **Kimmeridge:**
locally plentiful in village. **Church
Knowle:** Bradle hamlet; also plentiful
for 50m on E side of N end of path20.
Ridge: plentiful both sides of road
from crossroads first NE-wards and
then NW-wards to Redcliffe Farm.
Hartland Moor: E side of Slepe Road
for 5m N of path80; along N side of
first 30m of path80 E of road. **Corfe:**
S side of Sandy Hill Lane 400m E of
Challow car park. **Worth:** wall SE of
village green. **Studland:** plentiful on
SE side of Beach Road 100-200m
from Ferry Road; SE side of Coast
Path from car park to Middle Beach.

**Houseleek, Welcome-home-hus-
band-though-never-so-late**
Sempervivum tectorum
Introduction. Rare. Planted. June to
July.
Hartland Moor: S side of tall old wall
N of old Middlebere Farm buildings.

Autumn Joy
Sedum spectabile cv. Herbstfreude
(*S. spectabile* x *telephium?*)
Introduction. Rare. Planted.
September to October.
Hartland Moor: one in W end of
White House Wood 5m from W edge
3.5m NE of old apple tree (plant gets
eaten). This dates from a garden from
before the early 1940s when White
House (now demolished) was last
inhabited.

Lesser Mexican Stonecrop
Sedum confusum
Introduction. Rare. Escape.
Swanage: E end of copse W of

D'Urberville Drive (not flowering
because of shade).

Reflexed Stonecrop
Sedum rupestre (*S. reflexum*)
Introduction. Occasional. Escape.
June to September.
Stoborough: scattered on E side of
Furzebrook Road S of start of path24
especially 60-80m and 150-190m S of
that path. **Worth:** on wall E of road at
N end of Renscombe Farm buildings.
Wares (east): on rock on N side of
Priest's Way 50m E of junction with
bridleway16 and path17. **Canford
Cliffs:** by cliff-top fence 100m NE of
SW corner of Cliff Drive; at foot of
cliff below in gap between beach
chalets; on cliff-top shortly before top
of steps 100m NE of first site.
Branksome Chine: low on sea-cliff
100m NE.

Rock Stonecrop *Sedum forsterianum*
Native, but introduced here. Rare.
Escape. June to July.
Lilliput: by start of E of two paths
running N from Lilliput Road near
Lilliput Church of England School.

Biting Stonecrop *Sedum acre*
Native. Occasional. Calcareous cliff-
tops (take care) and rocks; escape on
road curbs, pavements; sometimes
planted on walls, roofs. June.
Holme: on SE side of B3070 200m
NE of 27m trig point on NE side of
concreted area. **Tyneham:** on remains
of a wall by corner of wire fence on
Tyneham Cap summit. **Stoborough:**
NE side of A351 50m SE of Grange
Road junction. **Worth:** roof of
Renscombe Farm large old barn E of
road; near Coast Path both SW and
W of row of houses at St. Aldhelm's
Head. **Wares (west):** near fence in
front of caves in Seacombe Quarry;

(east) 30m S of gate from Hay Brimble to Balston Wear; SE of lower Western Mile Post. **Durlston:** clifftop SW of SE corner of Field 10A. **Swanage:** roof of The Globe pub at N end of Bell Street.

White Stonecrop *Sedum album*
Early Introduction. Occasional. Planted or escape here. July.
Holme: by bridleway W of gate to Rifle Range. **Corfe:** junction of Mead Road and Jubilee Gardens. **Langton:** where path14 leaves Steppes Hill (road) 80m S of B3069. **Swanage:** N side of main road from Corfe 200m E of junction with road from Langton; NE corner of Northbrook Road cemetery; behind beach huts W of Shore Road 20m S of end of Victoria Avenue. **Ulwell:** NW side of Ulwell Road 50-75m SE of path15. **Durlston:** plenty 10m S of lighthouse enclosure. **Sandbanks:** small amount halfway between rock gardens and two-storey beach chalets 125m NE of main car park. **Canford Cliffs:** near top of stepped path from Cliff Drive to beach.
   Leaves 4-12mm long, mid-green; flowering stems with several branches.

English Stonecrop *Sedum anglicum*
Native. Occasional. Acid sand, cliffs and rock. June to August.
Dorset Scarce.
Hartland Moor: in NE corner of South Middlebere along 12m of centre of grassy track 100m SSE of SE corner of conifer plantation. **Ower:** by bridleway8 S of Game Copse.
Godlingston Heath: on S side of Agglestone itself; below its S side.
Studland Heath: banks of Redhorn Bay 50m S of Brand's Bay Hide; 200 and 350m N of same hide; 150m SE of Redhorn Quay; also along 30m of

shore 300m SW of Sandy Point; here and there on fixed dunes for 250m N of Knoll Beach main N car park.
Brownsea: plentiful on and near SW beach for 800m SE of Pottery Pier.
Branksome Chine: S of cliff-top path at bend 275m SW of chine (at base of Monterey Pine); on bank W of car park at sea end of chine.
   Leaves 3-5mm long, dull greyish dark green, sometimes with tinge of red; flowering stems with only one or two branches. See Plate 13.

SAXIFRAGE FAMILY
Elephant Ears *Bergenia crassifolia*
Introduction. Rare. Escape. January to April.
Swanage: small amounts on W side of Cowlease (road) 30m S of Priests Road; W side of Taunton Road 10m N of Bon Accord Road.
   Often disappears under other vegetation in summer.

Rue-leaved Saxifrage
Saxifraga tridactylites
Native. Occasional. Walls, thin soil over calcareous rock. March to May.
Hartland Moor: NW side of Soldiers Road 300m NE of S cattle grid.
Norden: N-facing wall in Norden Farm Pets Corner. **Worth:** W side of bridleway15 just N of St. Aldhelm's Head (working) Quarry; at least three places near top of E side of valley N of Renscombe Farm. **Langton:** on old spoil heap opposite Bower's quarry entrances; S side of B3069 from 10-50m W of village shop. **Wares (east):** near exposed flat rocks level with ground on W-facing slope in S of Sherwood's Wear; 30m S of gate from Hay Brimble to Balston Wear.
Swanage: some roofs of The Globe pub at N end of Bell Street (easiest to see on porch roof). **Townsend**

Reserve: several places – especially plentiful S of Orchid Bastion.

Fringecups *Tellima grandiflora*
Introduction. Occasional. Escape on verges. April to May.
Studland: plentiful in village near sea, especially by path1and by E half of Watery Lane. **Studland Heath:** by stream S of Knoll Beach car park. **Branksome Chine:** 500m up chine from road at SE end.

Opposite-leaved Golden Saxifrage *Chrysosplenium oppositifolium*
Native. Occasional. Wet places under or near trees. March to May.
East Creech: W of path32 by stream along N side of Caldecot's Wood; 75m NE of same path by stream on N side of Creech Wood. **Furzebrook:** very plentiful in wet woodland in Kilnwood Reserve N of central field; some in ditch on S side of path13 S of Blue Pool car park. **Stoborough Heath:** by streams on E edge120m E of Dismantled Tramway 300m N of A351; by bridleway23 225m SW of A351 2m W of fence where birch grows out of old oak. **Rempstone:** S side of bridge over small stream at E end of Breaches Lane; by bend in stream 30m N of previous site. **King's Wood:** on little used track (covered with Ramsons in season) which branches ESE-wards off bridleway16 20m E of National Trust sign at W end of wood – 175 and 350m along track.

ROSE FAMILY
Confused Bridewort *Spiraea* x *pseudosalicifolia* (*S. salicifolia* x *douglasii*)
Introduction. Occasional. Planted and spreading. June to July.
Furzebrook: N of track 40m W of stile into central field on Kilnwood

Reserve. **Herston (north):** visible (especially with binoculars) to W from path2 in hedge (in front of Monkey Puzzle) 200m N of stile which is at S end of path. **Studland:** hedge N of Agglestone Road 80m W of bend. **Branksome Chine:** halfway along N side of S (highest) area of Beach Road car park.
Leaves are hairy but not felted underneath and leaf-edges toothed for three-quarters of way from apex to stalk.

Steeple Bush *Spiraea douglasii*
Introduction. Rare. Planted and spreading. June to July.
Canford Cliffs: towards foot of cliff 100m NE of Canford Cliffs Chine (binoculars, view from E).
Leaves felted with hairs underneath, leaf-edges toothed for half of way from apex to stalk.

Dropwort *Filipendula vulgaris*
Native. Rare. Calcareous grassland. June to July.
Hartland Moor: small amount at unusual site on calcareous verge on N side of Arne Road 10m W of Arne Triangle (known there since 1973, but site may have been accidentally destroyed in 2007). **Wares (west):** E side of Seacombe Bottom 175m N of sea-cliff 50m E of path11 one-third way up slope (flowers only when valley not grazed in early summer).

Meadowsweet *Filipendula ulmaria*
Native. Frequent. Ditches, very wet fields. June to August.

Raspberry *Rubus idaeus*
Native. Occasional. Woods, verges; often an escape or remnant from cultivation. June.
Creech: sides of road through Great

Wood. **Wareham:** N of Purbeck Way 450m E of South Bridge. **Stoborough Heath:** NE side of path5 300m NW of small square field through which path passes. **Corfe:** by stream SW of castle at point where stream flows closest to Purbeck Way; 60m N of S end of Byle Copse. **Swanage:** SE corner of car park at N end of De Moulham Road; at W edge of dell 80m NE of gate at SW corner of The Downs. **Studland:** both sides of Watery Lane 75m NE of junction with Manor Road. **Canford Cliffs:** by track between Haven Road and Bessborough Road. **Branksome Chine:** E side of Western Road 30m N of junction with Pinecliff Road.

Loganberry *Rubus loganobaccus*
Cultivated species. Rare. Escape. June. **Swanage:** N side of Court Road 50m W of railway bridge by low concrete railway building.

Bramble *Rubus fruticosus* agg.
Native. Abundant. Woods, hedges, cliffs, verges, heaths, downs, commons, neglected fields, waste ground. June to August.

Brambles are divided into about 320 microspecies in the British Isles, about 100 of which occur in Dorset. Latter are listed in *The Flora of Dorset*, including about 17 references to this area, particularly to Corfe Common. One is named *Rubus purbeckensis*. Microspecies of brambles have been omitted in this book.

Cut-leaved Blackberry
Rubus laciniatus
Introduction. Rare. Escape. June to August.
Canford Cliffs: by path from Nairn Road to Brudenell Road 30m from latter.

Dewberry *Rubus caesius*
Native. Occasional. Wood edges, verges; often with other brambles. June to August.
Harman's Cross: on W side of Haycraft's Lane 100m N of B3069; on E side of same lane 30 and 50m N of path22. **Langton:** E of Crack Lane beyond gate of vehicular entrance to cemetery; by track leading W-wards from second gate close by; in Talbot's Wood N of gate on path5 at S side of wood (not W but N of cemetery). **Ulwell:** E side of Darkie Lane 40-80m S of junction with Brickyard Lane (not producing fruit). **Studland:** E side of bridleway12 10m N of SE corner of Glebeland Estate.

It is probably more common than records suggest, but in *The Flora of Dorset* Bowen (2000) wrote that it is 'perhaps confused with some of its hybrids.' Often sterile, or nearly so.

Marsh Cinquefoil *Potentilla palustris*
Native. Occasional. Ditches, wet places on heaths, lakeside ponds. May to June.
Holme: East Holme Meadows – see p.23. **Furzebrook:** much in pond midway between paths8, 10 and 11 and Purbeck Way. **The Moors:** p.27. **Corfe:** occasional in wet areas in NW of West Common; 10-30m S of bridleway30 E of scrub bordering W stream on Little East Common; by tiny E stream 30m further E 20m SE of bridleway30. **Studland Heath:** NW side of N arm of Little Sea – visible with binoculars across water from opposite side 200m SW of track to nudists' area.

Often only few plants flower.

Silverweed *Potentilla anserina*
Native. Frequent. Open damp ground including verges and tops of beaches. May to August.

Hoary Cinquefoil *Potentilla argentea*
Native. Rare. Dry sandy ground with
bare patches. Late June to mid-July.
Dorset Scarce. Near Threatened.
Hartland Moor: both sides of bridle-
way4 140-160m NE of gate at W end.
Godlingston Heath: small amount
sometimes found by rabbit holes in
rectangular fenced area 150m N of
field gate on N side of bridleway36.

Very difficult to find when not in
flower; hoary undersides of leaves face
ground.

Tormentil *Potentilla erecta*
Native. Frequent. Heaths, commons,
verges, tracks on non-calcareous soils.
April to September.

Trailing Tormentil *Potentilla anglica*
Native. Occasional. Permanent grass-
land, tracks, verges. June to
September.
Creech: on Creech Heath on W-E
track for 125m E-wards from its junction with path34 halfway along latter.
Stoborough Heath: on W side of
Soldiers Road 10-20m W of gate
140m from N end of road. **Corfe:**
100m S of gate at N corner of Middle
Common; thinly 20-100m SE of
Middle Common Pond (with
Tormentil at both sites). **Rempstone:**
along 50m of both sides and track of
bridleway8 750m SW of junction
with bridleway9 (Oil Road) (with
Tormentil); E side of bridleway9 (Oil
Road) 120m N of where crossed by
bridleway10; here and there on SE
side of bridleway34 (Oil Road) 400-
500m NE of same crossing. **Durlston:**
100m E from W wall of Field 3 thinly
scattered along 40m of S side of W-E
grass track near S side of southern of
two large open areas in field.
Studland: on Harmony Farm NW
Field near where track crosses stream

on E side of field. **Brownsea:** N of
track 350m W of junction of Deer
Park Road and Beech Valley track.

Flowers have 4 or 5 petals; for more
details see hybrid next below. See
Plate 13.

Hybrid Cinquefoil *Potentilla* x *mixta*
(*P. anglica* x *reptans*)
Native. Rare. Open ground, especially
man-made sites. June to September.
Herston (north): on E side of path2
along 55-75m N of stile at S end of
path (especially by drain hatch); 30m
further N. **Studland:** on bridleway38
90-130m W of Ferry Road.

Flowers have 4 or 5 petals; differs
from Trailing Tormentil above in
readily rooting from its stem joints
(Trailing Tormentil roots to a small
degree in late summer), having no or
very few swollen seed-cases in older
flowerheads and having leaf-stalks
much longer than older leaves.

Creeping Cinquefoil
Potentilla reptans
Native. Frequent. Grassland. June to
September.

Barren Strawberry *Potentilla sterilis*
Native. Frequent. Dry banks and
woods. February to May.

Distinctions sometimes given
between this and next species are
noticeable gaps between petals in this
species and shorter length of tooth at
tip of leaflets relative to two adjacent
teeth. Those do not always give right
answer. However, this species has
hairs under leaves mostly on veins and
which project at various angles,
whereas Wild Strawberry has hairs
under leaves both on and between
veins and all those hairs are pressed
flat against leaves. This species has
flowers 10-14mm across and petals

mostly indented at outer end, whereas Wild Strawberry (below) has flowers 12-18mm across with petals pointed and often toothed.

Wild Strawberry *Fragaria vesca*
Native. Occasional. Verges, gardens. March to June.
Creech: several places on SE side of road going through Great Wood near old quarry halfway up hill.
Furzebrook: plentiful N of entrance track in Kilnwood Reserve where it passes through woodland.
Stoborough: 75m SE of New Road on NE side of track leading to Stoborough Heath (track later crosses heath SE-wards). **Langton:** by middle of E-W ride in S of West Wood; also NW of church tower. **Knitson:** by wet area on N side of bridleway8 400m W of bridleway12 (with Barren Strawberry). **Godlingston:** N side of Burnham's Lane 130m E of SW corner of Marsh Copse. **Studland:** W side of Ferry Road 30m N of end of Beach Road on opposite side; NW side of Watery Lane 50m NE of junction with Manor Road. **Luscombe Valley:** W side 80m SW of wooden bridge at N end of reserve.

For differences from Barren Strawberry see above.

Yellow-flowered Strawberry
Duchesnea indica
Introduction. Rare. Escape or planted. May to June.
Lilliput: near N end of path between Alington Close and Shore Road along 8m of W side.

Flowers up to 22mm across.

Wood Avens, Herb Bennet
Geum urbanum
Native. Frequent. Woods, verges. May to August.

Agrimony *Agrimonia eupatoria*
Native. Frequent. Verges, rough grassland, wood rides. June to August.

Fragrant Agrimony
Agrimonia procera
Native. Occasional. Verges. June to August.
Holme: East Holme Meadows – see p.23. **Stoborough:** Soldiers Road scattered along 100m of S end both sides; plentiful on W side 350-500m from S end of same road. **Hartland Moor:** N side of Arne Road 30m E of Soldiers Road; plentiful along 50m of sides of old tramway just NE of gate 550m NNE of Langton Wallis; N of W corner of Arne Triangle; on W side of Slepe Road 200m N of corner near Scotland. **Corfe:** SW side of path79 70m SE of sharp bend in path opposite old tramway bridge; small amount near NE of Outer Bailey in castle.
Godlingston Heath: S side of bridleway35 opposite private track to Goathorn Farm; 30m W of that site (compare with Agrimony nearby); on NE side of bridleway36 325m from Ferry Road along 4m.

Can be identified in leaf by numerous tiny stalkless glands under the leaves (lens).

Great Burnet *Sanguisorba officinalis*
Native. Rare. Banks of ditches. Mid-July to August.
East Holme Meadows: see p.23.

Salad Burnet *Sanguisorba minor*
subsp. *minor*
Native. Abundant. Calcareous grassland. May to August.

Fodder Burnet *Sanguisorba minor*
subsp. *muricata*
Introduction. Rare. Escape. May to August.

Branksome Chine: cliff-top E of first way down cliff E of Library.

Pirri-pirri Bur
Acaena novae-zelandiae
Introduction. Occasional. Escape on sandy soil. May to August.

It displaces native species. Each of the many spines of its globular seed-heads has four tiny backward pointing barbs on the end (lens). If found outside its centre of population in the Knoll area of **Studland** where it is plentiful, please dig it up and dispose of it safely, so as to stop it spreading further. It particularly needs to be kept out of Shell Bay car park and off War Hill, both of which have several interesting small species.

Parsley Piert *Aphanes arvensis*
Native. Frequent. Bare places in dry short grassland, anthills. April to September.

<u>Usually fairly upright rather than spreading.</u> Told, with experience, from next species by flowers not being nearly out of sight (lens), and sepals being longer than broad and fairly erect.

Slender Parsley Piert *Aphanes australis* (*A. microcarpa, A. inexspectata*)
Native. Occasional. Bare places in dry short grass, including on firm sand; on more acid soil than previous species. April to September.
Arne: by bridleway1 650 and 975m from W end. **Ower:** by bridleway8 S of Game Copse. **Studland:** in front of beach huts at South Beach 100m SE of Joe's Café. **Shell Bay:** both sides Ferry Road along 200m S of roundabout. **Brownsea:** especially plentiful on tracks. **Canford Cliffs:** between road and cliff-top at SW corner of Cliff Drive; in grass near head of W

path down Canford Cliffs Chine.
Branksome Chine: by cliff-top path 200m SW of chine.

<u>Usually fairly upright rather than spreading.</u> Told, with experience, from previous species by flowers being tucked down nearly out of sight (lens); sides of sepals being same length as their base and usually folded over flower. <u>(Stipule lobes vary in shape even on one plant, and are so not a distinctive feature).</u>

Roses
It is only possible to identify wild roses with certainty when the hips (fruit) have developed, so the time to do so is between late July and early November. The excellent BSBI handbook on Roses (Graham & Primavesi, 2005) is essential for anyone interested.

Species and fertile hybrids are identified by the shape of their hips, presence of glands on them, the shape and colour of their outer end (disk), appearance of stigmas (hairy or not, columnar or not) and the orifice through which they come, any glands on stalks, shape, spacing, edge teeth and appearance of any glands on leaves, and shape of prickles on new and older growth. It is fun, but it is not the place to start flower recognition.

Most species of the wild rose interbreed, forming a puzzling number of wild hybrids. They vary in appearance depending upon which parent supplied pollen and which seed but are usually more like the seed (female) parent. Most of these hybrids are themselves also fertile, unlike most other hybrids. Fertile hybrid roses can in turn breed with either of their parent species (called backcrossing), producing plants which are mostly one species with some characteristics of another. If in doubt ask an expert, who will need to see a couple of short stems with hips and leaves, and a piece of stem of previous year's growth.

When recording, the seed parent is named first – for example *Rosa stylosa* x *canina* means that Long-styled Rose is the seed parent. If it is not clear which parent supplied seed and which pollen, the hybrid name is used – *Rosa* x *andegavensis*.

In Good's Flora (1948) species were subdivided into numerous varieties and forms. However, in the second half of the 20th century it became widely accepted that hybridisation and back-crossing are the cause of the many types of wild roses.

Centuries of breeding and artificial hybridisation have also added very many cultivated varieties. They often do not form good hips, being infertile. These are difficult to name, as along several m of NE side of **Wareham** bypass opposite Grange Road; by the building by bridleway 300m NE of **Chapman's Pool**; on cliffs of **Swanage** Bay 250 and 500m N of N end of Shore Road; above South Beach at **Studland** beyond straight row of beach huts SE of Joe's Café; plentiful on Evening Hill at **Lilliput**; at **Canford Cliffs** on cliff-top 75m NE of SW corner of Cliff Drive.

Field Rose *Rosa arvensis*
Native. Frequent. Hedges, woods. June to July.

Field Rose x Long-styled Rose –
hybrid *Rosa* x *pseudorusticana* (*R. stylosa* x *arvensis*)
Native. Rare. Hedges. June to July.
Swanage: E side of Northbrook Road 40m N of Battlemead.

More like Long-styled Rose, which is the female parent of this plant. Some hips are medium size, some small. Taller than Field Rose, with some young stems wine-red like that parent, but less so. Some prickles are broad-based like Long-styled Rose, others smaller and more curved like Field Rose.

Field Rose x Dog Rose – hybrid *Rosa* x *verticillacantha* (*R. arvensis* x *canina*)
Native. Rare. Hedges. June to July.
Norden: SW of roundabout by track permissive bridleway. **Swanage:** SW side of Ulwell Road opposite house no.70.

Taller than Field Rose, with some young stems stained wine-red like that parent, but less so. Hips larger than Field Rose, with stalks shorter, averaging 2cm rather than 3.5cm in length, and with only few glands on them.

Burnet Rose *Rosa spinosissima* (*R. pimpinellifolia*)
Native. Occasional. Verges, hedges, grassland. May to July.
Stoborough: E side of Furzebrook Road 350m N of railway bridge.
Stoborough Heath: here and there on both sides of Dismantled Tramway 100-300m N of A351; on W side of Soldiers Road 300m from S end for 10m. **Hartland Moor:** E side of Soldiers Road 600m from S end for 20m; 40m E of Jubilee Bridge; by and N of S cattle grid on Slepe Road; on E side of Slepe Road 200 and 400m N of corner near Scotland; by old tramway especially by Hart Hide. **Kingswood:** by bridleway87 50m from B3351.
Durlston: on W side of Field 10 30m S of footbridge over gully. **Townsend Reserve:** very plentiful. **Studland Heath:** W side of Ferry Road 250m N of bridleway36. **Lilliput:** centre of fenced area of Evening Hill.

**Burnet Rose x Common Dog Rose –
hybrid** *Rosa* x *hibernica*
(*R. spinosissima* x *canina*)
Native. Occasional. Habitat as Burnet
Rose, with which it grows. Mid-May
to June.
Hartland Moor: 400m N of corner
near Scotland on E side of road.
Townsend Reserve: above bank
25m NNW of crossing of permissive
bridleway and path59; 15m S of
Twayblade Bank on W side of
path59; several N of SE Bastion.

Specimens at most of these sites are
backcrosses (see introduction to Roses
above), with features of Burnet Rose
predominating. Petals usually tinged
pink; hips are globular like Burnet
Rose, but turn deep red, not black.
First Townsend site specimen lacks
pink-tinged petals but has some
broader-based curved prickles, and
some leaves with 7 leaflets rather than
9 or 11.

Japanese Rose *Rosa rugosa*
Introduction. Occasional. Planted,
suckering and self-sown. June to
August.
Kimmeridge: W side of main car
park 30m N of Coast Path. **Studland:**
on E side of bridleway38 60m N of
junction with Wadmore Lane.
Lilliput: here and there in fenced area
of Evening Hill. **Sandbanks:** SE end
of raised dune SW of main car park;
two on upper shore opposite W end
of Chaddesley Glen. **Branksome
Chine:** cliff-top SE of Library.
Branksome Dene Chine: up sea cliff
75m NE of chine (binoculars).

Red-leaved Rose
Rosa ferruginea (*R. glauca*)
Introduction. Rare. Planted and suck-
ering. June to July.
Sandbanks: roses on raised dune SW

of main car park are closest to this
species, but have some features of the
next species.

Virginia Rose *Rosa virginiana*
Introduction. Rare. Planted and
suckering. June to July.
Lilliput: roses on fenced slope of
Evening Hill are closest to this species,
but have some features of previous
species. **Sandbanks:** bank E of main
car park S of café.

**Long-styled Rose, Short-styled Field
Rose** *Rosa stylosa*
Native. Occasional. Hedges, downs.
June to July.
Norden: S side of path78 125m from
W end. **Kingston:** on W side of
B3069 75m NW of path40 on oppo-
site side. **Bushey:** SE side of
Thrasher's Lane at sharpest bend NW
of Lower Bushey Farm. **Durlston:**
100m S of Recycling Centre on W
side of path59. **Knitson:** on S side of

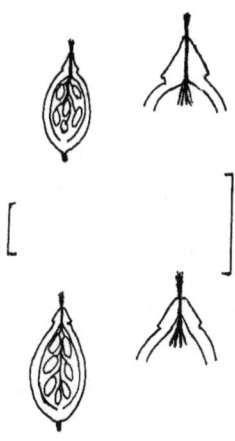

*Dissected hips of Long-styled Rose (above) and
its hybrid with Dog Rose, with enlargements of
each on right to show difference in internal
shape.*

bridleway8 200m W of bridleway12.
Godlingston: S side of Washpond
Lane 100m W of Darkie Lane.
Ulwell: 150m ENE of SW corner of
Round Down. **Durlston:** 50m E from
W wall of Field 3 near track along S
side (brow); S side of track at S end of
Herren Ground 30m from SE corner;
halfway along Tasker's Path.

The author prefers the old name
(listed first) to the modern one
because this species is neither short-
styled nor closely related to the Field
Rose. Hybrids with Dog Rose are
usually found nearby.

**Long-styled Rose x Dog Rose –
hybrid**
Rosa x *andegavensis* (*R. stylosa* x
canina, and less often vice versa)
Native. Frequent. Hedges, verges,
scrub, downs, wood edges, often with
Dog Rose. June to July.
Ridge: NW side of New Road 50m
from N end. **Church Knowle:** N side
of path3 50m W of bridleway39.
Norden: S side of path78 50m from
W end. **Corfe:** N side of bridleway30
just W of rail bridge; N side of Sandy
Hill Lane just W of UCR. **Bushey:**
few on sides of Bushey Lane within
200m E of bridleway10. **Wares
(west):** albino near stile at W edge of
Taylor's Ware by NE corner of East
Plain. **Knitson:** here and there along
bridleway8 W of bridleway12.
Durlston: thinly scattered in hedges
of Country Park. **Swanage:** several on
NE side of Ulwell Road 200m NW
of Whitecliff Road (perhaps one
Long-styled Rose there too).

Very many more bushes present
than of the Long-styled Rose. They
usually appear more like Long-styled
Rose than Dog Rose; so presumably
the former is more often the female
parent. Their styles are close together

in a column (see drawing), their disks
are flat or conical but without a
mound at the centre, their flower-
stalks are shorter than Long-styled
Rose, their leaves are somewhat hairy
beneath, some less pointed than
Long-styled Rose, some of their prickles are broad-based like Long-styled
Rose. Many records of Long-styled
Rose in *The Flora of Dorset* are probably this hybrid.

Dog Rose *Rosa canina*
Native. Frequent. Downs, hedges,
verges, scrub, wood edges. June to
July.

Albinos plentiful in wide area S and
SW of **Swanage.**

Dog Rose x Sweet Briar – hybrid
Rosa x *nitidula*
(*R. rubiginosa* x *canina*)
Native. Occasional. Downs, verges.
June to July.
Ridge: six plants by Dismantled
Tramway – on W side 290m S of
Arne Road; on E side 390, 400, 450
and two at 620m S of road. **Hartland
Moor:** E side of Soldiers Road 50m N
of Isolation Cottages entrance.
Church Knowle: 20m NW of gate at
E end of UCR S of trig point on
Down. **Herston (north):** two 60m
from A351 on S side of path23; one
on W side of path2 160m N of stile at
S end of path. **Godlingston Heath:**
150m from E end of bridleway36 on
SW side of bridleway. **Studland
Heath:** both sides of Ferry Road
120m SW of track to Redhorn Quay.

Leaves with few glands underneath;
stems with groups of small straight,
very thin prickles and with mixture of
Dog Rose-like triangular prickles and
Sweet Briar-like longer thinner curved
prickles. Not clear which rose is the
seed parent.

Dog Rose x Small-flowered Sweet Briar – hybrid
Rosa x *toddiae* (*R. micrantha* x *canina*)
Native. Occasional. Verges, scrub–often but not always with parents. June to July.
Stoborough Heath: NW side of Soldiers Road both at S cattle grid; 75m SW of that. **Hartland Moor:** W side of Soldiers Road 10m from N end; N side of Arne Road 250m E of Soldiers Road. **Wares (west):** E side of Coast Path 20m S of top of steps on W side of Seacombe Bottom; E bank of Seacombe Bottom 70m S of junction of path11 and track from near Eastington; by track down E side of Triangular Ware (with Small-flowered Sweet Briar); **(east)** in Golter 120m ENE from gateway into Middle Field. **Langton:** W side of unmade road to Castle View 65m N of B3069; by gate on path5 at S side of Talbot's Wood (N not W of cemetery). **Rempstone:** E side of bridleway9 (Oil Road) 125m S of junction with bridleway8 (one year with a large number of Robin's Pin Cushion galls, caused by the gall wasp *Diplolepis rosae*). **Durlston:** on N-facing edge of scrub 60m SSW of Visitor Centre 10m E of track (with parents nearby). **Studland Heath:** NW side of Ferry Road 80 and 140m SW and 100 and 200m NE of start of track to Redhorn Quay; SE side of road 140m SW and 110m NE of start of track to Redhorn Quay on opposite side of road; also E side of Ferry Road 30, 70 and 280m N of Knoll Beach Road. **Shell Bay:** NW side of Ferry Road 40 and 80m SW of roundabout sign.

It has a mixture of hybrid features: some small urn-shaped hips (Small-flowered Sweet Briar), some unevenly-shaped larger hips (Dog Rose), less glands and hairs underneath the leaves than Sweet Briar, mixture of triangular and narrow prickles on stems. Records have not been kept of which rose is the seed parent.

Sweet Briar *Rosa rubiginosa*
Native. Occasional. Verges, scrub. June to July.
Ridge: over 60 plants along sides of Dismantled Tramway mostly 150-650m S of Arne Road (with two other species and four types of hybrid). **Stoborough Heath:** NW side of Soldiers Road 175m NE of S cattle grid. **Swanage:** near SE corner of long Playing Field W of Northbrook Road cemetery.
Studland Heath: here and there on both sides of Ferry Road from bridleway36 N-wards for 1200m (about 80 Sweet Briar bushes, with three other species and three types of hybrid); SE side of Ferry Road 350m SW of roundabout. **Studland:** E side of Ferry Road 40m S of bridleway38 on opposite side. **Brownsea:** S of The Villa.

Sweet Briar and Small-flowered Sweet Briar both have many stalked glands underneath their leaves. Sweet Briar is distinguished by its large hips, hairy styles, sepals pointing forwards or sideways and remaining on hips until they are ripe, and straight stems with clusters of short straight prickles (acicles) on them. It is often only about 1m high. Compare with Small-flowered Sweet Briar p.132.

The dot map in *The Flora of Dorset* shows *Rosa rubiginosa* agg. – it includes *R. micrantha.*

Sweet Briar x Small-flowered Sweet Briar – hybrid *Rosa* x *bigeneris* (*R. rubiginosa* x *micrantha* or vice versa) Native. Rare. Verges. June to July.
Ridge: W side of Dismantled

Tramway 210 and 290m S of Arne Road (latter 10m S of hide on opposite side); E side of tramway 320 and 620m S of road (group of six at latter site).

Most hips are urn-shaped like Small-flowered Sweet Briar, but often larger and with plenty of stalked glands all over them; with groups of short straight prickles on branches like Sweet Briar. Not clear which rose is the seed parent. See Plate 14.

Small-flowered Sweet Briar
Rosa micrantha
Native. Occasional. Verges, scrub, top of shores. June to July.
Creech: E side of Grange Road W of Icen Barrow Pond S of gate.
Stoborough Heath: on W side of path5 20m N of junction with path6; several on NW side of Soldiers Road from 50-125m NE of S cattle grid.
East Creech: two near N side of E end of Stonehill Down. **Norden:** S side of path78 200m from W end.
Arne: NW side of Arne Road 200m NE of Bank Gate Cottages. **Corfe:** several by Purbeck Way on N side of West Hill around 450m W of path72.
Bushey: several on both sides of Bushey Lane 250m W of Forest Lane.
Wares (west): E bank of Seacombe Bottom 100m from sea 30m from E wall; by track down E side of Triangular Ware (hybrid with Dog Rose nearby). **Langton:** near path44 in scrubby area between West Wood and Talbot's Wood (area marked as wood on O.S. map). **Studland Heath:** SE shore of Bramble Bush Bay 10m S of row of concrete blocks; E side of Ferry Road 100m N of Knoll Beach Road. **Studland:** W side of Ferry Road 20m S of bridleway38. **Shell Bay:** NW side of Ferry Road 80m SW of roundabout sign. **Luscombe**

Valley: 60m N of SE corner entrance.

This species is told from Sweet Briar p.131 by its small urn-shaped hips, hairless styles, sepals pointing backwards and mostly dropping before hips are ripe, arched stems and lack of acicles. It is usually 2-3m high.

Cherry Plum *Prunus cerasifera*
Introduction. Occasional. Planted. Hedges, wood edges. February to March.
Kimmeridge: on N side of W-most of three copses near path14 (late-flowering tree). **Stoborough:** here and there on S side of path9 for 120m E of Grange Road. **Church Knowle:** 10m W of path18 90m S of public road.
Norden: SE side of road opposite S end of Slepe Road. **Wytch:** several on W side of Thrasher's Lane 60-170m N of entrance to Oil Gathering Station. **Rempstone:** E side of Forest Lane S of Breaches Lane for length of 100m. **Godlingston:** N side of Washpond Lane 75m W and 50m E of cemetery entrance. **Durlston:** S of W side car park on N side of path50. **Ballard Down:** large group on clifftop 350m NE of Shep's Hollow. **Studland:** E side of N end of path4.

Pissard's Plum
Prunus cerasifera cv. Pissardii
Cultivar planted. February to April.
Worth: E of road at N end of Renscombe Farm buildings. **Swanage:** NE side of Ulwell Road 70m NW of Whitecliff Road.

Dark red leaves.

Blackthorn, Sloe *Prunus spinosa*
Native. Abundant. Hedges, woods, scrub, cliffs. March to May.

Flowers appear before leaves, usually singly on stem, not grouped, compare with next species. Petals are usually 8mm or less in length. Some bushes have larger flowers than usual; they need to be checked later to see if they have larger fruits and if so are the next species (though some do not fruit, or not every year.) Some with larger flowers may be hybrids with the next species; others are difficult to name; the situation is complex. One group flowers later (mid-May to June) with small partially pink flowers – at **Creech:** in RSPB fields W of Grange Road W of gateway between fields (enter from N field) – this may be due to a virus (E.J. Clement, pers. com.)

Wild Plum, Bullace and Damson
Prunus domestica
Native (Bullace) or Early Introduction. Frequent. Usually planted. Hedges, scrub. March to May.

In the past, this species has traditionally been divided into subspecies, but hybridisation has confused distinctions.

Flowers appear with the leaves, usually 2 or 3 in a group; petals are usually 9mm or more long. Fruits vary considerably in size between one tree and another; often they do not fruit.

Wild Cherry *Prunus avium*
Native, but mostly planted here. Occasional. Waysides (often near former buildings). April to May.
Holme: along 10m of N side of Holme Lane 400m E of junction with minor road to East Holme. **Steeple:** W of road at right-angled bend N of Steeple Leaze Farm. **Stoborough:** W side of Grange Road just N of railway bridge. **Norden:** 375m from A351 along 10m of N side of bridleway77. **Arne:** SE side of Arne Road 425 and 500m NE of

Bank Gate Cottages. **Worth:** escaped cultivar plentiful by Coast Path at Winspit Quarry (there used to be a building there). **Swanage:** S side of Victoria Avenue just W of Pitch and Putt entrance. **Durlston:** on S side of path50 100m E of Lighthouse Field. **Studland:** triangle of land between Ferry Road and SE end of Wadmore Lane. **Brownsea:** few 100m SW of church. **Branksome Chine:** near E end of path on cliff-top SW of chine.

A deep pink Cherry *Prunus* species
Introduction. Rare. Planted. April to May.
Arne: W of road 150m NW of church (national experts have not yet been able to identify this).

Bird Cherry *Prunus padus*
Native, but planted here. Rare. May.
Durlston: W side of Long Meadow both 30 and 100m S of NW corner.

Rum Cherry *Prunus serotina*
Introduction. Rare. Escape. May to June.
Stoborough Heath: 20m from Grange Road by path7 (not yet flowering).
Orange-brown hairs either side of the central vein at the stalk end of the leaf underside.

Portugal Laurel *Prunus lusitanica*
Introduction. Rare. Planted. June.
Durlston: one plant 10m E of Durlston Road on N bank of summer-dry stream. **Brownsea:** one with several of next species E of track W of Maryland ruins; also in NE part of Venetia Park.
Leaf stalks are crimson.

Cherry Laurel *Prunus laurocerasus*
Introduction. Frequent. Planted and self-seeding, often with

Rhododendron on soils N of chalk ridge. March to May.
Holme: plentiful along Holme Lane. **Kingston:** plentiful around junction of paths49, 50 and 51. **Durlston:** plentiful in N of woods in NE of Country Park (with Spotted Laurels and one Portugal Laurel). **Studland:** site of Harmony Farm. **Brownsea:** by Maryland ruins; also large trees on E side of Vinery ruins.

Leaf stalks are green. When not in flower or fruit, it can be distinguished from Rhododendron by its broader and shinier leaves.

Cathay Quince
Chaenomeles cathayensis
Introduction. Rare. Planted. May.
Brownsea: 20m NW of Visitor Centre.

It is about 2m high, with short stocky thorns, leaves with forward-pointing teeth and with crimson edges (at least when young), has blunt sepal-lobes, pink buds, pink-flushed white flowers up to 40mm across.

Pear *Pyrus communis*
Early Introduction. Occasional. Planted. April to May.
Stoborough: NE side of bypass 200m SE of River Frome bridge; E side of Furzebrook Road 25m S of path24. **Norden:** E side of Slepe Road 550m N of roundabout. **Langton:** can be seen from A351 in field between B3069 and A351 W of their junction; N of A351 in field 200m NW of same junction. **Durlston:** sides of path48 – N side just E of bridge; S side 20m E of bridge; S side of path52 40m W of quarry. **Swanage:** E side of Victoria Avenue 30m N of railway bridge.

It is conspicuous in flower in late April but easily missed at other times. Some trees do not fruit.

Crab Apple *Malus sylvestris*
Native. Occasional. Woods. May.
Church Knowle: wooded N side of road to West Orchard Farm 200 m E of T-junction. **Studland:** NE corner of The Warren Wood.

Mature leaf underside is hairless. Escaped domestic apple trees are often thought to be Crab Apple; at least 95% of apples in the wild in this area are *Malus domestica*, (see below).

Hybrid Apple
Malus sylvestris x *domestica*
Langton: in N-S ride on E side of West Wood 200m NNE of SE corner of wood; 15m S of N edge of Talbot's Wood 75m W of path5.

These trees have features of Crab Apple (thin twigs and buds, small fruit, thorns on first tree) yet the undersides of mature leaves are not smooth but hairy.

Apple *Malus domestica*
Early Introduction. Frequent. Escape in woods, hedges, verges, downs, cliffs, dunes – any ground where apple-core might be thrown, though sometimes remnant of old orchard. May.

Mature leaf underside is downy (lens).

Japanese Crab (Apple)
Malus floribunda
Introduction. Rare. Planted. Smothered with blossom around late April.
Brownsea: 50m SW of churchyard.

Rowan *Sorbus aucuparia*
Native. Occasional. Heaths, hedges, woods on acid soil; planted elsewhere. May.
Holme: on open access part of Battle Plain 100m NW of entrance at

Doreys Farm. **Stoborough Heath:** W of stream SW of Hartland Stud.
Hartland Moor: N side of Arne Road 500m E of Soldiers Road; E side of Slepe Road both N and S of Slepe Copse. **Arne:** NW side of Arne Road 250 and 800m NE of Bank Gate Cottages. **Kingswood:** visible S of B3351 30m E of bridleway16.
Studland Heath: here and there on heath E of Ferry Road and NW of Western Arm of Little Sea.
Brownsea: scattered through island.
Luscombe Valley: near track on W edge of Reserve 150m N of metal bridge. **Branksome Dene Chine:** behind beach chalets SW of café.

Swedish Whitebeam
Sorbus intermedia
Introduction. Occasional. Planted. May.
Tyneham: middle of picnic area W of car park. **Kingston:** visible (from W edge of open access land) in NE corner of Broadley Wood. **Worth:** several in field on N side of Weston Road W of Playing Field; by path23. **Knitson:** on E side of bridleway12 near N end; NE side of Burnham's Lane 430 and 450m SE of Knitson Farm. **Durlston:** hedge between Smith Field and Skipworth Meadow 50m W of E end.

Common Whitebeam *Sorbus aria*
Native at first site below, otherwise planted in this area. Woods on chalk. May.
Creech: SE side of road through Great Wood 5m E of lower of two tall Lawson's Cypresses. **Church Knowle:** two on S edge of old quarry N of Cocknowle. **Worth:** by short path23.
Knitson: N of N end of bridleway12; SW side of road 300m SE of Knitson Farm. **Herston (north):** NE of path1 80m from SE end.

Wild Service Tree *Sorbus torminalis*
Native, but planted in this area. Rare. May.
Studland: triangle of land between Ferry Road and SE end of Wadmore Lane. **Brownsea:** SW corner of Venetia Park.

Juneberry *Amelanchier lamarckii*
Introduction. Rare. Planted. April to May.
Branksome Chine: two trees S of Pinecliff Road 80m E and SE of Library.

Cotoneasters
Stace (1997) lists 67 species of Cotoneaster which have escaped into the wild and one native species. Blamey, Fitter and Fitter (2003) describe 12 of them, including 8 of the 12 found in this area, though their illustrations are not much help for the shape or colour of the berries, see drawing. Descriptions of the other four species are given below. In the drawing the leaves shown are full-grown, late summer leaves; plants will also be bearing smaller ones.

Tree Cotoneaster
Cotoneaster frigidus
Introduction. Occasional. Planted. June.
Tyneham: two planted behind ruined cottages NW of pond near telephone box. **Church Knowle:** in old quarry N of Cocknowle. **Knitson:** NE side of Burnham's Lane 15-25m NW of W end of path2 (with two other Cotoneaster species). **Studland:** N side of Agglestone Road 20m W of bend. **Brownsea:** N side of track opposite E end of Maryland ruins.

Hairs on the undersides of the leaves wear off as season progresses, except from veins.

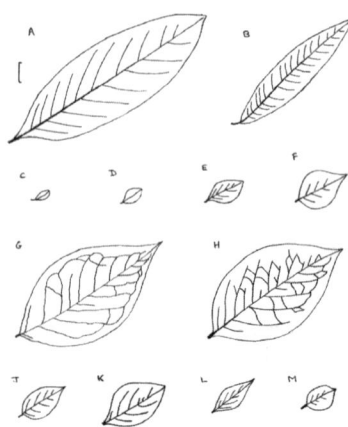

Cotoneaster leaves: A - Tree, B - Waterer's, C - Entire-leaved, D - Wall, E - Spreading, F - Himalayan, G - Hollyberry, H - Bullate, J - Maire's, K - Stern's, L - Diel's, M - Showy.

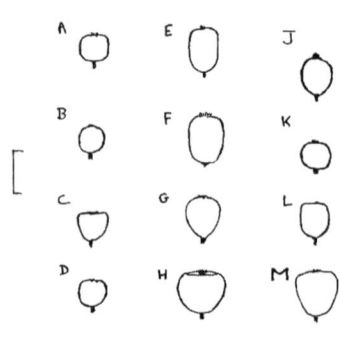

Cotoneaster fruit: A - Tree (red), B - Waterer's (red), C - Entire-leaved (matt red), D - Wall (shiny red), E - Spreading (deep glossy red), F - Himalayan (orange), G - Hollyberry (deep red), H - Bullate (deep red), J - Maire's (orange-red), K - Stern's (orange-red), L - Diel's (orange-red), M - Showy (orange-red).

Waterer's Cotoneaster *Cotoneaster* x *watereri* (*C. frigidus* x *salicifolius*) Introduction. Rare. Planted and self-seeding. June.
Swanage, N of path in rough grass-land 100m SE of S end of Benlease Way.

Entire-leaved Cotoneaster, Rock Cotoneaster *Cotoneaster integrifolius* Introduction. Rare. Escape June to July.
East Creech: conspicuous on E end of Stonehill Down Reserve 20m W of road 20m N of worked quarry.

Wall Cotoneaster
Cotoneaster horizontalis
Introduction. Occasional. Escape on verges, downs. June to July.
East Creech: by fence above worked quarry 50m W of road at E end of Stonehill Down Reserve. **Church Knowle:** above old quarry N of Cocknowle (with next species).

Corfe: NE corner of The Pound (growing lower than mower cuts!).**Worth:** E side of Kingston Road opposite car park. **Langton:** in field just W of unmade-up road to Castle View just S of houses (view from road). **Rempstone:** NW side of Oil Road where bridleways9 and 10 cross. **Townsend Reserve:** 80m SE of NW entrance. **Durlston:** S of path50 in NE of Field 10; in shallow quarry in NE of Field 14. **Ballard Down:** 125m NE of where bridleway14 crosses Purbeck Way on NW side of former (see Map 20, not O.S. map). **Branksome Chine:** on bank on W side of car park by sea.

Spreading Cotoneaster
Cotoneaster divarticus
Introduction. Rare. Planted and self-seeding. June to July.
Church Knowle: very large plant (planted) in old quarry N of Cocknowle; several smaller plants just

to SW and N of quarry, (with Wall Cotoneaster to N of quarry).

Leaves 8-26mm long, flat and shiny upperside, sparsely hairy underside, fall in winter, (beautiful variety of colours in November). Flowers mostly 2 to 3 together, anthers white. Fruit mostly 9-12mm long, oblong, deep red, with 2 stones.

Himalayan Cotoneaster
Cotoneaster simonsii
Introduction. Occasional. Escape on verges, downs, heathy woodland; not fussy about soils. June to July.
Stoborough: 20 and 35m from Grange Road by path7. **Creech Heath:** on S side of path34 150m W of Furzebrook Road. **Stoborough Heath:** NE side of A351 at E side of start of Dismantled Tramway; area W of Dismantled Tramway up to 175m N of A351. **Harman's Cross:** E side of Haycraft's Lane 70m NW of bridleway6. **Knitson:** NE side of Burnham's Lane 20m NW of W end of path2 (with two other Cotoneaster species). **Townsend Reserve:** 40m SE of NW entrance; 75m W of E (path) entrance. **Swanage:** on NE side of Ulwell Road 150 and 180m NW of Whitecliff Road. **Studland Heath:** E side of Ferry Road just N of Knoll Beach Road. **Luscombe Valley:** by track 70m NW of metal bridge in centre of Reserve. **Canford Cliffs:** by path from Nairn Road to Brudenell Road 30m from latter.

Leaves with hairs flat against underside, not downy.

Hollyberry Cotoneaster
Cotoneaster bullatus
Introduction. Rare. Escape or planted. June to July.
Stoborough: SW side of path7 just E of kissing-gate at Grange Road; 50m

further SE; NE side 30m SE of gate.

Leaves 6.5-10.5cm long, slightly blistered (veins impressed on upperside), sparsely downy underside, fall in late winter. Flowers seen 8 to 11 together, anthers purple. Fruit 8-9mm wide, 9-10mm long, with 5 stones. Leaves and fruit of these three specimens are larger than described by Stace (1997) and Blamey *et al.* (2003); there are several forms currently grouped under *C. bullatus* (J. Fryer, pers. com).

Bullate Cotoneaster, Blistered Cotoneaster *Cotoneaster rehderi*
Introduction. Rare. Escape. June to July.
Townsend Reserve: on N edge of flat-topped mound 20m SW of where paths46 and 56 cross.

Next three species are similar in appearance to each other.

Maire's Cotoneaster
Cotoneaster mairei
Introduction. Rare. Escape in scrub. June to July.
Sandbanks: raised dune SW of main car park (with next species).

Leaves 15-35mm long, veins impressed on upperside, very downy on underside, some fall in winter; flowers 3 to 7 together; fruit 8-10mm long, with 2 to 3 stones.

Stern's Cotoneaster
Cotoneaster sternianus
Introduction. Occasional. Escape in scrub and on verges. June to July.
Stoborough: E side of Grange Road 400m N of railway bridge; 35 and 60m SE of Grange Road by path7. **Stoborough Heath:** by fence on W edge of Hyde Hill 50m S of N track to Heath from Furzebrook Road.

Langton: on old spoil heap N of Bower's Quarry. **Swanage:** in small copse by S end of Benlease Way. **Townsend Reserve:** 15m SW of crossing of paths 46 and 56 (view from S); 10m E of SW corner of Manwell Field just N of reserve fence; near same fence 100m W of reserve E entrance. **Luscombe Valley:** in woodland W of metal bridge. **Sandbanks:** raised dune SW of main car park (with previous species); near E end of path from Brudenell Avenue to Dornie Road.

Leaves 25-50mm long, veins deeply impressed on upperside, very downy on underside, do not fall in winter; flowers 5 to 15 together; fruit 8-10mm long, with 2 to 3 stones.

Diel's Cotoneaster, Chinese Cotoneaster *Cotoneaster dielsianus* Introduction. Occasional. Escape in scrub and on verges. June.
Corfe: 60m N of S end of Byle Copse. **Townsend Reserve:** two plants 75m SE of NW entrance on N edge of large open area. **Durlston:** E side of Durlston Road 20m N of Long Meadow. **Studland:** N side of bend in Agglestone Road.

Leaves 12-35mm long, veins deeply impressed on upperside, very downy on underside, fall in winter; flowers 3 to 7 together; fruit 6-8mm long, with 3 to 4 stones.

Showy Cotoneaster
Cotoneaster splendens
Introduction. Rare. Planted. June to July.
Knitson: NE side of Burnham's Lane 15 and 20m NW of W end of path 2 (with two other Cotoneaster species).

Leaves 10-20mm long, almost flat on upperside, greyish downy on underside, fall in winter; flowers 2 to

3 together, anthers white; fruit 8-11mm long, with 4 stones.

Firethorn *Pyracantha coccinea*
Introduction. Rare. Planted or escape. June to July.
Stoborough: on N side of path 7 10m E of Grange Road.

Hawthorn, May *Crataegus monogyna*
Native. Abundant. Woods, hedges, scrub, downs, verges, neglected fields. May to June.

Hybrid Hawthorn *Crataegus* x *media* (*C. monogyna* x *laevigata*)
Native, but planted here. Rare.
Ballard Down: W of lowest point of Coast Path when passing second field N of Shep's Hollow.

Some flowers and fruit have two styles and stones, some one. Fruit is larger than Hawthorn. Some leaves like one parent, some like other parent.

ACACIA FAMILY
Mimosa *Acacia dealbata*
Introduction. Rare. Escape.
Sandbanks: near W end of path parallel to and between Grasmere Road and Seacombe Road (sucker from tree in adjacent garden).

PEA FAMILY
Robinia *Robinia pseudacacia*
Introduction. Rare. Planted.
Brownsea: NE part of Venetia Park; W and NW sides of Church Field; several N of Visitor Centre.

Goat's Rue *Galega officinalis*
Introduction. Rare. Escape. Late June to July.
Swanage: albino just over gate SE of junction of Northbrook Road and Washpond Lane.

Sainfoin *Onobrychis viciifolia*
Native, but more often a relic of culti-
vation. Occasional. Calcareous grass-
land. June.
Near threatened.
Worth: by Coast Path 625m S of
path18; 600m E of Coastwatch
Station. **Wares (east):** by path64
200m N of Belle Vue East Ware.
Townsend Reserve: between permis-
sive bridleway and Orchid Bastion
NW of latter; SW of SE Bastion.
Durlston: W of path56 25 and 140m
S of where it leaves Townsend Reserve
(plentiful at latter site); on W-facing
bank near SE corner of Eight Acres;
in W and NW of Centenary
Meadow; in South Field 20m NE of
NE corner of Small Copse; E side of
South Field towards SE corner. See
Plate 14.

Kidney Vetch
Anthyllis vulneraria subsp. *vulneria*
Native. Frequent. Calcareous grassland, cliffs. May to August.
Holme: here and there on B3070
verges across West Holme Heath.
Worth: patches on West Hill. **Corfe:**
by W steps on path79 N of car park.
Wares: here and there in short grassland. **Durlston:** in SW of Johnston
Meadow; W of path56 140m S of
where it leaves Townsend Reserve
(supports population of Small Blue
butterfly); in Field 10 E of stone stile
on top of Down. **Godlingston
Heath:** small road island where road
from Swanage meets B3351.
Studland: very plentiful in Old Nick's
Ground (supports good population
of Small Blue butterfly, best seen
along edge of wood).

Anthyllis vulneraria subsp. *polyphylla*
Introduction. Rare. Calcareous grassland. June to July.

Wares (west): one near SW corner of
Cliff Field 26m N of tenth fence post
from corner.

Narrow-leaved Birdsfoot Trefoil
Lotus glaber (*L. tenuis*)
Native. Occasional. Grassland, verges.
June to September.
Wares (west): S side of Priest's way
100m E of path30; here and there
near N edge of East Plain and Taylor's
Ware; E side of pond S of Priest's Way
250m E of path30; by entrance to old
quarry workings E of new route of
path27 E of Sea Spray; N side of
Priest's Way 200m E of previous
pond; by path25 in Dancing Ledge
North Ware 50m N of Dancing
Ledge Ware; (east) in SE corner of
Sherwood's Wear. **Durlston:** near
diagonal track in SE part of Johnston
Meadow. **Studland:** W end of
Agglestone Road in front of large
gate. **Luscombe Valley:** 12-20m W of
metal bridge in centre of Reserve.

Upper leaves usually at least 4 times
as long as wide in summer, but sometimes only 3 times as long as wide.
Upper sepal-tube (calyx) points bend
towards each other. Often grows near
next species which does have similar-
sized flowers.

Common Birdsfoot Trefoil
Lotus corniculatus
Native. Abundant. Grassland, verges.
May to September.

Distinction in the shape of the
notch between upper sepal-tube
(calyx) points, for this and next
species, does not work well. Sepal
points are flat on flower-bud (see next
species). Lower stalks are solid.

Greater Birdsfoot Trefoil
Lotus pedunculatus
Native. Frequent. Usually in wet

places, except acid ones, but sometimes at dry sites. June to August.

Sepal tube points are raised off flower-bud (see previous species) Lower stalks are hollow except when young.

Hairy Birdsfoot Trefoil
Lotus subbiflorus (*L. hispidus*)
Native. Occasional. Dry, bare sandy soil. May to August.
Nationally Scarce.
Norden: just NE of roundabout on track. **Ower:** by SW side of bridleway7 10m N of crossing of bridleways7 and 8; here and there by bridleway8 from same crossing to Game Copse. **Godlingston Heath:** 10m NW of gate on N side of bridleway36 opposite E end of bridleway35. **Studland Heath:** N side of Knoll Beach Road just W of coach park. **Shell Bay:** NW corner of car park. **Lilliput:** on triangle where Minterne Road, Alington Road and Bingham Avenue meet. **Luscombe Valley:** on bank at junction of Shore Road and Brudenell Avenue. **Sandbanks:** in lawn 10m S of entrance from Banks Road to small triangular garden S of junction of Banks and Shore Roads. **Branksome Dene Chine:** above promenade 100m NE of chine.

Not at all sites every year. See Plate 14.

Birdsfoot *Ornithopus perpusillus*
Native. Occasional. Dry, sandy soil. May to July.
Stoborough Heath: very plentiful from Nature Reserve notice 50m N of S cattle grid on Soldiers Road on track up to cairn. **Hartland Moor:** plentiful on parts of South Middlebere. **Kingston:** unusual site 100m SW of Polar Wood on SE facing rocks below bridleway46. **Arne:**

here and there in N end of triangular field S of car park. **Ower:** here and there by bridleway8 from crossing of bridleways7 and 8 to Game Copse. **Godlingston Heath:** in field N of bridleway36 400m along bridleway from Ferry Road. **Studland Heath:** W and E of Heather Walk 250m N of Knoll Beach main N car park. **Shell Bay:** E of centre of E side of car park. **Lilliput:** triangle at junction between Alington Road, Minterne Road and Bingham Avenue. **Branksome Chine:** near E end of path on cliff-top W of chine.

Examine flowers with lens to see details of their beautiful colouring.

Horseshoe Vetch *Hippocrepis comosa*
Native. Abundant. Downs, chalk cliffs. May to July.

Tufted Vetch *Vicia cracca*
Native. Frequent. Hedges, scrub, verges.

(**Wood Vetch** *Vicia sylvatica*
Native. Old woods. July to August.
Langton: perhaps one place in Talbot's Wood – which can be shown on request to author (see Appendix); do not step on its trailing stems – but it has not appeared since 2005).

Hairy Tare *Vicia hirsuta*
Native. Occasional. Verges, grassland. May to July.
Steeple: scattered along NE side of road which ascends Down NW of Steeple from 100m from top 125m SE-wards. **Kimmeridge:** plentiful NE of Coast Path SW of Gaulter Cottages; SW of Coast path 150m further NW (with Smooth Tare). **East Creech:** N side of road here and there S of worked quarry from 150-180m W of E end of quarry.

Stoborough Heath: here and there on W side of Soldiers Road for 700m N from Three Barrows. **Corfe:** scattered on E side of castle mound outside walls. **Herston (north):** N side of path23 10m E of path1 stile. **Studland:** N side of Coast Path N of The Warren Wood; in Old Nick's Ground especially on W edge along S half of Studland Wood. **Luscombe Valley:** 10m W of gate in SE corner (Smooth Tare also present). **Sandbanks:** 125m NE of main car park NW of two-storey block of beach chalets.

Flowers are off-white, and pods usually 2-seeded.

Slender Tare
Vicia parviflora (*V. tenuissima*)
Native. Occasional. Meadows and verges on calcareous clay. June to July. *Nationally Scarce. Vulnerable.*
Wares (west): here and there on SW part of Nicholas Down; by Coast Path along SE edge of Nicholas Down where path passes rocks left from quarrying 100m S of top of steps; scattered in SE part of Cliff Field; **(east):** on E side of path46 125m S of Priest's Way. **Durlston:** W side of Centenary Meadow near S end; E side of same meadow 50m N of SE corner.

See next species for differences.

Smooth Tare *Vicia tetrasperma*
Native. Occasional. Verges, clay cliffs, rough grass. May to July.
Kimmeridge: SW of Coast Path between Gaulter Cottages and Oil Well 25m NW of stone seat in memory of Paul Curtis (with Hairy Tare). **Wares (west):** 10m W of track along E side of Long Close 50m S of junction of walls. **Rempstone:** NW side of bridleway34 (Oil Road) 150m SW of where crossed by bridleway31.

Swanage: foot of cliff 50m N of N end of promenade. **Luscombe Valley:** here and there in S half of reserve (Hairy Tare also present); near track at N end of E side of reserve.

Has one or two flowers together 4-8mm long, whereas previous species often has three or four 8-9mm long. Four (sometimes 3) seeds can be seen as bumps in Smooth Tare pods, whereas Slender Tare usually has 5. Smooth Tare has 3 to 6 pairs of leaflets, whereas Slender Tare has 2 to 4.

Bush Vetch *Vicia sepium*
Native. Frequent. Verges. May to August.
Holme: N side of Holme Lane 600m W of B3070 for 5m; SW side of Holme Lane 700m W of B3070 for 20m. **Steeple:** N side of W-E road 25m E of road into Steeple hamlet. **Church Knowle:** 180m S of road on E side of path18 for 5m. **Kingston:** both sides of path44 through The Plantation especially on NW side 190-250m from West Street; E side of South Street 75 m S of end of The Plantation, including albino. **Bushey:** S side of B3351 40m W of bridleway14 for 5m. **Langton:** few places in rides in Langton West Wood. **Woolgarston:** S side of road 100m SE of Ailwood Farm along 10m. **Wares (east):** along 40m of S side of Priest's Way from 200m W of junction of Way with path46. **Studland:** here and there 200-400m S of Watery Lane on E side of bridleway12.

Narrow-leaved Vetch
Vicia sativa subsp. *nigra*
Native. Frequent. Grassland, verges. May to July.

The upper leaves are usually narrower than the lower ones, but the best way to tell this from the two sub-species below is that its petals are all the same colour. Small plants have been recorded as Spring Vetch, but Narrow-leaved Vetch has smooth seeds, unlike that species.

Common Vetch
Vicia sativa subsp. *segetalis*
Early Introduction. Frequent. Verges. May to July.

Upper petal paler than others.

Cultivated Vetch
Vicia sativa subsp. *sativa*
Early Introduction. Occasional. Verges near arable fields. May to August.
Kimmeridge: field edge 50m SE of junction of path6 and 7. **Church Knowle:** on W side of bridleway16 375m N of road. **Kingston:** by stile on path42 before it descends cliff to Chapman's Pool. **Worth:** W side of path13 150m N of junction with path14. **Bushey:** N side of Bushey Lane opposite Higher Bushey Farm buildings. **Wares (west):** N side of Priest's Way 130m E of path26; **(east):** here and there on W side of path46 500-700m N of Belle Vue West Ware. **Herston (north):** E side of path24 on its short length on private road to Sludge Works. **Durlston:** S side of Hoggett Mead near SW and SE corners. **Ballard Down:** by Coast Path from stone seat at bottom of steps up Down here and there for 200m SW-wards.

It is a larger plant in all respects. Formerly grown as crop.

Broad Bean *Vicia faba*
Ancient cultivated species, never found native anywhere in the world. Occasional. Casual escape. April to August.

Spring Pea *Lathyrus vernus*
Introduction. Rare. Escape.
Langton: 5m S of bridleway42 on SW side of path44.

Bitter Vetch
Lathyrus linifolius (*L. montanus*)
Native. Occasional. Rough grassland, verges. April to June.
Furzebrook: few in NE of central field in Kilnwood Reserve within 5m N of bramble patch (finishes in May). **Hartland Moor:** in drier part of Middle Fen 75m E of Jubilee Bridge. **Corfe:** several on drier part of West Common S of W half of First Valley (thinly scattered); 150m SE of Middle Common pond. **Langton:** in N of West Wood where path44 ascends N-wards with steps towards bridleway42.

Meadow Vetchling *Lathyrus pratensis*
Native. Frequent. Verges. May to August.

Two to 12 flowers in a group – compare with Yellow Vetchling p.143.

Narrow-leaved Everlasting Pea
Lathyrus sylvestris
Native. Rare. Verges. June to August.
Dorset Scarce.
Steeple: two groups in scrub on Steeple Down (east) one 10m N of bottom fence 300m E of W fence; other 2m N of bottom fence 350m E of W fence. **Kimmeridge:** N side of road to Bradle 80m from T-junction NE of Kimmeridge; also from there take correct route of bridleway18 for 25m SE-wards then turn S along grassy track for 35m to site on its W side. See Plate 15.

Broad-leaved Everlasting Pea
Lathyrus latifolius
Introduction. Occasional. Escape. June to August.

Norden: NE side of A351 80m SE of bridleway77. **Swanage:** Victoria Avenue opposite Triangle Garage; on cliff (binoculars help) in at least two places – high up 100m N of N end of Shore Road; 75m N of E end of path down cliff from Burlington Road. **Durlston:** at bottom of Zigzag Path.

Grass Vetchling *Lathyrus nissolia*
Native. Occasional. Rough grassland on calcareous clay. Mid-June to early July.
Kimmeridge: 125m WSW of junction of bridleways11 and 12 on N side of track down slope. **Wares (west):** here and there on SW part of Nicholas Down; by Coast Path along SE edge of same Down 100m S of top of steps; by Coast Path half way along Cliff Field. **Herston (north):** on N side of path23 10m E of path1 stile; on E side of path24 on its short length on private road to Sludge Works. **Durlston:** W side of Centenary Meadow 30m N of SW corner; E side of Ox-eye Daisy Field near NE corner; E side of South Field S of central gateway; 60m NE of SW corner of area 34.

Plants are very rarely noticed until they flower; these rubies in the grass then look delightful. Short flowering period in dry seasons. It is an annual species, so it varies in quantity from year to year. See Plate 15.

Yellow Vetchling *Lathyrus aphaca*
Native or introduced. Occasional. Calcareous grassland and verges. June to July.
Nationally Scarce. Vulnerable.
Worth: by Coast Path due W of row of houses at St. Aldhelm's Head. **Wares (west):** SW of Nicholas Down several on both sides of fence

W of pit quarry (view from Down); **(east):** on E side of path46 125m S of Priest's Way. **Herston (north):** on N side of path23 10m E of path1 stile; on E side of path24 on its short length on private road to Sludge Works. **Durlston:** on E side of path59 35m N of gate into NE of Field 3; S side of Hoggett Mead 75m W of SE corner; on S side of path50 65m W of gate from Field 10 into Lighthouse Field; 40m W of gate in SE corner of South Field; on N side of same gateway; on E side of path54 300m N of Holecombe (field); by path43 130m S of junction with path42; 35m S of W end of terrace S of Visitor Centre; near NE corner of Smith Field on N side of track 12m W of gate; W side of Long Meadow 70 and 80m S of NW corner.

Flowers are borne singly – compare with Meadow Vetchling p.142. It is an annual species, so some sites change from year to year. See Plate 15.

Common Restharrow *Ononis repens*
Native. Frequent. Grassland, verges. Mid-June to September.

Tall Melilot *Melilotus altissimus*
Early Introduction. Frequent. Verges, waste ground. June to August.
Holme: very plentiful on verges of B 3070 across West Holme Heath. **Steeple:** SW side of road 125m NW of S end of bridleway3. **Worth:** near bridleway19 above beach at Chapman's Pool. **Corfe:** plentiful at N and S ends of SE side of B3069 where it crosses Common. **Durlston:** plentiful both sides of S end of Panorama Road near Recycling Centre. **Ulwell:** E side of path4 20m from S end.

Distinguished from Ribbed Melilot (p.144) by having wing and keel petals of roughly equal length and by hairy seedpods (though hairs disappear when pods are old).

White Melilot *Melilotus albus*
Introduction. Rare. Disturbed ground. June to August.
Wareham: N side of Priory Meadow by Rotary Seat (may not persist).
Luscombe Valley: N of road just E of SE entrance gate.

Ribbed Melilot *Melilotus officinalis*
Native. Rare. Arable fields. June to August.
Stoborough Heath: along S side of Roebuck Meadow beginning just W of Dismantled Tramway (when disturbed). **Worth:** 200m N of B3069 on E side of bridleway2 (when field cultivated).

Keel petals are shorter than wing petals; seedpods are wrinkled, not hairy (compare with Tall Melilot, p.143).

Black Medick *Medicago lupulina*
Native, or relic of cultivation. Frequent. Short grass, verges, gardens, pavements. May to August.

Like Lesser Trefoil (p.146), but downy, with black ripe seedpods, and each leaflet has a tiny point in its notch.

Lucerne *Medicago sativa* subsp. *sativa*
Introduction. Rare. Relic of cultivation in grassland, verges. Mid-June to July.
Worth: on W side of Coast Path where it runs through edge of field 500-625 m S of path18. **Corfe:** W side of UCR up Rollington Hill 12m S of gate at junction with bridleway20. **Durlston:** near NE corner of Smith Field 20m W of gate 2-3m N of track.

Toothed Medick
Medicago polymorpha
Native. Rare. Open dry grassland and verges. June to September.
Nationally Scarce.
Durlston: on lawn of The Lookout café near terrace (with much more of next species).

Seedpods are in looser spiral than the next species.

Spotted Medick, Calvary Clover
Medicago arabica
Native. Frequent. Grassland, including lawns. May to August.

Leaves are not always spotted, seedpods in neat tight spirals.

Clovers
Almost everyone knows Red Clover and White Clover, but only they, Zigzag Clover, Alsike and Hop Trefoil have conspicuous flowers. Details of most other clovers listed below need to be appreciated at ground level, and some of them will only be found on hands and knees.

Birdsfoot Clover
Trifolium ornithopodioides
Native. Occasional. Very short grassland, verges, lawns, car parks. May to August.
Tyneham: on Coast Path 200m N of S end of Worbarrow Bay. **Arne:** in car park extension (N of car park) 5m from N end. **Ower:** on SW side of bridleway7 20m NW of where bridleways7 and 8 cross. **Godlingston Heath:** on both sides of bridleway25 200m N of B3351. **Durlston:** on SE side of path52 10m SW of E edge of Lighthouse Field; on N-going track 35m N of Dry Stone Walling Centre. **Studland:** E side of Ferry Road opposite S entrance to Knoll House Hotel. **Studland Heath:** here and there on

Redhorn Quay; here and there in Knoll Beach car parks especially in dinghy park; E side of Heather Walk 200m N of main N car park. **Shell Bay:** W side of Ferry Road 50m N of roundabout sign; SE corner bays in car park. **Brownsea:** low wall opposite Visitor Centre; plentiful on café lawn. **Sandbanks:** in lawn on N side of entrance from Banks Road to small triangular garden S of junction of Banks and Shore Roads. **Branksome Chine:** by cliff-top path 200m SW of chine.

Flowers are usually borne singly, pale pink and always tiny.

White Clover *Trifolium repens*
Native. Abundant. Grassland, verges, fixed shingle, cliffs. June to September.

Alsike (Clover) *Trifolium hybridum*
Introduction. Occasional. Grassland, verges. June to September.
Ulwell: meadow SW of Ulwell Road opposite Ulwell Farm Caravan Park – but often close grazed (binoculars from road). **Luscombe Valley:** plentiful 20m from SE gate along S side of Reserve.

Sometimes it is mistaken for White Clover (above), but it is larger, lower part of flowerheads are always pink when in full flower, and it has broad papery bracts (stipules) at bases of leaf-stalks.

Clustered Clover
Trifolium glomeratum
Native. Occasional. Fairly bare places, verges. June to July.
Nationally Scarce.
Hartland Moor: on bridleway4 50m NE of gate at W end; along 5m of two shallow ruts of grassy track just W of gate NW of White House

Wood (with other clovers). **Arne:** N end of triangular field S of car park 10m from kissing-gate along 8m S-wards on partly bare ground. **Ower:** S side of bridleway8 opposite centre of Game Copse. **Knitson:** on SW side of Purbeck Way 100m NW of top of zigzag track. **Studland Heath:** NW side of Ferry Road 250 and 260m NE of start of track to Jerry's Point; S-facing bank W of Knoll Beach toilets.
Shell Bay: NW side of Ferry Road 90m NE of roundabout sign; SE side of Ferry Road 100m SW of round-about; E of roundabout. **Lilliput:** by Scout Jubilee Stone on Evening Hill. **Branksome Chine:** by cliff-top path for over 200m SW of chine especially near seats; S-facing bank N of road at sea end of chine.

Usually prostrate and fairly incon-spicuous.

Suffocated Clover
Trifolium suffocatum
Native. Occasional. Fairly bare: sandy places near coast. April to July (August in wet year).
Nationally Scarce.
Hartland Moor: in shallow ruts of grassy track just W of gate NW of White House Wood (with other clovers). **Studland:** between car park rows both N and S of rise in middle of Middle Beach car park. **Studland Heath:** NW side of Ferry Road 300m NE of start of track to Jerry's Point; SE side of same road 100 and 425m NE of track to nudists' area.
Sandbanks: plentiful on NW verge of Banks Road 250m NE of round-about. **Canford Cliffs:** much by Cliff Drive near top of stepped path to beach. **Branksome Chine:** near E end of path on cliff-top just SW of chine. **Branksome Dene Chine:** in lawn SW of café.

The tiny flowers are almost hidden (lens). Best found by learning to recognise the light green rosette of the leaves.

Strawberry Clover
Trifolium fragiferum
Native. Occasional. Grassland and verges damp in winter because of clay soil. July to August.
Corfe: plentiful near gate at N of Middle Common. **Worth:** plentiful by path13 along 175m N-wards from junction with path14. **Wytch:** on S side of new route of path5 (Oil Road) at N end of Wytch Moor 10m E of stream bridge. **Wares (west):** by Coast Path through Hedbury Ware for up to 50m E of Cliff Field. **Langton:** at junction of paths15 and 21. **Ulwell:** NW of Purbeck Way 100 and 190m SE of Ulwell Road. **Townsend Reserve:** near gate at W end of permissive bridleway. **Durlston:** plentiful in Long Meadow 20-60m S of NE corner. **Studland Heath:** shore of Redhorn Bay 50m N of Brand's Bay Hide for 40m N-wards. **Sandbanks:** verge W of Banks Road 50 and 550m S of junction with Shore Road.

It is often not noticed until its distinctive fruiting pale-pink, raspberry-like heads appear.

Hop Trefoil *Trifolium campestre*
Native. Frequent. Grassland, verges. Mid-June to early October.

Lesser Trefoil *Trifolium dubium*
Native. Abundant. Grassland, paths. May to September.
Can be confused with Black Medick (p.144) and Slender Trefoil (see below). It has no tiny point in the notch of its leaflets.

Slender Trefoil *Trifolium micranthum*
Native. Occasional. Verges, pavements, car parks, short grass including lawns. June to July.
Tyneham: on S side of Army Range path (N of picnic table) 550m WSW of Whiteway Hill trig point (with much Lesser Trefoil). **Stoborough Heath:** 20m NW of gate between Heath and Hartland Stud. **Norden:** on permissive path leading NNE from near New Line Farm 20m N of S end of track. **Hartland Moor:** here and there on South Middlebere including on grassy track just W of gate NW of White House Wood (with other clovers). **Kingston:** by path41 80m S of gate at S end of South Street. **Corfe:** much on E side of UCR across West Common at E-most sharp bend at S of Common. **Worth:** near W edge of Worth Cowleaze 80m S of Langton Road. **Rempstone:** N side of bridleway35 (Oil Road) 100m E of junction with bridleway34. **Knitson:** on SW side of Purbeck Way 100m NW of top of zigzag track. **Godlingston Heath:** on both sides of bridleway25 200m N of B3551; in field N of bridleway36 400m along bridleway from Ferry Road. **Durlston:** between pavings on patio S of Visitor Centre. **Studland:** in Middle Beach car park particularly between payment booth and central rise. **Brownsea:** low wall opposite Visitor Centre. **Branksome Chine:** by cliff-top path 20m SW of chine.

Often confused with the small flowerheads of Lesser Trefoil (see above), but each of the 2 to 6 flowers in heads of Slender Trefoil has a longer stalk of *c*.1.5 mm, compared with the 5 to 20 flowers in the heads of Lesser Trefoil with stalks of *c*.1mm (lens). Flowers of Slender Trefoil are not grouped so closely in their head because of the longer stalks.

Red Clover *Trifolium pratense*
Native. Abundant. Grassland, verges.
May to September.
Albinos have been seen at following
sites: **Stoborough Heath:** on W side
of Furzebrook Road by short track to
path5; on E side 150m N of path24;
Durlston: NW corner of Field 2. The
leaflets close under each flower distinguish it from the next species; they
also separate albinos from White
Clover.

Zigzag Clover *Trifolium medium*
Native. Occasional. Grassland, verges.
June to September.
Hartland Moor: along 15m of S side
of Arne Road 50m E of Soldiers
Road. **Corfe:** in very shallow valley
30m W of path51 on West Common
130m N of stream along S edge of
Common; 20m SW of SW corner of
S end of Middle Common Pond.
Bushey: along 20m of N side of
Bushey Lane 200m E of bridleway10;
along 40m of S side opposite previous
site (on S side it grows with Red
Clover and can be compared).
Harman's Cross: plentiful by track to
N platform of station 40m W of
Haycraft's Lane. **Swanage Railway:** S
side just E of Harman's Cross bridge.
Langton: by bridleway42 near
path44.
    This species has shortly-stalked
heads, and its leaves are hairless on the
upperside. Stems are only slightly
zigzag and usually hidden by other
vegetation. See Plate 15.

Knotted Clover *Trifolium striatum*
Native. Occasional. Verges, grassland.
May to June.
Kimmeridge: by NE side of bridle-
way18 near field corner 450m along
bridleway from road. **Worth:** N of
path18 20m W of where crossed by

Coast Path; near W edge of Worth
Cowleaze 80m S of Langton Road.
Knitson: on SW side of Purbeck Way
100m NW of top of zigzag track.
Godlingston Heath: on E side of bri-
dleway25 10m S of junction of bridle-
way25 and 27; near rabbit holes in rectangular fenced area 150m N of field
gate on N side of bridleway36.
Studland Heath: W side of Ferry
Road 250m N of Sewage Works
entrance; NW side of Ferry Road
250m NE of start of track to Jerry's
Point. **Sandbanks:** plentiful in lawn
from 5m S of entrance from Banks
Road to small triangular garden S of
junction of Banks and Shore Roads.
Branksome Chine: S-facing bank N of
road at sea end of chine.
    The only small pink clover with
leaves downy on both sides. Always in
small amounts; absent some years in
any given place.

Rough Clover *Trifolium scabrum*
Native. Occasional. Short grass, verges,
car parks. May to June.
Stoborough Heath: W side of
Furzebrook Road at paths5 and 37.
Hartland Moor: near gate at SW end
of bridleway4. **Wares (west):** near
Coast Path in SE of Nicholas Down;
very plentiful near Coast Path SE of
Seacombe Bottom; (east) on mound in
NE of Middle Field; on track up bottom of valley in White Ware 25m N of
Coast Path. **Knitson:** on SW side of
bridleway9 250m from SE end of bridleway. **Durlston:** on S side of path50
30m E of Lighthouse Field. **Townsend
Reserve:** on mound W of SW corner
of Manwell Field. **Studland Heath:**
bank SW of Knoll Beach toilets.

Haresfoot Clover *Trifolium arvense*
Native. Occasional. Verges, heaths, sta-
bilised dunes. June to August.

Hartland Moor: thinly scattered on South Middlebere. **Godlingston Heath:** plentiful in rectangular fenced area 150m N of field gate on N side of bridleway36. **Studland Heath:** SE side of Ferry Road 90m NE of track to Brand's Bay Hide on opposite side; also on War Hill. **Shell Bay:** W side of car park; E side of Ferry Road W of toilets; same side 100m and 150m N of ferry offices. **Luscombe Valley:** just S of pond. **Branksome Chine:** above promenade 525m SW of chine; by cliff-top path 210m SW of chine.

Subterranean Clover
Trifolium subterraneum
Native. Occasional. Short grassland. April to June.
Stoborough Heath: near top of NE side of track up to cairn from Soldiers Road. **Hartland Moor:** 5m E of Slepe Road opposite W end of White House Wood; by grassy track just W of gate NW of same wood (with other clovers). **Corfe:** SW of Monkey's Hump. **Worth:** plentiful by path16 N of St. Aldhelm's Head (working) Quarry 100m from bridleway15. **Arne:** in N end of triangular field S of car park 10 to 15m S of gate. **Godlingston Heath:** along 10m on E side of bridleway25 200m N of B3351. **Swanage:** lawn S of Health Centre. **Studland:** plentiful by path19 across field E of bridleway23. **Brownsea:** 20m E of churchyard. **Sandbanks:** around edge of lawn S of entrance to main car park. **Branksome Chine:** few scattered in lawn N of road at sea end of chine.

Often only two flowers together in the head, but they are conspicuous when flowering. See Plate 16.

Tree Lupin *Lupinus arboreus*
Introduction. Rare. Escape on dunes.

June to July.
Shell Bay: near ferry mostly E of road. **Sandbanks:** SE end of walled raised dune SW of main car park; inside fenced dunes 80m S of main car park.

Subject to mortal attack by blue-green Lupin aphid (*Macrosiphum albifrons*), so sites change.

Laburnum *Laburnum anagyroides*
Introduction. Rare. Escape on pavements. June.

Hybrid Laburnum *Laburnum* x *watereri* (*L. anagyroides* x *alpinum*)
Neophyte. Rare. Planted. June.
Herston (north): one can be seen at distance W from 200m N of stile at S end of path2.

Broom *Cytisus scoparius*
Native. Frequent. Verges, heaths. April to June.

Conspicuous and beautiful in bloom, north of chalk downs.

Dyer's Greenweed *Genista tinctoria*
Native. Rare. Grassland. June to July.
Swanage Railway: two in cutting on N side just E of A351 bridge SE of Corfe (fleeting glimpse from train). **Durlston:** many in S end of Johnston Meadow (spread from seed collected in Durlston); one plant 100m NNE of SW corner of Field 14. See Plate 16.

Petty Whin *Genista anglica*
Native. Occasional. Heaths. May to June.
Dorset Scarce. Near Threatened.
Stoborough Heath: in area of heath lacking scrub 200m due E of A351 roundabout 15m N of fence. **Hartland Moor:** about 10 plants on N side of Middle Fen 250m W of

Jubilee Bridge; over 25 plants for distance of 25m W of same bridge; few 60m E of same bridge; few on heath SW of Scotland by cattle track 130m ENE of the gateway located 180m NE of Slepe Road S cattle grid; few 400m N of Scotland Barn 60m E of Slepe Road (20m E of copse); more 75m E of Slepe Road 75m N of bridleway3 on E side of damp area.

Surprisingly difficult to find when not in flower. See Plate 16.

Mount Etna Broom *Genista aetnensis*
Introduction. Rare. Planted or self-seeding. August.
Sandbanks: on upper shore opposite W end of Chaddesley Glen.

No spines, few small leaves. When in flower it is a wonderful sight.

Gorse species are reputed to flower throughout the year, hence the old saying 'When gorse is out of bloom, kissing's out of season'. Western Gorse and Dwarf Gorse begin to flower in second week of July and former continues until November. Before they finish some Gorse (*Ulex europaeus*) bushes have begun to flower in mid-September. This latter species can be found in flower brightening up winter months and reaching its peak in late April, with some bushes continuing until early June. However, there are then four weeks when all gorse species are 'out of bloom' – so no kissing?

On **Godlingston Heath** all three species can be found in flower together in one place in late September and early October. Coming from Studland, follow bridleway23 until gate through fence into field S of Greenland Farm. Instead of going through gate, turn left and follow fence to its corner, then go SE for 75m. See Plate 17.

Gorse, Furze *Ulex europaeus*
Native. Abundant. Heaths, downs, woods, dunes, waste ground. Mid-September to early June.

Major problem on downs, where it screens out other species.

Western Gorse *Ulex gallii*
Native. Frequent. Heaths, verges, sandy cliffs, rarely on acid places on chalk downs; always with previous species. Mid-July to November.
Stoborough Heath: along 125m of SE edge of heath 100m NW of Halfway Inn; W side Soldiers Road 100m N of Hartland Stud private entrance. **Hartland Moor:** E side Slepe Road 220m S of start of track to Middlebere Farm. **Godlingston Heath:** by bridleway25 both just after gate to Heath itself from Golf Course; 200m further on. **Ulwell:** large area on top of down 175m SE of Obelisk. **Studland Heath:** small numbers thinly scattered on heath NW of Ferry Road between track to Brand's Bay Hide and track to Redhorn Quay. **Brownsea:** thinly scattered in long E-W stretch of Heather inland in SW of island. **Lilliput:** plentiful on Evening Hill (with some of next species). **Branksome Chine:** above esplanade 550m SW of chine.

Flowers are more golden than the previous and next species, though that is not always easy to assess unless they are seen together. Examine several flowers – longest petal usually 13-15mm; sepal tube usually over 9mm.

Dwarf Gorse *Ulex minor*
Native. Abundant. Heaths, commons, acid woodland tracks, sandy cliffs. July to October.
Grows to over 1m high on S side of **Corfe Common**, where it has been

mistaken for Western Gorse.

Examine several flowers – longest petal usually 8-12mm; sepal tube usually under 9mm; foliage distinctly smaller than the species above.

SEA-BUCKTHORN FAMILY
Sea-buckthorn
Hippophae rhamnoides
Introduction. Occasional. Planted or self-sown. April.
Worth: N side of road 50m W of Playing Field. **Langton:** several in recently planted National Trust wood S of junction of B3069 and E road to Worth (where they are doing much the best of several species planted, because deer respect their prickles!). **Swanage**: two just above promenade near its N end. **Sandbanks:** W of road at junction of Shore Road and Banks Road.

Hybrid Oleaster *Elaeagnus* x *submacrocarpa* (*E.* x *ebbingei*) (*E. macrocarpa* x *glabra* x *pungens*?) Introduction. Rare. Planted. October to November.
Evening Hill: low on slope towards SE end. **Sandbanks:** both near centre of raised dune at SW end of main car park; towards sea end of same dune. **Branksome Dene Chine:** slope on NE side near sea (binoculars).

WATER-MILFOIL FAMILY
Parrot's Feather
Myriophyllum aquaticum
Introduction. Rare. Escape in ponds. June to August.
Corfe: Middle Common Pond; private pond E of minor road NE of Afflington Farm (binoculars for detail). **Durlston:** Johnston Pond.

A distinctive invasive species that smothers ponds and should be controlled when found.

Spiked Water-milfoil
Myriophyllum spicatum
Native. Rare. River. June to August, but not seen flowering.
Wareham: in River Frome 450m upstream of South Bridge (boat).
Each leaf has 13 to 38 segments.

Alternate Water-milfoil
Myriophyllum alterniflorum
Native. Rare. Lakes, ditches. May to August, but not seen flowering.
Dorset Scarce.
The Moors: see p.27. **Studland Heath:** near two beaches of Western Arm of Little Sea; by Second Beach at SE of Little Sea; off many other parts of Little Sea shores.
Each leaf has 6 to 18 segments.

GIANT-RHUBARB FAMILY
Giant-rhubarb *Gunnera tinctoria*
Introduction. Rare. Planted.
Church Knowle: visible to W from path18 200m S of road.
It can be told from Brazilian Giant-rhubarb by the mainly cylindrical shape of the infloresence, rather than an oval shape; also by the spines which do not fully cover the leaf-stems.

PURPLE LOOSESTRIFE FAMILY
Purple Loosestrife *Lythrum salicaria*
Native. Occasional. Wet places, except bogs. July-August.
Holme: by ford in East Holme hamlet. **Creech:** E side of Grange Road opposite bridleway2. **Kimmeridge:** W side of road 25m S of T-junction N of Blackmanston Farm.
Stoborough: W of W-most part of path13. **Wareham:** W side of B3075 20m S of South Bridge. **Norden:** NE corner of Michael's Pond. **Corfe:** by A351 on SW side of Little East Common. **Harman's Cross:** by

path26 in second field N of A351 (between woods). **Swanage:** by Swan Brook at SW corner of main car and coach park. **Studland Heath:** by stream S of Knoll Beach car park.

Water-purslane *Lythrum portula*
Native. Occasional. Open acid places wet in winter. June to October.
Creech: by Army fence on Grange Heath SW of Drinking Barrow; bed of pond which dries in dry summer 250m from Grange Road on S side of bridleway1. **Hartland Moor:** much on NW side of N end of Upper Fen 550m NE of Isolation Cottages. **The Moors:** see p.27. **Corfe:** in places by Middle Common Pond. **Wytch:** on path80 50 and 70m W of Thrasher's Lane. **Godlingston Heath:** 100m SSW of true E junction of bridleways35 and 36 on right hand fork of field track. **Studland Heath:** S end of First Beach on SE side of Little Sea.

DAPHNE FAMILY
Spurge-laurel *Daphne laureola*
Native. Occasional. Woods over limestone. February.
Langton: here and there in NW of West Wood near stream and S of it (best site). **Durlston:** E of N-S track running between and roughly parallel to Durlston Road and Coast Path (probably planted) in two places – 65m S of main glade and 10m N of Long Meadow. **Swanage:** two escaped under hedge of E side of De Moulham Road 45m S of Walrond Road.

It is neither a Spurge nor a Laurel! Poisonous.

WITCH-HAZEL FAMILY
Sweet Gum *Liquidambar styraciflua*
Introduction. Rare. Planted.
Studland: triangle of land between Ferry Road and SE end of Wadmore Lane.

Leaves have splendid autumn colour.

WILLOWHERB FAMILY
Confusing specimens of *Epilobium* genus may be hybrids, some of which have been recorded in the past – see *The Flora of Dorset* (Bowen, 2000).

Great Willowherb
Epilobium hirsutum
Native. Abundant. Wet but not acid places, verges, waste ground. July to August.

Stem leaves (as for all *Epilobium* species) are opposite each other – compare with Rosebay (p.152).

Hoary Willowherb
Epilobium parviflorum
Native. Occasional. Wet places. July to September.
Wareham: on track 15m E of SW corner of Priory Meadow. **Furzebrook:** S side of E-most of three ponds in S of Kilnwood Reserve. **Hartland Moor:** thinly scattered through Middle Fen. **Corfe:** some wet areas of the Common. **Worth:** near top of flush in S end of Worth Field. **Wares (west)** and **(east):** in several flushes. **Langton:** by vehicular track to Crack Lane cemetery 30m from road entrance. **Herston (north):** N of path78 in SE corner of field SE of Herston Halt. **Swanage:** by path from Cauldron Barn Road to Victoria Avenue where it passes through E side of allotments (with three other species of Willowherb). **Studland:** 20m W of Ferry Road by bridleway38. **Brownsea:** by SE part of boardwalk through Orchid Meadow.

Four lobes of stigma are close together on young flowers and so are difficult to see.

Broad-leaved Willowherb
Epilobium montanum
Native. Frequent. Verges, arable fields, other disturbed ground. June to August.
Kimmeridge: plentiful by path2.
Corfe: along 15m of NW side of UCR beginning 15m SW of cattle grid at N edge of West Common.
Woolgarston: sides of bridleway23 especially 180-200m N of road.
Harman's Cross: by track to S platform of railway station; on W side of Haycraft's Lane 100m S of railway bridge; on NE side 150m SE of road to Downshay Farm. **Luscombe Valley:** 50m W of metal bridge by track in woodland. **Canford Cliffs:** towards N end of path between Brudenell and Nairn Roads.
Branksome Chine: plentiful on SW side of SE end of Chine gardens N of road.

Spear-leaved Willowherb
Epilobium lanceolatum
Native. Rare. Verges, gardens, other disturbed ground. July to August.
Dorset Scarce.
Wareham: on path near SW corner of Priory Meadow (much more Hoary Willowherb nearby). **Studland:** SE side of Beach Road 30-50m NE of junction with Rectory Lane.

Square-stalked Willowherb
Epilobium tetragonum
Native. Frequent. Arable fields, other disturbed ground. July to August.
   No glandular hairs on sepals or seedcase (lens). Leaves usually <u>but not always strap-shaped</u>.

Short-fruited Willowherb
Epilobium obscurum
Native. Occasional. Wood rides, verges. July to August.

Hartland Moor: by fence corner post on S side of Snag Valley 300m W of Slepe Road; along small stream in NW of heath SW of Scotland.
Wytch: on SW side of bridleway4 275m NW of Thrasher's Lane.
Swanage: by path from Cauldron Barn Road to Victoria Avenue where it passes through E side of allotments (with three other species of Willowherb). Single specimens elsewhere have not been listed because of impermanence.
   Glandular hairs on sepals, and sometimes a few on the top end of the seedcase (lens).

American Willowherb
Epilobium ciliatum
Introduction. Frequent. Arable fields, other disturbed ground. June to August.
   Glandular hairs on sepals and on the whole of the seedcase (lens).

Marsh Willowherb
Epilobium palustre
Native. Occasional. Marshes – often with other willowherbs. July to August.
Hartland Moor: thinly scattered in Upper and Middle Fens; on Langton Wallis Heath 300m NNE of Langton Wallis close to Bog Myrtle. **Corfe:** thinly scattered through NW side of West Common – e.g. at map references SY95478118 and 95498132; by Middle Common Pond. **Shell Bay:** in marsh 150m S of NE end of boardwalk
   Leaves are very narrow, flowers usually bent over.

Rosebay *Chamerion angustifolium*
Native. Frequent. Verges, cleared woodland, burnt heath. July to August.

Steeple: along 20m N of road 60m E of viewpoint. **Kimmeridge:** SW of bridleway18 50m from road at NW end. **Church Knowle:** near top of down slope N of junction of bridleway39 and paths3 and 5. **Norden:** N side of bridleway77 by W cattle grid. **Swanage Railway:** between A351 bridge W of Woodyhyde Farm and Harman's Cross (good displays); on S side E of Herston Halt station. **Worth:** near S end of path13. **Langton:** by path31 S of Acton village. **Kingswood:** B3351 viewpoint. **Townsend Reserve:** several areas near Burry's Circle. **Brownsea:** recently cleared areas.

Stem leaves alternate, not opposite each other as in Great Willowherb (p.151).

Some years ago it occurred in vast quantity on part of Hartland Moor after a fire, but within a year or two it was very much reduced by beetles.

Large-flowered Evening-primrose
Oenothera glazoviana
Introduction. Occasional. Escape on verges, dunes. June to September.
Stoborough: SW side of A351 just NW of Blue Pool Exit Road. **Norden:** NE side of A351 250m NW of bridleway77. **Worth:** by Renscombe Farm. **Harman's Cross:** by permissive bridleway S of large barn at Quarr Farm. **Swanage:** N of centre of Northbrook Road Cemetery. **Studland Heath:** dunes around three sides of Knoll Beach café. **Lilliput:** plentiful on Evening Hill. **Sandbanks:** here and there inside and outside wire-fenced dunes behind beach SW of main car park; scattered in dunes up to 450m NE of main car park (with Fragrant Evening Primrose at some sites). **Branksome Chine:** near top and bottom of first way down cliff E of Library.

Intermediate Evening-primrose
Oenothera x *fallax*
(*O. glazoviana* x *biennis*)
Introduction. Rare. Escape on verges. June to September.
Sandbanks: towards E end of path between and parallel to Grasmere and Seacombe Roads.

Evening-primroses are very prone to hybridisation, as is helpfully explained in both *The Wild Flower Key* (Rose & O'Reilly, 2006) and *Wild Flowers of Britain and Ireland* (Blamey, Fitter & Fitter, 2003).

Small-flowered Evening-primrose
Oenothera cambrica
Introduction. Occasional. Escape on verges, dunes. June to September.
Studland: 350m SW-wards along B3351 from crossroads in village centre on NE side of road. **Shell Bay:** roadsides N and S of toll-booths. **Sandbanks:** top of beach 130m NE of Midway Path; SE side of main car park 40m SW of hedge across middle of car park. **Canford Cliffs:** above promenade 300m NE of Canford Cliffs Chine.

Fragrant Evening-primrose
Oenothera stricta
Introduction. Rare. Escape on dunes. June to September.
Sandbanks: here and there behind wire-fenced dunes at top of beach for 100m SW of main car park; scattered in dunes for 300m NE of main car park (with Large-flowered Evening Primrose at both sites).

Flowers turn orange when going over; narrow leaves.

Fuchsia *Fuchsia magellanica*
Introduction. Rare. Escape. June to October.
Swanage: high on cliff 10-15m N of N end of promenade (binoculars).

Enchanter's-nightshade
Circaea lutetiana
Native. Frequent. Woods, shady
verges, gardens. June to July.

If you walk through it when it is in
seed (especially in July and August)
you may spend much time picking its
little burs off your clothing after-
wards.

DOGWOOD FAMILY

Dogwood *Cornus sanguinea*
Native. Frequent. Hedges and scrub
on calcareous soils, roadsides. June.
Ridge: plentiful along N half of SE
side of New Road. **Church Knowle:**
W of village N of crossroads along
first 50m of E side of road to
Cocknowle. **Corfe:** along 15m of S
side of Sandy Hill Lane 75m E of railway bridge. **Bushey:** S side of B3351
50-250m W of UCR which passes
Rollington Farm. **Langton:** by
Haycraft's Lane (especially S end); on
N side of bridleway42 80m E of NW
corner of Langton West Wood. **Wares
(west):** N edge of Scratch Arse Ware
140-160 and 220-230m E of N corner
at W end. **Herston (north):** S side of
path23 opposite S end of path2.
Swanage: plenty on N side of
Washpond Lane for some distance E
of Northbrook Road. **Ulwell:** around
Y-shaped road junction N of Round
Down.

Twigs are crimson, fruits purplish-
black.

Red-osier Dogwood *Cornus sericea*
Introduction. Rare. Planted or escape.
Mid-June to August.
Corfe: SW of path18 (which runs
along field edge – not across field)
70m N of stream bridge.

Twigs deep red or olive; fruits
white. Stace (1997) thinks it may be
same species as next.

White Dogwood *Cornus alba*
Introduction. Rare. Planted. Mid-June
to August.
Church Knowle: E side of path69
opposite NE part of camping site.
Studland Heath: SE of Knoll Beach
dinghy park N of stream E of bridge.

Twigs are bright red, fruits white.

Spotted Laurel *Aucuba japonica*
Introduction. Occasional. Planted
and sometimes self-seeding. April to
May.
Kingston: by junction of paths50 and
51. **Durlston:** several unspotted near
summer-dry stream in NE of Country
Park within 25m of gate from
Durlston Road (with Cherry Laurels
and one Portugal Laurel); two further
E. **Swanage:** SW corner of the Downs
50m N of gate. **Studland:** W side of
permissive path towards SE end of
South Beach 10m up from beach.

Leaves are usually, but not always,
variegated. At flowering times, female
bushes still carry fruit from the previous year.

SANDALWOOD FAMILY
Stars-in-grass *Thesium humifusum*
Native. Occasional. Short calcareous
grassland. June to August.
Nationally Scarce.
Steeple: very plentiful on Steeple
Down (west) from 80-120m E of
bend in bridleway3 from bottom
of Down upwards for 20m. **Corfe:**
scattered on Down N of Purbeck Way
150m W of radio mast on Rollington
Hill. **Wares:** widely scattered at at
least 35 sites – main groups of sites as
follows: **(west)** towards S tip of Long
Close; towards SE corner of Long
Close; towards S end of steep W-
facing slope in Cliff Middle Field;
adjoining S-facing slope at W extremity of Hedbury Ware; **(east)** in W of

both Middle Field and Middle Ground; on SW-facing slopes of Golter; scattered in SW of Verney Ware; near E end of track across middle of Western Mileposts Ware; 10m E of stile half way up W side of Belle Vue West Ware; several places near Coast Path in Belle Vue West Ware; N of Coast Path in Belle Vue Middle Ware 40m from W wall; scattered in NW of same Ware. **Townsend Reserve:** 90m SE of NW entrance; at Burry's Circle; W of path56 40m S of where paths46 and 56 cross; on bank 10m W of SW corner of SE Bastion. **Durlston:** by track 40m E of Belle Vue East Ware 20m N of Coast Path; S of path53 in NE corner of Field 6; NE of shallow quarry in NE of Field 14; in NE of Lighthouse Field 40m from NE gate 15m S of path50; just W of Eastern Mile Posts; between them.

Quite unlike Toadflaxes, except perhaps when in young leaf and very small. It is deserving and worthy of its new name. See Plate 17.

MISTLETOE FAMILY
Mistletoe *Viscum album*
Native. Rare. Parasitic on trees.
Bushey: N side of Bushey Lane on Hawthorn 75m E of bridleway10; 175m further E on S side of Lane high up on two Hybrid Black Poplars.

Poisonous. May be grown on apple tree by rubbing the berries into the cracks of the bark, and waiting two or three years to germinate.

SPINDLE FAMILY
Spindle *Euonymus europaeus*
Native. Occasional. Hedges, woods, scrub. May to June.
Steeple: in two places on NE side of road by Beach Coppice. **Kingston:** on NW side of path44 40m from N end

of path. **Harman's Cross:** E side of Haycraft's Lane 20m N of path22.
Woolgarston: S side of road 150m E of N end of Tabbit's Hill Lane.
Bushey: by bridleway15 – 200, 300 and 400m from SE end. **Langton:** SE corner of Langton West Wood.
Kingswood: S side of B3351 10m W of bridleway16. **Godlingston:** S side of Washpond Lane 50m E of cemetery entrance. **Durlston:** E side of Lighthouse Road 60, 110 and 160m S of NW corner of Long Meadow (introduced form – its autum colour is more dramatic). **Studland:** several NW of Studland Wood near Coast Path.

Poisonous.

Evergreen Spindle
Euonymus japonicus
Introduction. Occasional. Planted and self-seeding. June.
Wareham: SW of South Bridge.
Langton: W side of Durnford Drove 40m before car park at S end.
Durlston: much – especially on W side of Lighthouse Road.

HOLLY FAMILY
Holly *Ilex aquifolium*
Native. Abundant. Woods, hedges, scrub, cliffs.

BOX FAMILY
Box *Buxus sempervirens*
Native in few places in S England, but introduced here. Rare. Planted.
Ulwell: several on E side of path16 by ruined building 175m N of S end of path. **Brownsea:** NE part of Venetia Park E of path.

SPURGE FAMILY
Dog's Mercury *Mercurialis perennis*
Native. Abundant. Woods, verges, by walls. February to May.

Annual Mercury *Mercurialis annua*
Early Introduction. Frequent. Arable
fields, beaches, other disturbed
ground especially in gardens and
allotments (when not weeded). All
year.
Stoborough Heath: few 20m W of
Furzebrook Road on N side of track S
of houses connecting road to path5.
Church Knowle: N side of road
150m W of path2. **Worth:** E side of
road E of village pond. **Harman's
Cross:** by road and path6 at New
Barn. **Durlston:** flowerbeds of Visitor
Centre. **Swanage:** flowerbeds near
Health Centre. **Studland:** near NE
corner of Middle Beach car park.
Shell Bay: in front of toilets.
Brownsea: flowerbeds by track W of
Landing Pier; plentiful on beach from
100m NW of SW corner of island
round to 300m E of same corner.

Broad-leaved Spurge
Euphorbia platyphyllos
Early Introduction. Rare. Arable
fields. June to October.
Dorset Scarce.
Kingston: here and there by S side of
West Street along 500m beyond W
edge of The Plantation. **Wares (east):**
usually visible over gate at NE corner
of Golter field in field to E (especially
with short range binoculars).

Similar, and in similar habitat, to
next species. Leaf-bases heart-shaped
rather than tapered and fruits warted
rather than nearly smooth (lens).

Sun Spurge *Euphorbia helioscopia*
Early Introduction. Frequent. Arable
fields, other disturbed ground. April
to October.
Wares (east): unusually small plants
on SE-facing slope of White Ware
50m NE of SW corner.

Compare with species above.

Caper Spurge *Euphorbia lathyris*
Early Introduction. Occasional.
Gardens, verges, waste ground. June
to July.
Holme: by churchyard gate
(approach via Holme Priory drive).
Swanage Railway: N side 50m W
of Victoria Avenue bridge (binoculars); S side 300m W of Northbrook Road bridge (from train).
Swanage: halfway up E side of
Sentry Road. **Studland:** visible
when plants are tall from middle of
path5 looking S. **Shell Bay:** one or
two on W side of car park some
years. **Brownsea:** near entrance to
The Villa. **Sandbanks:** E end of
path from SE end of Chaddesley
Glen to beach on both sides of
upper steps.

Poisonous.

Dwarf Spurge *Euphorbia exigua*
Early Introduction. Occasional.
Arable fields, gardens, other disturbed ground, steep downs, pavements. June to October.
Near Threatened.
Church Knowle: small areas of
steep Down N of village at map references SY93988222 and 94428223.
Kingston: by N side of West Street
450m W of edge of The Plantation.
Wares (west): 250m from sea on
upper half of SW-facing slope on E
side of Seacombe Bottom 80m from
path11. **Woolgarston:** at high point
on bridleway20 120m SE of N end
of bridleway24 go N-wards through
scrub onto rough area of Ailwood
Down – plants are 50m N of
bridleway20 at map reference
SY99728126 on W side of cattle
track. **Durlston:** infrequently on
mound by track in SE corner of
Holecombe (field) when ground
disturbed.

Petty Spurge *Euphorbia peplus*
Early Introduction. Frequent.
Arable fields, gardens, other disturbed ground. All year.

Portland Spurge
Euphorbia portlandica
Native. Occasional. Cliffs, cliff-tops. May to August.
Tyneham: SW corner of Worbarrow Tout (from top of Tout descend path on SW side; use binoculars before path gets too narrow).
Durlston: one on S side of Coast Path 40m W of E wall of Field 6A; here and there by narrow climbers' track above cliff-top (S of Coast Path) S of Field 10A for 180m (take care). **Swanage:** bare crumbling cliff 50m N of E end of path down cliff from Burlington Road (binoculars). **Ballard Down:** base of chalk cliffs 150m E of W end of chalk (easiest site but longish walk).

Sea Spurge *Euphorbia paralias*
Native. Rare. Sandy shores. July to September.
Dorset Rare.
Sandbanks: back of dunes at both 130m SW and 450m NE of main car park.

Figert's Spurge
Euphorbia x pseudoesula
(*E. esula x cyparissias*)
Introduction. Rare. Escape. June to July.
Ballard Down: N side of Shep's Hollow W of top of steps to beach (very much reduced since landslip). Originally misidentified by this author and therefore wrongly recorded in *The Flora of Dorset* as Twiggy Spurge, *Euphorbia x pseudovirgata*. This is the first site in Dorset.

Wood Spurge
Euphorbia amygdaloides
Native. Occasional. Old woods.
March to May.
Creech: plentiful on NW side of road above Great Wood 50m NE of '20' sign; here and there on SE side of same road passing through wood. **Bushey:** by bridleway14 30m SW of junction of bridleways14 and 15. **King's Wood:** here and there but especially by bridleway16 100m NW of lower gate at top of wood.

Leathery Wood Spurge *Euphorbia amygdaloides* subsp. *robbiae*
Introduction. Occasional. Spreading on to verges from gardens. February to May.
Ridge: S side of Barnhill Road 150m W of Sunnyside (road).
Corfe: plentiful by brook in open area in middle of Byle Copse.
Swanage: W side of Ulwell Road opposite No.38. **Studland:** SW corner of village crossroads; E side of Ferry Road 40m N of same crossroads; N side of W end of Beach Road.

Mediterranean Spurge *Euphorbia characias* subsp. *characias*
Introduction. Rare. Escape. March to May.
Canford Cliffs: one clump high on cliff 275m SW of Flaghead Chine (a telescope is necessary to identify the subspecies by the dark colour of its glands).

Euphorbia characias subsp. *wulfenii*
Introduction. Rare. Escape. March to May.
Canford Cliffs: two clumps high on cliff 250m SW of Flaghead Chine (a telescope is necessary to identify it by the pale colour of its glands).

BUCKTHORN FAMILY

Alder Buckthorn *Frangula alnus*
Native. Occasional. Acid woods and
hedges. Late May to mid-June.
Stoborough Heath: N side of track to
Stoborough Heath from New Road
20-40m E of road (small plants).
Ridge: NW side of Barnhill Road N
of path12; N side of Arne Road 250m
E of Sunnyside (road). **Hartland
Moor:** halfway along E side of E part
of Arne Triangle (with other trees); on
island of scrub in Tramway Bog 75m
SE of Post Pool; NE side of Slepe
Road 30m NW of N cattle grid; E side
of Slepe Road 575m N of sharp corner
by Scotland; both sides of bridleway4
along S side of White House Wood.
Arne: SE side of Arne Road 900m NE
of Bank Gate Cottages. **Brownsea:**
near S end of short-cut track from near
Two-level Hide to The Villa.
Poisonous.

VINE FAMILY

False Virginia Creeper
Parthenocissus inserta
Introduction. Occasional. Planted or
escape.
Godlingston: by path1 near its NW
end. **Townsend Reserve:** by E end of
permissive bridleway (mistakenly
recorded as Boston-ivy in *The Flora of
Dorset*). **Brownsea:** W end of
Maryland ruins. **Branksome Dene
Chine:** E-facing car park bank near
sea.
Tendrils do not have adhesive discs
on the ends.

FLAX FAMILY

Pale Flax *Linum bienne*
Native. Frequent. Calcareous mead-
ows, verges, quarries. May to July.
Holme: scattered along NW side of
B3070 375-550m SW of Holme Lane.
Rempstone: here and there on verges

of bridleway34 (Oil Road). **Wares
(west and east):** plentiful on slopes
above Coast Path. **Durlston:** plentiful
in meadows in Country Park.
Swanage: NW corner of Playing Field
N of Swan Brook S of Victoria
Avenue. **Luscombe Valley:** plentiful at
S end.
As many flowers drop petals around
midday, they need to be seen in their
glory in the morning.

Flax *Linum usitatissimum*
Introduction. Rare. Escape. June to
July.

Fairy Flax *Linum catharticum*
Native. Frequent. Downs, lime-based
verges. May to August.

Allseed *Radiola linoides*
Native. Occasional. Tracks on acid
soil, short vegetation on heaths, firm
sand at rear of dunes; always where wet
in winter. June to September.
Dorset Scarce. Near Threatened.
Stoborough Heath: thinly scattered
along 140m of SW side of track which
leads NW from its junction with
Purbeck Way 250m S of A351; on and
near track running S 350 and 400m S
of junction just to E of previous junction; along 120m S-N of permissive
bridleway 10m E of and parallel to
Dismantled Tramway NW of
Hartland Stud; along 30m S-N 30m
W of gate from Stud to heath.
Hartland Moor: on track E of Soldiers
Road parallel to it both 325m SW of S
cattle grid and 150m NE of same grid;
20m SW of Slepe Road on track N of
and parallel to old tramway. **Wytch:** on
path80 130, 290-300, 320 and 410m
W of Thrasher's Lane; near NW corner of open access part of Thrasher's
Heath; especially plentiful towards SW
corner of same Heath. **Studland:** near

track in NE of Harmony Farm NW Field; plentiful along track in Harmony Farm NE Field. **Studland Heath:** SW of Study Centre at Knoll Beach; E of Heather Walk 200m N of Knoll Beach main N car park.

Amounts vary greatly from year to year according to weather and open-ness of ground. When found, look for the inconspicuous species Chaffweed and Yellow Centaury which may be nearby. See Plate 17.

MILKWORT FAMILY
Common Milkwort *Polygala vulgaris*
Native. Frequent. Short, usually slop-ing, grassland – mainly on calcareous or neutral soil. April to July.
Wares (west and east), Durlston, Ballard Down: plentiful on each.

Inner sepals are dull blue, purple or white, with several veins making loops, which can still be seen when sepals have turned green (see drawing). Upper stems are usually slanting. Usually no rosette of leaves on the lower stem (compare with Chalk Milkwort, see below).

Heath Milkwort *Polygala serpyllifolia*
Native. Frequent. Heaths, wood rides on acid soil, acid places on top of downs. May to July.
Studland: several albinos on Harmony Farm NW Field 150m N of gate at

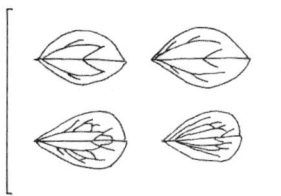

Inner Sepals of Milkworts – Common (below) and Chalk (above).

centre of E-W part of Agglestone Road.

Lower leaves usually opposite, if not fallen from old plants.

Chalk Milkwort *Polygala calcarea*
Native. Frequent. Short calcareous grassland, though more on Purbeck limestone than on chalk. April to July.
Wares (east): E side of White Ware.
Godlingston Hill: S-facing slope of N arm of E end of hill 200-400m W of road. **Durlston:** beautiful patches on brow of downland; by old shallow quarry in NE of Field 14.

Inner sepals are bright blue, pink or white, with one loop each side or none, which can still be seen when sepals have turned green (see drawing). Upper stems are usually upright, rosette of leaves on lower stems (com-pare with Common Milkwort, above).

HORSE CHESTNUT FAMILY
Horse Chestnut
Aesculus hippocastanum
Introduction. Frequent. Planted and self-seeding. May.
Fruits are round, with prickles.

Indian Horse Chestnut
Aesculus indica
Introduction. Rare. Planted. June.
Brownsea: NW side of Church Field; W of Visitor Centre; S of track 150m W of Landing Pier.

Flowers later than previous species; fruits are oblong-oval or pear-shaped, without prickles.

MAPLE FAMILY
Norway Maple *Acer platanoides*
Introduction. Occasional. Planted and self-seeding. Woods, verges.
Stoborough Heath: 50m E of Grange Road on N side of path9.
Corfe: by stream W of castle.

Leaves of Norway Maple (above) and Sycamore. Former can be 35% larger, latter 45% larger.

Harman's Cross: W side of Haycraft's Lane on N side of road to Downshay Farm. **Knitson:** W side of road to New Barn 50 and 150m S of T-junction at N end. **Swanage Railway:** on S side just E of Herston Halt station. **Swanage:** in small young copse on SW side of S end of Benlease Way; middle of copse W of D'Urberville Drive on both sides of path. **Durlston:** SE of pedestrian entrance to woods in NE of Country Park 10m NE of shed. **Studland Heath:** E side of Ferry Road just N of Knoll Beach Road. **Canford Cliffs:** E side of Bessborough Road 150m from S end. See drawing.

Sycamore *Acer pseudoplatanus*
Introduction. Abundant. Planted and self-seeding. Woods, hedges, verges, dunes.
   Attractive when seedcases are turning red on some trees in June.

Field Maple *Acer campestre*
Native, also planted. Frequent. Woods, hedges, verges.
   Yellow leaves stand out in autumn.

Red Maple *Acer rubrum*
Introduction. Rare. Planted.
Holme: junction of Holme Lane with road to East Holme.

SUMACH FAMILY
Stagshorn Sumach *Rhus typhina*
Introduction. Occasional. Escape; usually suckers from nearby gardens.
Stoborough: SW side of B3075 25m S of N part of Old Furzebrook Road.
Swanage: E side of Sentry Road more than halfway up; N side of Peveril Point Road at E-most bend.
Sandbanks: by S half of W of two paths between Grasmere and Seacombe Roads. **Canford Cliffs:** N side of Bodley Road towards E end.

WOOD SORREL FAMILY
Procumbent Yellow Sorrel
Oxalis corniculata
Introduction. Rare. Escape. May to September.
Durlston: by The Lookout café.
Studland: junction of Watery Lane and Manor Road.
   Creeping, with stems frequently rooting; leaves are often purple, with simple hairs; 2 to 8 flowers together, each 9-16mm across; seed capsule is cylindrical.

Least Yellow Sorrel *Oxalis exilis*
Introduction. Rare. Escape. June to September.
Kimmeridge: S side of path through Kimmeridge Farm. April to September.
   Creeping, with stems frequently rooting; leaves are never purple, have simple hairs; flowers singly, 4-8mm across; seed capsule is nearly round.

Upright Yellow Sorrel *Oxalis stricta*
Introduction. Rare. Escape. June to
September.
Stoborough: pavement edge towards
NE end of NW side of Tuckers Mill
Close. **Swanage:** by E end of front of
Cricket Ground pavilion (off Ulwell
Road).

Fairly upright, with stems rarely
rooting; leaves are sometimes purple,
with more than one hair from common base.

Pink Sorrel *Oxalis articulata*
Introduction. Frequent, especially in
Poole. Escape on verges, waste
ground, cliffs. March to October.

Wood Sorrel *Oxalis acetosella*
Native. Occasional. Woods. April to
May.
East Creech: by stream on N side of
Caldecot's Wood 130m W of
path32. **Furzebrook:** plentiful in
old woodland in Kilnwood Reserve
especially E of central field.
Langton: scattered in West Wood
by rides. **Bushey:** 10m SW of gate
on bridleway14 at S side of wood.
Rempstone: on E side of bridle-
way16 25m S of B3351.
Kingswood: SE of bridleway87
30m SW of E corner of King's
Wood.

Pale Pink Sorrel *Oxalis incarnata*
Introduction. Rare. Escape. May to
July.
Swanage: much in middle of little-
used passageway between Kings
Road East and Spring Hill (S of
Eldon Terrace). **Studland:** on
stonework by toilets at junction of
Manor road and Watery Lane.
Sandbanks: by W end of path
between and parallel to Grasmere
and Seacombe Roads.

GERANIUM FAMILY
Druce's Cranesbill *Geranium* x
oxonianum (*G. endressii* x *versicolor*)
Introduction. Occasional. Escape.
June to August.
Hartland Moor: behind Early
Goldenrod 4m N of Arne Road
opposite gate at N end of Soldiers
Road. **Corfe:** on path between
Tilbury Mead and Battle Mead 25m
from latter. **Swanage:** W end of copse
W of D'Urberville Drive. **Studland:**
10m N of SE corner of Glebeland
Estate on E side of bridleway12.
Brownsea: S of track W of buildings
near Landing Pier. **Lilliput:** near N
end of path from Alington Close to
Shore Road.

A fertile hybrid which has been
interbred with its parents to produce
various intermediate cultivars. Petals
are a shade of pink, usually with darker veins; if veins are not darker, the
length of style is usually greater than
4mm, compared with 2.5-3mm for its
plain pink parent *G. endressi.*

Round-leaved Cranesbill
Geranium rotundifolium
Native. Occasional. Roadsides. April
to June.
Swanage: N side of Court Road 10-
20m W of railway bridge; on N side
of E end of Washpond Lane; sometimes at W end of Ballard Way.
Ulwell: numbers vary (due to spray-
ing) on NE side of Ulwell Road from
Ulwell Farm to Whitecliff Road
(especially by end of path15, 100m SE
of that; also near Whitecliff Road).

Meadow Cranesbill
Geranium pratense
Native, but probably escape in this
area. Rare. Verges. June to July.
Ridge: S side Arne Road 200 m E of
New Road. **Kingswood:** S side of

B3351 50m W of end of bridleway29 opposite (sometimes gets mown). See Plate 18.

Long-stalked Cranesbill
Geranium columbinum
Native. Occasional. Grazed S-facing limestone especially near scrub; best sites are where Gorse is controlled by burning from time to time. May to July.
Steeple: on Steeple Down (west) 225m E of bend in bridleway3.
Church Knowle: plentiful on section of downland through which bridle-way39 runs N of village especially by bridleway (joint best site). **Corfe:** below SW side of UCR 110m SE of mast at top of Rollington Hill (with Field Pepperwort). **Wares (west):** upper half of SW-facing slope on E side of Seacombe Bottom both opposite start of S-running track branching off path11 100m S of junction of valleys and also 250m from sea 80m from path11. **Knitson:** plentiful on downland between bridleways8 and 9 (joint best site, despite Gorse); halfway on N side of lower section of zigzag track.
Ballard Down: widely scattered on S side especially by Purbeck Way.

Flowers are bell-shaped, not usually pointing upwards.

Cut-leaved Cranesbill
Geranium dissectum
Early Introduction. Frequent. Grassland, verges, gardens. May to July.

Hedgerow Cranesbill
Geranium pyrenaicum
Introduction. Occasional. Escape on verges, where it gets cut. June to October.
Norden: along 7m of NE side of A351 250m SE of railway bridge. **Harman's Cross:** along 15m of N side of A351

50m W of path41. **Swanage:** SW side of Ulwell Road 10m SE of Washpond Lane (nearly albino). **Studland:** E verge of road by Clayton Meadow (small flowers). **Branksome Chine:** E of Library on E side of road to cliff-top car park.

Small-flowered Cranesbill
Geranium pusillum
Native. Occasional. Grassland, verges. May to September.
Wareham: N of Purbeck Way by E side of South Bridge. **Kimmeridge:** by bridleway18 near field corner 450m along from road at NW end.
Stoborough: NE side of A351 by metal hatch 300m NW of Dismantled Tramway. **Norden:** W side of S end of Slepe Road in field gateway (with next species). **Durlston:** in grass around S end of W side car park. **Branksome Chine:** in grass strip on pavement on SE side of Westminster Road just E of path to Promenade.

Not appearing each year in each place. Flowers are mauve, hairs on flower stalks are all short (lens) – compare with next species. Lack of anthers on outer five filaments is difficult to see.

Dove's-foot Cranesbill
Geranium molle
Native. Frequent. Grassland, arable fields, other disturbed ground, gardens. April to September.
Albinos as follows – **Worth:** frequent in valley W of St. Aldhelm's Head working quarry; **Wytch:** E side of Thrasher's Lane 100m S of SE corner of Thrasher's Heath; **Studland Heath:** NE corner of Redhorn Quay; **Lilliput:** NW of area of seats on centre of Evening Hill.

Flowers are pink; hairs on flower stalks are both short and long (lens).

Shining Cranesbill
Geranium lucidum
Native. Rare. Verges. May to July.
Corfe: W end of W arm of Battle
Mead (road). **Worth:** in Hill Bottom
hamlet usually one on bank or wall
opposite Rose Cottage. **Studland:**
few on verge by SW corner of
Clayton Meadow.
Impermanent at other sites where it
has occurred.

Herb Robert *Geranium robertianum*
Native. Abundant. Woods, verges,
gardens, shingle beaches. March to
October.
Albinos as follows – **Hartland Moor:**
E side of Soldiers Road 425m N of
track to Isolation Cottages, **Langton:**
W side of western ride at map reference SY99057949 10m N of a W-E
ride, **Studland:** near junction of
bridleway23 with path20; by E end
of path3 down cliff to South Beach,
Canford Cliffs: in N of grounds of
church in Chaddesley Glen.

Sea Storksbill *Erodium maritimum*
Native. Occasional. Bare, dry places,
usually near sea. May to August.
Brownsea: plentiful – especially in
suitable places on and near S and W
shore; present on low wall NW of
Visitor Centre; in NW of churchyard.
Most flowers lack petals; when
present they are tiny.

Musk Storksbill
Erodium moschatum
Early Introduction. Rare. Short grass
near the sea. March to July.
Dorset Scarce.
Canford Cliffs: plentiful between
Cliff Drive and cliff-top especially at
SW end. **Branksome Chine:** cliff-top
100m SW of chine.

Common Storksbill
Erodium cicutarium
Native. Frequent. Bare, dry, usually
sandy soil, usually near sea. April to
August.
Flower size varies considerably. Can
be sticky, and mistaken for Sticky
Storksbill. (Latter needs to be identi-
fied by examining the seeds with a lens;
then check with an expert.)

BALSAM FAMILY
Indian (Himalayan) Balsam
Impatiens glandulifera
Introduction. Occasional. Escape on
damp verges, streamsides. July to
October.
Worth: E of path13 75m S of junction
of paths13 and 14; several places S of
that by same path. **Ower:** SW of
Newton Copse by bridleway35.
Studland: both sides at low point in
Ferry Road N of centre of village; small
amount by stream NE of Middle
Beach car park 15m upstream from
beach; plentiful by Watery Lane from
junction of Manor Road towards
beach. **Studland Heath:** S side of
Knoll Beach Road W of S car park.
Attractive invader that dominates
watersides in some parts of Britain, yet
it cannot spread much further at most
sites above; popping its nearly ripe seed
heads is fun.

IVY FAMILY
Ivy *Hedera helix*
Native. Abundant. Woods, hedges,
rocks, quarries, cliffs, walls. September
to November.
The national collection of Ivies at
Pebworth, Worcester, featured 365
named species and varieties by 2004,
most of them are cultivars of this
species. No cultivar is recorded as having escaped in this area yet.
Poisonous.

CARROT FAMILY

The shape of seeds in this family is a useful aid for identification; sometimes overlooked.

Marsh Pennywort *Hydrocotyle vulgaris*
Native. Frequent. Wet ground except acid bogs. June to August.

Flowers are inconspicuous.

Sanicle *Sanicula europaea*
Native. Occasional. Old woods, shady places. May to June.
Holme: in open access woodland SW of East Holme 20m NE of SW corner of wood. **Creech:** SE side of road through Great Wood in several places. **East Creech:** by sides of path32 through woods N of Stonehill Down 60-65m S of N edge of wood. **Langton:** E of large marshy pond in NW of West Wood. **Harman's Cross:** by path44 steps down railway embankment into The Wilderness. **Bushey:** here and there by SW half of bridleway14. **Rempstone:** on E side of bridleway16 100m S of B3351. **Knitson:** on S side of bridleway8 just W of junction with bridleway12. **Godlingston:** on E side of Burnham's Lane W of Marsh Copse 10m S of entrance to caravan field on opposite side. **Studland Heath:** with Primroses on Primrose Way. **Branksome Chine:** E side of stream 500m up Chine from road at SE end.
Usually few.

Blue Eryngo *Eryngium planum*
Introduction. Rare. Escape. July to August.
Shell Bay: W side of Ferry Road 5m S of restaurant.

Rough Chervil
Chaerophyllum temulum
Native. Frequent. By hedges. June to July.

Holme: NE side of bridleway3 at Doreys Farm. **Furzebrook:** on E side of Furzebrook Road just S of Purbeck Way SSE of Blue Pool. **Church Knowle:** SW side of road 65-80m NW of bridge at Puddle Mill Farm. **Corfe:** NW side of road to Church Knowle 20m SW of lay-by at NE end of road (with Hedge Parsley); plentiful on both sides of Sandy Hill Lane 350m W of Sandyhills Farm. **Worth:** by gate on Coast Path just S of Hill Bottom hamlet. **Wares (east):** SE side of junction of Priest's Way with path46. **Durlston:** by hedges both in Hoggett Mead; in S end of Johnston Meadow. **Townsend Reserve:** 10m N of S edge 80m from W edge.
Stems blotched purple.

Queen Anne's Lace, Cow Parsley
Anthriscus sylvestris
Native. Abundant. Woods, verges, except on acid soils. April to June.

Bur Chervil *Anthriscus caucalis*
Native. Rare. Stable sand with some shade. May to June.
Dorset Scarce.
Hartland Moor: under hedge N of large barns on E side of track to Middlebere Farm. **Shell Bay:** S edge of copse N of restaurant (permission has been given to go over low wire fence to view).

Shepherd's Needle
Scandix pecten-veneris
Early Introduction. Rare. Arable fields, other disturbed ground. April to May.
Dorset Rare. Critically Endangered.
Worth: S side of Coast Path in two patches 600m E of Coastwatch Station.

Alexanders *Smyrnium olusatrum*
Early Introduction. Frequent. Verges, rough ground. March to May.

Church Knowle: plentiful by road up hill by Cocknowle. **Corfe:** particularly plentiful on W side of Castle Mound. **Swanage:** plentiful on SW side of Ulwell Road SE of Washpond Lane.

Pignut *Conopodium majus*
Native. Frequent. Woods, verges, undisturbed fields. May to June.
Holme: W side of East Holme churchyard (approach via Priory drive). **Kingston:** by path41 50m S of S end of South Street. **Corfe:** plentiful on N face of castle mound opposite railway viaduct; on higher parts of West and Middle Commons. **Wytch:** side of Thrasher's Lane 50m N of SE corner of Thrasher's Heath. **Langton:** by path44 25m SE of bridleway42. **King's Wood:** along S side (top) of wood here and there between bridleways16 and 87. **Godlingston Heath:** by bridleway27 at S corner of wood W of greenkeepers' private depot. **Swanage:** S side of path through copse W of D'Urberville Drive 20m W of road. **Studland Heath:** with Primroses on Primrose Way.

Shares with Early Purple Orchid ability to be at home in woods and in open grassland.

Burnet-saxifrage *Pimpinella saxifraga*
Native. Frequent. Calcareous grassland including verges. July to August.

This and Pepper Saxifrage below are not Saxifrages.

Ground-elder *Aegopodium podagraria*
Early Introduction. Occasional (but too frequent in gardens !). Gardens, escape on verges – usually near past or present buildings. May to July.
Holme: W side of road at East Holme 225m NW of ford. **Kimmeridge:** in N end of withybed E of path15 along 15m. **Stoborough:** N side of Holme Lane at E end along 200m. **Steeple:** N of Manor House on S side of road 60-70m E of T-junction. **Creech:** along SW side of bridleway2 – 20-40m from Grange Road. **Kingston:** N side of West Street opposite car park in The Plantation. **Corfe:** NE side of Purbeck Way NW of National Trust tearoom. **Worth:** S side of Weston Road opposite Playing Field. **Woolgarston:** E side of bridleway23 at S end. **Swanage:** W end of path down cliff from Burlington Road. **Studland:** S side of E end of Rectory Lane.

Lesser Water-parsnip *Berula erecta*
Native. Rare. Water-meadow ditches. July to September.
Holme: East Holme Meadows – see p.23.

When not in flower its leaves can be confused with Fool's-watercress (p.168), but those of Lesser Water-parsnip have a transverse membrane near base of leaf-stalk (see drawing), with clear white flowers.

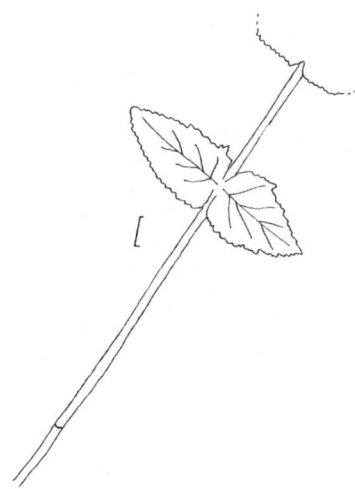

Lesser Water-parsnip leaf-stalk, showing mark indicating transverse membrane

Rock Samphire
Crithmum maritimum
Native. Frequent. Sea cliffs, rocks, sea-walls. June to October.
Kimmeridge: plentiful on cliffs E of Charnel (only open when Range Walks open). **Wares (west):** large quarries. **Durlston:** plentiful S of lighthouse. **Swanage:** by promenade in front of café below Grand Hotel. **Sandbanks:** around S tip of peninsular by Haven Hotel. **Branksome Chine:** above promenade 500m SW of chine. **Branksome Dene Chine:** here and there on sea-front. See Plate 25.

Tubular Water-dropwort
Oenanthe fistulosa
Native. Rare. By ditches in water-meadows. July to September. *Vulnerable.*
Holme: East Holme Meadows – see p.23. **The Moors:** see p.27.

Corky-fruited Water-dropwort
Oenanthe pimpinelloides
Native. Abundant. Verges, undisturbed grassland; not on acid soil. June to early August.
Corfe Charity's Meadows: present in all fields – very plentiful in most. **Corfe:** plentiful in W corner of Little East Common near A351. **Bushey:** plentiful on N side of Bushey Lane opposite Higher Bushey Farm. **Harman's Cross:** by path26 in S end of second field N of A351 (between woods). **Wares (west):** plentiful in Spyway Meadow. **Durlston:** many in several meadows: S half of Centenary Meadow, N half of South Field, E side of Long Meadow. (**Swanage:** plant once found flowering and fruiting on Pitch and Putt course (players only) when only about 1cm high 11m towards 16th green from 16th tee.)

Flowers are always white, not pink here; stems are narrowly hollow except for their lowest and highest (of six or more) sections late in their season (compare with next species); flower-heads press together when in seed; fruit shape, rather than its tiny corky base, is a distinctive feature.

Parsley Water-dropwort
Oenanthe lachenalii
Native. Occasional. Top of salt-marshes. June to September.
Arne: here and there along shore S of RSPB beach noticeboard. **Wytch:** here and there in NE of Wytch Moor. **Studland Heath:** here and there in salt-marshes in Brand's Bay (below Brand's Bay Hide; in Bramble Bush Bay for example). **Shell Bay:** towards SE of Shell Bay N of plank-bridge over usually summer-dry stream.
Some are very short because of deer-grazing. Upper halves of stems are narrowly hollow at flowering time.

Hemlock Water-dropwort
Oenanthe crocata
Native. Frequent. By watercourses, in wet woods. May to mid-July.
Poisonous.

Fool's Parsley *Aethusa cynapium*
Native. Occasional. Arable fields, other disturbed ground, including gardens. July to September.
Kingston: scattered along first 400m of edge of field S of West Street W of The Plantation. **Worth:** few near village green. **Studland:** E bank of Manor Road near junction with Watery Lane.
Poisonous.

Fennel *Foeniculum vulgare*
Early Introduction. Occasional. Verges, usually near houses. July to October.

Stoborough: in Holme Lane N side lay-by 300m from E end of Lane. **Kimmeridge:** N side of path through Kimmeridge Farm 15m E of field gate. **Kingston:** E side of The Lane just N of West Street. **Corfe:** near 50th to 75th of steps up East Hill. **Worth:** SE side of road NE of village pond. **Langton:** N side of B3069 both 100m W of path1; pavement edge up to 20m W of Serrell's Mead. **Studland:** look over gate (which may be partly hidden by Nettles) on middle of W side of South Beach car park. **Sandbanks:** near Brownsea Ferry jetty; cultivar on W edge of fenced dune 200m NE of main car park.

Pepper-saxifrage *Silaum silaus*
Native. Occasional. Permanent grassland on clay – often but not always where damp in winter. June to August.
Corfe: 50m W of Purbeck Way S of path61; 40 and 70m E of Purbeck Way on Middle Common 100m N of stream along S edge. **Wares (west):** S-facing slope of Long Close 130m N of S corner; **(east)** near SE corner of Western Mile Posts Ware; on W side of path46 425m N of Belle Vue West Ware; 40m SW of NE corner of Belle Vue Middle Ware; two areas N of actual route of path55 in Belle Vue East Ware. **Swanage:** NE side of Ulwell Road for 25m opposite houses numbered 59 and 61. **Durlston:** area towards SE corner of Field 13; in SE of Field 14 40m NNW of gateway into South Field; 50m SW of Visitor Centre.

Hemlock *Conium maculatum*
Early Introduction. Occasional. Verges, waste ground. June to July.
Holme: on NW side of B3070 175m

NE of 27m high trig point. **Kimmeridge:** along S side of bridleway12 125-85m W of road. **Wareham:** by Purbeck Way 60m E of South Bridge. **Kingston:** by Coast Path 500m E of South Gwyle. **Worth:** by path17 both through and S of Weston Farm. **Corfe:** at foot of N side of castle mound near A351.
Corfe Charity's Meadows: along Corfe River (stream) 25-35m S of Sharford Bridge. **Wares (west):** on N edge of Hedbury Ware 70m from NE corner of Cliff Middle Field. **Townsend Reserve:** at S end of Panorama Road. **Durlston:** below stone chart on plinth S of castle.

Poisonous. Ribbing of fruit exaggerated in most drawings in identification books. Keble Martin (1965) shows it correctly.

Wild Celery *Apium graveolens*
Native. Occasional. Flushes near coast. June to August.
Tyneham: around some anti-invasion blocks at Pondfield beach (known there since early 1930s). **Kimmeridge:** beach E of Charnel (only open when Range Walks open) at foot of cliff 10m before danger notice to W. **Wares (west):** near top of S-most of central southern group of flushes in Long Close; flush 100m SSE of main gateway at N end of Long Close; halfway down W-running flush in SE of Long Close; in four places in Hedbury Ware – in upper half of lower flush in W; just beyond NW extremity of Scratch Arse Ware; in second flush from E; at top of E-most flush; also in E part of Dancing Ledge Quarry towards E end of quarry face; **(east)** in five flushes on sloping cliff S of Verney Ware.

Its short-stalked or unstalked umbels grow at intervals off its nearly vertical stems.

Fool's-watercress *Apium nodiflorum*
Native. Frequent. Wet places, except acid ones. July to August.

Dull white flowers. Compare with Lesser Water-parsnip (p.165).

Corn Parsley *Petroselinum segetum*
Native. Occasional. Pasture disturbed by stock, arable field verges. August to September.
Kimmeridge: N side of bridleway12 along S side of large field N of village 225-250m W of road (when crop was Rape). **Wares (west):** very plentiful by and below flush towards SW corner of Nicholas Down; near track 60m SE of stile at N of Long Close; near SE corner of Long Close; along NE edge of Seacombe Bottom SW of Seacombe Field fence; by fence 110m E of SW corner of Cliff Field. **Durlston:** either side of path59 E of both S half of Field 1 and N half of Field 2.

Difficult to find; flowers and grey-green leaves and stems are inconspicuous, despite moderate height. Lower leaves with 4 to 12 pairs of leaflets; stalks of umbels and of flowers very unequal. Compare with next species.

Stone Parsley *Sison amomum*
Native. Frequent. Verges. July to September.
Church Knowle: here and there by path24 up to 200m S of NW end; W side of bridleway39 close to road. **Corfe:** SE side of UCR across West Common 20m NE of First Valley. **Wytch:** on S side of path5 25m W of Wytch Farm buildings. **Worth:** both sides of path11 near top of steps 350m E of village. **Langton:** along 15m of W side of path1 100m N of B3069. **Godlingston:** on N side of path2 20m W of Washpond Lane. **Swanage:** N corner of junction of Northbrook Road and Beach Gardens. **Durlston:** by stone steps of top of Zigzag Path.

Lower leaves are green, with 2 to 5 pairs of leaflets, smelling unpleasant when crushed; stalks of umbels and of flowers are nearly equal. Compare with previous species.

Whorled Caraway
Carum verticillatum
Native. Rare. Wet grassland. Late June to August.
Dorset Rare.
The Moors: see p.27. See Plate 17.

Wild Angelica
Angelica sylvestris
Native. Frequent. Wet places, including ditches. July to August.
Wareham: in Priory Meadow especially by track along S side. **Furzebrook:** along 30m on S side of Kilnwood Reserve entrance track where it reaches Reserve. **Stoborough Heath:** on E side of Dismantled Tramway 30m from N end. **Stoborough:** on SW side of A351 50-150m SE of Halfway Inn entrance. **Worth:** by stream in Hill Bottom 20-60m NE of junction of UCR and Purbeck Way (with Hogweed). **Corfe:** near SE corner of Little East Common. **Worth:** W of Kingston Road S of start of private track to Swanworth Quarry. **Harman's Cross:** by track to S platform of station. **Bushey:** S side of B3351 50-130m E of Meadus' Lane on opposite side. **Kingswood:** S side of B3351 70-110m E of bridleway16. **Studland:** by bridleway38 20m W of Ferry Road.

Domed flowerheads are conspicuous at distance.

Wild Parsnip *Pastinaca sativa*
Native. Abundant. Dry grassland, verges, on calcareous soil. July to August.

Handling it leads to skin irritation for some people.

Hogweed *Heracleum sphondylium*
Native. Abundant. Verges, wood rides,
permanent grassland. June to September.

Handling it leads to skin irritation
for some people. Not usually over 2.5m
tall.

Giant Hogweed
Heracleum mantegazzianum
Introduction. Rare. Escape. June to
July.
Corfe: S of Challow Farm SW of
path18 (which runs along field edge –
not across field).

Do not touch it; it can lead to skin
irritation; usually over 3m tall, and
larger than the previous species in most
of its parts.

Upright Hedge Parsley
Torilis japonica
Native. Frequent. Verges, scrub, woodland paths. July to October.
Kimmeridge: plentiful along S fence
of oil well by Coast Path. **Holme:** both
sides of bridleway between Doreys
Farm and Rifle Range. **Creech Heath:**
plentiful by path34 80m W of
Furzebrook Road. **Corfe:** NW side of
road to Church Knowle 20m SW of
lay-by at NE end of road (with Rough
Chervil). **Worth:** here and there by
bridleway19. **Wytch:** plentiful along
100m of one or other side of bridle-
way4 NW of its crossing of private Oil
Road. **Langton:** in scrub by path5 W
of Crack Lane cemetery. **Herston
(north):** by stile at S end of path1.
Townsend Reserve: 60m SE of NW
entrance. **Studland:** sides of Wadmore
Lane 120-140m from SE end.

Flowers are pinky-purple when in
bud; stems are rough.

Knotted Hedge Parsley *Torilis nodosa*
Native. Frequent. Dry grassland and
verges. May to July.

Tyneham: plentiful beside Army
Range path for over 300m when
approaching Tyneham Cap from E.
Stoborough: back of village pump
at N end of The Green (when not
strimmed). **Church Knowle:** near
steps at church gate. **Corfe:** half way
along N side of Colletts Close.
Worth: fringing Coast Path 350-
650m E of Coastwatch Station;
along E edge of Worth Field from
175-550m from NE corner. **Wares
(west):** especially in Cliff Field both
along S part of W side; here and
there near Coast Path; also **(east)** by
Coast Path fence in White Ware
along 40m in SW corner. **Durlston:**
by kerbs of W side car park. **Ballard
Down:** 100m NE of gate by eastern
tumuli.

Inconspicuous. Its leaves are only
sparsely hairy; this distinguishes it
from small plants of the next species
when no flowers or fruit are present.

Wild Carrot *Daucus carota*
Native. Abundant. Rough grassland,
verges. June to October.

Height may be 1cm in grazed
areas near sea or approaching 1m
on verges! Enjoy looking for the
scarlet, crimson or black flowers in
the centre of each white umbel;
(compare with subspecies below).
See Plate 18.

Sea Carrot
Daucus carota subsp. *gummifer*
Native. Rare. By the sea. June to
August.
Studland: cliff-top near Handfast
Point (take care) (with very much
more Wild Carrot).

Umbels remain convex when in
seed, in contrast to the concave
(saucer-shaped) Wild Carrot seed-
heads (see above).

GENTIAN FAMILY
Yellow Centaury
Cicendia filiformis
Native. Rare. Bare places on heaths which are wet in winter; similar sites as for Allseed and Chaffweed, but rarer. Late June to July.
Nationally Scarce. Vulnerable.
Stoborough Heath: 260-300m from NW end on both sides of track which runs SE from path9 to join Purbeck Way 250m S of A351.
Wytch: on S side of path80 – 190, 290, 320 and 410m W of Thrasher's Lane. **Studland:** Harmony Farm NE Field 15m SE of NE gateway into field from bridleway17.

Flowers, 2-4mm across, only open in the mornings and in full sun. Numbers vary greatly from year to year according to the weather and openness of the ground.

Common Centaury
Centaurium erythraea
Native. Frequent. Stable sand, thin grassland, wood rides, verges. June to October.
Wares (west): few albinos in Seacombe Field 70m NW of SE corner.

The basal rosette mentioned as a distinctive feature in identification books has often disappeared at flowering time! It is easier to distinguish Common from Lesser Centaury (below) by the tiny leaves (bracts) under its sepal-tube (calyx) either immediately or with a gap of up to 1mm (compared with 1-4 mm for Lesser Centaury), and by the petal (corolla) lobes which are 4.5mm or more long (4mm or less for Lesser Centaury), and by the lobes being paler pink and more rounded at their ends. Also compare with variety below.

Tufted Centaury *Centaurium erythraea* var. *capitatum*
Native. Rare. Very short exposed grassland near sea. Late June to early August.
Durlston: scattered in Lighthouse Field in an arc SE-S-W-N around the rocky knoll 50m W of NW corner of lighthouse enclosure; 60m NW of same corner on NE side of path48; also 15m SE of lighthouse enclosure.

The stamens of each flower are joined to the petal-tube near its base, rather than at the top of the tube as in Common Centaury above (lens). Plants are only up to 1.5cm high, usually little larger than a 50-pence piece. Ignore plants 2cm or more in height with stalks that can be seen – they are Common Centaury. See Plate 19.

Lesser Centaury
Centaurium pulchellum
Native. Occasional. Short grassland (especially S-facing), verges, tracks, stable dunes, quarry floors – sometimes places that are wet in winter due to the clay in the subsoil. June to September.
Wytch: in SW of open access part of Thrasher's Heath. **Corfe:** on West Common between E end of Second Valley and UCR. **Rempstone:** NW side of junction of bridleways31 and 34 (Oil Road). **Worth:** just E of top of flush in S end of Worth Field. **Wares (west):** floors of both W and E parts of main cliff quarry at Hedbury; (**east**) in short grassland in many places especially near Coast Path. **Godlingston Heath:** by bridleway25 200m N of B3351. **Durlston:** NE of shallow quarry in NE of Field 14. **Ulwell:** along Purbeck Way NE of lower lay-by on Ulwell Road. **Ballard Down:** widely and thinly scattered. **Studland:** 130m N of Agglestone

Road by S-N track in Harmony Farm NW Field.

Flowers close early afternoon unless the sun is bright. See Common Centaury p.170 for other differences.

Yellow-wort *Blackstonia perfoliata*
Native. Frequent. Limestone – grassland, sloping cliffs, car parks and roadsides. June to September.
Tyneham: S of Coast Path between outer and inner ramparts on W side of Flowers Barrow; N side of Coast Path passing through outer E rampart.
Steeple: here and there on Steeple Down (west). **Corfe:** in old quarry N of bridleway20 SW of UCR up Rollington Hill. **Wares (west):** E half of Cliff Field; other slopes above Coast Path: likewise slopes in **Wares (east). Durlston:** field slopes above Coast Path; S-facing slope N of lighthouse. **Townsend Reserve:** 10m W of SW corner of Manwell Field. **Ballard Down:** thinly scattered on S side. **Studland Heath:** S end of car park at Knoll Beach.

Autumn Gentian, Felwort
Gentianella amarella
Native. Occasional. Short calcareous grassland. Mid-July to September.
East Creech: on Stonehill Down both scattered 50-150m from E end on N-facing slope near crest of Down; at E end of Down just above E-facing old quarry (some plants pale). **Wares (west):** on Nicholas Down 30m from W edge both 300 and 400m S of NW corner of Down; steep W-facing slopes in Long Close firstly in NW 130m from N wall 110m from W hedge; secondly larger colony in SE 200m N of S wall halfway up slope opposite largest rock W of track below; 40m N of stile in SE of Cliff Middle Field on low part of lower of

two W-facing banks (colony length 3m N-S). **Ulwell** (late July to early August best): plentiful up to 35m NW of track halfway up steep slope above right-angled bend of Purbeck Way (that bend is by height number 62 on O.S. map). **Durlston:** few both 7m W of shallow quarry in NE of Field 14; 5-10m N of quarry near its W end. **Townsend Reserve:** near W end of 'Orchid Scrub' in SW of reserve; few on mound 25m W of Orchid Bastion; on NE part of Burry's Circle.

Flowers are fairly deep purple; varies in numbers from year to year; appears to be an annual.

Early Gentian *Gentianella anglica*
Native. Occasional. Short calcareous grassland. April to June, usually peaking in last week of May.
Nationally Scarce.
Wares: recorded in over 20 sites, including **(west)** SW-facing slope of Long Close 150m E of SW corner; in Hedbury Ware near SE corner of Cliff Middle Field; SW-facing slope of Hedbury Ware halfway between SE corner of Cliff Middle Field and main Hedbury Quarry entrance; W end of Scratch Arse Ware 30m NE of Coast Path gate; 30m SW of NE corner of same ware; **(east)** S-facing bank above track S of path55 in NW of Verney Ware; in SE of Belle Vue East Ware. **Durlston:** 80m from W wall of Field 3 near path55; slightly W of centre of field 10A above halfway between bottom of field and path55; near path48 NW of lighthouse; NE of shallow quarry in NE of Field 14; on and near bank between Mile Posts. **Townsend Reserve:** on N side of top of mound 70m NE of horses' shed (early June best). **Ballard Down:** here and there above Purbeck Way 400-700m E of

gate to Down above Whitecliff Farm; just N of fence 220m W of trig point; on bank running 40m W from right-angle in same fence 110m W of trig point; at S end of N-S ditch just W of trig point.

Flowers are fairly deep purple, opens in the sun; otherwise can be difficult to spot; varies in numbers from year to year; appears to be an annual. See Plate 19.

Marsh Gentian
Gentiana pneumonanthe
Native. Occasional. Damp heaths (often near bogs but not in them); not in marshes! Mid-August to September. *Nationally Scarce.*
Stoborough Heath: in large area 400-500m NNW of S end of Dismantled Tramway either side of conspicuous N-S band of Black Bog-rush; in small area 50m further NNW of that 50m NE of track; in smaller area 600m N of S end of Tramway 50m W of it. **Norden:** on Norden Heath 30m S of path10 for 100m E-W 150-250m W of junction of paths10 and 12. **Hartland Moor:** here and there on N side of Moor towards E end especially 75m NW of Post Pool; also SE of Tramway Bog. **Bushey:** between Gorse on Brenscombe Heath 100m N of point on Bushey Lane which is 80m W of gate near SE corner of Heath; good colony near NW corner of Brenscombe South Heath. **Godlingston Heath:** 40 and 90m W of path32 180m N of its junction with bridleway27; 60 m E of bridleway26 100 and 200m N of quarry; 100 and 200m E of same quarry; 400m along track running NW from SW of Puckstone 30m W of track; 130m NW of Puckstone; scattered in small numbers in various other sites above edges of bogs. **Studland Heath:** Spur

Bog 190-220m ESE of entrance best. There are many other sites with small numbers of plants. Spur Bog is the best site, followed by Brenscombe South Heath, Tramway Bog and Post Pool.

Rose, Clarke and Chapman (1998) examined the longevity of this species and found that numbers of plants that reach maturity (4 years old) live for over 20 years, though without flowering every year. Undisturbed colonies gradually decrease, and, if undisturbed by fire, mowing or grazing, may die out within 50 years; disturbance, especially fire, leads to growth of new plants. See back cover and Plate 19.

PERIWINKLE FAMILY
Lesser Periwinkle *Vinca minor*
Early Introduction. Occasional. Escape on verges and in woods. April to May.
Holme: NE side of junction of Holme Lane with road to East Holme. **Ridge:** N side of Nutcrack Lane 70m from E end; corner of Arne Road and Barnhill Road. **Kingston:** very large amount 100m N of West Street by path50. **Studland:** 100m S of NE corner of Glebeland Estate on E side of bridleway12. **Sandbanks:** by path from Brudenell Avenue to Dornie Road 50m from former.

Leaf edges are hairless (lens).

Greater Periwinkle *Vinca major*
Introduction. Frequent. Escape on verges, usually not far from houses. February to May.

Often with variegated leaves; leaf edges are hairy (lens).

NIGHTSHADE FAMILY
Apple-of-Peru *Nicandra physalodes*
Introduction. Rare. Casual. June to October.

Poisonous.

Duke of Argyll's Teaplant
Lycium barbarum
Introduction. Occasional. Planted or escaped near coast. April to August.
Tyneham: 20m E of picnic area above S end of Worbarrow Bay on S side of path from Tyneham; N side of same path 70m further E. **Wares (west):** above W side of Seacombe Bottom 2m E of fence 125m S of top of Coast Path steps; E side of Seacombe Bottom towards top of slope 100m N of sea. **Studland:** on E side of bridleway12 in hedge 30-45m from N end of bridleway.

Henbane *Hyoscyamus niger*
Early Introduction. Occasional. Disturbed farmland (but not when heavily winter-grazed), cliff-tops, beaches. June to July.
Vulnerable.
Tyneham: beside 10m of Coast Path above Hobarrow Bay. **Worth:** some years near small building by bridleway19 NE of Chapman's Pool. **Wares (west):** 100 and 120 and 180m SW of stile on N edge of Long Close by rabbit warrens; 200m S of first site by water trough. **Knitson:** by bridleway9 especially S of it near its SE end; on N side of bridleway8 100m E of bridleway12; near foot of zigzag track. **Studland Heath:** some years near neck of Redhorn Quay.

Irregular in appearance at some sites. Trampling by cattle in winter kills the plants, but seed is long-lived. Poisonous.

Black Nightshade *Solanum nigrum*
Native. Abundant. Arable, especially maize, fields, other disturbed ground, rubbish heaps. July to October.

Poisonous.

Bittersweet (Woody Nightshade)
Solanum dulcamara
Native. Frequent. Hedges, verges. May to September.
Sometimes thought to be Deadly Nightshade, which is not in this area.
Poisonous.

Potato *Solanum tuberosum*
Introduction. Occasional. Escape. June to August.

Thorn-apple *Datura stramonium*
Introduction. Rare. Casual. July to October.
Brownsea: has occurred on S shore 60m E of SW corner of island.
Poisonous. Irregular in appearance.

Tobacco cvs. *Nicotiana* cvs.
Cultivated. Occasional. Escape. July to October.
Difficult to tell cultivars apart.

Petunia *Petunia* x *hybrida*
(*P. axillaris* x *integrifoli*a)
Introduction. Rare. Escape. July to October.

BINDWEED FAMILY
Field Bindweed
Convolvulus arvensis
Native. Abundant. Grassland, verges, gardens. June to September.
See drawing of leaf p.174.

Sea Bindweed *Calystegia soldanella*
Native. Occasional. Fore-dunes. June to August.
Dorset Scarce.
Studland Heath: just beyond areas of fenced fore-dunes 375m N of Knoll Beach Café and continuing for 175m N-wards; 150m further N at start of Sand Dune Nature Trail.
Shell Bay: from 30m N of E end of boardwalk NW-wards for 50m.

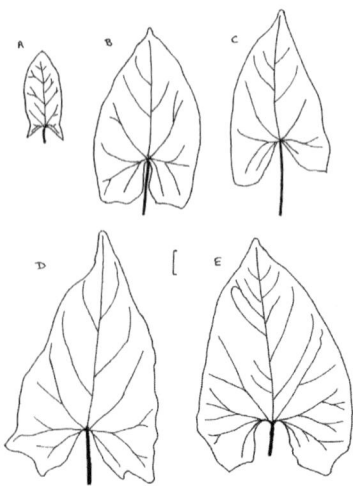

Leaves of Bindweed: A - Field, B and C - Hedge, D and E - Large. Note variation in base of leaves by stalk in latter two species.

Sandbanks: dunes 80m SW of main car park; also both 125 and 400m NE of car park.

Hedge Bindweed *Calystegia sepium*
Native. Frequent. Hedges. July to September.

Outer sepals (actually bracts) under flowers are only slightly inflated; tips of some inner sepals are visible; flower width 3-6cm.

Large Bindweed *Calystegia silvatica*
Introduction. Frequent. Hedges, usually near houses. July to September.

Outer sepals under flowers are inflated into a wide pouch, hiding inner sepals; flower width 6-9cm.

Dodder *Cuscuta epithymum*
Native. Occasional. Dry heaths, usually parasitic on Heather. June to July. *Vulnerable.*
Stoborough Heath: on higher

ground in centre and E of Sunnyside Mire; on and near track in SE of Heath here and there 150-550m NW-wards from Dismantled Tramway.
Hartland Moor: E side of Soldiers Road 300m S of N end; on open access land 175-225m W of Slepe Road S of track just N of the main area of the Moor; on W side of Slepe Road below electricity lines marked on maps (parasitic on Dwarf Gorse).
Godlingston Heath: N of W-E track S of tumulus 120m E of bridleway26; up to 15m SW of bridleway23 150m SE of grass field (some on Bell Heather and some on Dwarf Gorse); W side of track 200m SW of Puckstone; by bridleway17 150m SW of junction of bridleways17 and 23.
Studland Heath: 20m W of Ferry Road 220m S of track to Brand's Bay Hide; on SE side of Ferry Road from Shell Bay car park SW-wards for 425m from 5m to 100m from road (including one on Gorse and another on Bell Heather) (largest population in this area); by track on SE side of Third Ridge 50 and 100m SW of track to nudists' area.

Numbers vary considerably from year to year.

BOGBEAN FAMILY
Bogbean *Menyanthes trifoliata*
Native. Occasional. Bogs, marshes, lakes, ponds (sometimes planted in latter). April to May.
Holme: East Holme Meadows – see p.23. **Hartland Moor:** scattered across it; **The Moors:** open access pond 250m W of Bank Gate Cottages.
Corfe: several places including on W side of West Common; area 30m W-E 15m N-S 75m SW of Middle Common Pond. **Godlingston Heath:** near centre of Knoll Bog; in bog near fence 450m SW of bridleway to

Greenland. **Durlston:** planted in Johnston Pond. **Studland Heath:** narrowest neck at N end of Little Sea.

Fringed Water-lily
Nymphoides peltata
Native, but planted or escaped here. Occasional. July to August.
Tyneham: W and middle ponds E of ruined Rectory. **Creech Heath:** in small pond 75m ENE of crossing of path34 by W-E track (best approached from track to S). **Norden:** Michael's Pond. **Wares (west):** pond S of Priest's Way 250m E of path30.

PHACELIA FAMILY
Phacelia *Phacelia tanacetifolia*
Introduction. Rare. Casual; also sown for winter bird feed. May to August.
Congested coiled clusters of blue flowers.

BORAGE FAMILY
Common Gromwell
Lithospermum officinale
Native. Occasional. Scrubby calcareous grassland and verges. Late May to July.
Woolgarston: on track parallel to and 5m N of bridleway20 10m NW of N end of bridleway24. **Knitson:** on S side of bridleway9 400m NW of junction of bridleways8 and 9; S of same junction. **Ulwell:** NE side of Round Down 80m SE of Purbeck Way 10m from Ulwell Road; near steps on path4 up to Obelisk.

(Field Gromwell
Lithospermum arvense
Early Introduction. Arable fields, other disturbed ground. May to July.
Dorset Rare. Endangered.
Worth: seen 1986 S of and close to Renscombe Farm; in 1970s in E edge of largest field on W side of bridle-way15 – so look out for it from bridleways and paths in that area.)

Viper's Bugloss *Echium vulgare*
Native. Occasional. Open rough ground, sandy or calcareous, including cliff-tops. June to August.
Holme: here and there on verge B3070 across West Holme Heath. **Kingston:** by Coast Path 150m E of junction with path44. **Hartland Moor:** by both cattle grids on Slepe Road. **Worth:** by bridleway19 500m SW of junction with Coast Path; by Coast Path in three areas at St. Aldhelm's Head – W and SW of row of houses and E of Coastwatch Station. **Corfe:** slope near top of outer bailey of castle. **Langton:** by path36 200m NW of B3069; at passing place on W side of road from B3069 to Acton. **Wares (west):** Dancing Ledge; **(east)** top of Balston Wear near gate to Hay Brimble. **Ballard Down:** on cliff-top S of trig point. **Branksome Chine:** cliff-top 210m SW of chine.

Lungwort *Pulmonaria officinalis*
Introduction. Rare. Escape. March to May.
Corfe: near Byle Brook 30m S of N end of S half of Byle Copse.
Durlston: outside NW corner of Long Meadow (not seen flowering).

Narrow-leaved Lungwort
Pulmonaria longifolia
Native. Rare. Verges. April to May.
At one private site. The farmer has given permission for the author to show people this site once a year (see Appendix).

Common Comfrey
Symphytum officinale
Native. Frequent. Verges, banks of

watercourses. April to June.
Holme: in several colours both sides of road S of ford in East Holme hamlet.

Much more common in this area than the hybrid below. Leaf-bases run down the stems as wings to at least the next leaf-base (compare with hybrid below).

Russian Comfrey *Symphytum* x *uplandicum* (*S. officinale* x *asperum*)
Introduction. Occasional. Verges. May to June.
Hartland Moor: plentiful along 100m W of track S of entrance to Middlebere Farm old buildings (now holiday cottages). **Kingston:** at corner of UCR 300m S of Orchard Hill Farm; N side of same UCR 200-300m W of car park; W side of South Street 120m S of West Street. **Swanage:** E end of copse W of D'Urberville Drive; by Swan Brook near E end of Kings Road East.

Leaf-bases run down stems as wings for only a short distance (compare with species above).

Tuberous Comfrey
Symphytum tuberosum
Introduction. Rare. Planted. June to July.
Langton: S side of B3069 200m W of junction with A351.

Hidcote Comfrey
Symphytum cv. Hidcote Blue
Introduction. Rare. Escape. March to June.
Bushey: on top of bank 15-30m E of Brenscombe Farm entrance on S side of B3351 (view from road).

Creeping Comfrey
Symphytum grandiflorum
Introduction. Rare. Escape. March to May.

Durlston: plentiful in middle of N edge of wood at NE of Country Park.
Durlston: on E side of path43 150m from Russell Avenue.

White Comfrey *Symphytum orientale*
Introduction. Rare. Verges. April to May.
Studland: E side of Ferry Road just S of bus shelter N of Beach Road.

Teeth of sepal-tube less than half the length of the tube, in contrast to other Comfreys.

Great Forget-me-not
Brunnera macrophylla
Introduction. Rare. Planted. March to May.
Durlston: outside NW corner of Long Meadow.

Like Forget-me-nots, but with pointed wide oval leaves.

Bugloss *Anchusa arvensis*
Early Introduction. Occasional. Arable fields, other disturbed ground. June to September.
Ower: by bridleway7 just N of where bridleways7 and 8 cross. **Studland:** N of Coast Path in grassland around 600m E of The Warren Wood (soil disturbed by moles). **Brownsea:** bank of S shore 200m E of SW corner of island.

Green Alkanet
Pentaglottis sempervirens
Introduction. Frequent. Verges, especially in built-up areas. March to July.

Borage *Borago officinalis*
Early Introduction. Occasional. Waste ground near buildings, casual. May to mid-August.
Corfe: some years here and there outside castle high on long SW side of castle mound (can get hidden by

Alexanders or eaten by stock); inside castle on SW-facing bank 30m NW of entrance gate; (it has been known at castle for over 100 years – perhaps it is a relic of cultivation from the time before the castle was built, as Mabey (1972) writes in *Food for Free*, 'Borage once had a great reputation as a sort of herbal pep-pill'. **Kingston:** on W side of B3069 150m N of N end of path40 on opposite side. **Swanage:** cliff 100m N of N end of Shore Road.

Water Forget-me-not
Myosotis scorpioides
Native. Occasional. Watersides. May to September.
Holme: S edge of River Frome between old and new bridges; plentiful on East Holme Meadows – see p.23. **Stoborough:** by Cobbs Lake watercourse at NW end of path13. **Wareham:** E side of River Frome both by and 20m N of bypass bridge (binoculars, or boat). **Corfe:** by stream along SW side of West Common just E of UCR; at S end of Greater Tussock Sedge area in NW of West Common; along 20m of stream 120m W of road at SE corner of West Common; by stream near S edge of Middle Common 10 and 50m E of B3069. **Durlston:** Johnston Pond. **Swanage:** in Swan Brook alongside St. Mary's churchyard. **Studland Heath:** by stream S of Knoll Beach car park.

Creeping Forget-me-not
Myosotis secunda
Native. Occasional. Wet places. May to August.
Stoborough Heath: E of path5 550m SE of bypass; by stream S of A351 250m NW of Halfway Inn. **Corfe:** (pale form), several places on

Commons: near edge 125m NE of SW corner of West Common (with next species); in Second Valley 50m NW of UCR; in three places in First Valley – 100m SE of UCR (sometimes with next species), 30m NW of path53, 75-125m SE of same path; also E of scrub bordering W stream on Little East Common 10m S of bridleway30; by tiny E stream 10m S of same bridleway. **Hartland Moor:** E of copse 400m N of Scotland Barn.

Creeping runners are not always present early in the season; best distinguished from the next species by the hairs on lower stem sticking out, rather than being flat on the stem; petal size overlaps occasionally with the next species.

Tufted Forget-me-not *Myosotis laxa*
Native. Occasional. Wet places. May to October.
Furzebrook: S side of E-most of three ponds in S of Kilnwood Reserve. **Hartland Moor:** here and there in Upper Fen; by Pillwort Pond; on Langton Wallis Heath 300m NNE of Langton Wallis close to Bog Myrtle; scattered along S side of Snag Valley W of Slepe Road; scattered along stream in NE of heath SW of Scotland. **The Moors:** see p.27. **Norden:** SW edge of Michael's Pond 100m from road. **Corfe:** with previous species in two places – see above; also with Water Forget-me-not 125m WNW of SE corner of West Common; by stream near S edge of Middle Common 100 and 140m E of B3069 (latter site is by boards across wet ground); much around Middle Common Pond.

Petals can be pale like those of previous species; see above regarding hairs on the stem.

Wood Forget-me-not
Myosotis sylvatica
Native elsewhere but garden escape
in this area. Frequent. Verges. April
to June.

Field Forget-me-not
Myosotis arvensis
Early Introduction. Frequent.
Arable fields, disturbed dry ground.
April to August.

Early Forget-me-not
Myosotis ramosissima
Native. Occasional. Anthills, thin
calcareous soil, sand. April to June.
Tyneham: on bank on N side of
Army Range path 700m WSW of
W end of bridleway12.
Stoborough: here and there on The
Green. **Hartland Moor:** NW side of
Soldiers Road 300m NE of S cattle
grid; NW side of old tramway 100m
SW of Slepe Road. **Corfe:** N side
Sandy Hill Lane 300m W of
Sandyhills Farm. **Worth:** plentiful
near top of E side of valley N of
Renscombe. **Woolgarston:** plentiful
10m N of N end of bridleway22.
Wares (west): especially near SE
corner of Dancing Ledge Ware;
widely scattered elsewhere especially
on anthills (also in **east**). **Knitson:**
on N side of bridleway8 both for
10m at 125m W of bridleway12 and
for 20m at 425m E of bridleway12.
Durlston: just NW of The Globe.
Townsend Reserve: at least six
places especially S and E sides of
Orchid Bastion. **Ballard Down:**
here and there. **Studland:** much
between Middle Beach car park payment booth and rise in middle of car
park.

Flowers are bright blue; teeth at
the ends of the sepal-tubes point
outward when in fruit.

Changing Forget-me-not
Myosotis discolor
Native. Occasional. Thin dry grass-
land, pavements. May to June.
Stoborough: SW corner of The
Green. **Stoborough Heath:** by S cat-
tle grid on Soldiers Road. **Hartland
Moor:** scattered in N end of large
unfenced field E of Soldiers Road
700m N of A351; by Dartford Hide.
Corfe: in grass verge on S side of
Colletts Close 75m from E end.
Wares (west): few albinos 100m N of
sea towards top of slope on E side of
Seacombe Bottom. **Rempstone:** N
side of bridleway35 100m E of junc-
tion with bridleway34. **Godlingston
Heath:** near gates that are opposite
each other N and S of bridleway36.
Durlston: here and there on E side of
Ox-eye Daisy Field. **Ballard Down:**
here and there – near bottom of
Down 550m E of gate on bridleway14
for example. **Studland:** in grass in
Middle Beach car park opposite
National Trust offices. **Studland
Heath:** here and there around Knoll
Beach car parks. **Brownsea:** plentiful
– petals of some under trees 100m SE
of church are particularly bright
yellow.

Flowers are cream-coloured and
later turn blue; teeth at the ends of
the sepal-tubes point forward when in
fruit.

Houndstongue
Cynoglossum officinale
Native. Frequent. Calcareous grassland near scrub or rabbit holes. May
to July.
Near Threatened.
Steeple: several places in central area
of Steeple Down (west) especially
near rabbit holes. **Wares (west):** here
and there, especially in W of Hedbury
Ware; along wall at N of Hedbury

Ware and East Plain; in NE of Taylor's Ware; (east) along N of Chillmark Ware; in SE of same ware. **Woolgarston:** by bridleway20 250m SE of N end of bridleway24. **Ulwell:** plentiful near SE corner of Round Down. **Ballard Down:** here and there, especially near steepest part of bridleway14 up S-facing Down; in shallow coomb crossed by Purbeck Way 400m NE of gate on bridleway14; on lower slopes three-quarters of way from bridleway14 to path11.

VERBENA FAMILY

Vervain *Verbena officinalis*
Early Introduction. Frequent. Verges, wood rides, rough grassland – especially along southern foot of chalk downs. June to September.
Stoborough Heath: on heath near NW corner S of hotel. **Church Knowle:** here and there by paths30 and 3 and NE part of bridleway39. **Corfe:** here and there by path70. **Arne:** road verge 15m S of car park entrance. **Worth:** by stile on Coast Path just W of Hill Bottom hamlet. **Langton:** by track leading W from Crack Lane cemetery vehicular entrance. **Woolgarston:** here and there along bridleway20 at foot of Ailwood Down. **Knitson:** N of N end of bridleway12. **Godlingston Heath:** W side of bridleway36 near entrance to Greenlands Farm. **Ulwell:** very plentiful in field N of S lay-by; much along foot of Down above that field.

Argentinian Vervain
Verbena bonariensis
Introduction. Rare. Escape. June to October.
Kimmeridge: one in withybed on W side of path15 25m S of N edge of withybed. **Langton:** plenty on W side of Durnford Drove near S end.

Swanage: N side of junction of Northbrook Road and Washpond Lane.

LABIATE FAMILY

Betony *Stachys officinalis*
Native. Occasional. Permanent grassland, verges. Late June to September.
Steeple: plentiful on upper part of Steeple Down (west) 425-525m E of W end. **Creech:** NE side of bridleway2 opposite cricket pavilion. **Furzebrook:** plentiful in N half of field in Kilnwood Reserve. **Corfe:** abundant on higher parts of West and Middle Commons (albinos 200m S of S end of West Street). **Bushey:** along 20m of E side of Thrasher's Lane 600m from B3351. **Wares (west):** towards top of slope on E side of S end of Seacombe Bottom. **Knitson:** on N side of path13 225m W of Burnham's Lane. **Kingswood:** on S side of B3351 30m W of viewpoint (take care). **Durlston:** SE corner of Johnston Meadow; NE of lighthouse. **Ballard Down:** on grazed S-facing grassland above Ballard Cliff.

Lambsear *Stachys byzantina*
Introduction. Rare. Escape. July to August.
Durlston: on E side of path54 450m N of Holecombe (field).

Hedge Woundwort *Stachys sylvatica*
Native. Frequent. Verges, wood rides. June to September.
Upper leaves have long stalks.

Hybrid Woundwort *Stachys* x *ambigua* (*S. sylvatica* x *palustris*)
Native. Occasional. Verges, usually in absence of parents. June to September.
Tyneham: N side of path to Worbarrow Bay 140m E of picnic area above bay. **Wareham:** on W side of

B3075 110m S of South Bridge. **East Creech:** SW side of T-junction where road from East Creech meets Furzebrook Road. **Ballard Down:** sides of bridleway14 just N of second bend in bridleway N of Whitecliff Farm.

Upper leaves have short stalks. See Plate 19.

Marsh Woundwort *Stachys palustris*
Native. Occasional. Damp or dry verges, watersides, grassland. June to September.
Creech: on both sides of bridleway2 250m NW of Grange Road.
Hartland Moor: here and there in N end of Upper Fen. **Woolgarston:** N side of road 120m W of N end of Tabbit's Hill Lane. **Rempstone:** along S side of Breaches Lane 100 to 160m E of Forest Lane. **Kingswood:** S side of B3351 just E of bridleway29 on opposite side. **Wares (east):** by path64 225m N of Belle Vue East Ware. **Godlingston:** N side of Burnham's Lane 30m W of Washpond Lane. **Durlston:** here and there around sides of N half of Long Meadow. **Studland:** by bridleway38 20m W of Ferry Road. **Sandbanks:** top of shore in edge of reeds opposite end of Haven Road (colony with unusually sharp-toothed leaves and rough hairs).

Upper leaves have no stalks.

Field Woundwort *Stachys arvensis*
Early Introduction. Rare. Arable fields, other disturbed ground, often with Sharp-leaved Fluellen (p.189). May to October.
Near Threatened.
Ballard Down: when Maize is being grown by Coast Path both in edge of first and third fields N of Shep's Hollow.

Black Horehound *Ballota nigra*
Early Introduction. Occasional. Verges, by gates. June to September.
Kimmeridge: N side of path through Kimmeridge Farm by field gate.
Church Knowle: by junction of bridleway39 with paths3 and 5. **Corfe:** on N side of bridleway70 10m W of gate at SW corner of West Hill. **Worth:** N side of Weston Road 100m E of corner at Weston Farm. **Wares (west):** by gate at SE corner of Long Close. **Knitson:** N side of road 10m W of bridleway12. **Durlston:** by kissing-gate in NW corner of Lighthouse Field. **Swanage:** SW of Health Centre. **Ballard Down:** E side of bridleway14 just S of stone cottage NW of Whitecliff Farm. **Studland:** E side of Church Road 20m N of Watery Lane.

Many sites are by gates or buildings. It has been associated with human settlements since the Iron Age. The plant is not eaten by cattle because of its smell. It was used for treating coughs and colds, but was powerful medicine to be used sparingly. It was also used for people bitten by rabid dogs – but only to alleviate a symptom before death; its site near Swanage Health Centre is probably coincidental! Flowers are dull purple, <u>not pink</u>.

Yellow Archangel *Lamiastrum galeobdolon* subsp. *montanum*
Native. Occasional. Light areas in ancient woods. May to June, two weeks later than the subspecies below.
Creech: small numbers of plants scattered on SE side of road through Great Wood. **East Creech:** 1m W of path32 in Caldecot's Wood 40m N of Beech around which path bends.
Furzebrook: 125m SE of Furzebrook Road along 10m of wood edge W of stile on path5. **Bushey:** one on S side of path13 60m from path's entrance to

wood S of Brenscombe Farm. **King's Wood:** near S edge of wood 150, 240 and 500m SE of lower of two gates near top of bridleway16. **Ulwell:** 5m SW of road 40m NW of lay-by by Currendon Chalk Pit.

Variegated Yellow Archangel
Lamiastrum galeobdolon
subsp. *argentatum*
Introduction. Occasional. Escape. April to May.
Stoborough: here and there along path9 between Grange Road and heath. **Hartland Moor:** N side of Arne Road 10m W of N end of Soldiers Road. **Corfe:** on S side of path32 60-80m E of A351.
Woolgarston: N side of road 100m W of N end of Tabbit's Hill Lane; S side of road on N edge of Higher Grove Wood. **Rempstone:** on NW side of bridleway11 50m SW of Foxground Cottage. **Swanage:** E side of Washpond Lane 80m N of High Street; by path at S end of Bell Street; 100m from Russell Avenue along 10m on E side of path43. **Studland:** 50m S of NE corner of Glebeland Estate on E side of bridleway12.

White Dead-nettle *Lamium album*
Early Introduction. Frequent. Verges. March to December; peak in April to May.

Spotted Dead-nettle
Lamium maculatum
Introduction. Rare. Escape.
Studland: NE side of Manor Road 10m N of path5 on opposite side. April to September.

Red Dead-nettle *Lamium purpureum*
Early Introduction. Frequent. Verges, arable fields, other disturbed ground. February to October.

Henbit Dead-nettle
Lamium amplexicaule
Early Introduction. Rare. Arable fields, other disturbed ground. April to August.
Worth: field edge by path21 S of St. Aldhelm's Chapel.

Common Hemp-nettle
Galeopsis tetrahit
Native. Occasional. Verges, hedge-banks. July to September.
Stoborough: one seen on SW side of bypass 60m NW of path13. **Hartland Moor:** one seen by fence corner post on S side of Snag Valley 300m W of Slepe Road. **Harman's Cross:** N here and there both sides of track to S platform of station; W side of road 30m S of railway bridge at New Barn; on NW side of path6 – 3, 30 and 45m SW of stile near junction of paths6 and 13. **Woolgarston:** 225m S of road at Ailwood Farm along 50m of W edge of grass field crossed by path26 (farmer allows close viewing). **Kingswood:** on W side of bridle-way87 100m from B3351. **Knitson:** on S side of path13 250m W of Burnham's Lane.

An annual species; not necessarily at the same site every year.

Lesser Hemp-nettle *Galeopsis bifida*
Native. Rare. Verges. July to September.
Holme: East Holme Meadows – see p.23.
Surprisingly there are no written records to support entries elsewhere in this area in *The Flora of Dorset*.

This species may just be a variety of the previous species. A plant has been reported by Smith (2007) from else-where which produced Lesser Hemp-nettle flowers at first and then Hemp-nettle flowers.

Jerusalem Sage *Phlomis fruticosa*
Introduction. Rare. Planted. April to
July.
Sandbanks: raised dune SW of main
car park.

White Horehound
Marrubium vulgare
Native. Rare. Cliff-tops. June to July.
Nationally Scarce.
Worth: by Coast Path at Emmetts
Hill mainly 130m N of steps down to
valley.

There is one other cliff-top site that
demands head for heights and sure
footwork.

Skullcap *Scutellaria galericulata*
Native. Occasional. Marshes, beaches
(where it is short). June to September.
Stoborough Heath: in valley 50m
SW of A351 250m NW of Halfway
Inn. **The Moors:** see p.27. **Corfe:**
small amount 150m WSW of W end
of First Valley on West Common
(near Marsh Valerian). **Arne:** above
top of shore along 50m N-wards from
Telegraph Cable Notice (small flowers). **Shell Bay:** towards SE of Shell
Bay in area N of plank-bridge over
stream. **Brownsea:** plentiful for 1km
on and near beach running first SE
from Pottery Pier and then E.

Lesser Skullcap *Scutellaria minor*
Native. Occasional. Woods, verges,
marshes. July to September.
Creech Heath: on path34 400m W
of Furzebrook Road. **Stoborough
Heath:** along first 40m of permissive
bridleway10m E of and parallel to
Dismantled Tramway NW of
Hartland Stud. **Norden:** NW bank of
Michael's Pond. **Corfe:** West
Common in NW wet area; in First
Valley by stream precisely 50m SE of
UCR; near S edge of West Common

400m W of B3069; by little stream S
of Middle Common Pond 100m SW
of A351. **Godlingston Heath:** at
slight dip on NE side of bridleway27
near W edge of W of two small
woods N of golf course. **Studland
Heath:** on both beaches in Western
Arm of Little Sea; various places by
Woodland Nature Trail.

Wood Sage *Teucrium scorodonia*
Native. Frequent. Thin scrub on sand
or calcareous soil, wood rides. July to
September.

Bugle *Ajuga reptans*
Native. Frequent. Verges, grassland,
open woods. April to June.
Steeple: by path6 S of stream N of
field N of Hyde Wood. **Furzebrook:**
side of Furzebrook Road 75m NE of
right-angled bend in Purbeck Way.
Kingston: plentiful here and there
along NW side of path44 where it
passes through The Plantation.
Corfe: scattered in several sites in
NW of West Common NW of cattle
grid; in several sites in N of Middle
Common. **Rempstone:** N side of
Breaches Lane 15m E of Forest Lane.
Langton: here and there in rides of
West Wood. **Godlingston Heath:**
several places by bridleway27 from
wood W of greenkeepers' private
depot to E end of bridleway.
Swanage: here and there in
Northbrook Road Cemetery.
Canford Cliffs: just N of church
between two parts of Chaddesley
Glen.

Leaves are oval, some slightly
toothed. See Ground-ivy p.183.

Garden Catmint *Nepeta* x *faassenii*
(*N. racemosa* x *nepetella*)
Introduction. Rare. Escape. April to
August.

Ground-ivy *Glechoma hederacea*
Native. Frequent. Woods, verges, grassland. March to May.

When growing upright in open grassland, it can be mistaken for Bugle (p.182), but leaves are kidney-shaped, with large blunt teeth.

Self-heal *Prunella vulgaris*
Native. Frequent. Tracks, grassland including lawns. June to September.

Balm *Melissa officinalis*
Introduction. Occasional. Escape. August to September.
Stoborough Heath: by path5 140m NW of N side of small field crossed by path. **Langton:** pavement at SE corner of old cemetery on B3069. **Godlingston Heath:** on S side of bridleway35 10m W of S end of private track to Goathorn Farm. **Durlston:** near bottom of stone steps at top of Zigzag Path. **Studland:** E of bridleway12 30m N of middle W-E road of Glebeland Estate; on E side of Ferry Road S of path2 at horse warning sign.

Common Calamint
Clinopodium ascendens
(*Calamintha ascendens, C. sylvatica*)
Native. Occasional. Calcareous grassland and verges. July to September.
Stoborough: NE side of bypass from 20m SE of path13 here and there for 100m SE-wards. **Corfe:** here and there plentiful inside castle; much on S slopes outside of it including near bridge on road to Church Knowle W of castle and also by S end of path2 (form of this species – *baetica* – at castle was once considered to be separate species). **Ulwell:** near stepped path to Obelisk with relatives Wild Basil and Wild Marjoram; field bank 60m NE of lower lay-by. **Ballard**

Down: NE of true junction of Purbeck Way and bridleway14 – both by Purbeck Way where it passes through first band of scrub and also on N side of bridleway14 250m from junction.

Flowers are in loose, not densely hairy whorls (compare with next species).

Wild Basil *Clinopodium vulgare*
Native. Occasional. Calcareous grassland, scrub and verges. July to September.
Steeple: many places on Steeple Down (west). **Church Knowle:** on NW side of bridleway39 – 175-200m NE of junction with paths3 and 5. **Furzebrook:** both sides of track to Kilnwood Reserve 40m E of gate. **Norden:** N side of Purbeck Way along N foot of West Hill 30-40m E of bend at W end. **Corfe:** E of steps up East Hill about 100 steps from top. **Woolgarston:** E side of bridleway23 at its N end. **Wares (east):** scattered along N side of Priest's Way from junction with path26 E-wards for 500m. **Townsend Reserve:** NE of SE Bastion. **Ulwell:** by stepped path4 between Purbeck Way and Obelisk with relatives Wild Marjoram and Common Calamint. **Ballard Down:** above path10 500m E of its junction with bridleway14.

Few at most sites above: Wares and Ulwell are the best. Flowers are in tight, densely hairy whorls (compare with previous species). <u>There are usually only a few flowers out together in any whorl.</u>

Wild Marjoram *Origanum vulgare*
Native. Frequent. Undisturbed calcareous grassland, scrub and verges. July to September.
Steeple: on Steeple Down (west)

225m E of bend in bridleway3.
Corfe: plentiful on castle mound
(albino by path2); much inside castle;
with albinos 40m and more N of
Purbeck Way just E of gate at junction
of Purbeck Way with Sandy Hill
Lane. **Worth:** E side of bridleway19
from 300m SW of Coast Path for
100m. **Wares (west):** plentiful at
middle of E edge of Long Close.
Woolgarston: E side of bridleway23
at its N end. **Knitson:** plentiful on E
side of N end of bridleway12. **Ulwell:**
plentiful by Purbeck Way for 500m E
of path4. **Ballard Down:** very plentiful along S edge of Down. **Durlston:**
on rocks on W side of Caravan
Terrace. See Plate 20.

Wild Thyme *Thymus polytrichus*
Native. Frequent. Calcareous short
grassland, rocky outcrops and verges.
May to September.
Hartland Moor: albinos on old
tramway particularly 220m SW of
Slepe Road. **Durlston:** near albinos in
E side of Lighthouse Field between
path52 and Mile Posts. **Ballard
Down:** many albinos 40m ESE of
J.A.A. seat.
     Large plants are sometimes mis-
taken for Large Thyme.

Gypsywort *Lycopus europaeus*
Native. Frequent. Wet places, except
most acid ones. June to early
September.
Stoborough: by bend in W part of
path13. **Hartland Moor:** 125m E of
Jubilee Bridge along 15m. **Corfe
Charity's Meadows:** by gateway from
Home Mead (W) into Paddle Dock
meadow. **Wytch:** by path80 50m W
of Thrasher's Lane. **Studland:** W side
of bridleway23 just S of junction with
bridleway17; by stream at Middle
Beach. **Studland Heath:** on Third

Beach at SE of Little Sea. **Shell Bay:**
on NW side of boardwalk in two
places. **Brownsea:** S of track 50m W
of The Villa; N of track near Public
Hide.

Corn Mint *Mentha arvensis*
Native. Rare. Arable fields, other
disturbed ground. July to August.
Studland: 20m W of Ferry Road by
bridleway38. **Studland Heath:** S end
of Knoll Beach car park on E side of
track 10m N of stream bridge
(decreasing).

Tall Mint *Mentha* x *smithiana*
(*M. arvensis* x *aquatica* x *spicata*)
Introduction. Rare. Escape. August to
September.
Hartland Moor: N corner of Arne
Triangle S of road.

Whorled Mint *Mentha* x *verticillata*
(*M. arvensis* x *aquatica*)
Native. Rare. Verges. July to August.
Hartland Moor: S side of Arne Road
20m E of Soldiers Road. **Wytch:** on
NE side of bridleway4 30-80m NW
of private road to Oil Gathering
Station; 5-50m W of Thrasher's Lane
on path80. **Godlingston Heath:** by
bridleway27 425m W of junction of
bridleways26 and 27 (adjacent building now gone).

Water Mint *Mentha aquatica*
Native. Frequent. Wet places. July to
October.

Spear Mint *Mentha spicata*
Early Introduction. Occasional.
Escape. August to October.
Langton: old cemetery wall on N side
of B3069. **Kingswood:** S side of
B3351 opposite bridleway29. **Ulwell:**
SW side of road by Currendon Chalk
Pit.

Apple Mint *Mentha* x *villosa*
(*M. spicata* x *suavolens*)
Introduction. Occasional. Escape on verges, waste ground, grassland. July to August.
Kimmeridge: N side of path at W end of Kimmeridge Farm buildings.
Stoborough: on W side of short road which is former route of Grange Road 80m S of bypass. **Church Knowle:** W side of road at Cocknowle. **Corfe:** S side of bridleway30 just W of tiny E stream on Little East Common.
Worth: NW side of Purbeck Way 50m NE of its junction with Coast Path at Hill Bottom. **Langton:** E end of Castle View; E of path1 100m N of B3069. **Ulwell:** just over field fence on SW side of Ulwell Road opposite Ulwell Farm Caravan Park. **Swanage:** (form with few hairs) N side of path near NW corner of green E of Ballard Estate. **Studland:** (form with few hairs) on E side of bridleway12 65-70m N of middle W-E road of Glebeland Estate.

(**Pennyroyal** *Mentha pulegium*
Native, but introduced here. Former claypits. August to September.
Nationally Rare. Endangered.
Creech Heath: it has apparently disappeared from former clay workings in SE of Heath; it may reappear with the introduction of grazing.)

Rosemary *Rosmarinus officinalis*
Introduction. Rare. Walls. February to May.
Corfe: E wall of Village Pound (on E side of A351 just N of path32).

Wild Clary *Salvia verbenaca*
Native. Frequent. Downs, calcareous verges. May to August.
Corfe: S of West Hill on N side of bridleway70 from 10-70m W of Purbeck

Way; on long SW side of castle mound outside walls; on bank on E side of A351 N of junction with B3069.
Worth: on roadside bank N of village pond. **Wares (east):** by Coast Path through White Ware; scattered through wares E of that – especially by Coast Path. **Ulwell:** here and there near S edge of Round Down.
Durlston: S of path50 in NE corner of Field 10; on top of Down at SW corner of same field; near The Globe.

Dorset supplied stone for the forts at Portsmouth in the 18th and 19th centuries. Within Fort Cumberland at Portsmouth there is a colony of Wild Clary, which is absent from downland in E Hampshire, Sussex W of Arundel, and the E chalk ridge in The Isle of Wight. When dry, Wild Clary's seeds roll freely, but when wet they become sticky and adhere easily. So presumably Wild Clary seeds were carried to Portsmouth stuck to stone. Likewise, stone from Dorset probably accounts for its presence in Portchester churchyard, and in some Isle of Wight churchyards.

WATER-STARWORT FAMILY
It is difficult to identify these species. Ripe fruit is helpful; it is not easy to see, but it can often be found if enough plant material is examined carefully. *The Wild Flower Key* (Rose & O'Reilly, 2006) is useful. More detail is given in *Plant Crib 1998* (Rich & Jermy, 1998).

Common Water-starwort
Callitriche stagnalis
Native. Frequent. Ponds, streams, ditches, mud. May to September.

Various-leaved Water-starwort
Callitriche platycarpa
Native. Occasional. Streams and

ditches; often with previous species.
June to September.

The Moors: see p.27. **Corfe:** all in same stream but positions vary yearly – on S side of West Common both 5m E of bridge on UCR (often there); at SE corner of common 100m W of B3069; close to B3069 bridge; on S side of Middle Common both 40-50m E of B3069 and by Purbeck Way footbridge.

Pedunculate Water-starwort
Callitriche brutia
Native. Rare. Ditches. April to September.
Holme: East Holme Meadows – see p.23.

PLANTAIN FAMILY
Buck's-horn Plantain
Plantago coronopus
Native. Frequent. Cliff-tops, cliff quarries, tracks, salted roadsides. May to July.

Sea Plantain *Plantago maritima*
Native. Occasional. Muddy shores, salt-marshes. June to August.
Wytch: N end of path6; plentiful on Wytch Moor 100-150m S of NW corner. **Studland Heath:** scattered in Brand's Creek; along Redhorn Bay; NE corner of Redhorn Quay; S corner of Dyke Bay; SW shore of Bramble Bush Bay (deer keep it down, except at Redhorn Quay). **Sandbanks,** large plant 80m W of junction of Shore Road and Banks Road. **Lilliput,** SE end of Evening Hill by seawall.

Greater Plantain
Plantago major subsp. *major*
Native. Frequent. Verges, tracks. June to September.
Leaves have heart <u>or wedge</u>-shaped

bases and are hairless to slightly hairy on upper and undersides; the inflorescence is long <u>or short</u>, with up to 15 seeds per capsule. The subspecies *intermedia*, in contrast, always has leaves with wedge-shaped bases with slightly hairy undersides, and a short inflorescence, but usually over 15 seeds per capsule. Latter has not yet been found in the area by the author. Leaves die off in winter, unlike other plantain species.

Hoary Plantain *Plantago media*
Native. Frequent. Calcareous grassland. May to August.
Leaves with hairy upper and undersides.

Ribwort Plantain *Plantago lanceolata*
Native. Abundant. Grassland including lawns. April to August.
Sometimes, the aberrant form with large irregular heads occurs, especially at **Studland** between The Warren Wood and Studland Wood, in grassland between the Coast Path and the cliff-top path, but not at the same spot year on year.

Shoreweed *Littorella uniflora*
Native. Occasional. Shallow fresh water and shores. June to August.
Dorset Scarce.
Studland Heath: on and off two beaches of Western Arm of Little Sea; on and off most of beaches in SE of Little Sea; submerged near many other parts of its shore.
Submerged leaves are filled with pith without large hollows – compare with Spring Quillwort p.53. Shoreweed has two types of leaves: larger and thicker ones when submerged, and smaller ones when exposed (when it flowers). When the plant becomes exposed, the thicker first type dies

back and smaller one then grows. When the plant is submerged again those smaller leaves and flowering stems wither and a new set of thicker leaves is grown (M. Gillham, pers. com.).

BUDDLEIA FAMILY
Butterfly Bush *Buddleja davidii*
Introduction. Frequent. Cliffs, waste ground, pavements, buildings. June to October.

If it is allowed to grow on walls of gardens or buildings, it will crack them, and should be removed as soon as it is noticed. On roofs especially it can lead to Dry Rot.

Orange Ball Tree *Buddleja globosa*
Introduction. Rare. Planted or escaped. May to July.
Kimmeridge: W of path15 halfway through withybed. **Kingston:** NE side of B3069 just after first left hand bend going downhill from village. (**Durlston:** one recorded in *The Flora of Dorset* was deep in the scrub SE of N end of Diagonal Path – it may have died.)

OLIVE FAMILY
Forsythia *Forsythia* x *intermedia* (*F. suspensa* x *viridissima*)
Introduction. Occasional. Planted. March to April; some again in mid-August to September.
Holme: N side of Holme Lane 25m W of junction with minor road to West Holme Manor. **Ridge:** NE side of Purbeck Way E of Redcliffe Farm. **Church Knowle:** E side of path18 SW of West Buncknowle House just S of garden. **Bushey:** on E side of bridle-way10 250m N of Bushey Lane. **Langton:** E side of unmade road from B3069 to Castle View 20m S of Norman's Quarry.

Ash *Fraxinus excelsior*
Native. Abundant. Woods and hedges, mostly on calcareous soil.

Male and female flowers usually separate. Some trees wholly of one sex, some mostly so but with few branches with flowers of other sex. Some branches bear male flowers one year, female next year (Mitchell, 1978)!

Lilac *Syringa vulgaris*
Introduction. Rare. Planted. May to June.
Worth: E of road at N end of Renscombe Farm buildings. **Ulwell:** visible E of road 60m S of Currendon Farm. **Herston (north):** in hedge of former caravan park which can be seen from path2 looking W 200m N of stile at S end of path.

Wild Privet *Ligustrum vulgare*
Native. Frequent. Hedges, woods and scrub, mainly on calcareous soils. Late May to early July.
Kimmeridge: near bay on S side of road SE of S car park. **Stoborough:** NE side of A351 opposite Halfway Inn. **Church Knowle:** NW side of road for 300m NE of path69. **Corfe:** NE side of car park N of castle. **Arne:** variegated form 50m N of church on W side of road. **Worth:** S side of Coast Path 400 and 450m E of Coastwatch Station. **Wares (west):** N edge of Scratch Arse Ware 25-30m E of W end. **Langton:** N side of Wilkswood Lane here and there for 80m W of A351. **Herston (north):** E side of Washpond Lane 200m N of A351. **Durlston:** across road from N end of Diagonal Path. **Ulwell:** W side of steps of path4 N of Purbeck Way; variegated form on S side of Purbeck Way 85m W of stile which is 500m E of previous site.

Poisonous. Bushes most noticed when in flower. Very short dense hairs on the end of the twigs (lens), or on the edges of the bud-scales only by the end of winter.

Garden Privet *Ligustrum ovalifolium*
Introduction. Frequent. Planted, self-sown in woods and scrub. Mid-June to late July.

Poisonous. Bushes most noticed when in flower, peaking 2 to 3 weeks later than Wild Privet. Few very short sparse hairs on newest growth only, otherwise hairless.

FIGWORT FAMILY

Moth Mullein *Verbascum blattaria*
Introduction. Rare. Escape (sporadic). June to August.
Wytch: one in 2007 on W side of Thrasher's Lane 100m S of SE corner of Thrasher's Heath. **Brownsea:** sometimes albinos just beyond 'NO ENTRY' gate N of pond E of The Villa (confirming record which was doubted by Bowen (2000) in *The Flora of Dorset*).

Great Mullein *Verbascum thapsus*
Native. Occasional. Arable fields, other disturbed ground including rabbit warrens, verges. June to August.
Holme: SE edge of East Holme churchyard (approach via Holme Priory drive). **Steeple:** plentiful on Steeple Down (west) above old quarry 250m E of W end. **Arne:** here and there along 100m of SE side of Arne Road 250m SW of car park. **Worth:** car park S of Renscombe Farm. **Corfe:** for 40m along bridleway20 W of fence gate SW of mast on Rollington Hill. **Wares (west):** steep S-facing bank in Long Close 175m S of Eastington Farm. **Godlingston:** by bridleway84 – 400 and 440m W of

junction of bridleway84 and Purbeck Way. **Studland:** just E of entrance to Middle Beach car park. **Shell Bay:** W side of Ferry Road N of toll-booth. **Brownsea:** on S shore 75-150m E of SW corner of island. **Canford Cliffs:** above promenade 175m NE of Flaghead Chine.

Biennial; it does not appear in some of the sites every year.

Common Figwort
Scrophularia nodosa
Native. Occasional. Woods, verges. June to September.
Tyneham: by W end of Woodland Walk 225m W of Tyneham Farm. **Stoborough Heath:** W of path23 225m SW of A351. **Norden:** NE side of A351 by W corner of Gallows Plantation; where bridleway77 meets Slepe Road. **Harman's Cross:** few by track to S platform of railway station; on W side of path26 50m N of A351. **Kingswood:** by bridleway87 50m from B3351. **Knitson:** SW side of Burnham's Lane 300m SE of Knitson Farm. **Ulwell:** SW side of road 300m SE of Currendon Farm. **Studland:** near SE gate of Studland Wood. **Canford Cliffs:** towards N end of path between Brudenell and Nairn Roads.

Not at the same sites every year. It is less common in this area than the next species. Leaves are pointed, with fairly pointed teeth.

Water Figwort
Scrophularia auriculata
Native. Frequent. Wet places in woods, verges, flushes, gutters. June to mid-September.
Wareham: W side of B3075 just S of South Bridge; on side of inlet just W of same bridge. **Furzebrook:** W end of E-most of three ponds in S of

Kilnwood Reserve. **Corfe:** just N of Copper Bridge. **Worth:** flush on W edge of Abbott's Combe 125m S of path11. **Wares (west):** much in top of W-running flush in SE of Long Close; in most other flushes including at N of W end of Scratch Arse Ware.
Durlston: near ticket machine in E side car park; by Coast Path NE of castle. **Brownsea:** N of track 175m W of The Villa.

Leaves have rounded ends and rounded teeth.

Balm-leaved Figwort
Scrophularia scorodonia
Introduced. Rare. Beaches, verges. June to August.
Rempstone: few seen between bridle-ways34 (Oil Road) and 35 on W side of their junction (species having spread S-wards down private road from beach W of Goathorn Pier).
Brownsea: small non-flowering plants found both on beach near SW corner of island and also behind sea defence fence at middle of S shore 50m W of 'Easy Way Down' sign. It is spreading from its sites near the coast in the SW of Britain. The author thinks that its discovery on a small island in Portsmouth Harbour and the evidence from this area indicates that the increase may be partly due to plant material or seeds being carried in the sea.

Leaves are wrinkled, downy and double-toothed.

Snapdragon *Antirrhinum majus*
Introduction. Occasional. Pavements. June to September.

Small Toadflax *Chaenorhinum minus*
Early Introduction. Occasional. Railtracks, arable fields, other disturbed ground. May to October.

Swanage: visible on rail track with short-range binoculars looking from Court Road to N – both from road bridge over Swan Brook and from road 20m W of that bridge; may be seen by patrons as weed in flowerbeds of Pines Hotel.

Weasel's Snout *Misopates orontium*
Early Introduction. Rare. Verges, arable fields, other disturbed ground. July to October.
Vulnerable.
Stoborough: NE edge of bypass 50m NW of path13 along 2m (gets mown), (look out for it in other places near Stoborough, where it has had casual sites in the past).

Ivy-leaved Toadflax
Cymbalaria muralis
Introduction. Frequent. Usually walls, sometimes railway ballast, rarely rocks. April to September.
Swanage Railway – fleeting glimpses, N side of railtrack near New Barn both 110m W of bridge and 150m E of bridge; S side of track 250m E of bridge. **Swanage:** on rock on W side of bridleway just E of Belle Vue Farm (contrasting with usual sites on walls).

Sharp-leaved Fluellen *Kickxia elatine*
Early Introduction. Occasional. Arable fields, other disturbed ground on calcareous and on sandy soils, often with Field Woundwort. July to October.
Corfe: NW side of path19 just SW of railway crossing. **Wares (east):** by path22 in E edge of second field N of Priest's Way (with next species).
Ballard Down: by Coast Path in edge of first field N of Shep's Hollow when Maize is being grown. **Studland:** near where track crosses stream on E side of Harmony Farm NW Field; on bri-

dleway38 both 85-90m and 100-110m W of Ferry Road.

Leaves with three pointed corners.

Round-leaved Fluellen
Kickxia spuria
Early Introduction. Occasional. Disturbed calcareous ground, especially field edges. July to October. **Kingston:** sometimes by sides of West Street W of The Plantation. **Woolgarston:** from high point on bridleway20 120m SE of N end of bridleway24 go N-wards through scrub onto rough area of Ailwood Down – plants are 25m N of bridleway20. **Wares (east):** by path22 in E edge of second field N of Priest's Way (with previous species). **Ballard Down:** by Coast Path in edge of field just S of Down when Maize is being grown. At three sites over the Purbeck Limestone it has occurred with its normally 2-lipped flowers and also with small trumpet-shaped (peloric) flowers. One of the sites was below the low wall at the right-hand top of the path to **Durlston** Visitor Centre's toilets; the other two sites were on private land. It is worth looking out for this aberration.

Leaves are rounded at the base, usually slightly pointed at the apex.

Common Toadflax *Linaria vulgaris*
Native. Occasional. Verges, rough grassland. Late June to October. **Steeple:** N side of road along hilltop NW of Steeple 100m E of viewpoint. **Corfe:** N side of Sandy Hill Lane 60m E of railway bridge. **Bushey:** N side of Bushey Lane 100m E of Higher Bushey Farm. **Langton:** W side of unmade road to Castle View 70m N of B3069. **Swanage Railway:** S side 50m W of A351 bridge W of New Barn. **Knitson:** halfway on N side of lower section of zigzag track. **Swanage:** NE side of Ulwell Road 90-105m NW of Whitecliff Road. **Townsend Reserve:** NE and E of Orchid Bastion. **Durlston:** many along 10m of Caravan Terrace. **Studland:** in Old Nick's Ground 40m SE of NE corner of Studland Wood. See Plate 20.

Common x Pale Toadflax – hybrid
Linaria x *sepium*
(*L. vulgaris* x *repens*)
Native. Rare. Railbank. Late June to August.
Swanage Railway: fleeting views from the train of single specimens which may occur (with Pale Toadflax populations) either side of track within 300m E of bridge at New Barn.

Pale flowers, leaves intermediate size.

Purple Toadflax *Linaria purpurea*
Introduction. Frequent. Escape on verges, pavements, railbanks. June to September.

Purple x Pale Toadflax – hybrid
Linaria x *dominii*
(*L. purpurea* x *repens*)
Native. Rare. Railbank. Late June to August.
Swanage Railway: fleeting views from train of single specimens which may occur (with Pale Toadflax populations) within following three stretches of railway – both sides of rail track for 100m E of crossing of path4 (or binoculars from path4 well off rail track); on N side 150m E of same crossing; either side of track for 300m E of bridge at New Barn.

It has pale flowers, but is taller than Pale Toadflax; the upper stem is branched like Purple Toadflax.

Pale Toadflax *Linaria repens*
Native. Occasional. Railway sides.
June to August.
Swanage Railway: N end of NE side
of Corfe cutting; bank on N side 20m
E of Harman's Cross platform; two
places on bank on N side just E of
bridge at Harman's Cross (binoculars
from bridge); both sides for 100m E
of crossing of path4 (with hybrid
above); both sides for 300m E of
bridge at New Barn. **Harman's Cross:**
sides of rail track for 100m E of crossing of path4 (with hybrid above)
(binoculars from path well off rail
track); SE buttress of bridge at New
Barn (**easiest site**).

In light of the previous five entries,
and the one three before them,
Swanage Railway could be subtitled
'The Toadflax Line'.

Foxglove *Digitalis purpurea*
Native. Frequent. Woods, heaths,
scrub, verges – plentiful after clear-
ances. June to July.
Holme: N side of Holme Lane for
some distance W of railway bridge.
Stoborough Heath: here and there by
N half of path5. **Arne:** plentiful in
several places by tracks. **Godlingston
Heath:** plentiful in Harmony Farm
West just E of private house garden.
Studland Heath: plenty N of Curlew
Cottage ruins. These sites all have
good displays at present. See Plate 20.

Thyme-leaved Speedwell
Veronica serpyllifolia
Native. Frequent. Woods, heath
tracks, short grass including lawns.
April to October.

Heath Speedwell *Veronica officinalis*
Native. Occasional. Heaths, grassland.
May to August.

Stoborough: plentiful on Stoborough
Heath Reserve W of Soldiers Road N
of S cattle grid. **Hartland Moor:** plen-
tiful near permissive bridleway in field
E of Isolation Cottages. **Corfe:** here
and there on drier parts of West
Common. **Rempstone:** N of bridle-
way35 (Oil Road) 100m E of junc-
tion with bridleway34 (Oil Road).
Godlingston Heath: W end of
Harmony Farm W Fields. **Studland:**
Harmony Farm NW Field; E side of
Ferry Road 130m S of Knoll Beach
Road. **Studland Heath:** 125m SE of
Ferry Road by track opposite that to
Brand's Bay Hide. **Brownsea:** here
and there in grassland and thin wood-
land along S side of island.

Germander Speedwell, Birdseye
Veronica chamaedrys
Native. Abundant. Woods, verges,
fields. April to June.
Townsend Reserve: albino on anthill
15m SE of gate at W end of permissive bridleway.
  Many plants have stems with hairs
in two lines along their whole length,
but in some the upper and/or lower
stem is covered with hairs and only
the middle part of the stem has hairs
in two lines, whether in sun or shade.

Wood Speedwell *Veronica montana*
Native. Frequent. Woods, mostly
ancient ones. May to June.
  Stems hairy all round.

Marsh Speedwell *Veronica scutellata*
Native. Occasional. Marshes, damp
verges. June to August.
Dorset Scarce.
Holme: East Holme Meadows – see
p.23. **Hartland Moor:** few in E side of
Upper Fen 350m NE of Isolation
Cottages; small plants 5m S of SW cor-
ner of Jubilee Bridge 3m W of track.

Corfe: 5m S of bridleway30 200m from A351 (just W of tiny E stream) (may be grazed). **Shell Bay:** here and there under and on edge of willows for 200m S of E end of boardwalk (only flowers in lighter places and not often then; larger plants are grazed); rather more of it (blue flowers) 200m SE of E end of boardwalk between end of line of Grey Willows and area dominated by rushes.

Narrow pointed leaves in opposite pairs, with next pair at right angle to the previous pair. Leaves are usually green in this area, but sometimes olive-brown.

Brooklime *Veronica beccabunga*
Native. Occasional. Wet places, except on heaths. May to August.
Corfe: by stream at E-most sharp bend of UCR in S of West Common; in First Valley 20m SE of UCR; by stream on S side of Middle Common 50 and 100m from SW corner. **Wytch:** S side of path5 by W corner of Wytch Farm buildings. **Worth:** flush on W side of Abbott's Combe 150m S of path11. **Wares (west and east):** in most flushes. **Langton:** 50m E of NW corner of Langton West Wood in middle of bridleway42. **Woolgarston:** on E side of path26 50m S of road at Ailwood Farm. **Harman's Cross:** 60m NE of stile E of New Barn at low point of path6. **Herston (north):** N of path78 in SE corner of field SE of Herston Halt.

Blue Water Speedwell
Veronica anagallis-aquatica
Native. Occasional. Watersides. June to September.
Holme: plentiful in East Holme Meadows – see p.23. **Stoborough:** by Cobbs Lake watercourse at NW end of path13. **Wareham:** on SE side of River

Frome both sides of bypass bridge (binoculars); here and there for 750m downstream from bridge especially 400m downstream (boat); here and there on S side of river along 50m immediately E of South Bridge; along 5m 140m E of bridge. **Hartland Moor:** on edges of Pillwort Pond. **Corfe:** by E side of Copper Bridge.

Wall Speedwell *Veronica arvensis*
Native. Abundant. Arable fields, other disturbed ground, including anthills, gardens, also wall-tops. April to September.
Plants are often very small.

American Speedwell
Veronica peregrina
Introduction. Rare. Garden weed. April to September.
Kimmeridge: albino path weed in S end of Smedmore House walled garden (open one Sunday afternoon in May and one in September).
Flowers alternate up the stem; they are 2-3mm across; fruitcase is hairless and leaves narrowly oblong. See drawing.

Grey Field Speedwell *Veronica polita*
Introduction. Rare. Arable fields, other disturbed, non-acid ground, including gardens; walls. All year.
Brownsea: low wall bordering track NW of Visitor Centre.
Flowers not always as dark blue as in

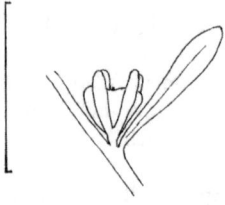

American Speedwell seedcase and leaf.

published illustrations, and leaves not always greyish. Lower leaves are usually wider than long; crucially it has very small, mostly arched hairs on the seed capsule as well as straight glandular hairs (lens). Over 4 times more frequent in Dorset than Green Field Speedwell, which has not been seen recently in this area.

Common Field Speedwell
Veronica persica
Introduction. Abundant. Arable fields, other disturbed, non-acid ground. All year.

Sometimes, the flowers are smaller than usual; check the shape of the seedpods.

Slender Speedwell *Veronica filiformis*
Introduction. Occasional. Lawns. April to June.
Church Knowle: N side of road W of path69 (with previous species – compare their differences). **Kingston:** in churchyard halfway along N wall. **Langton:** small patch near S end of old cemetery N of B3069. **Godlingston:** in cemetery (with rather more Germander Speedwell) especially on W side of main drive 80m S of gates. **Swanage:** much in Day's Park near entrance from Ulwell Road (near entrance to Cricket Ground). **Ulwell:** SW side of Ulwell Road opposite lower lay-by. **Durlston:** E of road near entrance to wood in NE of Country park; in main glade in same wood. **Canford Cliffs:** E side of Bessborough Road 100m from S end. **Branksome Chine:** 200m up chine from road at SE end for example.

Ivy-leaved Speedwell
Veronica hederifolia
Early Introduction. Frequent. Woods, arable fields, other disturbed ground. March to May.

Sometimes two subspecies are described, but as Bowen (2000) wrote in *The Flora of Dorset*, 'The distinction between them is not clear-cut.'

Koromiko *Hebe salicifolia*
Introduction. Rare. Planted.
Swanage: N side of W corner of copse W of D'Urberville Drive – beyond brambles (take secateurs).

Long narrow leaves up to 7cm long; 6 to 7 times as long as wide – see drawing.

Dieffenbach's Hebe
Hebe dieffenbachii
Introduction. Rare. Planted and self-sown.
Branksome Chine: cliff-top SW of car park S of Library.

Most leaves are 5-8cm long, 3 to 5 times as long as wide.

Hedge Veronica *Hebe* x *franciscana* (*H. elliptica* x *speciosa*)
Introduction. Rare. Escape on cliffs, pathways.
Sandbanks: by shops and toilets near ferry. **Branksome Chine:** seedlings sometimes around flights of steps on

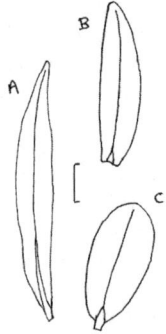

Leaves of Hebe genus: A - Koromiko, B - Dieffenbach's Hebe, C - Hedge veronica.

cliff path and top of path down cliff 150m SW of chine.

Most leaves over 7 cm long, 2 to 4 times as long as wide; partially fertile.

For other Hebes see Stace (1997).

Eyebrights *Euphrasia* species
Eyebrights are currently divided into 21 species (formerly 25) and 63 hybrids in the British Isles. Only one species is easily distinguishable from the rest, and that is only found in Eire. Seven species and two hybrids are recorded in this area in *The Flora of Dorset* (Bowen, 2000). It is difficult to get help with identifying Eyebrights, and they are therefore often recorded as '*Euphrasia* agg.'. Some books do not separate them. Blamey, Fitter and Fitter (2003) gives them brief and insufficient treatment; however, their maps are very helpful. Some colonies are hybrids and so do not fit descriptions of species, e.g. W of Middle Common Pond at Corfe.

Eyebrights are semi-parasitic. They use many plant species as hosts: clovers, birdsfoot trefoils and plantains are some favourites; Eyebrights that grow on clovers and birdsfoot trefoils may be larger than usual, because of the extra nitrogen available from members of the pea family; small plants may be small because they have no host (A. Silverside, pers. com.).

Identification features are the overall size of ungrazed and uncut plants, position and thickness of their branches, spacing of leaves on them, leaf size, flower size, position of the lowest flower on the main stem and length of the seedcase in relation to sepal-tube tips. However, these features vary and an average for each of them in a population needs to be determined. The shape of the teeth of the lowest bract – i.e. leaf-like structure under the lowest flower – is used in some identification books, but is too variable to be of much use in some species.

English Sticky Eyebright
Euphrasia anglica
Native. Occasional. Commons. June to July.
Dorset Scarce. Endangered.
Corfe: few in grassland near SW corner of West Common; very plentiful on higher ground between First and Second Valleys 20-150m NW of UCR; very plentiful to SE of UCR S of First Valley streamlet as far E as path51; some on N-facing slope above flushes S of Middle Common Pond (Little Kneeling Eyebright is nearby at some sites).

This is the easiest species to identify: it has tiny glands on the ends of the hairs which are at least 6 times the length of the glands (lens); the only species in this area which has this gland/hair length ratio.

Short-haired Eyebright
Euphrasia arctica subsp. *borealis*
Native. Occasional. Verges. June to September.
Dorset Scarce.
Holme: NE (open access) corner of Battle Plain 90m WNW of entrance to it at Doreys Farm. **Creech Heath:** here and there along path34; by track on map running E from midway along same path. **Stoborough:** on Dismantled Tramway 150-350m N of A351. **Hartland Moor:** S side of Arne Road 300m E of Soldiers Road; scattered on Arne Triangle verges especially NE of Triangle; NE side of Slepe Road both 20m SE of bridge at NE of Moor and at 20m NW of N cattle grid; also 20m SW of Slepe Road on

SE side of track N of and parallel to old tramway. **Godlingston Heath:** here and there either side of first 200m of bridleway36 NW of Ferry Road.

It is usually the tallest of the species in this area, with long gaps (internodes) on the stems between the leaves, and with branches only from the lower to middle part of the stem.

Broad-leaved Eyebright
Euphrasia tetraqueta
Native. Occasional. Short calcareous grassland. May to August.
Tyneham: N side of Coast Path E of stream at Arish Mell. **Corfe:** N side of Purbeck Way 150-325m W of radio mast on Rollington Hill. **Wares (west and east):** scattered patches in many S-facing sloping fields, especially towards Coast Path; especially throughout slopes in both Belle Vue Middle and Belle Vue East Wares. **Knitson:** few in between Gorse halfway up near W end of steep part of Down between bridleways8 and 9. **Durlston:** scattered on S-facing sloping fields; on S-facing rocks N of lighthouse; N of track which forms boundary between Fields 13 and 14; NE of shallow quarry in NE of Field 14. **Ulwell:** plentiful on Down from NW of path4 to road to Studland. **Ballard Down:** here and there in short grassland especially above fence above Ballard Cliff W of trig point.

A squat plant; leaves longer than the lengths between them on the stem and sometimes flushed purple; its earliest flowers are low on the stem; it begins flowering in May before other Eyebrights. It grows wider and taller later if the summer is wet.

Common Eyebright
Euphrasia nemorosa
Native. Frequent. Grassland, verges,

grazed heaths. June to September.

Often much-branched, with branches coming from anywhere up the stem; the leaf underside is not dark; lowest flower usually at the 9th or higher node up the stem (when counting check for node-scars of fallen leaves); seedcases are shorter than the sepal-tube. It sometimes grows near the previous species.

Little Kneeling Eyebright
Euphrasia confusa
Native. Occasional. Well-grazed grassland. June to August.
East Creech: along N-facing N side of Stonehill Down W of path32.
Stoborough Heath: along 50m of SW side of Rabbits' Meadow beginning 60m SE of gate near NW corner of Meadow. **Corfe:** widely scattered along NE side of West Common between UCR and B3069; on Monkey's Hump; scattered in area SW of Purbeck Way for 100m NW of B3069. **Wares (west):** probably this species near track along S end of E side of Long Close.

A squat plant with thin wavy branches, with small leaves at their bases; the foliage is sometimes flushed with purple; the flowers are not usually opposite each other.

Red Bartsia *Odontites vernus*
subsp. *serotinus* (*O. vulgaris*)
Native. Frequent. Rough grassland, woodland rides, tracks, verges. Semi-parasitic. June to August.
Corfe: near NE edge of West Common 15m NW of UCR; plentiful near W end of bridleway30.
Langton: by path35 in field W of road to Acton; by road to Acton; S of gate on path5 on S side of Talbot's Wood (N not W of cemetery). **Wares (east):** N side of Priest's Way 10m W

of path 68. **Durlston:** plentiful along sides of W half of track which is boundary between Fields 13 and 14; very plentiful near path50 along N side of Lighthouse Field. **Townsend Reserve:** very plentiful. **Luscombe Valley:** 6-18m N of gate at SE corner; 30m SW of pond.

Has up to 8 pairs of branches, at angles of 50-85° to the main stem. The number of pairs of leaves on the main stem between the topmost branches and lowest flower is not significant in distinguishing it from the subsp. *vernus*, which has up to 4 pairs of branches, at angles of 30-50 ° to the main stem and which has not yet been recorded in this area.

Yellow Bartsia *Parentucellia viscosa*
Native. Occasional. Heaths, verges and tracks. Semi-parasitic. June to September.
Holme: NE (open access) corner of Battle Plain 70-85m WNW of entrance at Doreys Farm; East Holme Meadows – see p.23. **Stoborough Heath:** here and there in Rushy Hollow field and Sandlings field.
Hartland Moor: scattered in large area of Stoborough Heath W of Soldiers Road W and SW of the name 'Slepe Heath' on O.S. map; on Slepe Heath 25-50m N of gate from Soldiers Road. See Plate 20.

Yellow Rattle *Rhinanthus minor*
Native. Occasional. Permanent grassland, except on acid soils; semi-parasitic on grasses and various other plants. May to August.
Hartland Moor: here and there both sides of Arne Road from 450m W of N end of Soldiers Road all the way E to Arne Triangle. **Corfe Charity's Meadows:** plentiful in meadow SW of Sharford Bridge; in Long Meadow

and in Close Next The Barn.
Langton: at junction of roads to Kingston and Worth in field between them (view from roads); near path37 in N side of field N of B3069.
Bushey: here and there on N side of Bushey Lane S of Brenscombe Heath.
Wares (east): Sherwood's Wear especially. **Durlston:** very plentiful in some meadows.

Marsh Lousewort
Pedicularis palustris
Native. Occasional. Marshes. Semi-parasitic. Mid-June to August.
Dorset Scarce.
Furzebrook: along 60m of valley in SE of Norden Heath SW-wards from just E of junction of paths11 and 12. **Corfe:** in three places in large low wet area in middle of W side of West Common; in First Valley both at W end; 100m SE of UCR; also in Second Valley 80 and 100m NW of UCR; in Third Valley 90m NW of UCR; in Middle Common mostly by 20m long streamlet running N-wards down middle of slope S of Pond.

Flowers later than the next species; stems are upright; lower lip is longer than the upper. (Some flowers have 2 pairs of 'teeth' either side of the apex of the upper lip, but others have only 1 pair, like the next species.)

Lousewort *Pedicularis sylvatica*
Native. Frequent. Wet heaths, bogs and acid fields. Semi-parasitic. End April to mid-June.
Stoborough Heath: here and there on part of Heath between Grange Road and Furzebrook Road. **Hartland Moor:** E of copse 400m N of Scotland Barn. **Corfe:** plentiful on Common especially W and E of Middle Common Pond (albino 15m N of concrete path marker on ridge

SW of Middle Common Pond).
Studland: plentiful in SW end of
Harmony Farm NE Field. **Studland
Heath:** Spur Bog.

Stems mostly close to ground.
Upper lip longer than lower. See Plate
21.

BROOMRAPE FAMILY

Toothwort *Lathraea squamaria*
Native. Occasional. Old woods –
parasitic chiefly on Hazel, also on
Field Maple and other trees. February
to May (first appearance varies from
late January to mid-April according to
the weather).
Creech: one seen on NW side of road
through Great Wood 100m NE of
lower of two tall Lawson's Cypresses
on other side of road. **East Creech:**
plentiful here and there near S (top)
edge of woods N of Stonehill Down
in some of areas where Ramsons is
not dominant especially 50m E of
path32 and from 200-400m E of same
path – very good population. **King's
Wood:** by bridleway16 80m NW of
lower gate near top of wood; SE of
bridleway87 30m SW of E corner of
wood. See Plate 21.

Ivy Broomrape *Orobanche hederae*
Native. Occasional. Parasitic on Ivy.
June to July.
Corfe: few on left 5-10m beyond gate
to West Bailey of castle. **Worth:** by
Coast Path 200, 300 and 425m E of
Coastwatch Station; by and E of junc-
tion of path13 with Coast Path.
Townsend Reserve: by path entrance
on E side of Reserve; 50m W of that
near fence. **Swanage:** close to Health
Centre (with Common Broomrape
nearby); W side of Newton Road near
N end. **Durlston:** by lower half of
Zigzag Path; on W side of Lighthouse
Road opposite S-most house; both

sides of Solent Road 40m from
Lighthouse Road. **Studland:** NE side
of Wadmore Lane 20m NW of Ferry
Road. **Branksome Chine:** halfway
along N side of S (highest) area of
Beach Road car park.

Has dull yellow stigma lobes. Does
not occur every year at some sites. See
Plate 21.

Common Broomrape
Orobanche minor var. *minor*
Native. Occasional. Parasitic, particularly on members of the pea family.
June to July.
Worth: near W edge of Worth Mead
300m S of London Row. **Wytch:** E
side of Thrasher's Lane 10m N of NE
corner of Thrasher's Heath.
Durlston: near SE corner of Hoggett
Mead; good number near track
halfway down W side of Centenary
Meadow. **Swanage:** regular in
flowerbeds near Health Centre especially one nearest light-controlled
pedestrian crossing of Kings Road on
Shrub Ragwort (Ivy Broomrape nearby). **Studland:** S edge of track along
cliff-top (N of and parallel to Coast
Path) 250m and more W of Studland
Wood; widespread in Old Nick's
Ground. **Branksome Chine:** on bank
on W side of car park by sea.

Has purple stigma lobes. Often not
at a given site every year.

Carrot Broomrape
Orobanche minor var. *maritima*
Native. Occasional. Parasitic on <u>Wild</u>
Carrot on and near cliffs. May to
June.
Nationally Scarce.
Tyneham: plenty on low cliff at
Pondfield beach. **Kimmeridge:** along
200m of sloping cliffs above beach E of
Charnel (accessible when Army Range
Walks open). **Worth:** plentiful by

Coast Path in open triangular area 400m SW of W end of Winspit quarries. **Wares (west):** by large spoil-heap near sea-cliff at E side of Seacombe Quarry; near Coast Path gate from Seacombe Bottom to Cliff Field; few widely spaced near Coast Path in W half of Cliff Field; near fence above cliff 100m SW of entrance to Hedbury main cliff quarries; S of stile of path down to Dancing Ledge Quarry; **(east)** near cliff-top in White Ware 60m E of W wall; few thinly scattered near Coast Path in Chillmark Ware and Balston Wear; at various hazardous sites on edge of cliffs from below Nicholas Down to below Balston Wear. **Durlston:** SE of lighthouse between Coast Path and corner of lighthouse enclosure. **Swanage:** SE-facing broken low cliffs near Peveril Point.

This variety was first described for the British Isles from a plant at Seacombe. It differs from Common Broomrape by having yellow bosses in the throats of the flowers. There is much less of it in years with dry springs.

ACANTHUS FAMILY

Bear's Breech *Acanthus mollis*
Introduction. Rare. Escape. July to August.
Swanage: edge of cliff at Ballard Green; some below it (view latter from beach, binoculars help). **Lilliput:** by N end of path from Alington Close to Shore Road.

BUTTERWORT FAMILY

Pale Butterwort *Pinguicula lusitanica*
Native. Occasional. Bogs, sides of ditches, marshes. May to August.
Stoborough Heath: 140m W of NE corner of Sandlings field 40m S of N edge. **Hartland Moor:** 200m NE of Isolation Cottages; on S side of S part

of Arne Triangle 40m from E end. **Corfe:** 150m WSW of W end of First Valley on West Common; in Second Valley 100m NW of road; 30m W of S end of path53 plank bridges in E of First Valley; much in parts of Southwest Valley of Middle Common; on same common in wet area on NE-facing slope SSE of pond 75m SW of A351. **Kingswood:** in Kingswood Bog (wrongly marked as woodland on O.S. map) 25m E 160m S of final 'h' in the name 'Kingswood Heath' on O.S. map. **Studland Heath:** thinly scattered in NW part of Spur Bog; closer together in N half of Wood Heath.

Inconspicuous plants with one small flower per stem.

Bladderwort, Wavy Bladderwort
Utricularia australis
Native. Occasional. Ponds, ditches, swampy woodland, lake edges. Mid-July to September.
Dorset Scarce.
The Moors: see p.27. **Studland Heath:** scattered off E half of N shore of Western Arm of Little Sea; here and there off some less accessible shores of Little Sea; scattered in shallow pools along SE edge of Second Ridge for distance of 250m SW of track to nudists' area.

It flowers sporadically in the open but does not flower in the shade; it flowers well in the first year after overhanging scrub has been cleared. Flowers in Little Sea are easily damaged by waves. Leaves look all the same, with both segments and bladders (compare with next species).

Nordic Bladderwort
Utricularia stygia
Native. Occasional. Bogs. Mid-July to September.
Dorset Rare.

Hartland Moor: NW edge of West Bog 100m E of S cattle grid on Soldiers Road; W end of hat-shaped pond in SE of West Bog; in two small pools 125m W and 80m WSW of bend in electricity lines just below 'H' of 'Hartland Moor' printed on O.S. map (approach from dry heath to N); SW of island of scrub 75m SE of Post Pool; much in pools 175m N of Fire Pond E of Tramway Bog; many 200m E of Post Pool; 100m W of Slepe Road somewhat S of stream in NE of Moor; 30m W of Slepe Road in same stream.

Flowers are bright yellow, <u>not orange</u>, similar to but slightly smaller than the previous species. It flowers more in the Purbeck area than at any other British site. It has 2 leaf types: one without bladders, often green (and pretty), just under the water surface, and the other with bladders and few segments, deeper in the water (compare with previous species). See Plate 21.

Lesser Bladderwort
Utricularia minor
Native. Occasional. Bogs. July to September.
Stoborough Heath: here and there in wettest parts of bog E of Dismantled Tramway 900m N of A351. **Hartland Moor:** NW edge of West Bog 100m SE of S cattle grid on Soldiers Road; W end of hat-shaped pond in SE of West Bog; small pools at bog edge 30m NE of prominent red diamond-shaped 'EWS' sign in NW (not W) of Moor; several places both in and S of stream in NE of Moor; in open access area 75m E of N end of Arne Triangle. **The Moors:** pools and muddy edges in open access area 80m SW of Bank Gate Cottages; W side of large pond 250m W of same cottages; **Godlingston Heath:** much in pools

of Brand's Bog from 50m S of bridle-way36 for 450m SW – more on W side of bog than E side.

Flowers pale yellow.

BELLFLOWER FAMILY
Peach-leaved Bellflower
Campanula persicifolia
Introduction. Rare. Escape. June to August.
Studland: S side of Heath Green Road 50m W of Agglestone Road on opposite side.

Adria Bellflower
Campanula portenschlagiana
Introduction. Rare (frequent in gardens). Temporary escape on walls, pavements. April to October. See drawing.

Trailing Bellflower
Campanula poscharskyana
Introduction. Occasional (frequent in gardens). Escape on walls and paths, banks. June to October.
Woolgarston: N side of road 100m W of N end of Tabbit's Hill Lane.
Langton: Norman's Quarry; W side of S end of path2; S side of B3069

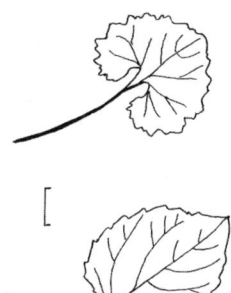

Leaves of Bellflowers: Adria (above) and Trailing.

50m W of Leeson House entrance. **Sandbanks:** W side of W path between Grasmere Road and Seacombe Road 20m from former road. **Canford Cliffs:** near S and N ends of path between Brudenell and Nairn Roads. **Branksome Chine:** several places on walls of stream in chine.

Nettle-leaved Bellflower
Campanula trachelium
Native. Occasional. Verges, woods. July to August.
Kimmeridge: W side of road 70 and 80m S of entrance to car park near junction of road to Bradle. **Creech:** plentiful on SE side of upper part of road through Great Wood. **East Creech:** S side of road E of East Creech for 50m W of T-junction with Furzebrook Road; W side of road S of same T-junction; SE side of road beyond that as far as worked quarry (these three sites are best). **Church Knowle:** N side of road 25m W of N end of path23. **Bushey:** on N side of bridleway14 – 30 and 200m SW of junction of bridleways14 and 15. **Woolgarston:** on W side of bridleway23 50m N of road. **Langton:** by bridleway42 140m E of path44. **Knitson:** by bridleway8 500m W of bridleway12. **Ulwell:** E side of path4 shortly S of Purbeck Way (with albino in past). **Studland:** here and there in Studland Wood. See Plate 22.

Harebell *Campanula rotundifolia*
Native. Occasional. Dry ground on verges, downs, commons. July to September.
Tyneham: scattered by Coast Path along top of Gad Cliff (albino seen 200m W of junction with path which goes N to Tyneham village). **Church Knowle:** here and there on down NW of Cocknowle. **Kingston:** on

Swyre Head tumulus viewpoint. **Hartland Moor:** E side of Slepe Road by S cattle grid. **Corfe:** scattered on Central Ridge of West Common. **Worth:** plentiful in places on steep down NW of Hill Bottom. **Wares (west):** on E side of S end of Seacombe Bottom towards top of slope. **Knitson:** on SW side of bridleway9 250m NW of SE end of bridleway. **Kingswood:** on N side of B3351 E of viewpoint for 100m. **Durlston:** on N side of Coast Path near closed steps to Tilly Whim Quarry. **Ballard Down:** widely scattered along top of S-facing slope.

Sheepsbit *Jasione montana*
Native. Frequent. Fixed dunes, sandy heaths and banks. May to September.
Corfe Charity's Meadows: N side of path80 10m E of gate at Slepe Road. **Corfe:** on ridge of West Common 30m W of path51; N side of Sandy Hill Lane 450m W of Sandyhills Farm. **Studland** and **Shell Bay:** frequent on fixed dunes. **Sandbanks:** inside fenced dunes both 80m SW of main car park; 200m NE of it.

Do not confuse with Scabiouses, which are larger-flowered, paler blue, much taller plants, with spine-like sepal teeth and all leaves in opposite pairs.

Garden Lobelia *Lobelia erinus*
Introduction. Occasional. Casual. June to September.

BEDSTRAW FAMILY
Field Madder *Sherardia arvensis*
Native. Frequent. Arable fields, other disturbed ground, short grass, verges and paths. May to September.
Worth: albinos have been seen on SE-facing slope NW of North Hill.

Flowers are four-pointed, as with all

Bedstraws. Do not confuse with Cornsalads (p.205), which have five-pointed flowers.

Squinancywort *Asperula cynanchia*
Native. Frequent. Short calcareous permanent grassland. June to August.
    Albinos are frequent.

Woodruff *Galium odoratum*
Native. Occasional. Calcareous old woods and verges. May to June.
Creech: NW side of road through Great Wood 100m NE of '20%' sign; SE side of same road both halfway down hill near lower of two tall Lawson's Cypresses; near bottom of wood. **East Creech:** along 10m near S edge Furlong's Coppice around 100m from E end of it. **Corfe:** near Byle Brook 30m S of N end of S half of Byle Copse. **Langton:** near stream in West Wood 150m from W edge of wood; NW of large pond in centre of N of West Wood; by middle of E-W ride in S of West Wood. **Bushey:** here and there by SW half of bridleway14. **Rempstone:** S side of Breaches Lane 120m E of Rempstone Farm new buildings.

Fen Bedstraw *Galium uliginosum*
Native. Occasional. Marshes. July to August.
Hartland Moor: here and there in Upper Fen; here and there in W half of Middle Fen; by Pillwort Pond; S side of Arne Road – both 400 and 450m E of Soldiers Road; 200m W of Arne Triangle; SW side of Slepe Road 20m NW of N cattle grid. **The Moors:** see p.27. **Corfe:** frequent in NW parts of West Common; by and near Middle Common Pond; also in wet area NE of stream on Little East Common.
    The ends of the leaves drawn out

into long points; the stem is usually very rough. Marsh Bedstraw (below), with its less pointed leaves and variably but less rough stems, is sometimes found at the same sites.

Marsh Bedstraw
Galium palustre subsp. *palustre*
Native. Frequent. Wet places except bogs. June to July.
    Buds may be pink. The minute prickles on leaf-edges may point <u>forwards and/or backwards</u>. In fact, they often point backwards in about the lower two-thirds of a leaf-edge and forwards in the upper third; sometimes they point all in one direction. Rarely, they point forwards on one edge of a leaf and backwards on the other edge (A. Mundell, pers.com).

Lady's Bedstraw *Galium verum*
Native. Abundant. Dry, usually calcareous, grassland. June to August.

Lady's x Hedge Bedstraw – hybrid
Galium x *pomeranicum*
(*G. verum* x *mollugo*)
Native. Rare. With both parents. Late June to mid-July.
Steeple: 10m above long grass at foot of Steeple Down (west) 200m ESE of bend in bridleway3. **Durlston:** up to 5m S of path50 in NW of Lighthouse Field 70m E of gate to Field 10.
    Flowers are primrose colour, intermediate between parents. See Plate 22.

Hedge Bedstraw *Galium mollugo*
Native. Frequent. Hedges, wood edges, verges, calcareous and neutral grassland. June to August.
    Ends of 'petals' (trumpet lobes) are drawn out into a point of at least 0.3mm and usually more; fruit is minutely wrinkled (lens).

It is divided into two subspecies in some identification books, but doubted by Stace (1997).

Heath Bedstraw *Galium saxatile*
Native. Frequent. Heaths, acid grassland, including some clay tops of downs given below. June to August.
Tyneham: by picnic table S of Army Range path 550m SW of Whiteway Hill trig point. **Kingston:** Swyre Head. **Woolgarston:** on and near some tumuli on top of Ailwood Down. **Ballard Down:** in S-facing area near top of Down 250m W of path7.
Ends of 'petals' may have a short point, but of less than 0.3mm; fruit has minute warts.

Cleavers, Goosegrass
Galium aparine
Native. Abundant. Anywhere except dark or very acid sites. April to August.

Crosswort *Cruciata laevipes*
Native. Frequent. Calcareous scrub, verges and grassland. May to June.
Surprisingly there is much less of it in other calcareous areas in Dorset.

Wild Madder *Rubia peregrina*
Native. Occasional. Rough grassland and climbing in scrub on calcareous coastlands. June to August.
Worth: in places near Coast Path 300-400m E of St. Aldhelm's Head; by path13 100m S of Winspit Cottage private drive. **Wares (west):** near Coast Path SE of Nicholas Down 100m S of top of steps; **(east)** on low rock face 35m S of gate from Hay Brimble to Balston Wear; by Coast Path 80m E of W edge of Verney Ware. **Durlston:** plentiful by

much of Diagonal Path; by Coast Path from closed steps to Tilly Whim Quarry to Durlston Head; both sides of Solent Road. **Ballard Down:** here and there in ungrazed grassland area S of fence between eastern tumuli and trig point.

HONEYSUCKLE FAMILY
Elder *Sambucus nigra*
Native. Abundant. Woods, hedges, waste ground. May to July.

Dwarf Elder, Danewort
Sambucus ebulus
Early Introduction. Rare. Verges. July to August.
Langton: E side of S end of lane to Castle View; N side of B3069 E of lane to Castle View up to 70m further E.

Guelder-rose *Viburnum opulus*
Native. Occasional. Hedges, scrub; some planted. June to July.
Ridge: S side of Arne Road here and there for 450m between New Road and opposite Sunnyside (road).
Corfe Charity's Meadows: NW side of meadow SW of Sharford Bridge 75-100m SW of bridleway4.
Bushey: near N end of Meadus' Lane both sides; on S side of Bushey Lane 175 and 700m E of bridleway10. **Langton:** in NE of recently planted National Trust wood S of junction of B3069 and E road to Worth; by bridleway42 N of Wilkswood Farm. **Godlingston:** N side of path2 where it meets Washpond Lane. **Godlingston Heath:** by 'GIVE WAY 50 yds' sign on road from Swanage to Studland SW of junction with B3351; N side of B3351 just W of W part of same junction. **Studland:** S side of bridleway38 close to Ferry Road.

Wayfaring Tree *Viburnum lantana*
Native. Frequent. Hedges, scrub, cliffs, downs; mostly on calcareous soils. May to June.

Laurustinus *Viburnum tinus*
Introduction. Occasional. Planted, and self-seeding. Mid-October to April.
Furzebrook: S of new bridleway41 just SW of railway bridge. **Durlston:** some in woodlands in E of Country Park. **Branksome Chine:** E side of Western Road at junction with Pinecliff Road.

Southern Arrowwood
Viburnum dentatum
Introduction. Rare. Planted. May to June.
Branksome Chine: seen in 2005 20m S of Pinecliff Road 190m ENE of Library (has been cut down; may grow again).

Snowberry *Symphoricarpos albus*
Introduction. Occasional. Planted and suckering. Woods, hedges. June to September.
Creech: on SW side of bridleway2 70m NW of Grange Road. **Stoborough:** on E side of S part of Old Furzebrook Road near junction with new Furzebrook Road. **Kingston:** by The Plantation car park. **Godlingston Heath:** by bridleway27 425m W of junction of bridleways26 and 27. **Swanage:** W side of path extending S from Taunton Road 25m S of Queens Road. **Durlston:** here and there 60-100m N of Long Meadow by N-S track running N between and roughly parallel to Durlston Road and Coast Path. **Ulwell:** N of gate to path4 from lower lay-by. **Studland:** N side of bend in Agglestone Road; E side of Ferry Road both 10m S of path2; 40m N of village crossroads.

Hybrid Coralberry
Symphoricarpos x *chenaultii*
(*S. microphyllus* x *orbiculatus*)
Introduction. Rare. Planted and suckering. Hedges. June to September.
Worth: NW side of road NE of Village Green for 45m. **Swanage:** S side of Victoria Avenue 20m E of W end of Prospect Crescent. **Durlston:** N of path46 30m E of junction with path54.
Berries pink with some white on them.

Himalayan Honeysuckle
Leycesteria formosa
Introduction. Occasional. Verges, scrub; escaping increasingly frequently. July to October.
Creech Heath: on N side of path34 60m from Furzebrook Road. **Harman's Cross:** NE side Haycraft's Lane 70m NW of bridleway6. **Woolgarston:** N side of road 200m W of N end of Tabbit's Hill Lane; on N side of bridleway20 25m W of bridleway24. **Swanage:** W side of path which extends S from Taunton Road 30m S of Queen's Road. **Studland:** E of bridleway12 50m S of NE corner of Glebeland Estate; by path2 50m E of Ferry Road; near path behind beach huts 250m S of Knoll Beach car park.

Wilson's Honeysuckle
Lonicera nitida
Introduction. Occasional. Hedges, woods, scrub. April to May. Most British plants descend from an originally sparsely flowering import.
Kingston: plentiful along path44 through The Plantation. **Worth:** S side of gate to Hill Bottom hamlet where Purbeck Way meets Coast Path; large-leaved cultivar on SW side of path13 100m NW of Coast Path.

Bushey: on E side of bridleway10 250m N of Bushey Lane. **Swanage:** S side of Victoria Avenue 5m W of Pitch and Putt entrance (flowers well); E side of path which runs S from S end of Townsend Road 150m from end of pavement. **Studland:** at SW corner of Clayton Meadow (flowers well); here and there E of Glebeland Estate on E side of bridleway12; near junction of path2 with Beach Road. **Durlston:** opposite stone seat commemorating 200 years of American independence on old (blocked) route of Coast Path NE of woods in NE of Country Park.

May be mistaken for Cotoneaster species.

Tartarian Honeysuckle
Lonicera tatarica
Introduction. Rare. Planted. April to May.
Swanage: E side of Northbrook Road near top of rise S of Beach Gardens (does not flower every year).

Japanese Honeysuckle
Lonicera japonica
Introduction. Occasional. Escaped or planted in hedges. June to August.
Stoborough: in N side lay-by 300m from E end of Holme Lane. **Creech:** N of bend in road S of Creech Barrow Hill. **Stoborough Heath:** by fence on W edge of Hyde Hill 140m N of path24. **Ridge:** on NE side of Purbeck Way 50m NW of Redcliffe Farm; SE side of Barnhill Road 50m from SW end. **Ulwell:** SW side of road by Currendon Chalk Pit. **Swanage:** open area 10m SW of path 50m SE of S end of Benlease Way; S side of Victoria Avenue 90 and 50m W of Pitch and Putt entrance; on cliff N of E end of path from Burlington Road to beach (binoculars).

Honeysuckle
Lonicera periclymenum
Native. Abundant. Woods, hedges, scrub. June to September.

Weigela
Weigela (cultivated hybrid)
Introduction. Rare. Planted. June to July.
Worth: E side of road at N end of Renscombe Farm buildings. **Woolgarston:** S side of W-E road 120m W of short road to Woolgarston Farm.

Beauty Bush *Kolkwitzia amabilis*
Introduction. Rare. Planted. June to September.
Swanage: S side of Victoria Avenue 20m E of Pitch and Putt entrance.

ADOXA FAMILY
Moschatel, Town Hall Clock
Adoxa moschellina
Native. Frequent. Woods and hedge-banks. March to May.
Steeple: by bridleway11 100m S of Steeple Leaze Farm; by path6 where it crosses stream N of field N of Hyde Wood. **Furzebrook:** here and there by Purbeck Way to S of Blue Pool, including near right-angled turn of Way at Furzebrook Road. **Corfe:** by path79 through square wood; several places in S half of Byle Copse. **Langton:** several places in West Wood; in W end of Talbot's Wood. **King's Wood:** by bridleway87 just N of wood. **Studland:** here and there in The Warren Wood.

VALERIAN FAMILY
Do not confuse cornsalads with Field Madder (p.200), which has four-pointed flowers rather than five-pointed ones.

Common Cornsalad
Valerianella locusta
Native. Occasional. Verges, near rock outcrops on downs. April to May.
Corfe: at SE corner of West Hill just N of bridleway70; by path2 E of castle entrance tower; here and there on N side of Sandy Hill Lane E of railway bridge. **Worth:** E of bridleway15 near entrance to St. Aldhelm's Head working quarry; scattered near top of W and N facing slopes N of Renscombe Farm (where it looks like Hairy-fruited Cornsalad at first glance).

Keeled-fruited Cornsalad
Valerianella carinata
Early Introduction. Frequent. Roadsides, gardens. April to May.
Corfe: along side roads in SE of village. **Swanage:** around streets. **Sandbanks:** around streets. **Canford Cliffs:** E side of path in Canford Cliffs Chine 80m from promenade.

Fruit has prominent groove on one side (lens).

Hairy-fruited Cornsalad
Valerianella eriocarpa
May be native here. Occasional. Thin soil – over Purbeck and Portland Limestone or hard Chalk. May. *Nationally Rare*. New sites have been discovered in the last 10 years; more is known in this area than anywhere else in Britain; it is found at a few similar sites in Portland, Isle of Wight, Devon and N Wales and it is a sporadic introduced field weed elsewhere (Pearman & Edwards, 2002; Pratt, 2002).
Corfe: E side of castle mound (opposite columnar cypresses in garden across A351) stretching from path2 for 15m up mound in an area of a width of 10m (short walk only – easy site, late May, later and pinker than on

Limestone sites). **Worth:** by Coast Path 300m E of Coastwatch Station. **Wares (west):** scattered (except in dry years) in two areas in Seacombe Bottom – firstly on SSW-facing slope S of Seacombe Field around 70m NNE of path11 and 250m from sea; secondly near top of W-facing slope around 100m from sea; also in Hedbury Ware at map reference SY99297707 for 15m down SW-facing slope; Scratch Arse Ware just N of Coast Path 180m SW of entrance to Dancing Ledge Quarries; on cattle track at E edge of Dancing Ledge Ware 100m S of N wall; **(east)** various places near and below path23 along N edge of Chillmark Ware/Balston Wear; scattered both near S edge of Second Hayfield and in SE of Sherwood's Wear. **Townsend Reserve:** 40m NE of horses' shed on two anthills and bank (short walk only – easy site). **Ballard Down:** three banks on N side of path10 N of N-S hedge on W side of first field W of Coast Path – 40m W of that hedge along 10m, 15m W of hedge along 5m and 10m E of hedge along 5m; also up slope above and below E-W track 16m N of path10 30m NW of N end of hedge.

Fewer plants appear in dry years. Varies in pale colour – but usually pinky-mauve. Capsules are usually hairy but occasionally hairless, despite the species' name; however, hairless ones have not yet been found on land open to the public in this area. See Plate 22.

Common Valerian
Valeriana officinalis
Native. Occasional. Damp places, except acid ones, in tall vegetation. June to July.
Holme: N side of Holme Lane 250m W of Holme Lane Plantation.

Wareham: scattered on SE side of River Frome for 325m downstream from bypass bridge (boat); here and there by Purbeck Way from 250m E of South Bridge to Redcliffe Farm. **Stoborough Heath:** SE of path23 250m SW of A351. **Corfe:** NW side of road to Church Knowle 80m from A351; scattered along N half of NW side of West Common. **Hartland Moor:** by bridleway4 at SE corner of White House Wood. **Swanage Railway:** NE side 275 and 325m NW of bridleway30 bridge; N side 300m E of bridge over bridleway2. **Bushey:** E side of Thrasher's Lane 600m from B3351; at three other well-spaced intervals to N.

Marsh Valerian *Valeriana dioica*
Native. Occasional. Marshes, wet woods. May.
Stoborough: 10m ENE of sharp bend in W part of path13 on S side of ditch (binoculars). **Stoborough Heath:** 200m N of A351 in wet wood 120m E of Dismantled Tramway. **Norden:** in NW side of valley in SE of Norden Heath along 100m SW of bridge on path12 which is just E of junction with path11. **Hartland Moor:** in Upper Fen 250m SE of Isolation Cottages; in SE corner of White House Wood. **Corfe:** 150m WSW of W end of First Valley on West Common; in Middle Common 50-70m S of pond in area 30m W-E; Little East Common 100m NW of S corner 40m from A351 (once seen there with all male flowers eaten off).

As its scientific name indicates, male and female flowers are on separate plants. Male flowers are much wider, with umbels of 5mm wide flowers; female flowers of 1.5mm width are more often in tight heads than in umbels.

Red Valerian *Centranthus ruber*
Introduction. Abundant. Walls, buildings, cliffs, old quarries, verges. June to September.
Swanage Railway: colourful display in cutting at **Corfe. Ballard Down:** so plentiful on Ballard Cliff some years that a red patch could be seen from Swanage seafront.

Albinos are frequent. If allowed to grow on walls of gardens or buildings it will crack them.

TEASEL FAMILY
Wild Teasel *Dipsacus fullonum*
Native. Frequent. Rough grassland. July to August.

Field Scabious *Knautia arvensis*
Native. Frequent. Verges, meadows, downs; usually on calcareous ground. July to September.

Occasionally has untoothed leaves like those of Devilsbit Scabious (below). See also notes on Small Scabious (p.207) and compare them at the two sites given where they grow together.

Devilsbit Scabious *Succisa pratensis*
Native. Occasional. Wood rides, other tracks, commons, verges, wet fields, N-facing downs. July to November.
Wareham: few on bank on N side of Priory Meadow. **Furzebrook:** plentiful in N half of central field in Kilnwood Reserve (including one albino). **Stoborough Heath:** on Dismantled Tramway 150-350m N of A351. **Hartland Moor:** E side of Soldiers Road 40m from N end; E side of Slepe Road 450m N of corner near Scotland. **Corfe:** plentiful on drier parts of West Common and Middle Common (with few albinos). **Wytch:** on path80 at SW corner of Wytch Heath plantation. **Ower:** on

both sides of bridleway8 – 200-275m SW of crossing of bridleways7 and 8. **Harman's Cross:** by path26 in second field N of A351 (between woods). **Ulwell:** plentiful on Down NNE of where Purbeck Way meets road from Studland.

Do not confuse with Sheepsbit (p.200), which is low-growing, has royal blue flowers, with short-toothed sepals and some leaves not opposite to others.

Small Scabious *Scabiosa columbaria*
Native. Occasional. Downs. Late June to September.
Steeple: plentiful on Steeple Down (west). **Church Knowle:** here and there on Down NW of Cocknowle. **Corfe:** by E set of steps up railway embankment from National Trust Visitor Centre car park (with Field Scabious – good place to compare them. **Worth:** plentiful in places on steep Down NW of Hill Bottom. **Wares (west and east):** recorded in at least 25 sites in short grassland on thin soil. **Woolgarston:** on Down above bridleway20 between its junctions with bridleways21 and 23. **Ulwell:** 150m W of SE corner of Round Down. **Durlston:** NE of shallow quarry in NE of Field 14 (with Field Scabious). **Townsend Reserve:** scattered on several banks (with Field Scabious). **Ballard Down:** plentiful on sides of old rifle range ditch just SW of trig point.

It is distinguished from small specimens of Field Scabious (p.206) by more divided leaves, and by dark purple bristles in the flowerhead, which are best seen from underneath when in flower, and are very noticeable when in seed. See also note about Sheepsbit under previous species. See Plate 23.

DAISY FAMILY
Globe Thistle *Echinops exaltatus*
Introduction. Rare. Planted. July to August.
Corfe Charity's Meadows: under oak by hidden ruin S of Cowleaze 200m SE of Scotland 20m S of path80.

Carline Thistle *Carlina vulgaris*
Native. Frequent. Downs. July to October.
See Plate 23.

Great Burdock *Arctium lappa*
Early Introduction. Occasional. Rough grassland, verges. July to September.
Kimmeridge: by bridleway18 along edge of second field from NW end along 400m with Lesser Burdock. **Langton:** middle of area of scrub and rough grass (marked as wood on O.S. map) E of West Wood through which path44 runs NW-SE; near vehicle entrance to new cemetery off Crack Lane; E side of Crack Lane 20-50m N of that entrance on opposite side; near start of tractor rides on Putlake Adventure Farm (pay to enter). **Harman's Cross:** by stile on path6 40m E of road at New Barn; S of stile near junction of paths6 and 13.

This has wider and paler (apple-green) flowerheads than the next species and its lower leaf stalks are solid, not hollow. Often occurs with next species. See Plate 23.

Hybrid Burdock
Arctium x *nothum* (*A. lappa* x *minus*)
Native. Rare. Rough grassland. July to September.
Wareham: N side of Priory meadow 25m E of gate. **Worth:** W of Kingston Road S of entrance to Swanworth Quarry; by water tank in NE of Worth Mead.

Probably more widespread.

Lesser Burdock *Arctium minus*
Native. Frequent. Rough grassland, verges, wood rides. July to September.

Slender Thistle *Carduus tenuiflorus*
Native. Frequent. Calcareous pastures near sea, especially at warrens. June to August.

Musk Thistle *Carduus nutans*
Native. Frequent. Calcareous grassland. June to August.
   Tyneham: scattered by Army Range path from Coast Path to Tyneham Cap (with albino). **Church Knowle:** thinly on top of Down NW of Cocknowle. **Corfe:** by path73 in field E of Purbeck Way (including pink ones). **Worth:** beside path13 in NW part of Worth Mead; in field along SE side of Langton Road NE of W end of Priest's Way. **Wares (west):** plentiful in S end of Seacombe Bottom with other thistles. **Woolgarston:** between barrows on top of Ailwood Down. **Durlston:** S of gate from Field 3 into Belle Vue East Ware. **Ulwell:** valley NW of Round Down; open area E of top of path4 steps (with albino in 2002). **Ballard Down:** near junction of bridleways6, 12 and 14. See Plate 24.

Woolly Thistle *Cirsium eriophorum*
Native. Occasional. Calcareous grassland. July to August.
Worth: few on slopes N and NW of Renscombe Farm; plentiful near N extremity of Abbott's Combe (approach from S). **Wares (west):** near NW corner of Seacombe Bottom; **(east)** along N edge of Balston Wear; by path46 30m N of Belle Vue West Ware; here and there in N half of Belle Vue Middle Ware; by path64 200m N of Belle Vue East Ware. **Langton:** SE side of road to

Worth 250m from junction with B3069. **Durlston:** here and there on high downland and on edges of meadows nearest downland. See Plate 23.

Spear Thistle *Cirsium vulgare*
Native. Abundant. Grassland, verges, arable fields, other disturbed ground. July to October.

Meadow Thistle *Cirsium dissectum*
Native. Occasional. Wet grassland, marshes. May to July.
Furzebrook: towards NE corner of central field in Kilnwood Reserve. **Stoborough Heath:** by pond just W of Dismantled Tramway 275m N of A351. **Hartland Moor:** here and there in Upper Fen; along 20m of S side of Arne Road 225m W of Arne Triangle; along S side of S arm of Triangle itself 30-40m from W end. **Corfe:** here and there in wet places on West, Middle and Little East Commons. **Bushey:** scattered in some parts of S of Brenscombe Heath – especially plentiful near SW corner. **Harman's Cross:** by path26 in S end of second field N of A351 (between woods).

Dwarf Thistle *Cirsium acaule*
Native. Abundant. Calcareous grassland and verges. July to September.
East Creech: albinos on top of Stonehill Down 45m NE of NE (not E) corner of working quarry fence.

Marsh Thistle *Cirsium palustre*
Native. Frequent. Marshes, damp wood rides, damp grassland, dry calcareous grassland. July to September.
   Albinos are frequent.

Creeping Thistle *Cirsium arvense*
Native. Abundant. Grassland, verges, arable fields. July to September.

Cotton Thistle
Onopordum acanthium
Early Introduction. Occasional.
Downs, verges. July to August.
Godlingston: along bridleway84 from
60-150m W of junction with Purbeck
Way. **Ulwell:** plentiful near SW corner
of Round Down (but may be cut
there); halfway up down 250m E of
stepped path4. **Studland:** visible when
tall from middle of path5 looking S.

Milk Thistle *Silybum marianum*
Early Introduction. Occasional.
Disturbed calcareous grassland, arable
fields. July to August.
Tyneham: visible from Coast Path
along 20m of cliff-top on NE side of
Brandy Bay. **Kimmeridge:** by Coast
Path 450-550m E of Rope Lake
Head. **Worth:** by Coast Path both
100m NW of Coastwatch Station;
600-700m E of it. **Wares (west):**
Dancing Ledge Ware by gateway
halfway along boundary with Scratch
Arse Ware; (**east**) near gates on Coast
Path from White Ware to both
Dancing Ledge Ware and Chillmark
Ware; by path23 near SW corner of
Sheep's Leet; in Belle Vue West Ware
both in NW corner; 20m W of NW
corner of Belle Vue Middle Ware.
Knitson: on N side of bridleway8 –
100, 140, 220 and 350m E of bridle-
way12. **Ballard Down:** 50m NW of
gate on bridleway14 at foot of downland. Not in same places every year.
See Plate 24.

Saw-wort *Serratula tinctoria*
Native. Occasional. Grassland, commons, woodland rides. July to
September.
Hartland Moor: thinly scattered both
through N half of Upper Fen;
throughout Middle Fen. **Corfe:** very
plentiful on higher parts of West and

Middle Commons. **Wytch:** on
path80 at SW corner of Wytch Heath
plantation. **Durlston:** prominent
plant towards SW corner of short
grass in Field 13. **Ulwell:** on top of
down 75m SE of Obelisk.

Small flowers on grazed plants of
Common Knapweed can be mistaken
for this species, if the leaves are not
checked. A wild flower seed marketer
once pictured this species on the
fronts of packets of Common Knapweed seeds!

Greater Knapweed
Centaurea scabiosa
Native. Abundant. Downs, verges,
hay meadows. July to September.
Steeple: albinos at foot of down
175m SE of bend in bridleway3.

Flowers usually broad, but check
leaves.

Common Knapweed
Centaurea nigra
Native. Abundant. Grassland, verges.
June to September.

Broad-flowered form often seen, for
example at **Corfe Charity's Meadows**
and at **Durlston** Country Park.
Check leaves. See Plates 4, 24 and 25.

Cornflower *Centaurea cyanus*
Early introduction. Rare. Casual
(from bird-seed or wild flower seed
mixtures, or garden escape). June to
August.

Chicory *Cichorium intybus*
Early Introduction. Rare. Verges. July
to September.
Harman's Cross: on 10m of N side of
A351 50m W of path41. **Knitson:**
few on N side of road 50m E of S
sharp bend at Knitson Farm.
Durlston: N side of view from Visitor
Centre hide.

Blue Cupidone *Catananche caerulea*
Introduction. Rare. Escape on verge.
August to September.
Godlingston Heath: S side of road
10m E of two-way part of junction of
B3351 and road from Swanage.

Can be mistaken for Cornflower
(p.209). Each seed is surmounted by a
scale which narrows to a hair-like
point, and the seeds are surrounded
by other hair-like scales.

Dandelion-like species
The Durlston Visitor Center sells a
key to them compiled by the author
(20p).

Nipplewort *Lapsana communis*
Native. Frequent. Verges. April to
October.

Catsear *Hypochoeris radicata*
Native. Abundant. Dunes, verges,
grassland including lawns. June to
September.

Can be mistaken for next species.

Smooth Catsear *Hypochoeris glabra*
Native. Occasional. Acid grassland,
sand. Late May to early July.
Dorset Scarce. Vulnerable.
Hartland Moor: 90m W of Slepe
Road on track just N of Moor; just
over bank E of junction of Slepe Road
and track to Middlebere Farm and
also 35m further E; on both sides of
bridleway4 – 140-190m NE of gate at
its W end. **Godlingston Heath:** in
middle of rectangular fenced area in
field 150m N of field gate on N side
of bridleway36. **Studland Heath**: on
bank just W of Knoll Beach toilets
(flowers open little there because they
are under small trees); outlier 50m
NW of War Hill (with more Lesser
Hawkbit).

Flowers only open in the morning

and in bright sun; it is very difficult to
find it at other times. Can be confused with sparsely hairy specimens of
the previous species, especially on
sand, but Smooth Catsear flowers are
much smaller – only 4-8mm across
when open. Leaves are nearly hairless
except on edges; sepals are hairless.
See Plate 25.

Autumn Hawkbit
Leontodon autumnalis
Native. Frequent. Grassland, verges.
July to October.
Holme: plentiful in NE corner of
Battle Plain just W of Doreys Farm.
Norden: very plentiful on both sides
of bridleway77 towards its E end.
Corfe: on short grassland either side
of UCR across West Common.
Bushey: plentiful on SW side of
bridleway15 150m SE of NW end.
Langton: S end of old cemetery (all
three Hawkbit species occur in this
cemetery – Rough at S end and Lesser
at N end – but they may be mown).
Godlingston Heath: plenty on traffic
islands where road from Swanage
meets B3351. **Luscombe Valley:**
plentiful along W half of S end with
even more Lesser Hawkbit.

Flowers from late July onwards.
Often confused with Smooth
Hawksbeard (p.212).

Rough Hawkbit *Leontodon hispidus*
Native. Abundant. Calcareous grassland. May to November.

Very hairy all up the stem.

Lesser Hawkbit *Leontodon saxatilis*
Native. Abundant. Short grassland,
dunes. June to October.
Wares (west): floor of Seacombe cliff
quarry. **Wares (east):** Belle Vue Wares;
Durlston: – thousands on fields sloping towards sea. **Swanage:** plenty on

All Saints Church lawn. **Ballard Down:** very plentiful on top (with Catsear and Smooth Hawksbeard). **Shell Bay:** plentiful in car park. **Luscombe Valley:** plentiful at S end.

Usually violet-grey under the 'petals', with hairs markedly decreasing in numbers up the stem (rarely stem is hairless); outer row of seeds is usually without parachute of hairs.

Bristly Oxtongue *Picris echioides*
Early Introduction. Abundant. Grassland, verges, waste places, arable fields, other disturbed ground. June to November.

Hawkweed Oxtongue
Picris hieracioides
Native. Occasional. Near scrub in tall calcareous grassland. July to September.
Tyneham: scattered on S side of Coast Path along top of Gad Cliff. **Worth:** various places by path13 along Winspit Bottom; by Coast Path at Winspit where it ascends to W from junction with path13. **Wares (east):** scattered through area. **Townsend Reserve:** 60m NE of SW entrance; SE of 'Butterfly Hollow'; 35m W of SE entrance; also in other places. **Durlston:** by path56 E of NE corner of Jack Baiss Meadow; here and there along high-level downland from W boundary of Country Park to Visitor Centre. **Ballard Down:** 3m S of Coast Path 80m WSW of Trig Point.

Very hairy plant; some 'sepals' are spreading outwards.

Vipersgrass *Scorzonera humilis*
Probably native. Rare. Damp grassland. Late April to early July.
Nationally Rare. Vulnerable.
The Moors: site on closed land best

visited in June on application to RSPB, who will give directions (see Appendix). Wellingtons are essential. This was at one time the only remaining site in British Isles, but it has since been discovered in Glamorgan; at next site. **Corfe:** one on West Common with larger leaves which finishes flowering in May (first found by Steve O'Connell in 1997). See Plate 17.

Goatsbeard, Jack-go-to-bed-at-noon
Tragopogon pratensis
Native. Frequent. Tall calcareous grassland, verges. June to July.
Flowers only open in the mornings. The large seedheads ('clocks') repay close look.

Perennial Sow-thistle
Sonchus arvensis
Native. Frequent. Verges, arable fields and other disturbed ground, also above shores. Mid-July to October.

Smooth Sow-thistle
Sonchus oleraceus
Native. Frequent. Verges, arable fields and other disturbed ground. April to October.

Prickly Sow-thistle *Sonchus asper*
Native. Frequent. Verges, arable fields and other disturbed ground. June to October.

Prickly Lettuce *Lactuca serriola*
Early Introduction. Occasional. Verges, waste ground (increasing). July to September.
Corfe: on and by minor road bridge over stream W of castle. **Worth:** E of village green. **Knitson:** at Knitson Farm by path6. **Langton:** plenty on N side of B3069 opposite Steppes Hill (road); W and E of that. **Swanage:** N

side of main road from Corfe E of junction with road from Langton; both sides of bend in Mermond Place. **Lilliput:** near W end of Alington Road; at SE end of Evening Hill by sailing club. **Luscombe Valley:** along SW edge.

Great Lettuce *Lactuca virosa*
Native. Rare. Castle, verges; casual. July to September.
Dorset Rare.
Corfe: on and under viaduct leading from outer to middle ward of castle; W of castle keep; NE of keep (not always at all those sites every year). **Swanage Railway:** few on NE side of Corfe cutting.

Latex is mildly poisonous.

Wall Lettuce *Mycelis muralis*
Native. Occasional. Shady verges. July to early October.
Creech: few here and there on sides of road through Great Wood.
Bushey: by bridleway14 – 100m and 150m SW of junction of bridle-ways14 and 15. **Studland:** 5m N of Coast Path to Fort Henry 30m E of entrance to Middle Beach car park.
Brownsea: some years just beyond 'NO ENTRY' gate N of pond E of The Villa.

Dandelion *Taraxacum* agg.
Native. Abundant in aggregate. Grassland, verges, open or disturbed ground. All year.

Dandelions are currently divided into over 200 microspecies in the British Isles. In *The Flora of Dorset,* Bowen (2000) indicates that at least 17 have been recorded in this area. Microspecies of dandelions have been omitted from this book. Blamey, Fitter and Fitter (2003) summarise nine groupings of microspecies.

Smooth Hawksbeard
Crepis capillaris
Native. Abundant. Grassland, verges, disturbed ground. June to October.

Differs from Autumn Hawkbit (p.210) in the leaves with their arrow-shaped bases clasping the stems where they branch; flower-heads are widest near the base; there are white not brownish seed para-chutes; parachute hairs are simple rather than branched (lens). The size varies from small slightly-branched plants with thin stems 10cm high in sandy, grazed or mown sites, to vig-orous much-branched plants 120cm high in grassland.

Beaked Hawksbeard
Crepis vesicaria
Introduction. Frequent. Grassland, verges, waste ground. May to early June.

Can be confused with Rough Hawksbeard.

(**Shaggy Mouse-ear Hawkweed**
Pilosella peleteriana
subsp. *subpeleteriana*
Native. Rare. Calcareous banks near the sea. May to August.
Nationally Rare. Near Threatened.
Species only found on the Dorset Coast and in Montgomeryshire in mainland Britain, also in the Isle of Wight. Has been recorded at
Tyneham: on Worbarrow Tout; worth keeping an eye out for it by Coast Path on E and W of that at Gad Cliff and near Flower's Barrow. (Not difficult to find by Coast Path near **Durdle Door:** outside this area.)

Has much hairier leaves than the next species; any runners are short and thick, often ending in a rosette. Flowers are larger than most flowers of the next species.)

Mouse-ear Hawkweed
Pilosella officinarum
Native. Frequent. Undisturbed open ground, usually calcareous but also on sand. May to August.
Swanage: unusual site – small raised lawns on N side of Kings Road S of Cooperative supermarket.

It has thin runners with small leaves at intervals but no rosette at the end.

Fox-and-cubs *Pilosella aurantiaca* subsp. *carpathicola*
Introduction. Rare. Escape. June to October.
Stoborough: few on S side of The Green. **Swanage:** churchyard extension to SE of Church Hill (possibly indicating some past Rector's opposition to blood sports?).

Hawkweeds the genus *Hieracium*
Hawkweeds are currently divided into 261 microspecies in the British Isles. Faced with such complexity, one County Botanical Recorder in the Midlands, now deceased, told me that whenever she saw Hawkweeds she looked the other way! But only 6 have ever been recorded in this area, and of those only 3 recently, and another awaiting identification.

Leafy Hawkweed
Hieracium umbellatum
Native. Occasional. Verges, commons, dunes, downs. Late July to early September.
Steeple: patch on upper part of Steeple Down (west) 400m E of W end (with much more of an unidentified Hawkweed p.214). **Stoborough Heath:** area N and S of Purbeck Way railway crossing; NE side of path5 60m NW of small square field.
Hartland Moor: E side of Soldiers Road here and there 350-500m SW

of S cattle grid; 10-35m NE of same grid; along 15m of S side of Arne Road 275m E of Soldiers Road; near W end of bridleway4. **Corfe:** Middle Common above NE-facing wet slope SW of pond. **Wytch:** E side of Thrasher's lane 30m N of bridleway4. **Kingswood:** N side of B3351 40 and 150m E of viewpoint (near next species at latter site). **Shell Bay:** N of E end of boardwalk (with next species).

Usually with over 15 narrow leaves on the stem.

Hairy-stemmed Hawkweed
Hieracium trichocaulon
Native. Occasional. Rough grassland, verges, dunes, marshes. Late June to early August.
Hartland Moor: on small mounds in Middle Fen 100m W of Pillwort Pond; beside bridleway4 on SW side of White House Wood 70m from W end of wood. **Bushey:** NE corner of right-angled bend near E end of bridleway4. **Kingswood:** N side of B3351 125m E of viewpoint (near previous species). **Ulwell:** SE corner of Round Down. **Studland Heath:** scattered along NW side of bridleway36 up to 150m from Ferry Road; plentifully scattered on fore-dunes from Knoll Beach café all the way to Pilot Point. **Shell Bay:** E side of Ferry road just N of opposite restaurant; N of E end of boardwalk (with previous species). **Ballard Down:** along 5m of Coast Path 100m SW of Trig Point. **Branksome Chine:** in Bracken along 20m of top of cliff S of Library. **Branksome Dene Chine:** W side of entrance road 50m N of café.

Under 15 lancehead-shaped leaves on stem, upper ones with tapered bases.

Common Hawkweed
Hieracium vulgatum
Native. Rare. Downland. Mid-June to mid-September.
Woolgarston: area near top of Ailwood Down 150m SW of where Purbeck Way crosses E boundary of Down.

By no means the most common Hawkweed.

An unidentified Hawkweed
Hieracium species
Native or introduction. Rare. Downland. Mid-June to mid-September.
Steeple: here and there on upper parts of Steeple Down (west).

This species has been seen by four Hawkweed specialists but they have not yet been able to identify it.

Treasureflower *Gazania rigens*
Introduction. Rare. Escape. May to October.
Sandbanks: lawn S of entrance to main car park; in fenced dunes 100m NE of car park.

Variety *uniflora,* also present, has petals (actually ray florets) without a dark patch on the base.

Common Cudweed *Filago vulgaris*
Native. Occasional. Disturbed fields, dunes, heath tracks. July to August.
Near Threatened.
Holme: East Holme Meadows – see p.23. **Harman's Cross:** near path28 in second field SE of Westwood Farm 50m from gate. **Studland Heath:** E side of War Hill. **Canford Cliffs:** one seen at SE corner of Bessborough Road.

Small Cudweed *Filago minima*
Native. Occasional. Stable sand, sandy soil and tracks. June to September.

Stoborough Heath: 20m N of cairn W of Soldiers Road. **Hartland Moor:** on track 10m SE of and parallel to Soldiers Road – 75, 100 and 125m NE of S cattle grid. **Rempstone:** plentiful N of Green Pond along 550m of path5 W-wards from wooden barrier (with next species at E end). **Studland Heath:** W side of Ferry Road 250m N of entrance to Sewage Works; bank W of Knoll Beach shop; near tracks N of Knoll Beach main N car park; also on War Hill. **Shell Bay:** E of Ferry Road W of track leading S 40m from car park.

Marsh Cudweed
Gnaphalium uliginosum
Native. Frequent. Wet places on tracks and near gateways. July to August.
Creech: NE of bridleway2 between two gates just before Grange Heath. **Holme:** NE corner of Battle Plain just W of Doreys Farm. **Church Knowle:** by gate on W side of bridleway39 100m N of road. **Hartland Moor:** E side of Slepe Road by SE corner of Arne Triangle. **Wytch:** SW part of Thrasher's Heath. **Harman's Cross:** on path26 where it crosses stream flowing from Higher and Lower Grove Woods. **Kingswood:** on W side of bridleway29 100m N of B3351. **Godlingston Heath:** by bridleway35 15m E of W junction with bridleway36. **Shell Bay:** plentiful on summer-dry stream bed towards SE of Shell Bay – unusual site.

Shrubby Everlasting
Helichrysum stoechas
Introduction. Rare. Escape. Mid-June to July.
Sandbanks: behind wire-fenced dunes at top of beach 125m SW of main car park.

Low bush with grey foliage,

umbels of yellow disk florets of 3-3.5mm diameter.

Elecampane *Inula helenium*
Early Introduction. Rare. Escape.
Late July to September.
Worth: sides of entrance to private Swanworth Quarry on W side of Kingston Road (sometimes cut down, except in scrubby area 75m S of entrance).

Ploughman's Spikenard
Inula conyzae
Native. Occasional. Dry calcareous grassland and verges. July to September.
Steeple: plentiful in central section of Steeple Down (west).
Kimmeridge: W side of road 75m S of entrance to car park near junction of road to Bradle. **Church Knowle:** much in old quarry on down almost due N of Church Knowle church. **Corfe:** here and there in castle. **Worth:** by path11 SE of village green. **Wytch:** SE side of new route of path5 (Oil Road) 50m E of oil well NW of Wtych Moor. **Wares (west):** especially in Seacombe Quarry; **(east):** banks in NW of Verney Ware. **Durlston:** N side of Coast Path near closed steps to Tilly Whim Quarry. **Townsend Reserve:** here and there. **Ballard Down:** scattered on S-facing slope.

Golden Samphire
Inula crithmoides
Native. Frequent. Sea cliffs and cliff quarries. July to August.
Nationally Scarce.
Tyneham: cliff at Pondfield beach. **Wares (west and east):** most cliff quarries. **Durlston:** sea end of Gully. **Swanage:** foot of cliff just above N end of promenade. See Plate 25.

Common Fleabane
Pulicaria dysenterica
Native. Abundant. Marshes, verges.
Late July to September.

Goldenrod *Solidago virgaurea*
Native. Occasional. Acid verges.
July to September.
Hartland Moor: few on E side of Soldiers Road 275m S of N end; by S cattle grid on Slepe Road; on W side of Slepe Road opposite bridleway4; scattered N-wards from there for 250m. **Corfe:** S side of Sandy Hill Lane 400m E of Challow car park. **Rempstone:** sides of bridleway34 (Oil Road) 150-300m NE of where bridleway31 crosses it.

Early Goldenrod
Solidago gigantea
Introduction. Occasional. Escape on verges. July to August.
Stoborough Heath: by gate on W side of Furzebrook Road 600m S of A351. **Hartland Moor:** N side of Arne Road opposite end of Soldiers Road (may be cut before flowering). **Corfe:** SE side of B3069 20m SW of A351. **Bushey:** N side of Bushey Lane opposite Higher Bushey Farm. **Langton:** spoil heap opposite entrance to Bower's Quarry; E end of Castle View. **Godlingston:** by Washpond Lane 30m SW of where path2 crosses it. **Ulwell:** SW side of road by Currendon Chalk Pit. **Durlston:** S side of path42 near S end of Southcliffe Road. **Sandbanks:** much on W side of Shore Road 20m N of junction with Banks Road.

Stems are hairless. Usually 7 to 9 flowers in central disk of each little flowerhead (easiest to count them before they open).

Canadian Goldenrod
Solidago canadensis
Introduction. Rare. Escape on verges. August.
Creech: N side of road W of Great Wood by '20%' sign. **Kingston:** N side of West Street 50m E of path50. **Worth:** N side of B3069 nearly opposite lay-by.

Upper half of stems are downy. Usually 3 to 5 flowers in each central disk. Later species.

Michaelmas Daisies
There are at least 160 species and over 1000 cultivated varieties of Michaelmas Daisy, not to mention subspecies and naturally occurring varieties and hybrids. Common Michaelmas Daisy and Narrow-leaved Michaelmas Daisy are the most frequent escapes, and are not too difficult to identify. Other escapes usually do not match descriptions of the few species and hybrids (Stace, 1997; Rich & Jermy, 1998) and have been entered under Michaelmas Daisy cv. agg. (below). For further reading, Picton (1999) describes many, including over 500 cultivars.

Michaelmas Daisy cv. agg.
Aster cv. agg.
Introductions. Occasional. Escape on verges and cliffs. September to October.
Swanage: NE side of Ulwell Road 60m NW of Whitecliff Road (white). **Canford Cliffs:** behind beach chalets 250m NE of Flaghead Chine (with Narrow-leaved Michaelmas Daisy nearby); behind seafront toilets W of S end of Canford Cliffs Chine; behind beach chalets 50m SW of that chine.

Common Michaelmas Daisy *Aster* x *salignus* (*A. novi-belgii* x *lanceolatus*)
Introduction. Occasional. Escape on verges, cliffs and rough ground. August to October.
Wareham: by Purbeck Way E of South Bridge opposite Old Granary. **Worth:** N side of B3069 nearly opposite W end of lay-by. **Swanage:** by Swan Brook on W side of main car and coach park; on cliff 40m N of path from Burlington Road to beach; 30m N of N end of promenade. **Studland:** E of bridleway12 on E side of Glebeland Estate 75m N of SE corner of estate; in front of Middle Beach shop. **Luscombe Valley:** near SE corner of Reserve; E of metal bridge in centre of Reserve; on W side S of metal bridge.

Mauve or occasionally white; flowers are well spaced apart. The most common escape.

Narrow-leaved Michaelmas Daisy
Aster lanceolatus
Introduction. Occasional. Escape on verges and cliffs. October.
Wareham: N side of Priory Meadow 20m E of gate. **Worth:** 20m W of Kingston Road in scrub 75m S of entrance to Swanworth Quarries. **Studland:** E side of bridleway12 halfway down Glebeland Estate and at NE corner of it. **Canford Cliffs:** (mauve) behind beach chalets 250-280m NE of Flaghead Chine; by pavement of Cliff Drive near stepped path to beach.

Usually white; with many small flowers; leaves usually under 1cm wide.

Sea Aster *Aster tripolium*
Native. Frequent. Plentiful on sea cliffs and quarries, thin in upper salt-marshes. July to October.

Worth: by Coast Path 300 and 500m SW of W end of Winspit quarries. **Arne:** few very small deer-grazed plants flower in area S of RSPB beach noticeboard. **Wares (west and east):** most cliff quarries. **Durlston:** sea end of gully. **Godlingston Heath:** scattered 50-75m N of bridleway36 in rushes in Brand's Creek 20-30m E of edge of field. **Studland Heath:** few plants in rushes along S shore of Dyke Bay (some in SW corner only 10-12cm high). See Plate 25.

Seaside Daisy *Erigeron glaucus*
Introduction. Occasional. Cracks in stonework by the sea. June to October.
Swanage: wall cracks on Shore Road. **Sandbanks:** pavement between Shell Bay Ferry hut and shops; SW end of fenced dunes 175m NE of Midway Path; NW verge of Banks Road 150m NE of roundabout; sea wall 400m NE of main car park. **Canford Cliffs:** E side of Flaghead Chine near sea; clifftop near SW end of Cliff Drive; near stepped path from Cliff Drive to beach. **Branksome Dene Chine:** here and there by sea wall.

Mexican Fleabane
Erigeron karvinskianus
Introduction. Occasional. Cliffs, tracks, pavements, walls. April to October.
Kimmeridge: on path through Kimmeridge Farm. **Church Knowle:** by steps at church gate. **Kingston:** pavement at W end of Scott Arms. **Corfe:** E side of East Street 10m N of old cemetery. **Swanage:** near Mill Pond on Church Hill; S side of Kings Road opposite Co-op Supermarket including on wall of Swan Brook. **Canford Cliffs:** S of church between two parts of Chaddesley Glen; by stepped path down cliff from Cliff

Drive. **Branksome Chine:** 200m up chine from road at SE end.

Blue Fleabane *Erigeron acer*
Native. Occasional. Thinly-vegetated verges. July to August.
Holme: on NW side of B3070 175 and 250m NE of bridge over Luckford Lake stream. **Hartland Moor:** E side of Soldiers Road at N side of private forestry entrance NW of Slepe Heath. **Norden:** by track SW of and parallel to A351 W of roundabout. **Worth:** 10-20m W of Kingston Road 75m S of entrance to Swanworth Quarries. **Woolgarston:** from 120m ESE of N end of bridleway24 at high point on bridleway20 go N-wards through scrub onto rough area of Ailwood Down – plants are 50m N of bridleway at map reference SY99728126 on W side of cattle track through scrub. **Rempstone:** much on W side of junction of bridleways34 (Oil Road) and 35; here and there both on sides of bridleway34 (Oil Road) for 500m SW from that junction; on sides of bridleway35 NW of same junction. **Studland Heath:** on outlier 50m NW of War Hill.

Not eye-catching when in flower, but the delightful puffy 'clocks' are easily noticed.

Canadian Fleabane
Conyza canadensis
Introduction. Rare. Verges, pavements (decreasing). August to September.
Sandbanks: here and there along Panorama Road.

Leaves are yellowy green, hairless or sparsely hairy; stem is somewhat hairy; flowerheads are hairless or almost so; unopened flowerhead usually has 10 to 14 disk florets; opened head 5-9mm wide; disk florets usually four-lobed.

Hispid Fleabane *Conyza bilbaoana*
Introduction. Occasional, spreading rapidly since first discovery in England in 1992. Verges, bare ground. August to October.
Furzebrook: N side of Village Hall car park; both sides of Furzebrook Road near Clay Works S of railway. **Ridge:** Gover Close (branches off W side of Sunnyside) on pavement. **Wytch:** N of path5 (Oil Road) NE of Wytch Moor (with next species). **Harman's Cross:** by permissive bridleway S of large barn at Quarr Farm (with next species). **Herston (north):** N side of unnamed road near entrance to Prospect Farm farmyard. **Durlston:** S of castle by stone chart on plinth. **Lilliput:** Gardens Road; middle of fenced bank of Evening Hill.

Leaves are darkish green, almost hairless underneath; stem is thinly hairy; flowerheads are hairless or almost so; unopened flowerhead usually has 4 to 6 disk florets; opened head 5-8mm wide; disk florets usually five-lobed (Mundell, 2001).

Guernsey Fleabane
Conyza sumatrensis
Introduction. Occasional, spreading. Bare ground. August to October.
Wareham: N side of Priory Meadow. **Wytch:** N of path5 (Oil Road) NE of Wytch Moor (with previous species). **Harman's Cross:** by permissive bridleway S of large barn at Quarr Farm (with previous species). **Shell Bay:** plentiful N of car park. **Sandbanks:** SE side of main car park near café; upper shore opposite W end of Chaddesley Glen; S side of Shore Road car park. **Canford Cliffs:** by stepped path from Cliff Drive to beach. **Branksome Chine:** by first way down cliff E of Library.

Leaves are fairly pale green with short dense hairs underneath; stem is densely hairy; flowerheads are hairy; unopened flowerhead usually has 6 to 15 disk florets; opened head 7-12mm wide; disk florets usually five-lobed.

Daisy *Bellis perennis*
Native. Abundant. Short grassland. All year.
Likes certain amount of trampling, then it can turn ground white in May, for example on path27 approaching Dancing Ledge.
Godlingston Heath – rare aberration Hen and Chickens Daisy seen once in one of ploughed plots in grass field S of bridleway36 – normal-sized flower in seed, with smaller flowers, nine in the case seen, growing on short stalks from under the head of original flower. See Plate 26.

Feverfew *Tanacetum parthenium*
Early Introduction. Occasional. Escape in arable fields and other disturbed ground, usually near buildings. July to September.

Tansy *Tanacetum vulgare*
Native, but much planted as herb in the past, so natural distribution unknown. Occasional. Verges, tall grassland; probably escaped at all sites below; once used as infusion to kill roundworms in children (Bowen, 2000). July to September.
Kimmeridge: by Coast Path at steps to beach from main car park. **Creech:** S side of junction of Grange Road with path19. **Langton:** S side of B3069 – 75 and 175m E of road to Acton. **Ulwell:** W side of road just N of Currendon Farm. **Swanage:** S of easternmost houses at Peveril Point; between Coast Path and cliff-top near SE end of Ballard Estate.

Mugwort *Artemisia vulgaris*
Early Introduction. Frequent. Verges.
July to September.

The untoothed end lobe of the middle stem leaves is usually under 3cm long.

Chinese Mugwort
Artemisia verlotiorum
Introduction. Rare. Verges. October to December.
Knitson: at Knitson Farm both on S side of road opposite end of bridleway12; near N end of path6 on W side of path. **Swanage:** W side of Victoria Avenue 40m N of railway bridge; NE side of E end of Court Road 40-50m from Kings Road.

The untoothed end lobe of the middle stem leaves is usually greater than 3cm long. Species flowers late.

Wormwood *Artemisia absinthium*
Early Introduction. Occasional.
Calcareous verges and rough grassland. July to August.
Stoborough: NE side of bypass 20m NW of path13 (gets mown).
Furzebrook: W side of Furzebrook Road opposite Furzebrook House entrance. **Corfe:** by pavement on W side of A351 100m SE of B3351 junction. **Worth:** plentiful around Renscombe Farm; hillside just N of it. **Langton:** NW side of road to Worth 500m from junction with B3069.

Sneezewort *Achillea ptarmica*
Native. Occasional. Damp grassland, verges. July to August.
Holme: East Holme Meadows – see p.23. **Corfe:** on West Common on top of slope to SW of First Valley 35m NW of UCR; slope SW of First Valley 30-60m SE of UCR; several places in low N end of Middle

Common. **Ulwell:** NE side of Ulwell Road 10m SE of path15. See Plate 26.

Yarrow *Achillea millefolium*
Native. Abundant. Verges, grassland including lawns. June to August.

Chamomile *Chamaemelum nobile*
Native. Occasional. Grazed commons. June to July.
Dorset Scarce. Vulnerable.
Corfe: at top of third valley on West Common 25m NW of UCR; many areas on either side of bridleway36 along whole NE side of West Common; on NE side of First Valley 60m SE of UCR; in SE of West Common 20m SW of gate where paths53 and 57 meet road; near edge of West Common 50m NE of where Purbeck Way crosses B3069; 20m S of Purbeck Way on Middle Common just E of B3069; much 20m E of pond on Middle Common; near E edge of Middle Common 200m S of A351.

Perennial species which gives off pleasant odour; has yellow scales in between yellow disk florets, like other Chamomiles, but which are lacking in Mayweeds (e.g. p.220).

Sicilian Chamomile
Anthemis punctata subsp. *cupaniana*
Introduction. Rare. Escape. March to September.
Swanage: on cliff near top 50m N of end of path to beach from Burlington Road (binoculars).

Pale grey foliage.

Stinking Chamomile
Anthemis cotula
Early Introduction. Occasional.
Arable fields, other disturbed ground. July to September.
Vulnerable.

Kingston: in edge of field N of West Street – 350 and 425-450m W of edge of The Plantation. **Worth:** here and there in arable field edges at St. Aldhelm's Head near bridleway15, path21 and Coast Path; by Coast Path 1000 and 1200m E of Coastwatch Station.

Annual species, with a powerful smell which most find unpleasant, and with linear yellow scales in the flowerhead in between and slightly longer than the yellow disk florets in bud – in the central part of the disk only.

Corn Marigold
Chrysanthemum segetum
Early Introduction. Rare. Arable fields, other disturbed ground. June to August.
Vulnerable.
Church Knowle: one on N side of road just W of Playing Field entrance. **Studland:** visible from gateway S of Coast Path 325m E of NE corner of The Warren Wood; sometimes N of Coast Path 250m or so W of Studland Wood; sometimes S of hedge 50m E of same wood (depending on moles creating bare ground in last two sites); much seen from Old Nick's Ground on edge of field W of S half of Old Nick's Ground.

Ox-eye Daisy *Leucanthemum vulgare*
Native. Abundant. Calcareous grassland and cliffs, road banks. June to July (later if cut or grazed).
Steeple: good display in churchyard. **Norden:** many by A351.
Woolgarston: plants with large flowers and leaves low on Ailwood Down at map reference SY99458132.
Durlston: Centenary Meadow and Ox-eye Daisy Field are wonderful sights (originally sown). **Swanage:**

plentiful in Northbrook Road Cemetery.

Upper leaves are toothed, lower leaves spoon-shaped (compare with next species). See Plate 26.

Shasta Daisy *Leucanthemum* x *superbum* (*L. lacustre* x *maximum*)
Introduction. Occasional. Verges, waste ground, cliffs. July to September.
Creech: NE side of road 400m NW of East Creech. **Langton:** E end of Castle View. **Durlston:** E side of Smith Field. **Swanage:** plentiful on cliffs before and after N end of promenade. **Studland:** on E side of bridleway12 20m S of middle W-E private road of Glebeland Estate.

Upper leaves are not toothed and lower leaves not spoon-shaped (see previous species). Clement (2004) believes that Shasta Daisy may really be *L. lacustre*.

Pineappleweed *Matricaria discoidea*
Introduction. Frequent. Tracks, especially near gateways. June to July.

Sea Mayweed
Tripleurospermum maritimum
Native. Occasional. Shores. May to September.
Tyneham: much by upper shore at Worbarrow Bay near end of path from Tyneham. **Kimmeridge:** by steps to beach from main car park. **Studland Heath:** N half of shore of Redhorn Bay. **Brownsea:** here and there on W half of S (not SW) shore. **Sandbanks:** upper shore opposite W end of Chaddesley Glen; 100m S of junction of Banks Road and Shore Road. Perennial species, well rooted unless first year plant. No scales between disk florets.

The oil glands on one side of the seeds, as mentioned in some identification books, are difficult to make out, even with a lens.

Scentless Mayweed
Tripleurospermum inodorum
Early Introduction. Frequent. Arable fields, other disturbed ground. July to September.

Annual species – lightly rooted; no scales between disk florets; oil glands – as above.

Silver Ragwort *Senecio cinerea*
Introduction. Occasional. Escape on sea cliffs and dunes. June to September.
Swanage: plentiful on cliffs above promenade N of Shore Road. **Ballard Down:** near base of chalk cliffs 250m from W end of chalk. **Sandbanks:** top of beach 125m NE of Midway Path; dunes 300m NE of main car park. **Canford Cliffs:** E side of Flaghead Chine near sea. **Branksome Dene Chine:** low on sea cliffs 100m to NE.

Some plants have some leaves which are green on the upperside, looking like possible hybrids with the next species; but a key feature of the hybrid is the slightly downy seeds.

Common Ragwort *Senecio jacobaea*
Native. Abundant. Grassland, marshes, verges. Mid-June to October; at its best in July.

Sepals tipped almost black. Can be hoary when young.

Horses are attracted to it when cut or pulled, but it is poisonous for them, so dispose of it where they cannot find it, and where its seeds cannot blow away.

Common x Marsh Ragwort – hybrid
Senecio x ostenfeldii (*S. jacobaea* x *aquaticus*)
Native. Occasional. Damp commons. July to September.

Corfe: few down First Valley NW of UCR; up same valley on SE side of UCR; several along S edge of West Common near SE corner; scattered in NE corner of West Common; few near S edge of Middle Common; near gate at N corner of Middle Common; near gate at W corner of Little East Common; probably elsewhere on those three parts of Common.

Intermediate between its parents in leaf-shape, spacing of flowers, and especially in having a few short hairs on its seeds (Marsh Ragwort has hairless seeds, Common Ragwort has hairy seeds). This hybrid is 15% fertile, and therefore sometimes interbreeds with its parents, producing confusing plants which are mostly like one or other parent.

Marsh Ragwort
Senecio aquaticus
Native. Occasional. Wet fields, marshes, commons. July to September.
Holme: one on N side of Holme Lane 100m W of railway bridge on corner of private track; very plentiful in East Holme Meadows – see p.23
Corfe: plentiful in damp grassland on Common. **Corfe Charity's Meadows:** one at extreme NW corner of Cowleaze by gap in hedge; one in SW of meadow SW of Sharford Bridge at map reference SY96548469.

Poisonous to horses when cut – see under Common Ragwort.

Hoary Ragwort *Senecio erucifolius*
Native. Frequent. Verges, grassland. Late July to September; at its best in August (compare with Common Ragwort).
Sepals tipped very pale brown. Not as hoary as shown in some books.

Poisonous to horses when cut – see under Common Ragwort.

Oxford Ragwort *Senecio squalidus*
Introduction. Rare. Urban waysides. April to October.
Swanage: W end of Court Road;
sometimes in adjoining roads – not
far from railway. **Swanage Railway:**
S side W of Northbrook Road
bridge.

From Oxford Botanic Garden, it
spread around Britain along the
railway tracks.

Groundsel *Senecio vulgaris*
Native. Frequent. Arable fields,
other disturbed ground. All year.

Flowerheads are cylindrical and
short-stalked.

Heath Groundsel *Senecio sylvaticus*
Native. Frequent. Dunes, sandy
areas on heaths, clay cliffs, shores,
recently scrub-cleared areas on
downs, arable fields, other disturbed ground. June to September.
Tyneham: cliff-top above
Worbarrow Bay 300-525m NW of
SE end of bay. **Holme:** N side of
Holme Lane 100m W of railway
bridge. **Hartland Moor:** NE side of
Slepe Road 20-50m NW of
entrance to Slepe Farm (Natural
England offices). **Arne:** plentiful
along shore S of Shipstal Point.
Ballard Down: S-facing slopes after
scrub clearances. **Studland Heath:**
plentiful on shore of Redhorn Bay
from Brand's Bay Hide N-wards;
plentiful on spit of heath N of
Western Arm of Little Sea; also
here and there on dunes. **Canford
Cliffs:** cliff-top near SE corner of
Cliff Drive.

Each flower is about the same
size as the previous species, but
flowerheads are conical, with longer
stalks. The plant is usually much
larger and slightly sticky.

Sticky Groundsel *Senecio viscosus*
Native. Occasional. Beaches, verges.
July to September.
Wareham: bank by river inlet just W
of South Bridge. **Studland Heath:** E
side of S corner of Bramble Bush Bay.
Sandbanks: few 80m W of junction
of Shore Road and Banks Road.
Brownsea: few at top of beach just E
of SW corner of island (with previous
species – good place to compare
them); plentiful on beaches N and S
of Pottery Pier; plentiful on beach off
Maryland ruins.

Each flower fatter than Grounsel
and like Common Ragwort but
smaller; 10-12mm across (Common
Ragwort's flowers are 15mm or more
across). The plant is very sticky; its
seeds are slightly hairy so that does
<u>not</u> distinguish this species from the
previous one.

Shrub Ragwort
Brachyglottis compacta x *laxifolia*
(*B.* cv. Sunshine, *Senecio* 'Sunshine')
Introduction. Rare. Planted. July to
August.
Sandbanks: raised dune SW of main
car park. **Canford Cliffs:** cliff near
stepped path from Cliff Drive to
beach.

Coltsfoot *Tussilago farfara*
Native. Frequent. Cliffs, arable fields,
other disturbed ground. February to
April.
Swanage: plentiful on recently
slipped areas of cliffs N of Shore
Road. **Ballard Down:** plentiful like-
wise N and S of Shep's Hollow.

Winter Heliotrope *Petasites fragrans*
Introduction. Frequent. Verges,
woods, quarries. December to March.

Increasing problem, as it blankets
out native vegetation.

Garden Marigold
Calendula officinalis
Introduction. Occasional. Casual.
April to October.

Ragweed *Ambrosia artemisiifolia*
Introduction. Rare. Casual, usually
from bird-seed. August to October.
 Height is up to 1m but often much
less; leaves are deeply divided; male
flowers are a dull row of small bobbles
along ends of branches, female flowers
are inconspicuous.

Sunflower *Helianthus annuus*
Introduction. Rare. Casual, some-
times from bird-seed. August to
October.

Shaggy Soldier
Galinsoga quadriradiata
Introduction. Rare. Pavements. July to
December.
Stoborough: King's Arms car park.
Corfe: N side of The Square; also
down hill to NE of it. (**Swanage:** for-
merly both near NW end of
Mermond Place and in roads within
100m of corner shop on Redcliffe
Road, but gets sprayed).

Nodding Bur-marigold
Bidens cernua
Native. Rare. River and ditch sides.
July to September.
Holme: East Holme Meadows – see
p.23. (**Stoborough:** in past – where
path13 ends at Cobbs Lake water-
course.)

French Marigold *Tagetes patula*
Introduction. Rare. Casual. June to
October.

Hemp-agrimony
Eupatorium cannibinum
Native. Frequent. Woods, verges,

stream-sides, cliffs, damp places. July
to September.
Ulwell: albinos on NE side of Ulwell
Road 10-15m SE of path15.

FLOWERING-RUSH FAMILY
Flowering-rush *Butomus umbellatus*
Native. Rare. Watersides. July to
August.
Holme: East Holme Meadows – see
p.23. See Plate 27.

WATER-PLANTAIN FAMILY
Arrowhead *Sagittaria sagittifolia*
Native. Rare. Broad ditches. July to
August.
Holme: plentiful in East Holme
Meadows – see p.23.

Lesser Water-plantain
Baldellia ranunculoides
Native. Occasional. Edges of ponds,
ditches and streams. May to
September.
Dorset Scarce. Near Threatened.
Creech Heath: NW corner of second
pond W of Furzebrook Road N of
path34. **Furzebrook:** SE corner of E-
most of three ponds in S of Kilnwood
Reserve. **Hartland Moor:** by Pillwort
Pond. **The Moors:** see p.27. **Corfe:**
few in South-west Valley of Middle
Common 250m SW of Purbeck Way;
in N-wards flowing tiny stream in wet
area 40m S of Middle Common
Pond; 20m S of same pond; plentiful
on edges of that pond. See Plate 27.

Water-plantain
Alisma plantago-aquatica
Native. Frequent. Shallow freshwater
or mud beside it. June to August.
Holme Bridge: S edge of river
between old and new bridge. **Holme:**
plentiful in East Holme Meadows –
see p.23. **Stoborough:** W of path13
100m S of Cobbs Lake watercourse.

Creech Heath: in small pond 75m ENE of crossing of path34 by W-E track (best approached from track to S). **Hartland Moor:** Arne Road S side ditch at E side of junction with Soldiers Road. **Corfe:** much in Middle Common Pond. **Studland Heath:** scattered on edges of Little Sea including beaches, but grazed by deer. **Shell Bay:** by both ends of boardwalk.

FROGBIT FAMILY
Water Soldier *Stratiotes aloides*
Probably native, but planted here. Rare. Ponds. June to August.
East Creech: pond furthest SE on Creech Heath (not in woodland despite O.S. map). **Norden:** Michael's Pond. **Studland:** village pond.

Canadian Waterweed
Elodea canadensis
Introduction. Occasional. Ponds, ditches. July-August.
Tyneham: ponds E of ruined Rectory; pond near telephone box (with next species). **The Moors:** with next species – see p.27. **Norden:** Michael's Pond. **Swanage:** in Swan Brook by SW corner of main car and coach park; in same brook S of that W of cemetery. **Studland:** Westwood Pond (with much less Curly Waterweed). **Branksome Chine:** in stream in chine.

Leaves in whorls, with fairly blunt ends. See beautiful detail of flowers with lens.

Nuttall's Waterweed *Elodea nuttallii*
Introduction. Occasional. Ponds, lakes, ditches.
Tyneham: pond near telephone box (with previous species). **Holme:** East Holme Meadows – see p.23.
Wareham: in ditch on W side of B3075 S of South Bridge when cleared. **The Moors:** with previous species –

see p.27. **Studland:** plentiful along W edge of Little Sea from Spur Bog N-wards for 200m (visible from old jetty just N of Spur Bog), rooted 1m off shore at N end of Fourth Beach in SE of Little Sea; much can be found washed up on beaches in SE of Little Sea (there may be still some unexploded bombs and shells in Little Sea, but it is unlikely that they are close to shore).

Leaves in whorls, with sharply pointed ends. Not seen flowering, though it does flower in Little Sea.

Curly Waterweed *Lagarosiphon major*
Introduction. Rare. Ponds. Not seen flowering.
Creech Heath: plentiful in largest pond N of W-E track which crosses path34 halfway. **Studland:** Westwood Pond (with more Canadian Waterweed). **Durlston:** Johnston Pond.

Leaves are congested and very curved back, lower attached spirally, upper in whorls.

CAPE-PONDWEED FAMILY
Cape-pondweed
Aponogeton distachyos
Introduction. Rare. Streams. March to November.
Swanage: in Swan Brook N of St. Mary's Church.

Sometimes mistakenly called Water Hyacinth, which is a different species.

ARROWGRASS FAMILY
Marsh Arrowgrass *Triglochin palustre*
Native. Occasional. Marshes. June to August.
Corfe: both 250m SW and 150m WSW of W end of First Valley on West Common; by spring under W-facing slope 300m S of extreme NW of West Common; in Middle Common

both in South-west Valley (if not grazed); in wet slopes S of pond.
Wares (west): at least one near top of S-most of western group of flushes in Long Close; at least 30 plants 40m N of Scratch Arse Ware in part of N-most flush shown in Hedbury Ware on map 15.

Sea Arrowgrass *Triglochin maritimum*
Native. Occasional. Upper salt-marshes. May to September.
Wytch: N end of path6; plentiful 150m S of NW corner of Wytch Moor. **Godlingston Heath:** on SW shore of Brand's Creek NE of pentagonal fenced area. **Studland Heath:** here and there on E shore of Brand's Creek; thinly on shores of Bramble Bush Bay. **Sandbanks:** around head of inlet (not shown on O.S. maps) S of W end of Chaddesley Glen.

PONDWEED FAMILY
The BSBI handbook on Pondweeds (Preston, 1995) is one of the best of their handbooks.

Broad-leaved Pondweed
Potamogeton natans
Native. Frequent. Ponds, ditches, lakes.
Holme: East Holme Meadows – see p.23. **Creech Heath:** pond S of W-E track which crosses path34 halfway. **Furzebrook:** E-most of three ponds in S of Kilnwood Reserve; also W part of pond midway between paths8, 10 and 11 and Purbeck Way. **Norden:** Michael's Pond. **Bushey:** smaller pond on Brenscombe South Heath.
Studland Heath: two ponds S side of track to nudists' area 600m and 700m from Ferry Road. **Luscombe Valley:** in ditch along NW edge of Reserve adjoining golf course (next species is in ditch at N end of Reserve).
    Can be confused with the next

species which sometimes grows nearby, but floating leaves of this one often have a bend at the junction of leaf and stalk, have pale veins, and its submerged leaves do not look like leaves being hardly wider than the stalks (compare with next species); see identification books for other differences.

Bog Pondweed
Potamogeton polygonifolius
Native. Abundant. Bogs, acid streams, ponds and ditches.
    Leaves of various sizes and shapes, according to habitat. See drawing.

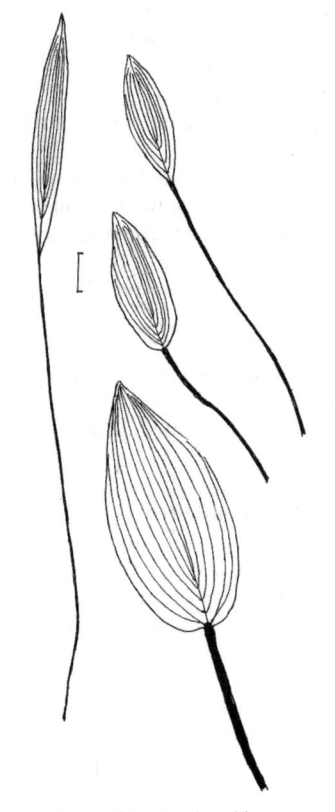

Various shapes of Bog Pondweed leaves.

225

Submerged leaves narrower than floating leaves, but are recognisably leaves (compare with previous species).

Shining Pondweed
Potamogeton lucens
Native. Occasional. Rivers.
Wareham: very plentiful in River Frome from bypass bridge (view best from W side of bridge) all the way to South Bridge (boat).

Leaves are short-stalked; they get covered with algae and so do not shine.

Willow-leaved Pondweed
Potamogeton x salicifolius
(*P. lucens* x *perfoliatus*)
Native. Rare. Rivers.
If hybrids were rated, this would be *Nationally Scarce*.
Holme: East Holme Meadows – see p.23. **Wareham:** in River Frome 200m downstream from bypass bridge (boat).

Like Shining Pondweed but leaves unstalked.

Red Pondweed *Potamogeton alpinus*
Native. Rare. Ditches.
Holme: East Holme Meadows – see p.23.

Perfoliate Pondweed
Potamogeton perfoliatus
Native. Rare. Lakes, rivers.
Wareham: here and there in River Frome for 200m downstream from bypass bridge (boat). **Studland Heath:** washed up on all beaches on both Western Arm and SE of Little Sea; rooted in sand 2m off shore 40m N of Fifth Beach (there may be still some unexploded bombs and shells in Little Sea, but it is unlikely that they are close to the shore).

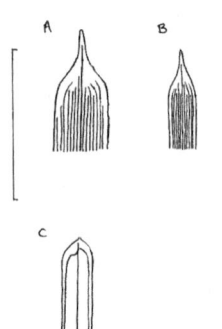

Pondweed leaf-tips: A- Sharp-leaved, B - Stoborough, C - Blunt-leaved.

Blunt-leaved Pondweed
Potamogeton obtusifolius
Native. Rare. Lakes with acid water.
Dorset Rare.
Studland Heath: rooted in sand 2m off shore at N end of Fourth Beach in SE of Little Sea; likewise 40 and 60m N of Fifth Beach; washed up on all beaches at SE of Little Sea (see Perfoliate Pondweed).

Small Pondweed
Potamogeton berchtoldii
Native. Occasional. Ditches, ponds, lakes.
Holme: East Holme Meadows – see p.23. **Furzebrook:** E-most of three ponds in S of Kilnwood Reserve. **The Moors:** see p.27. **Studland Heath:** rooted in sand 1m off shore 60m N of Fifth Beach; washed up on all beaches in SE of Little Sea (see Perfoliate Pondweed).

Dorset Pondweed
Potamogeton x sudermanicus
(*P. berchtoldii* x *acutifolius*)
Native. Rare. Ditches.
Nationally Rare. Vulnerable.
Plentiful on private land at the

only British site. Owner gives permission to individuals (not groups) to visit in late summer at own risk. Contact author for details (see Appendix). See drawing p.266.

Sharp-leaved Pondweed
Potamogeton acutifolius
Native. Rare. Ditches.
Nationally Rare. Critically Endangered.
Plentiful on private land with hybrid above.

Curled Pondweed
Potamogeton crispus
Native. Occasional. Ponds, streams.
Holme: East Holme Meadows – see p.23. **Bushey:** larger pond on Brenscombe South Heath (binoculars). **Wares (east):** S of Belle Vue Middle Ware halfway along in former cattle trough in large nettle-bed between fence and cliff-top (it has been there for at least 40 years). **Swanage:** in Swan Brook N of St. Mary's Church. **Studland:** village pond.

Fennel Pondweed
Potamogeton pectinatus
Native. Occasional. Rivers, ditches.
Holme: East Holme Meadows – see p.23. **Wareham:** very plentiful in River Frome from bypass bridge to South Bridge (boat); in river 125m E of South Bridge (boat).
With hollows either side of the central vein of the leaf (lens).

Opposite-leaved Pondweed
Groenlandia densa
Native. Rare. Ditches, ponds.
Dorset Scarce. Vulnerable.
The Moors: see p.27. **Corfe:** small amount in middle of Middle Common Pond (best approached from SW side when water level is low in dry summer).

TASSELWEED FAMILY
Beaked Tasselweed
Ruppia maritima
Native. Rare. Harbour shores. July to September.
Dorset Scarce.
Studland Heath: visible here and there at half or lower tide on mud just off shore S of neck of Redhorn Quay and here and there on mud for 275m SE of that in Redhorn Bay.

EELGRASS FAMILY
Eelgrass *Zostera marina*
Native. Abundant. Sandy sea and harbour floor. June to September.
Dorset Scarce. Near Threatened.
Studland: plentiful off whole length of South Beach especially N end where some is exposed at low spring tides and much more is in shallow water; off Middle Beach from near S end N-wards. **Studland Heath:** off Knoll Beach from N end of Middle Beach to 300m NE of Knoll Beach café, (vastly more further out in bay, as can be seen from usually blackened amount washed up). **Shell Bay:** near E end of rocks at low spring tides at Pilot Point; much more in both shallow and deeper water 150m W; much also for first 75m and also 175-250m S of those rocks. **Lilliput:** plentiful 200m off Evening Hill where some is exposed at low spring tides and much more is in shallow water.

PALM FAMILY
Chusan Palm *Trachycarpus fortunei*
Introduction. Rare. Planted.
Tyneham: garden of ruined Rectory. **Brownsea:** in NE of Venetia Park.

ARUM FAMILY
American Skunk-cabbage
Lysichiton americanus
Introduction. Rare. Planted or escaped; spreading. Wet shaded ground. April to May.

Ower: about 25 plants (some singly – some in groups) can be seen from broad W bank of stream, in open access area SW of bridleway7 (stream bank is accessible near its S end from open access area to W in Wellingtons with difficulty). **Brownsea:** few on N side of Middle Street 100m NW of church. **Luscombe:** several near track halfway up W edge of Reserve 80m N of metal bridge.

Poisonous.

Lords-and-ladies *Arum maculatum*
Native. Abundant. Woods, scrub, hedge-banks; not on acid soil. April to May (leaves <u>late December</u> to June).

Poisonous.

Italian Lords-and-ladies
Arum italicum subsp. *italicum*
Introduction. Occasional. On calcareous soil. May to June (leaves late September to July).

Worth: under trees by little stream 40m NW upstream of Sewage Works (with subsp. *neglectum*); on bank under Elders 50m W of S-most electricity post N of path11 in Abbott's Combe. **Wares (west):** 5m E of path11 in Seacombe Bottom 50m S of gate at S end of Long Close. **Wares (east):** two E of path61 under Sycamore 20m N of stone stile at NE corner of field N of Belle Vue East Ware. **Durlston:** in gully N of NE corner of lighthouse enclosure just W of overhead telephone wire (do not confuse with nearby electricity line) (steep approach).

Poisonous.

Arum italicum subsp. *italicum* cv. Marmoratum (synonym Pictum) Introduction. Occasional. Escape on any soils; prone to spreading. May to June (leaves from late September to July).

Ridge: plentiful 20m W of E end of Barnhill Road. **Corfe:** in Byle Copse 50m from N end. **Rempstone:** both sides of Breaches Lane 150m W of stream at E end; on NW side of bridleway11 50m SW of Foxground Cottage (with *Arum italicum* subsp. *neglectum*). **Swanage:** S side of Victoria Avenue 20m E of W end of Prospect Crescent opposite; W end of copse W of D'Urberville Drive (extreme form, in which paler areas around veins merge). **Studland:** 50m S of NE corner of Glebeland Estate E of bridleway12.

Poisonous.

Arum italicum subsp. *neglectum*
Introduction. Occasional. Rough pastures on limestone near sea, particularly on E side of drystone walls, on level areas beneath foot of slopes, and close to scrub, but sometimes out in open. Only larger sites of this local speciality are given below, with one exception at Rempstone. May to June (leaves from late September to July).
Nationally Scarce. Near Threatened.
Worth: E side of wall by Coast Path 450m SW of Winspit quarries; on W side of path13 10m N of private track to Winspit Cottage opposite; in W side of Abbott's Combe 70m N of path11; plentiful in same field under all seven E-facing strip lynchet banks within 200m S of path11. **Wares (west):** here and there both sides of W wall of Nicholas Down for 300m N-wards from Coast Path; also on E side of same wall for 75m

N of path11; unusual plants in Long Close under bramble at map reference SY98377764 lacking pale veins; scattered near stream W of track through Long Close both 250-300m SE of Eastington Farm; also 500-650m SSE of Farm; along W side of Cliff Field from 75-200m N of Coast Path; at W edge of Hedbury Ware for 200m NW of Coast Path; scattered across steepest part of Dancing Ledge Ware; (**east**) NW corner of Middle Ground N of gateway (easiest place because no descent involved); E of walls on W edges of both White Ware and Chillmark Ware for 150m N of Coast Path; scattered along E of walls on W edges of all three Belle Vue Wares. **Rempstone:** 50m SW of Foxground Cottage on NW side of bridleway11 (with *Arum italicum* subsp. *italicum* cv. Marmoratum). **Durlston:** E end of S-facing rocky escarpment N of lighthouse.

Poisonous. Introduced as a source of starch, probably from Spain (A. Diaz, pers. com), for preparing food from roots in times of famine, despite toxicity (Bowen, 2000).

Leaves have network of pale veins. See Plate 27. They begin to emerge from late September, making it easy to record in November, because leaves of *Arum maculatum* do not begin to emerge until around Christmas. Leaves of *Arum italicum* subsp. *neglectum* mostly get buried later in late spring under Bramble, Stinging Nettle etc. Few flowering spikes appear, and almost all of those get damaged, some by birds seeking insects trapped within. Possibly a proportion of these populations are hybrids with *Arum maculatum*; some leaves look intermediate (as in photo on Plate 27), and lack flowering spikes.

DUCKWEED FAMILY

If out of reach, use end of walking-stick or something similar.

Greater Duckweed *Spirodela polyrhiza* (*Lemna polyrhiza*)
Native. Rare. Ditches. Visible May to November.
Wareham: ditch on W side of B3075 from near South Bridge most of way S to Stoborough when ditch cleared (short range binoculars); under foot-bridge at E end of Priory Meadow (with three other Duckweed species).

Fat Duckweed *Lemna gibba*
Native. Rare. Ditches. Recognisable September to November.
Wareham: plenty under footbridge at E end of Priory Meadow (with three other Duckweed species).

Bowen (2000) wrote in *The Flora of Dorset*, 'Almost certainly under-recorded, as it does not fatten up until autumn.' It will probably be mistaken for Common Duckweed (see below) earlier than that.

Common Duckweed *Lemna minor*
Native. Occasional. Ponds, ditches. Visible all year, but very much less in winter.
Tyneham: pond near telephone box; ponds E of ruined Rectory (with Least Duckweed in W pond).
Stoborough: on W side of path13 where it goes through gate 110m W of bypass (correct path is in black not green on O.S. map). **Wareham:** ditch

Duckweeds: Common (left) and Least.

on W side of B3075 (when ditch cleared). **Corfe Charity's Meadows:** ditch on NW side of Paddle Dock meadow 175m SW of gateway from Home Mead (W). **Worth:** water tank in NE of Worth Mead; flush in S of Worth Field. **Ulwell:** ditch by lower lay-by. **Studland:** Westwood Pond – few; at Middle Beach on muddy track behind beach huts 50m N of footbridge. **Luscombe Valley:** pond.

Sometimes with Least Duckweed, two below. On average it is much bigger than that species, but the veins are very difficult to see.

Ivy-leaved Duckweed
Lemna trisulca
Native. Rare. Ponds, ditches. Visible April to July.
Wareham: under footbridge at E end of Priory Meadow (with Greater, Fat and Least Duckweed, but it can be blanketed out by them). **Studland:** village pond.

Least Duckweed *Lemna minuta*
Introduction, spreading fast. Occasional. Still or slow-moving water. Visible all year.
Tyneham: W of three ponds E of ruined Rectory (with Common Duckweed). **Wareham:** under footbridge at E end of Priory Meadow (with up to three other Duckweeds). **Furzebrook:** three ponds in Kilnwood Reserve SW of stile to field; pond S of Purbeck Way 600m E of Furzebrook Road. **Langton:** large pond in centre of N end of West Wood; downstream of it. **Studland:** village pond. **Brownsea:** very plentiful in ditches W and SW of Lagoon.

Sometimes with Common Duckweed, see two above. The shape is shorter than a grain of rice (see drawing p.229).

RUSH FAMILY
Flowering periods are given, but most species of the genus *Juncus* are easier to identify when in fruit, which they retain for several months after flowering.

Heath Rush *Juncus squarrosus*
Native. Occasional. Tracks and open areas on heaths. June to July.
Stoborough Heath: in Sandlings field 25m S of N edge 150m W of Dismantled Tramway. **Hartland Moor:** here and there on W half of Moor itself especially on tracks. **Wytch:** on new route of path5 200m SE of NE corner of Wytch Moor. **Rempstone:** along 5m of W side of bridleway31 375m N of crossing of bridleways31 and 34 (Oil Road); on SE side of bridleway33 100m NE of junction with bridleway31 in two places 10m apart. **Godlingston Heath:** middle of N-S track 825m S of its N end where Ferry Road meets bridleway36. **Studland Heath:** plentiful on track running NE from track to nudists' area 130 to at least 400m from latter. **Shell Bay:** in large depression 450m SSE of NE end of boardwalk 80m behind main foredunes; for several m on N-S track 100m W of that depression.

Slender Rush *Juncus tenuis*
Introduced. Occasional. Open wet tracks and verges. June to September.
Stoborough Heath: on Dismantled Tramway 20-35m N of gate at S end. **Hartland Moor:** on N side of Arne Road 250m W of Arne Triangle. **Studland Heath:** along 10m of NW side of Ferry Road 170m SW of track to Jerry's Point; on SE side of road opposite that site; 40m NE of there; by track to nudists' area close to Ferry Road. **Luscombe Valley:** tracks in S half of Reserve, especially near pond.

Salt-marsh Rush *Juncus gerardii*
Native. Frequent. Top of salt-marshes
and beaches. June to July.

Leafy Rush *Juncus foliosus*
Native. Rare. Damp places in non-cal-
careous woods and scrub. May to
September.
Dorset Scarce.
Corfe: several plants on N side of
First Valley stream just W of path53
board bridge under Grey Willow
(with rather more of next species).
Rempstone: on beginning of track on
SE side of bridleway34 (Oil Road)
500m NE of where bridleway31
crosses it. See drawing.

Toad Rush *Juncus bufonius*
Native. Frequent. Damp arable fields,
other disturbed ground, tracks and
watersides. May to September.
　　Can have a single dark band on the
petals – but rarely.

Frog Rush
Juncus ranarius (*J. ambiguus*)
Native. Rare. Damp places near
coast. May to September.
Dorset Scarce.
Wares (east): W arm of Y-shaped
flush in centre of Verney Ware (with
previous species).

Blunt-flowered Rush
Juncus subnodulosus
Native. Occasional. Fens, upper salt-
marshes. July to September.
Hartland Moor: plentiful towards S
end of Upper Fen; plentiful in
Middle Fen 200m W of Pillwort
Pond; SW side of Slepe Road both at
bridge over stream at NE of Moor;
10-15m SE. **The Moors:** see p.27.
Wytch: plentiful on E side of Wytch
Moor from 100m S of NE corner for
100m. **Godlingston Heath:** plentiful

here and there on W side of Brand's
Creek from 50m NW of bridle-
way36 for 130m NW-wards.
Studland Heath: in upper salt-marsh
on E side of Brand's Creek 120 and
210m N of bridleway36; halfway
along N shore of Western Arm of
Little Sea.

Jointed Rush *Juncus articulatus*
Native. Occasional. Wet places in
fields, tracks, heaths, cliffs; watersides. June to September.
Creech Heath: along W-E track 100-
150m E of junction with path34.
Hartland Moor: N side of Pillwort
Pond. **Corfe:** plenty on Common,
including 5m E of gate at N of
Middle Common. **Worth:** few in
flush on W edge of Abbott's Combe
125m S of path11. **Wares (west):** on
track where it passes through cutting
in NE of Long Close 200m down
track from stile at N edge; in flushes
furthest NW, NE and SE in Long
Close. **Godlingston Heath:** on S side
of bridleway27 – 90 and 110m E of
track to greenkeepers' private depot.
Shell Bay: near mouth of usually
summer-dry stream near SE end of
Bay. **Branksome Chine:** by promenade 550-570m SW of chine.

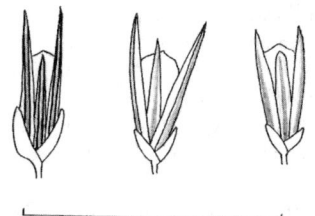

*Fruiting flowers of rushes (left to right): Leafy
(showing dark bands), Toad, Frog (showing
blunt inner petals)*

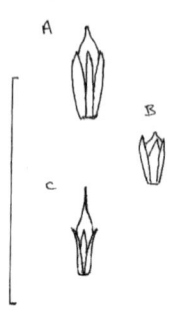

Fruiting flowers of Rushes: A - Jointed, B - Hybrid Jointed, C - Sharp-flowered.

Hybrid Jointed Rush *Juncus* x *surrejanus* (*J. articulatus* x *acutiflorus*)
Native. Occasional. Wet fields, heaths, verges; beaches; sometimes with parents. July to August.
Creech Heath: along W-E track 170-190m E of junction with path34. **Furzebrook:** N of pond in S of Kilnwood Reserve nearest to stile into central field. **Hartland Moor:** N side of Pillwort Pond (with Jointed Rush). **Norden:** depression just SW of Michael's Pond. **Wytch:** by new route of path5 450m SE of NE corner of Wytch Moor. **Wares (west):** second flush from E in Hedbury Ware. **Studland:** near where track crosses stream on E side of Harmony Farm NW Field. **Studland Heath:** NW side of Ferry Road 50m NE of track to Redhorn Quay; just N of junction of Heather Walk and track from car park by Study Centre; by Heather Walk 50-70m further N.

Flowerheads are often more congested than those of the parents. By September, most seed-cases still do not protrude beyond the petals. See drawing.

Sharp-flowered Rush
Juncus acutiflorus
Native. Frequent. Wet fields, heaths, dunes, verges; marshes. July to September.

Bulbous Rush *Juncus bulbosus*
Native. Frequent. Wet places on heaths. June to September.

Sea Rush *Juncus maritimus*
Native. Frequent. Upper salt-marshes. July to August.
Wares (east): unusual site in most flushes on sloping cliff S of Verney Ware.

Hard Rush *Juncus inflexus*
Native. Frequent. Wet fields, tracks, verges; marshes. June to August.

Soft Rush *Juncus effusus*
Native. Frequent. Watersides, wet fields, verges and heaths. June to August.
Compare with species below.

Compact Rush *Juncus conglomeratus*
Native. Frequent. Wet fields, verges and heaths. May to July.
The previous species, Soft Rush, can also have fairly compact heads, especially early in the season. However, the stem-ribs of Compact Rush can be felt, especially just below the flowerhead, whereas the finely-ribbed stem of Soft Rush feels smooth.

Hairy Woodrush *Luzula pilosa*
Native. Occasional. Old woods, verges. April to June.
East Creech: on top of one of the low banks in NW of Kilnwood Reserve 75m from W edge 100m S of Purbeck Way; on low bank 100m S of previous site. **Bushey:** SE side

of path13 one-third way up wooded area S of Brenscombe Farm.
Langton: S of largest pond in N of Langton West Wood plentiful on NE-facing bank slightly W of centre of pond; also few two-thirds of the way up the bank slightly E of centre of pond. **Rempstone:** on W side of bridleway16 100m S of B3351. **Canford Cliffs:** by E side of path in Flaghead Chine 20m N of upper seat.

Slight swelling at the blunt tip of the leaf (lens) <u>on fresh leaves.</u>

Great Woodrush *Luzula sylvatica*
Native. Rare. Woods. May to June.
Durlston: Country Park woods between Coast Path and Durlston Road 120m N of Long Meadow 8m NE of large Beech.

Field Woodrush, Good Friday Grass *Luzula campestris*
Native. Abundant. Grassland, including lawns, heaths, verges. March to May.

Anthers are conspicuous, 2 to 6 times as long as the filaments.

Heath Woodrush
Luzula multiflora subsp. *multiflora* and subsp. *congesta*
Native. Frequent. Heaths, verges. April to June.
The subspecies were not usually separately recorded – but at **Studland Heath,** subsp. *congesta* is plentiful.

Anthers are not very conspicuous, about as long as the filaments.

SEDGE FAMILY
The third edition of the BSBI handbook on Sedges by Jermy *et al.* (2007) is very helpful. This edition covers all genera, not just Carex – and hybrids too.

Common Cottonsedge
Eriophorum angustifolium
Native. Frequent. Bogs. April to May; conspicuous later when in seed.

Deergrass *Trichophorum germanicum* (*T. cespitosum* subsp. *germanicum*)
Native. Abundant. Heaths. May to June.

Common Spike-rush
Eleocharis palustris
Native. Occasional. Marshes, ponds. May to July.
Tyneham: ponds E of ruined Rectory. **Creech:** in pond 250m NW of Grange Road on S side of bridleway1. **Furzebrook:** S side of middle pond in S of Kilnwood Reserve. **Corfe:** here and there in wet areas in West, Middle, Little East and Big East Commons, especially plentiful S of Middle Common Pond. **Wares (west):** E side of pond S of Priest's Way 250m E of path30; **(east)** pond at junction of bridleways18 and 20. **Harman's Cross:** by path26 in S end of second field N of A351 (between woods). **Studland Heath:** halfway along W side of depressions N of main N car park at Knoll Beach. **Shell Bay:** 200m SE of E end of boardwalk. **Brownsea:** W of boardwalk through Orchid Meadow 50m N of SE end.

Stems are upright. The bases of the two lowest glumes each circle about half of the base of the flower spike. Stems vary greatly in height, 10cm up to 60cm.

Slender Spike-rush
Eleocharis uniglumis
Native. Rare. Top of salt-marshes. May to July.
Godlingston Heath: two sites 10m apart on SW side of Brand's Creek NE of pentagonal fenced area.

Studland Heath: from 250m S of Brand's Bay Hide running almost continuously S-wards for 110m; also S corner of Bramble Bush Bay.
Stems are upright. The base of the lowest glume almost encircles the whole base of the flower spike.

Many-stalked Spike-rush
Eleocharis multicaulis
Native. Frequent. Bogs, wet heaths, commons. July to August.
Godlingston Heath: fresh shoots were produced from the flowerheads (called viviparity) in wet summer of 2007 at pond at map reference SZ01958269.

Stems are at various angles, few are upright. The base of the lowest glume almost encircles the whole base of a flower spike.

Few-flowered Spike-rush
Eleocharis quinqueflora
Native. Occasional. Short vegetation in marshes. June to July.
Dorset Scarce.
Corfe: third Valley on West Common 90m from road; South-west Valley on Middle Common 150m SW of Purbeck Way within small area of Cottonsedge; also just E of it; 100m SSW of Middle Common Pond at map reference SY96458093; in S corner of Little East Common at middle of top of slope in front of Willows. It sometimes grows with many of the previous species. However, Few-flowered Spike-rush has a darker flowerhead, with the lowest glume usually more than half the height of the flowerhead. Stems are usually upright.

Sea Club-rush *Bolboschoenus maritimus* (*Scirpus maritimus*)
Native. Occasional. Salt-marshes;

occasionally by fresh water. July to August.
Studland Heath: most E point of Redhorn Bay; by fresh water S of beach at SW of Western Arm of Little Sea; few on W side of S corner of Bramble Bush Bay. **Studland:** by stream NE of Middle Beach car park 10m upstream from beach. **Sandbanks:** scattered on harbour edge S of W end of Chaddesley Glen.

Common Club-rush, Bulrush
Schoenoplectus lacustris
(*Scirpus lacustris*)
Native. Rare. Rivers, ditches, ponds. June to July.
Holme: East Holme Meadows – see p.23. **Wareham** (boat), S side of River Frome both 150 and 225m downstream from bypass bridge and 400m upstream from South Bridge. **Creech Heath:** NE corner of pond in extreme SE of open access area (probably planted).
Stems are dull darkish green; glumes are unspotted (lens).

Grey Club-rush, Glaucous Bulrush
Schoenoplectus tabernaemontani
(*Scirpus tabernaemontani, S. lacustris* subsp. *tabernaemontani*)
Native. Occasional. Ditches and other watersides, mostly near coast; may be planted in some sites. June to July.
Furzebrook: E-most of three ponds in S of Kilnwood Reserve. **The Moors:** see p.27. **Wytch:** along 40m of W-E stream 150m S of NW corner of Wytch Moor. **Bushey:** S end of smaller pond on Brenscombe South Heath. **Wares (west):** pond S of Priest's Way 250m E of path30. **Godlingston and Studland Heaths:** here and there around Brand's Creek. **Studland:** village pond. **Luscombe Valley:** by stream in SW corner of Reserve.

Stems are usually grey-green (pale green at one site in The Moors), glumes are minutely spotted (lens).

Bristle Club-rush
Isolepsis setacea (Scirpus setaceus)
Native. Occasional. Marshes, wet tracks. May to July.
Stoborough: E side Dismantled Tramway 300m N of A351. **Hartland Moor:** sides of Pillwort Pond; S side of Arne Road 50m W of Arne Triangle. **Corfe:** Second Valley in West Common 40 and 90m from road; under Grey Willow on N side of First Valley stream just W of path53 board bridge (with next species); many 100m W of SE corner of West Common 10m N of stream; halfway down South-west Valley of Middle Common; in East Valley in Big East Common 500m from railway fence. **Studland Heath:** SW side of track to Jerry's Point near where bridleway37 crosses it; on beach at SW of Western Arm of Little Sea.

Usually the flowerheads are mostly brown, often more than one per stem, with the stem projecting well beyond them; however, the only certain diagnostic feature is the several longitudinal ridges on the fruit, when viewed with x20 lens from certain angles (compare with species below) (rub flowerhead between finger and thumb to extract the fruits).

Slender Club-rush
Isolepsis cernua (Scirpus cernuus)
Native. Occasional. Wet ground, usually near coasts. June to August.
The Moors: see p.27. **Corfe:** under Grey Willow on N side of First Valley stream just W of path53 board bridge (with previous species); Middle Common NE-facing wet slopes S and SE of pond. **Arne:** near Telegraph

Cable notice. **Wares (east):** W arm of Y-shaped flush in centre of Verney Ware. **Studland Heath:** SE corner of Brand's Creek 40m from bridleway; on shore 350m S of Brand's Bay Hide.

Usually flowerheads are mostly green (brown later), only one per stem, with the stem projecting only just beyond it – but <u>sometimes</u> projecting further; however, the only certain diagnostic feature is that the fruit has no series of ridges, but tiny bumps (x20 lens), (compare with species above).

Floating Club-rush *Isolepsis fluitans (Eleogiton fluitans, Scirpus fluitans)*
Native. Frequent. By or in acid water, sometimes covering several square metres, but then with few flowers. May to September.
Creech Heath: near NW corner of Icen Barrow Pond; in pond S of W-E track which crosses path34 halfway. **Hartland Moor:** in pool 100m E of SE corner of Arne Triangle. **Corfe:** streamlet in First Valley on West Common 100m SE of UCR. **Godlingston Heath:** in pond W of gate into forest on bridleway33. **Studland Heath:** in low area N of main N car park at Knoll Beach very plentiful; on beaches on SE side of Little Sea; in edges of swamps N and S of track to nudists' area. **Shell Bay:** 200m SE of E end of boardwalk between end of line of Grey Willows and area dominated by rushes.

When not flowering it can be mistaken for pondweed or grass. See Plate 27.

Galingale *Cyperus longus*
Native. Rare. Wet meadows, verges. July to September.
Nationally Scarce. Near Threatened.
Stoborough Heath: NE side of path5

180m NW of small square field through which path passes (may be mown in some years). **Herston (north):** 30m N of path24 on W side of private road to Sludge Works (binoculars from path24). **Ulwell:** meadow SW of Ulwell Road opposite Ulwell Farm Caravan Park – often grazed, but in some years it is in flower close to pavement (binoculars from road); (maybe this is where it was first seen in Britain in 1688 – certainly known at this site since 1847).

Pale Galingale *Cyperus eragrostis*
Introduction. Rare. Escaped or planted. July to September.
Corfe: both sides of Tilbury Mead 30m E of A351. **Langton:** pavement edge on N side of B3069 up to 20m W of Serrell's Mead. **Canford Cliffs:** W side of S end of Bessborough Road.

Compact, greenish flowers, compared with the loose brown flowers of the previous species.

Black Bog-rush *Schoenus nigricans*
Native. Abundant. Bogs which are not too acid. May to June.

White Beak-sedge *Rhynchospora alba*
Native. Abundant. Open places in bogs, wet heaths. July to August.

Flowers are at the top of the stem; they turn brown in August and can therefore be confused with the next species.

Brown Beak-sedge *Rhynchospora fusca*
Native. Occasional. Small pools in bogs, wet heaths. Late May to July.
Nationally Scarce.
Stoborough Heath: scattered 8-19m E of W boundary of W part of Heath 275m N of railway in area 13m S-N with outliers to N (but with few flowers); on E part of Heath plenty by

track 250-280m SE of New Road (best site); by track for 12m in SW of same part of Heath 400m NW of Dismantled Tramway (few flowers); few scattered throughout length of Sunnyside Mire; few near NW corner of Sandlings field 30m S of fence 35m E of line of Gorse; in SW part of doughnut-shaped pond just E of Dismantled Tramway 190m N of A351 (may not flower there); two places 50m apart 40 and 70m E of tramway opposite gaps between letters 'm'-'w' and 'w'-'a' respectively in 'Tramway' on O.S. map. **Creech Heath:** 4m N of Purbeck Way 20m E of junction with path37 (few flowers). **Hartland Moor:** two sites just above letter 'p' of 'Slepe Heath' on O.S. map (not Map 5); one above second letter 'e' of same name. **Godlingston Heath:** at map reference SZ01958366; in S of Brand's Bog Extension at both SZ02338359 and 02368362; few 190m SSW of bridleway36 in 1m diameter hole10m E of lowest level of Brand's Bog 55m N of Scots Pine on mound. **Studland Heath:** N side of Spur Bog in depression 25m E of lone small Scots Pine; also a few 80m E of entrance of Spur Bog just above lower level (25m W of low trees) (with Marsh Clubmoss).

Leaf-like bract projects well above the group of flowers. This species is not easy to find, especially when they occur in low numbers, which is why sites are described in such detail above. The bright apple-green colour of the leaves in early summer helps to spot it. It can be confused with White Beak-sedge. See Plate 28.

Great Fen-sedge *Cladium mariscus*
Native. Rare. Fens. July to August.
Dorset Scarce.
The Moors: see p.27.

True Sedges. Flowering periods are given; most species of the genus *Carex* are best identified when in fruit, about one month after flowering.

Greater Tussock Sedge
Carex paniculata
Native. Rare. Wet woods and by heath streams. May to June.
The Moors: see p.27. **Corfe:** plentiful in various places along N two-thirds of NW edge of West Common.
Corfe Charity's Meadows: in wet strip of woodland W of Long Meadow 150m N of Close Next The Barn.

Lesser Tussock Sedge *Carex diandra*
Native. Rare. Ditches. May to June (fruit falls in early July).
Dorset Rare. Near Threatened.
The Moors: see p.27 – only site in Dorset – but the ditch it was in was dug out in 2007.

False Fox Sedge *Carex otrubae*
Native. Occasional. Marshes, verges, watersides. June to July.
Steeple: along 10m of N side of road just E of SW corner of Horse Coppice. **Hartland Moor:** S side of Arne Road 100m W of Arne Triangle. **Corfe:** in rushy area of The Rings between centre and SE bastion.
Worth: by pond on NE side of Renscombe Road. **Wytch:** W side of Thrasher's Lane 20m S of bridleway4.
Godlingston: N side of Washpond Lane 100m W of Darkie Lane.
Studland Heath: neck of Redhorn Quay. **Brownsea:** beside boardwalk through Orchid Meadow. **Lilliput:** by fence at bottom of Evening Hill 10m from SE end of fence. **Luscombe Valley:** W of stream 30m S of metal bridge in centre of Reserve.

Spiked Sedge *Carex spicata*
Native. Occasional. Dry but not acid banks and verges; often few. May to July.
Worth: on low bank on NE side of UCR 150m N of Renscombe Farm.
Bushey: N side of Bushey Lane opposite Higher Bushey Farm; along 15m of same side 110m E of bridleway10 (gets mown in both). **Woolgarston:** N side of W-E road just E of short road to Woolgarston Farm. **Ballard Down:** around head level on steep bank on N side of Purbeck Way 95m E of stile NE of Ulwell Farm.
Durlston: N side of track along S side of Herren Ground 20m from SE corner. **Luscombe Valley:** W and 60m N of metal bridge in centre of Reserve.

Ligules are longer than broad; female glumes are tawny; fruit is 4.5-5mm long.

Prickly Sedge
Carex muricata subsp. *pairae*
(*C. muricata* subsp. *lamprocarpa*)
Native. Occasional. Dry grassland (but not necessarily acid ground). June to July.
Hartland Moor: 85m NNE of gate at SW of Slepe Heath along 5m N-S 15m E of Soldiers Road (gets grazed by deer). **Studland Heath:** NW side of Ferry Road 225m SW of track to Jerry's Point. **Brownsea:** W end of low wall on edge of track NW of Visitor Centre; SW side of churchyard; plentiful 20m SE of churchyard.

Ligules are as broad as long; female glumes are pale; fruit is 2.5-3.5mm long.

Grey Sedge
Carex divulsa subsp. *divulsa*
Native. Frequent. Verges, banks; usually on neutral, but sometimes on calcareous soil. June to September.

Stoborough: by stone seat on The Green (gets strimmed). **Kingston:** NW side of path44 – 75 and 325m from N end; SE side 300m from N end. **Corfe:** 100m N of railway viaduct on W side of B3351. **Rempstone:** plentiful both sides of Breaches Lane from 300-500m E of Forest Lane (most gets mown). **Durlston:** several near entrance to The Lookout café. **Studland:** plentiful in at least four places – on N side of Heath Green Road between Agglestone Road and bridleway23; along W half of N side of Rectory Lane; on N side of School Lane opposite Old School House; by path leading N out of churchyard. **Branksome Chine:** several N of centre of Beach Road car park.

Compare with subspecies below.

Leer's Sedge
Carex divulsa subsp. *leersii*
Native. Occasional. Verges, banks; usually on calcareous, but sometimes on neutral soil. May to July.
Creech: plentiful on W side of Grange Road for 300m N of bridleway2. **Hartland Moor:** N side of Arne Road 20m W of Soldiers Road; NE side of Slepe Road 40m SE of Arne Triangle along 10m. **Corfe:** very plentiful outside castle on long SW side of castle mound; plentiful inside castle just NW of gateway into West Bailey; on steep slope below W side of keep; few patches outside castle high on SE side of mound; along much of N side of Townsend Road.

Compare with subspecies above.
Colours of glume are similar in both: silvery turning pale brown, with midrib green turning brown but always distinct. Notches at top of fruitcases vary. Both subspecies can, but do not always, have stalked lowest and next-to-lowest spikelets.
However, Leer's Sedge is more upright, with lighter foliage except when shaded, with stem longer than leaves, flowers spread not more than 8 cm down stem (up to 18cm in Grey Sedge), with lower two spikelets not more than 3.5cm apart; usually with mature female glumes and seedcases 25% larger than Grey Sedge.

Intermediates between the subspecies may be found, presumably because of interbreeding (M. Foley, pers. com.).

Sand Sedge *Carex arenaria*
Native. Abundant. Dunes, sandy grassland, sandy cliffs. June to July.

Brown Sedge *Carex disticha*
Native. Occasional. Wet grassland and verges, marshes. June to July.
Hartland Moor: S side of Arne Road both 250 and 500m W of Arne Triangle along 10m in each site; at both ends of NW side of Triangle. **The Moors:** see p.27. **Luscombe Valley:** 50m N of SE Reserve entrance; 60m SW of metal bridge in centre of Reserve; much N of W end of metal bridge; on E side 100m N of pond.

Remote Sedge *Carex remota*
Native. Frequent. Shady places by streams and wet places in woods. June.
East Creech: near path near N edge of woods N of Stonehill Down. **Stoborough Heath:** NE side of path5 300m NW of small square field through which path passes; plentiful in valley 250m W of Halfway Inn. **Hartland Moor:** plentiful in narrow wet wooded valley on E side of Langton Wallis Heath; N and E sides of White House Wood. **Langton:**

plentiful near stream in N of West Wood; here and there in rides of wood. **Brownsea:** N of Middle Street 100m NW of Reserve entrance.

Oval Sedge *Carex leporina* (*C. ovalis*)
Native. Occasional. Rough non-calcareous damp grassland. May to June.
Creech: on bridleway35 150m from Grange Road. **Stoborough Heath:** several within 80m to W of Dismantled Tramway in Sandlings field 20m S of north edge. **Corfe:** here and there in wide area near Middle Common Pond. **Hartland Moor:** E of copse 400m N of Scotland Barn. **Corfe Charity's Meadows:** on path80 35m NE of gateway between Great Close and Cowleaze. **Godlingston Heath:** thinly scattered in damper areas of grassland either side of bridleway33.
Studland: 130m NW of Wadmore Farm entrance near gate on SW side of bridleway23. **Brownsea:** near pond E of The Villa. **Luscombe Valley:** just W of metal bridge in centre of Reserve; E side of Reserve 100m N of same bridge.

Star Sedge *Carex echinata*
Native. Frequent. Boggy ground on heaths, marshes. May to June.

Dioecious Sedge *Carex dioica*
Native. Occasional. Bogs with open peat or water close by – go with a companion and take great care. May. *Dorset Scarce.*
Hartland Moor: 20m SE of prominent red diamond-shaped EWS sign in NW (not W) of Moor; 30m NE of same sign (with Bog Sedge); patches 400m E of Soldiers Road 60m S of electricity lines (marked on maps) in area 50m W-E 30m N-S (with Bog Sedge, approach from dry heath to

N); in NE of Moor S of stream 170 and 210m SW of Slepe Road; near SW corner of heath SW of Scotland 60m E of Slepe Road 40m N of fence.
Kingswood: scattered in Kingswood Bog (marked as open access but wrongly marked as woodland on O.S. map) in area 50m W-E and 20m N-S 180m S of final 'h' in words 'Kingswood Heath' on O.S. map.
Godlingston Heath: W side of bog in Western Valley 300m NW of junction of bridleway27 and path32 extending 250m N from that point; SE side of bog further N at map reference SZ01428367 for 20m N-wards and after 50m gap for 30m more NNE-wards; small patches 150m E of Agglestone; 250m ENE of it and 300m NE of it.

Hairy Sedge *Carex hirta*
Native. Frequent. Verges and tracks, damp grassland, flushes. May to June.
Steeple: 150m S of Steeple Leaze Farm by bridleway11 (just S of wood). **Wareham:** N side of Priory Meadow just E of Rotary Seat.
Hartland Moor: S side of path80 just E of gate from Slepe Road. **Corfe:** scattered in N area of Middle Common. **Worth:** towards S end of triangular NE part of Worth Mead.
Wares (west and east): in several flushes and other damp areas.
Durlston: plentiful among grass near vehicle exit from W side car park.
Studland: on Woodland Nature Trail in open area in NW part of loop.
Brownsea: plentiful by track leading W from Landing Pier. **Luscombe Valley:** SE of metal bridge in centre of Reserve. **Sandbanks:** on E side of lawn N of entrance to main car park.
   Hairs on foliage can be hard to find on some non-flowering plants, especially in winter.

Lesser Pond Sedge *Carex acutiformis*
Native. Occasional. By streams and
ponds, marshes, ditches, damp verges
and woods. May to July.
Stoborough: by Cobbs Lake watercourse NW end of path13. **Wareham:**
along W side of B3075 S of South
Bridge. **Ridge:** S side of Barnhill Road
20m W of N end of Sunnyside (road).
Corfe: by stream in NW of West
Common 350m S of Copper Bridge
(difficult to reach). **Hartland Moor:**
in SE corner of White House Wood.
Corfe Charity's Meadows: by bridle-
way4 on N edge of field W of
Sharford Bridge (with Greater Pond
Sedge – see drawing); S end of same
meadow. **Godlingston:** along 30m of
E side of path2 175m S of Washpond
Lane; along 10m of same path 350m S
of Lane. **Luscombe Valley:** by pond.

Greater Pond Sedge *Carex riparia*
Native. Occasional. Freshwater edges,
marshes, damp verges. April to May.
Stoborough: along NE side of 100m
of W end of path13. **Wareham** to
Ridge: plentiful both sides of Purbeck
Way along riverside. **Corfe Charity's
Meadows:** by bridleway4 on N edge
of field W of Sharford Bridge (with
Lesser Pond Sedge). **Studland:**
Westwood Pond. **Swanage:** by start of
boardwalk on N side of Playing Field
W of cemetery 125m W of car and
coach park; S of garden of white

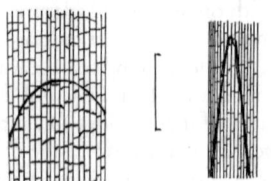

*Sections of leaves of Pond Sedges showing ligule
and vein pattern: Greater (left) and Lesser*

Downland flats on The Downs. **Shell
Bay:** 70m S of E end of boardwalk.
Brownsea: pond E of The Villa.

Cyperus Sedge *Carex pseudocyperus*
Native. Rare. Marshes, edges of ditches. May to June.
Stoborough Heath: on SW side of
depression 250m from A351 20m W
of path23 (but gets grazed). **The
Moors:** see p.27.

Bottle Sedge *Carex rostrata*
Native. Occasional. Marshes, bogs.
June to July.
Hartland Moor: patch 20m E of O.S.
map height figure '7' in NW of Moor;
other patches 70m WNW and 200m
ESE of that (approach from N). **The
Moors:** see p.27. **Corfe:** quite plenti-
ful here and there in marsh in middle
of NW side of West Common.

Pendulous Sedge, Drooping Sedge
Carex pendula
Native, sometimes escaped. Frequent.
Damp woods, verges. May to June.
Kimmeridge: plenty by path15
through withybed. **Stoborough
Heath:** NE side of path5 100m NW
of small square field through which
path passes. **Kingston:** SW side of
path48 – 150-300m from SE end.
Corfe: S side of path32 100m E of
A351; in Byle Copse. **Langton:** very
plentiful in Langton West Wood.
Harman's Cross: here and there by
path44 N and S of railway. **Swanage:** S
side of path through copse W of
D'Urberville Drive. **Studland:** by
stream by Middle Beach. **Branksome
Chine:** 30m SE of Pinecliff Road
opposite SE end of Beach Road.

Wood Sedge *Carex sylvatica*
Native. Abundant. Woods, verges.
May to July.

Thin-spiked Wood Sedge
Carex strigosa
Native. Rare. Damp parts of old woods where water has come from calcareous strata. May to June.
Langton: spread along 250m of stream valley in N of West Wood; several sites near W edge of Talbot's Wood S of Wilkswood Farm; colonies towards N edge of Talbot's Wood 75, 165 and 275m W of path5.

Glaucous Sedge *Carex flacca*
Native. Abundant. Usually downs, limestone based roadsides and tracks, but sometimes in wet pasture, woodland paths. April to June.
   Grey-green leaves distinctly greyer on undersides; see next species.

Carnation Sedge *Carex panicea*
Native. Frequent. Wet areas on heaths and commons. May to June.
   Similarly greyish on both sides of leaves, unlike previous species. Midleaf groove sometimes extends to the end of the leaf, and points of leaves are similar, so neither of these factors will always separate this species from the previous one. They grow together on Dismantled Tramway **Stoborough Heath** 250m N of A351 – a good opportunity to compare them.

Green-ribbed Sedge *Carex binervis*
Native. Occasional. Heaths, often near tracks. June.
Creech: on bridleway1 7m SE of Bridewell Plantation. **Stoborough Heath:** by track both 150m SE of New Road and along 10m at 400m SE of New Road. **Hartland Moor:** 90m E of S cattle grid on Soldiers Road. **The Moors:** towards S end of track across W end of rectangular open access area W of Bank Gate Cottages. **Wytch:** in middle of

path80 310m W of Thrasher's Lane.
Godlingston Heath: close to bridleway marker stone by bridleway27 150m W of junction with bridleways26. **Studland Heath:** 50 and 70m E of Ferry Road on track opposite track to Brand's Bay Hide; along 5-15m of bridleway37 S of previous track. **Brownsea:** 40m NE of SW corner of low-fenced area S of Baden-Powell Outdoor Centre.
   Look for dark red-brown leaf sheaths at the base of the plant.

Distant Sedge *Carex distans*
Native. Occasional. Damp places near the sea. May to June.
Tyneham: by path just N of central anti-invasion blocks at Pondfield beach. **Wares (west):** floor of W and E parts of main Hedbury Quarry (close to foot of SE descent track at latter site); floor of Dancing Ledge close to foot of descent track; also 15m ENE of that; **(east)** NW of meeting of arms of Y-shaped flush in centre of Verney Ware; on edges of five of the flushes on sloping cliff S of Verney Ware. **Godlingston Heath:** SW shore of Brand's Creek NE of pentagonal fenced area in two places 20m apart. **Studland Heath:** SE side of Ferry Road 10m SW of point opposite track to Redhorn Quay; NW side of road 200m SW of track to Jerry's Point.
   Fruits are at 30-40° to the axis of the female flower-spikes.

Dotted Sedge *Carex punctata*
Native. Occasional. Damp grassland, damp road and track sides, usually near the sea. June to July.
Nationally Scarce.
Rempstone: SE side of bridleway34 (Oil Road) 150m SW of where bridleway31 crosses it. **Godlingston**

Heath: 225m NE of Agglestone by path24 (unusually far from sea).
Studland Heath: by bridleway36 150m from Ferry Road; scattered along 125m of bridleway37 S-wards from point 40m S of track opposite track to Brand's Bay Hide; by track to Redhorn Quay 20 and 60m from Ferry Road; here and there on SE side of Ferry Road both from 40m SW of opposite track to Brand's Bay Hide to 400m NE of that track and scattered along 125m SW-wards from track to nudists' area; also NW side of Ferry Road 200 and 350m SW of track to Jerry's Point; by bridleway37 – 75-200m SW of track to Jerry's Point; by track to Jerry's Point 40 and 160m from Ferry Road; by some other tracks on heath both W and E of Ferry Road. **Luscombe Valley:** plentiful on E side of Reserve from 60m N of pond; plentiful on W side N and S of metal bridge in centre of Reserve.

Fruits are at 80-90° to the axis of the female flower-spikes; dots on fruits are not easy to see. See Plate 28.

Long-bracted Sedge *Carex extensa* Native. Occasional. Above saltmarshes. June to July.
Wares (east): in three of the flushes on sloping cliff S of Verney Ware.
Godlingston Heath: SW shore of Brand's Creek NE of pentagonal fenced area. **Studland Heath:** 275m S of Brand's Bay Hide; SW shore of Bramble Bush Bay particularly on shingle bank 225m NW of Ferry Road; on shore 50m WSW of that.

Tawny Sedge *Carex hostiana* Native. Occasional. Wet pastures, marshes. June.
Corfe: three sites on West Common – here and there in marsh in middle of NW side; on S side on S-facing

slopes E of UCR; in SE corner plentiful 60-200m NNW of gate; also four sites on Middle Common - here and there in South-west Valley; 130m SW and 50m SE of pond; 90m NW of NE corner 10m from A351; scattered in area 60 x 20m towards S corner of Little East Common. **Bushey:** in SW of Brenscombe Heath 100m N of slight bend in Bushey Lane; on S edge of Heath 150m from SE corner.

Compare with hybrid below.

Tawny x Yellow Sedge – hybrid *Carex x fulva* (*C. hostiana* x *viridula*) Native. Rare. With parents; numbers vary with the amount of grazing. June.
Corfe: 150m WSW of W end of First Valley on West Common; in SE of West Common scattered 90-200m NNW of gate; in South-west Valley of Middle Common 250m SW of Purbeck Way.

Looks like a smaller version of Tawny Sedge. Usually has just one spike of only male flowers at top of stem and two spikes with only female flowers below, whereas Tawny Sedge usually has one spike of only male flowers above two or three spikes which are mostly female but have some male flowers at the top. Stamens do not emerge. Leaf-like bracts of hybrid's female spikes are longer; one sometimes overtops male spike, unlike Tawny Sedge. Female spikes of the hybrid are paler because female glumes are paler.

Small-fruited Yellow Sedge *Carex viridula* subsp. *viridula* (*C. serotina*) Native. Occasional. Wet tracks on heaths. June to July.
Dorset Rare.
Studland Heath: track to Redhorn Quay 25m NW of Ferry Road; on 15m of track to Jerry's Point begin-

ning 30m NW of Ferry Road; here and there on bridleway37 SW from previous site (where there is much more of next subspecies affording good opportunity to compare them); on small W to E path through Heather running E from 'Heather Walk' SW of SW corner of nudists' area.

Male spike is usually stalkless; female spikes usually bunched together; fruits are 1.75-3.5mm long.

Common Yellow Sedge *Carex viridula* subsp. *oedocarpa* (*C. demissa*)
Native. Frequent. Wet places on grassland, commons, heaths – especially on paths. June.

Male spike is usually stalked; lowest female spike, at the base of the stem, is usually well apart from the rest; fruits are 3-4mm long.

Long-stalked Yellow Sedge
Carex viridula subsp. *brachyrrhyncha* (*C. lepidocarpa*)
Native. Rare. Marshes, ditch banks. May to June.
Dorset Scarce.
The Moors: see p.27 – numbers greatly vary with the amount of grazing.

Male spike often long-stalked at an angle to the main stem; fruits are 3.5-5mm long; the beak of the fruit is bent.

Spring Sedge *Carex caryophyllea*
Native. Occasional. Short but not acid grassland. April to May.
Church Knowle: scattered along 175m of lower part of Down NE of Cocknowle. **Hartland Moor:** few on SE side of old tramway 15 and 50m SW of Slepe Road. **Corfe:** many on West Common 15m E of path53 100m S of N cattle grid (for exam-

ple); on prominent anthill 1.5m E of Middle Common Pond (with Glaucous Sedge). **Woolgarston:** low at W side and rather more on E sides of old quarry N of bridleway20 just W of junction with bridleway21; on N side of bridleway20 – 10-20m NW of W end of Ailwood Down. **Wares (east):** in White Ware 3-10m N of Coast Path near bottom of W-facing slope. **Knitson:** plentiful on slopes below bridleway9 from 100-250m from SE end; N of bridleway8 – 35-40m W of bridleway12. **Durlston:** 100m SE of NW corner of Field 15; 30-40m NW of NW corner of lighthouse enclosure 2-8m SW of path48; many 6-11m N of upper Mile Post. **Townsend Reserve:** 45m slightly S of W from SE Bastion. **Ballard Down:** sites scattered near Purbeck Way for 700m E of gate to downland on bridleway14, especially below Way 575m from gate; many plants further E in area 30 x 30m 100m ESE of gates on top of Down by eastern tumuli.

It is difficult to see amongst grass; easiest in second half of April when anthers are noticeable. Usually two female spikes close under a male spike. Sometimes very few. Corfe, Knitson, Durlston and Ballard Down sites above are the easiest places to find it. Usually near Glaucous Sedge (p.241), which begins flowering at the same time.

Pill Sedge *Carex pilulifera*
Native. Occasional. Sandy areas on dry heaths. May to June.
Stoborough Heath: on track running NW from near S end of Dismantled Tramway 60 and 75-95m NW of second gate on tramway. **Hartland Moor:** 65m SW of S cattle grid on Soldiers Road on track E of and parallel to road; plenty on heath just E of

Slepe Road 20-80m S of S cattle grid.
Norden: on Norden Heath on track along E side of Blue Pool fence halfway between paths10 and 12.
Bushey: scattered in NW of Brenscombe Heath. **Godlingston Heath:** S side of bridleway27 20m W of junction with bridleway26.
Studland Heath: on bridleway37 – 115-135m S of track E of Ferry Road opposite track to Brand's Bay Hide; scattered in some open areas N and SW of Western Arm of Little Sea especially on tracks; plentiful in grassland E and SE of grey gate on E side of Ferry Road S of Spur Bog. **Brownsea:** 40m NE of SW corner of main low-fenced area S of Baden-Powell Out-door Centre. **Branksome Chine:** W side of S end of The Avenue just N of mown area (on tiny piece of relict grassland).

Has long flowering stems in relation to the leaves; stems curve outwards and downwards when in fruit, ending up almost flat on the ground.

Bog Sedge *Carex limosa*
Native. Occasional. In bog vegetation and on edges of wettest parts of bogs (take great care). May to June.
Dorset Scarce.
Hartland Moor: E end of hat-shaped pond in SW of West Bog; 30m NE of prominent red diamond-shaped EWS sign in NW (not W) of Moor (with Dioecious Sedge); 140m ESE of same sign; patches 400m E of Soldiers Road 60m S of electricity lines (marked on maps) in area 80m W-E 50m N-S (some patches with Dioecious Sedge, approach from N); scattered 60m SE of previous site for further 200m SE-wards in band 80m N-S. **Godlingston Heath:** leaves only in small area of soft bog in Western Valley (discovered by Bryan Edwards). See Plate 28.

Common Sedge *Carex nigra*
Native. Occasional. Wet grassland, verges and heath. May to July.
Creech: in SE of S RSPB field W of Grange Road (enter from N field) at E end of rushy area. **Hartland Moor:** along 5m of middle of NW side of Triangle. **Arne:** along 20m of NW side of Arne Road 600m NE of Bank Gate Cottages. **Corfe:** scattered in wide area around Middle Common Pond, especially near S corner. **Corfe Charity's Meadows:** 20-40m NE of gateway between Great Close and Cowleaze by path80; 20-30m S of gateway on N side of Bankes Mead.
Kingswood: large patch in Kingswood Bog (marked as open access but wrongly marked as wood-land on O.S. map) 165m S of letter 'a' in name 'Kingswood Heath' on O.S. map. **Brownsea:** towards N part of Orchid Meadow. **Luscombe Valley:** W side 15m N of boardwalk W of metal bridge in centre of Reserve; E side 100m N of pond.

Some leaves and bracts have distinctive grey ends.

Not the most common sedge; often few at its known sites.

Tufted Sedge *Carex elata* cv. Aurea
Introduction. Rare. Planted. May to June.
Studland: village pond.

Flea Sedge *Carex pulicaris*
Native. Occasional. Wet places that are not too acid. May to June.
Stoborough Heath: 40m E of Blue Pool Exit Road between Black Bog-rushes and Grey Willows at map reference SY93538432; on Dismantled Tramway 250m N of A351. **Hartland Moor:** widely and thinly scattered in Upper and Middle Fens; S side of Arne Road 15m W of Arne Triangle;

near SW corner of heath SW of Scotland 60m E of Slepe Road 40m N of fence. **Corfe:** here and there in marshes in West, Middle and Little East Commons – often on tussocks. **Bushey:** here and there along S edge of Brenscombe Heath. **Godlingston Heath:** S side of bridleway27 275m W of junction with bridleway26. **Studland Heath:** Spur Bog 50m E of entrance.

When flower spike is young all parts point up towards the end of the stem; female flowers only drop into position as shown in identification books when ready to flower.

GRASS FAMILY

Hubbard's *Grasses* has been the very useful standard book for over 50 years, but the forthcoming BSBI handbook will be right up-to-date.

Flowering periods are given, apart from bamboos; most species are just as easy to identify when in fruit, which they retain for a month or more after flowering.

Bamboos: always planted or discarded garden stock, rarely flowering; Stace (1997) describes many and there is a key. There is a longer key by Ryves, Clement and Foster (1996).

Chinese Fountain-bamboo
Fargesia murielae
Introduction. Rare. Planted.
Studland: 100m W of shore in wood 120m S of Knoll Beach car park (three other species of Bamboo nearby).

Three or more branches from each node; small leaves.

A Bamboo *Pleioblastus* species
Introduction. Rare. Planted.
Rempstone: unidentified plant of

this genus by E corner of Green Pond (O. S. map wrongly marks island in blue as if it is water).

More than one branch per node.

Broad-leaved Bamboo
Sasa palmata
Introduction. Rare. Planted.
Studland: 80m W of shore in wood 100m S of Knoll Beach car park.

One branch per node; leaves are large, up to 40cm long and up to 9cm wide.

Arrow Bamboo *Pseudosasa japonica*
Introduction. Occasional. Planted.
Stoborough Heath: 15m S of path23 375m from A351 by wooden fence. **Hartland Moor:** W end of White House Wood. **Church Knowle:** 20m W of path18 200m S of road. **Swanage Railway:** on S side E of Herston Halt. **Durlston:** E of Coast Path E of main glade in woods in NE of Country Park. **Studland:** S side of B3351 100m E of entrance to Woodhouse; 80m W of shore in wood 200m S of Knoll Beach car park; NW side of Watery Lane 75m NE of junction with Manor Road. **Brownsea:** in NE of Venetia Park. **Lilliput:** towards N end of short path between Lilliput Road and Greenwood Avenue (see Street Map for road name and O.S. map for path).

One branch per node from upper stem only; leaves up to 30cm long, up to 3.5cm wide.

Zigzag Bamboo
Phyllostachys flexuosa
Introduction. Rare. Planted.
Studland: 100m W of shore in wood 120m S of Knoll Beach car park.

Stem is flat on one side, somewhat zigzag; lowest nodes are symmetrical.

Mat Grass *Nardus stricta*
Native. Occasional. Heaths, commons. Late May to July.
Dorset Scarce.
Creech: W side of Grange Heath Reserve in depression 300m S of NW tumulus scattered from 15-80m E of army fence. **Stoborough Heath:** 12m N of Maritime Pine in area 3 x 1m on NE side of track 8m SW of fence around pond which is by path6.
Corfe: Middle Common both 50m SE of N gate and 100m S of N gate.
Godlingston Heath: S side of bridleway27 20m W of junction with bridleway26. **Brownsea:** plentiful 40m NE of SW corner of main low-fenced area S of Baden-Powell Outdoor Centre.

Easier to pick out in late summer when it is straw-coloured than during flowering when it is green and purple.

Wood Millet *Milium effusum*
Native. Occasional. Old woods. May to June.
Creech: 5m from N edge of Caldecot's Wood 25m W of path32.
Bushey: N side of path13 50m W of private track into Bushey Wood; on S side of bridleway14 150m SW of junction with bridleway15. **Langton:** much S and NE of largest pond in N of Langton West Wood; towards S side of Talbot's Wood 200m W of Crack Lane; on N edge of same wood 15m W of Lane. **Kingswood:** by bridleway16 both 75m S of B3351; near lower gate at top (S) of wood; in wood 150 and 250m ESE of same gate. **Studland:** several places in Studland Wood 15-75m S of Coast Path.

Meadow Fescue *Festuca pratensis*
Native. Occasional. Verges, neutral grassland. June.

Steeple: plentiful halfway up Steeple Down (west) along slope – best site.
East Creech: 50m NE of N end of path32 along 10m of NW side of road. **Hartland Moor:** N side of Arne Road 325m E of Soldiers Road; both sides of Slepe Road just S of S cattle grid. **Bushey:** here and there along N side of Bushey Lane S of Brenscombe Heath. **Wares (west):** on NW side of path25 225m NE of Dancing Ledge Quarry stile. **Durlston:** 50m SW of pond in Field 3 N of track; towards SW corner of Field 14; towards NE corner of South Field; E side of path on W edge of Skipworth Meadow 30m N of SW corner. **Studland Heath:** SE side of Ferry Road 40 and 100m SW of point opposite track to Redhorn Quay.

Short plants of Tall Fescue (see below) and tall plants of Red Fescue (p.247) can be mistaken for this species. Meadow Fescue has small hairless auricles; the shorter of the lowest pair of panicle branches has only 1 or 2 (or rarely 3) spikelets; it grows in small tufts.

Tall Fescue *Festuca arundinacea*
Native. Frequent. Verges, neutral grassland. June to August.

This has prominent auricles, with small hairs on the edges (lens) until old. The shorter of the lowest pair of panicle branches has at least 3 or usually 4 or more spikelets; it usually grows in large tufts. (Compare with Meadow Fescue.)

Giant Fescue *Festuca gigantea*
Native. Occasional. Woods, shaded verges. June to July.
Tyneham: here and there around ruined cottages in centre of village.
Creech: sides of road through Great Wood. **East Creech:** by path32 15-

20m S of N edge of wood. **Kingston:** S side of road 125m W of W car park; by path44 140m NE of S end of Quarry Wood. **Harman's Cross:** E side of Haycraft's Lane just S of path22. **Rempstone:** S side of Bushey Lane 250m W of Forest Lane. **Langton:** here and there along E-W ride in S of West Wood. **Godlingston:** N side of Burnham's Lane 50m W of junction with Washpond Lane. **Durlston:** 10m N of Coast Path at E end of small glade 50m E of entrance to wood at NE of Country Park. **Swanage:** S side of path through copse W of D'Urberville Drive 40-60m from E end.

Sometimes confused with Hairy Brome (p.259), with which it may grow. This species has very prominent auricles, hairless leaves and sheaths.

Rush-leaved Fescue
Festuca arenaria
Native. Abundant. Fore-dunes: rarely more than 20m back from the front of vegetation viewed from sea. May to July.
Nationally Scarce.
Studland Heath: here and there on fore-dunes with Marram all the way from Knoll Beach Café to Ferry. **Sandbanks:** on shore just N of opposite W end of Chaddesley Glen; dunes at top of beach both SW and NE of main car park.

Red Fescue *Festuca rubra*
Native. Abundant. Verges, grassland. May to July.

No auricles (compare with Meadow Fescue p.246). More detailed identification books describe subspecies, one of which is often blue-grey.

Sheep's Fescue *Festuca ovina* agg. (including *F. brevipila*)
Native. Abundant. Short calcareous grassland, anthills, verges, heaths. May to July.

Separating species reliably in this aggregate requires experience.

Fine-leaved Sheep's Fescue
Festuca filiformis
Native. Occasional. Heaths. May to June.
Corfe: on Purple Moor-grass tussocks here and there in South-west Valley of Middle Common; few in next valley to E. **Bushey:** in SW of Brenscombe Heath including 100m N of slight bend in Bushey Lane. **Studland Heath:** E side of Ferry Road 100m N of E end of bridleway36 opposite; on War Hill.

In *The Flora of Dorset* (Bowen, 2000) it is said to be present on dry areas of heath in many more areas, but this must be in low numbers.

Perennial Rye-grass *Lolium perenne*
Native. Abundant. Grassland. May to October.

Lemmas awnless.

Hybrid Rye-grass
Lolium x *boucheanum*
Introduction. Occasional. Grassland, verges. May to October.
Stoborough: by path13 W of bypass halfway across field. **Church Knowle:** by path29 in field N of Playing Field (with next species). **Corfe:** by path79 just N of square wood. **Knitson:** N side of path13 200m W of Burnham's Lane. **Studland:** visible from gateway S of Coast Path 325m E of NE corner of The Warren Wood (short range binoculars help).

Often sown. Lemmas with short unequal awns. Sometimes recorded as the next species.

Italian Rye-grass
Lolium multiflorum
Introduction. Rare. Casual remnant of sowing or seed spillage. May to October.
Church Knowle: by path29 in field N of Playing Field (with hybrid above).

Not used much by farmers now. Lemmas with long equal awns.

Dune Fescue *Vulpia fasciculata*
Native. Occasional. Stable dunes, sandy verges, grassland and car parks. June.
Nationally Scarce.
Studland Heath: beginning 40m NE of main N car park at Knoll Beach spread plentifully N-wards for 300m (see also Bearded Fescue below); E side of track on NE side of Second Ridge 350m NE of track to nudists' area; by second set of concrete ruins NW of that Second Ridge track (ruins which are 400m from track to nudists' area). **Shell Bay:** SE side of Ferry Road both from roundabout for 100m SW-wards and 100 and 150m N of ferry offices (not booths); also SW corner of car park.

Squirreltail Fescue
Vulpia bromoides
Native. Frequent. Grassland, especially if sandy; verges. May to July.
Kingston: Swyre Head tumulus.
Hartland Moor: on South Middlebere. **Ower:** by bridleway8 at Game Copse. **Godlingston Heath:** drier parts of grass field S of bridleway36. **Ballard Down:** S of bridleway6 125m W of junction with bridleways12 and 14 for example.
Studland Heath: centre of N end of Knoll Beach S car park; scattered by heath tracks. **Shell Bay:** SE side of

Ferry Road 175 and 275m SW of roundabout. **Brownsea:** grassland SE of church. **Sandbanks:** SE side of Banks Road 75m NE of roundabout. **Canford Cliffs:** SE side of Cliff Drive just NE of steps down cliff.

May have only few spikelets. As with other Vulpias, look carefully at the ratio of the lengths of the glumes with a lens; if plant has turned yellow, grasp the awns and pull the lemmas off; the glumes should remain and will be easier to see.

Ratstail Fescue *Vulpia myuros*
Early Introduction. Occasional. Arable fields, other disturbed ground, verges, gardens. May to July.
Corfe: much on N bank of private Oil Road where crossed by path79 just E of Park and Ride. **Rempstone:** on E side of bridleway31 70m S of crossing of bridleways31 and 34 (Oil Road); lay-by on NW side of bridleway34 (Oil Road) 200m NE of same crossing. **Sandbanks:** SE side of Banks Road 80m NE of roundabout. **Canford Cliffs:** NE side of Chaddesley Glen by church car park.

Bearded Fescue
Vulpia ciliata subsp. *ambigua*
Native. Occasional. Stable sand including verges. May to June.
Nationally Scarce.
Studland Heath: W side of Ferry Road 240m N of Sewage Works; plentiful on outlier 50m NW of War Hill; N of Knoll Beach barbeque area over distance of 100m (growing with Dune Fescue); E of Heather Walk 300m N of car park; by two sets of concrete ruins NW of track on SE side of Second Ridge 300 and 400m from track to nudists' area.
Shell Bay: just E of roundabout.

Crested Dogstail
Cynosurus cristatus
Native. Abundant. Permanent unfertilised grassland, verges. June to August.

Common Saltmarsh Grass
Puccinellia maritima
Native. Occasional. Near top of salt-marshes. June to early July.
Studland Heath: 40m W of inner corner of Plateau Bay; thinly scattered on SW shore of Bramble Bush Bay (sites vary). **Sandbanks:** plentiful around head of inlet (not shown on maps) S of W end of Chaddesley Glen.

Perhaps there are only a few flowering stems at Studland because it is eaten by deer.

Quaking Grass *Briza media*
Native. Frequent. Downland; calcareous based road and track sides. June to July.

Top of floret is slightly sloping down from the stalk; side shoots at the stem base (perennial species).

Lesser Quaking Grass *Briza minor*
Early Introduction. Rare. Arable fields, other disturbed ground. July.
Nationally Scarce.
Harman's Cross: may be visible from road N of New Barn in large field to E especially at gateway; from path6 W of gateway to same field W of path; here and there by same path from 175-375m NW of stile E of New Barn. **Studland:** one plant seen just S of gateway S of Coast Path 325m E of NE corner of The Warren Wood (short range binoculars help).

Top of floret is at a right angle to its stalk when it is mature; no side shoots at the stem base (annual species).

Greater Quaking Grass *Briza maxima*
Introduction. Occasional. Verges (increasing). June to July.
Wareham: N side of Priory Meadow just W of Rotary Seat. **Swanage:** S side of E end of Russell Avenue for 40m; on cliff between second and third groynes N of end of promenade (binoculars help). **Shell Bay:** NW side of Ferry Road 50m and more SW of roundabout. **Sandbanks:** behind wire-fenced dunes at top of beach 175m SW of main car park. **Canford Cliffs:** E side of path in Flaghead Chine 10m from S end; around stepped path from Cliff Drive to beach; by promenade 250-400m NE of Canford Cliffs Chine; here and there further NE. **Branksome Chine:** along cliff-top for 120m NE-wards from S of W end of Pinecliff Road.

Early Meadow-grass *Poa infirma*
Native. Rare. Open sandy turf. Late February to April.
Nationally Scarce.
Sandbanks: raised lawn W of café on SE side of main car park (easier to find in warmer snunny weather when new anthers show – they are the crucial distinguishing feature).

Anthers are only 1-1.5 times as long as wide; branches of fruiting flower-head usually point forwards. See Plate 28.

Annual Meadow-grass *Poa annua*
Native. Abundant. Bare ground. All year.
Anthers are 2 to 3 times as long as wide; fruiting branches usually at right angles to stem or pointing backwards.

Rough Meadow-grass *Poa trivialis*
Native. Abundant. Grassland, woods – where it can be mistaken for Wood Meadow-grass. All year.

Smooth Meadow-grass,
(including **Spreading Meadow-grass,
Narrow-leaved Meadow-grass**)
*Poa pratensis, P. humilis
(P. subcaerulea), P. angustifolia*
'This complex group ... perhaps best
recorded as *Poa pratensis* agg. The
three ... seem to be treated differently
by different botanists using different
characters' *Plant Crib 1998* (Rich &
Jermy, 1998).
Native. Frequent. Dry grassland,
walls. May to July.

Stem somewhat flattened, but not
as much as Flattened Meadow-grass,
which has not been seen lately.

Bulbous Meadow-grass *Poa bulbosa*
Native. Rare. Stable sand. April to
May.
Nationally Scarce.
Studland Heath: on level ground
above beach in Bramble Bush Bay
150m NE of row of concrete blocks
on shore. **Shell Bay:** Ferry Road NW
side scattered from toll roundabout
for 400m SW-wards; few in car park.

Easiest to find in the second half of
April when new flowering stems
appear, but deer graze most off.

Cocksfoot *Dactylis glomerata*
Native. Abundant. Grassland. March
to August.

Whorl-grass *Catabrosa aquatica*
Native. Occasional. Edges of slowly
moving water, ponds. May to July.
Corfe: by path58 plank bridge 100m
N of junction with path62; in 15m of
stream on S edge of West Common
120m W of B3069; at SE corner of
West Common 10m W of B3069; S
edge of Middle Common just W of
Purbeck Way footbridge; much flowering in Middle Common Pond when
not grazed – mostly in clumps.

Fern Grass *Catapodium rigidum*
Native. Frequent. Disturbed or thin
bare soil, verges, anthills, walls. May to
June.
Steeple: NE side of road 150m NW
of S end of bridleway3. **Creech
Heath:** halfway between Grange Road
and W end of Icen Barrow Pond.
Rempstone: along NW side of bridle-
way8 from 100-150m NE of end of
bridleway9. **Wares (west and east):**
some anthills. **Langton:** W side of
Durnford Drove. **Durlston:** by path54
40m S of NE corner of Ox-eye Daisy
Field. **Townsend Reserve:** E side of
South-east Bastion for example.
Studland Heath: bank W of Knoll
beach shop; also War Hill (with next
species). **Lilliput:** by N end of path
from Alington Close to Shore Road.
Canford Cliffs: plentiful under wall E
of Cliff Drive roundabout (The
Circle).

Sea Fern Grass *Catapodium marinum*
Native. Frequent. Cliff-edges, quarries
and slopes near sea, salted roadsides.
June to July.
Tyneham: in ruined house just above
beach at Worbarrow Bay.
Stoborough: NE side of A351 both
SE of River Frome bridge and NW of
Dismantled Tramway; SE of bridle-
way77 (benefiting from salt treatment
of road). **Wares (west and east):** in
thin grassland on slopes near sea; larger quarry floors. **Knitson:** here and
there on down NNE of Knitson Farm.
Studland Heath: War Hill (with previous species); outlier 50m NW.
Sandbanks: plentiful on NW verge of
Banks Road 200-300m NE of roundabout.

Hard-grass *Parapholis strigosa*
Native. Occasional. Near shores. Mid-
June to early July (difficult to find, but

easier when tiny anthers show in flower).
Arne: on shore 20m E of RSPB noticeboard. **Studland Heath:** 21-27m W of stern of rusting ship wreck on Redhorn Quay within 2m of S shore; 2m N of bow of wreck; easier to see on three low sandy hummocks inside shingle bar 200m SE of Jerry's Point; few near S corner of Bramble Bush Bay 20m NW of bridleway37; unusual site on outlier 50m NW of War Hill. **Sandbanks:** here and there on grass verge W of Banks Road from its start N of roundabout for 500m NE-wards (especially near NW edge of verge).

Anthers are 1.5mm or more long. Plants by the shores have slightly curved stems, and can be confused with the next species, e.g. at Sandbanks as in *The Flora of Dorset* (Bowen, 2000).

Curved Hard-grass
Parapholis incurva
Native. Occasional. Here and there on open-air floors of sea-cliff quarries, and banks near the sea. Mid-June to early July (dry and disintegrating by mid-July).
Nationally Scarce.
Worth: W side of Chapman's Pool on partly bare shelf 1m above rocks at map reference SY9538 7704/5 (inaccessible at high tide). **Wares (west):** Seacombe Quarry; W and E parts of main Hedbury Quarry; W and E parts of Dancing Ledge quarry, (and floors of several other smaller quarries that are less accessible). **Durlston:** 4m S of lowest point of Coast Path at gully; below third step of Coast Path up E side of gully; on bank N of Coast Path just W of closed steps to Tilly Whim quarry; on steps just W of The Globe.

Anthers are 1mm or less long.

Reed Sweet-grass *Glyceria maxima*
Native. Occasional. Watersides where not acid. July to August.
Holme: can be seen to W from old Holme Bridge on S side of river. **Stoborough:** by Cobbs Lake watercourse at NW end of path13. **Wareham:** on SE side of River Frome by E side of bypass bridge; here and there for 750m downstream from that bridge (boat). **Ridge:** by river N of Redcliffe Farm. **Worth:** variegated cultivar in village pond. **Durlston:** Johnston Pond. **Studland:** village pond.

Floating Sweet-grass *Glyceria fluitans*
Native. Frequent. Ponds, streams, flushes, ditches. May to August.
Tyneham: by ponds E of ruined Rectory (with some Hybrid Sweet-grass). **Holme:** by ford in East Holme hamlet. **Creech:** 250 and 300m NW of Grange Road on bridleway1 (hybrid nearby). **Stoborough Heath:** in Tramway Pond (with hybrid). **Corfe Charity's Meadows:** SE end of meadow SW of Sharford Bridge. **Corfe:** NW end of First Valley on West Common. **Wares (west):** pond S of Priest's Way 250m E of path30. **Swanage:** in Swan Brook NW of Northbrook Road cemetery. **Studland:** Westwood Pond (with hybrid). **Studland Heath:** wide ditch E of near N end of track to Woodland Hide. **Luscombe Valley:** 90m NE of W side of metal bridge in centre of Reserve (e.g.).

Hybrid Sweet-grass *Glyceria* x *pedicellata* (*G. fluitans* x *notata*)
Native. Occasional. Ponds, streamsides, wet tracks. May to July.
Tyneham: by ponds E of ruined Rectory (with much Floating Sweet-grass). **Holme:** East Holme Meadows

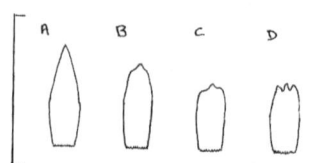

Outlines of lemmas of Sweet-grasses showing contrast in size and especially tips: A - Floating, B - Hybrid, C - Plicate, D - Small.

– see p.23. **Creech:** 200 and 325m NW of Grange Road on bridleway1 (Floating Sweet-grass nearby). **Stoborough Heath:** in Tramway Pond (with Floating Sweet-grass). **Corfe:** by path58 plank bridge 100m N of junction with path62; near S edge of Middle Common by boards across wet ground 150m E of B3069; at Middle Common Pond. **Studland:** Westwood Pond (with Floating Sweet-grass); pond W of path13 at S edge of small field S of Woodhouse (with Small Sweet-grass).

Not easy to distinguish from the parents. Anthers are empty (lens), but so are the parents' anthers as soon as the pollen is shed; be sure that anthers have only just emerged. Check lemma tips, and measurements of anthers, lemmas and spikelets. See drawing.

Plicate Sweet-grass
Glyceria notata (G. plicata)
Native. Occasional. Wet places in fields, by streams, ponds. May to June.
Tyneham: pond near telephone box.
Worth: in NW corner of triangular area in NE of Worth Mead; much by top of flush in S of Worth Field; in NW of Abbott's Combe; on W side of same field 100m S of path11.
Wares (west): top of flush in SW of Nicholas Down; third flush from E in

Hedbury Ware; **(east)** in W arm of Y-shaped flush in centre of Verney Ware. **Bushey:** NW corner of Brenscombe Heath. **Herston (north):** N of path78 in SE corner of field SE of Herston Halt.

Small Sweet-grass *Glyceria declinata*
Native. Occasional. Mud or shallow fresh water. June to September.
Corfe: in First Valley just W of UCR; at Middle Common Pond. **Wytch:** by path5 in S corner of triangular field by NW of Wytch Moor. **Wares (west):** by flush in Long Close protected by low square brick wall 175m NW of NW corner of Seacombe Field. **Studland:** pond W of path at S edge of small field S of Woodhouse (with Hybrid Sweet-grass).

Wood Melick *Melica uniflora*
Native. Occasional. Shady road and track sides. May to June.
Creech: plentiful on SE side of road descending hill through Great Wood; 40-55m S of N edge of woods by path32. **Corfe:** plentiful where shaded in Sandy Hill Lane between Challow Farm and Sandyhills Farm.
Bushey: N side of path13 50m W of private track into Bushey Wood; plentiful by SW half of bridleway14.
King's Wood: by bridleway16 200m SE of National Trust sign. **Langton:** by narrow track in centre of N of West Wood 50m S of large pond; W side of Crack Lane 200m S of A351.

Downy Oat-grass *Helicototrichon pubescens (Avenula pubescens)*
Native. Frequent. Calcareous grassland and verges. June to July.
Tyneham: by Coast Path along top of Gad Cliff from N of Wagon Rock for 500m E-wards (with next species – a good opportunity to compare lower

leaf-sheaths, leaves, spikelet size and grouping, and awns). **Creech:** around summit of Creech Barrow Hill. **Hartland Moor:** here and there on E side of Soldiers Road between track to Isolation Cottages and S cattle grid; both sides of Arne Road W of Arne Triangle; both sides of Slepe Road S of S cattle grid. **Corfe:** here and there outside of the castle around castle mound. **Langton:** SE side of triangular field between B3069 and road to Worth near Acton (view from latter) 100m SW of road junction (with next species). **Bushey:** here and there along N side of Bushey Lane S of Brenscombe Heath. **Swanage:** NE corner of Northbrook Road cemetery. **Ballard Down:** plentiful in S-facing grassland between eastern tumuli and Ballard Head.

Meadow Oat-grass *Helicototrichon pratense* (*Avenula pratensis*)
Native. Frequent. Calcareous grassland and verges. June.
Tyneham: by Coast Path along top of Gad Cliff from N of Wagon Rock for 500m E-wards (with previous species). **Church Knowle:** scattered along 175m of lower part of Down NE of Cocknowle. **Worth:** by Coast Path at St.Aldhelm's Head few metres from Coastwatch Station. **Wares (west):** among Gorse at S corner of Long Close; in Hedbury Ware 75m W of stile to Hedbury Quarry; on SW edge of East Plain 25m NW of SW corner. **Langton:** SE side of triangular field between B3069 and road to Worth near Acton (view from latter road) 100m SW of road junction (with previous species). **Knitson:** on Down either side of bridleway9. **Durlston:** near SE corner of Field 14 50m NW of gateway to South Field. **Ulwell:** by path4 near reservoir.

It can be picked out from other grasses by its leaves with grey-green uppersides and hooded tips, whether or not in flower. Leaves are green underneath, so their colouring is the opposite way round to the more common Glaucous Sedge p.241.

False Oat-grass
Arrhenatherum elatius
Native. Abundant. Grassland, verges, woods. June to August.

Onion Couch
Arrhenatherum elatius var. *bulbosum*
Native. Rare. Grassland, verges, woods. June to August.
Holme: SW corner of open access wood SW of East Holme. **Studland:** Old Nick's Ground 125m S of S end of Studland Wood.
   Would probably be found to be much more common if plants were checked for bulbs – and replanted.

Slender Oat *Avena barbata*
Introduction. Rare. Verges. June to July.
Sandbanks: casual towards E end of N side of Panorama Road both near The Horseshoe (road) with Oat nearby; 75-100m W of junction with Banks Road.
   Lower half of the lemmas densely clothed with long hairs.

Wild Oat *Avena fatua*
Early Introduction. Frequent. Arable fields, other disturbed ground. July to September.

Oat *Avena sativa*
Early Introduction. Occasional. Crop remnant in arable fields, casual in other disturbed ground. July to September.

Yellow Oat-grass *Trisetum flavescens*
Native. Abundant. Calcareous grassland. June to July.

Crested Hair-grass
Koeleria macrantha
Native. Frequent. Short calcareous grassland. June to July.

Tufted Hair-grass
Deschampsia cespitosa
Native. Frequent. Neutral grassland, verges, woods. June to August.

Bog Hair-grass *Deschampsia setacea*
Native. Rare. Marshes. July.
Nationally Scarce.
Hartland Moor: few plants in low area 200m NE of Isolation Cottages between damp heath to W and Black Bog Rush swamp to E 50m N of electricity lines (marked only on Map 5) just S of three isolated Grey Willows.
   Difficult to find; may be undiscovered elsewhere.

Wavy Hair-grass
Deschampsia flexuosa
Native. Rare. Dry acid open ground. June to July.
Shell Bay: W of track leading S 60m from car park; E of same track 20m further S. **Sandbanks:** 250m NE of main car park on NE side of first piece of narrow fenced dune between houses (not beach chalets) and beach.

Yorkshire Fog *Holcus lanatus*
Native. Abundant. Everywhere, except salt marshes. June to September.

Creeping Soft-grass *Holcus mollis*
Native. Occasional. Woods, shady verges. June to July.
Hartland Moor: SE side of Arne Road 50m SW of Bank Gate

Cottages on opposite side (with previous species). **King's Wood:** S of left part of letter 'W' in name 'King's Wood' printed on O.S. map; also S of upside-down '150' contour figure on same map. **Studland Heath:** on Woodland Nature Trail by start of part of trail which leads to Woodland Hide.
   Probably more but deer eat it.

Silver Hair-grass *Aira caryophyllea*
Native. Occasional. Short, dry, sparse grassland and verges. May.
Tyneham: plentiful by Coast Path where it passes through Flowers Barrow. **Holme:** here and there on B3070 verges across West Holme Heath. **Stoborough:** W side Furzebrook Road opposite track on to Hyde Hill. **Hartland Moor:** both sides of Slepe Road approaching Snag Valley from N or S. **Corfe:** on Monkey's Hump on West Common. **Durlston:** plentiful towards end of gully near sea. **Ballard Down:** especially on slightly S-facing top of down W of path 11. **Studland Heath:** War Hill. **Lilliput:** triangle at junction between Alington Road, Minterne Road and Bingham Avenue. **Sandbanks:** upper shore opposite W end of Chaddesley Glen (some is much taller than usual). **Canford Cliffs:** near top of stepped path from Cliff Drive to beach.
   Sometimes with next species, for which it can be mistaken when young flowerheads of Silver Hair-grass have not spread out.

Early Hair-grass *Aira praecox*
Native. Frequent. Heaths. April to May.

Sweet Vernal Grass
Anthoxanthum odoratum
Native. Abundant. Grassland. April to May.

Reed Canary-grass
Phalaris arundinacea
Native. Occasional. Watersides, damp
grassland and verges. June to July.
Holme: S edge of River Frome
between and either side of old and new
bridges. **Stoborough:** by Cobbs Lake
watercourse at NW end of path13.
Wareham: S side of River Frome just
W of South Bridge. **Ridge:** by river N
of Redcliffe Farm. **Corfe:** by E-ward
running part of stream 100m W of
bottom of First Valley on West
Common. **Corfe Charity's Meadows:**
SW edge of meadow SW of Sharford
Bridge 20m W of bridleway3. **Wytch:**
10m E of Sharford Bridge by bridle-
way4. **Brownsea:** E of track in nature
reserve just S of turning to two-level
hide. **Sandbanks:** on shore opposite
W end of Chaddesley Glen.

Canary-grass *Phalaris canariensis*
Introduction. Rare. Casual from bird-
seed. June to July.

Common Bent *Agrostis capillaris*
Native. Abundant. Dry grassland, gardens. July to August.
    No awns; flower spike does not con-
tract when in fruit; it is the only bent
grass with a short ligule.

Black Bent *Agrostis gigantea*
Early Introduction. Rare. Arable fields,
other disturbed ground. June to
August.
    No awns; flower spike does not con-
tract when in fruit; much taller than
other Bents.

Creeping Bent *Agrostis stolonifera*
Native. Abundant. Lawns, other grassland – dry or wet, arable fields, shores,
ponds. July to August.
    No awns; flower spike contracts
when in fruit.

Bristle Bent *Agrostis curtisii*
Native. Abundant. Dry heaths. June.
Ulwell: (unusual site) large area of
acid capping 175m SE of Obelisk.
    Awned; flower spike contracts
when in fruit; leaves are like bristles.
See Plate 29.

Velvet Bent *Agrostis canina*
Native. Occasional. Wet heaths and
acid watersides. July to August.
Creech: on Grange Heath Reserve in
depression 300m S of NW tumulus
here and there from army fence for
130m E-wards. **Stoborough Heath:**
halfway across N side of Sandlings
field (with much more Common
Bent). **Hartland Moor:** N side of
Snag Valley 200m W of Slepe Road.
Corfe Charity's Meadows: on bridle-
way3 through N end of second meadow SW of Sharford Bridge from 25-
45m S of gate (with Common Bent).
Corfe: 15m S of bridleway30 just W
of tiny E stream in Little East
Common. **Wytch:** on path80 across S
end of Wytch Heath plantation 175
and 400m W of Thrasher's Lane.
Studland Heath: low area W of
Heather Walk 130m N of main N car
park at Knoll Beach; on some beaches
along SE side of Little Sea.
    Awned; flower spike contracts little
when in fruit; distinctive tufts of narrow short leaves on creeping stems.
Often with only a few flower spikes,
which are smaller than those of
Common Bent, with which it sometimes grows.

Brown Bent *Agrostis vinealis*
Native. Occasional. Dry non-calcare-
ous grassland and verges. July to
August.
Stoborough Heath: around junction
of Purbeck Way and tracks 250m S of
A351; just S of N edge of Sandlings

field 200m W of Dismantled Tramway. **Hartland Moor:** scattered in S side of Middle Fen both for 250m W and for 250m E of Jubilee Bridge; plentiful along S side of Arne Road E of Soldiers Road (with fewer Bristle and Common Bents). **Corfe:** several places on West Common (though may be mown) including: wide band 75-200m NE of UCR stream bridge at SW of Common (with fewer Common Bent); 20m W of path51 10m N of stream on S edge of Common; near stone block by W-E track along highest ridge of Common 100m E of path51; near where that W-E track crosses path53; on tumulus 60m N of that just E of path53. **Studland:** plentiful in Harmony Farm NE Field (with Common Bent).

Awned; flower spike contracts when in fruit; tufted – no creeping stems.

Wood Small-reed
Calamagrostis epigejos
Native. Occasional. Damp grassland and verges; game crops. July to August.
Creech Heath: E of (overgrown) SW-running track which starts from path34 250m W of Furzebrook Road. **Hartland Moor:** 125m E of Pillwort Pond. **Corfe:** SW of UCR just beyond cattle grid on S side of West Common. **Swanage:** can be seen from gateway at SE side of mini-round-about where Northbrook Road meets Washpond Lane 5-15m from gate on E side of mown path (binoculars). **Studland:** by permissive path up cliff from S end of South Beach 50m from beach; by Coast Path at NW and NE corners of Studland Wood; E side of Studland Wood 150m S of Coast Path (view from Old Nick's Ground).

Marram *Ammophila arenaria*
Native. Abundant. Fore-dunes, sandy heaths. July to August.

Nit Grass *Gastridium ventricosum*
Native or Introduced. Occasional. Open areas in calcareous grassland. Late June to July (persists in seed until November).
Nationally Scarce.
Tyneham: many on S side of Coast Path ascending Gad Cliff beginning from 60m from bottom at Worbarrow upwards for 60m. **Steeple:** few seen on Steeple Down (west) at map reference SY91118158. **Church Knowle:** 35-70m NW of gate to bridleway71 thinly scattered on bank above and on Down below UCR. **Corfe:** here and there by top 70 steps up East Hill; plenty 40-50m N of Purbeck Way just E of gate at junction with Sandy Hill Lane. **Worth:** on W-facing slope of East Man 50m NW of 'E' of 'East Man' on O.S. map 5m W of isolated post with one large notch and one round hole above it. **Wares (west):** scattered on upper half of SW-facing lower slopes on E side of Seacombe Bottom 50-100m from path11 over distance of 200m NW-SE; W-facing slope from 50m S of SE end of previous site for over 100m finishing 150m from sea; in E end of Hedbury Ware on 20m of path below ruined building; on 5m of path 30m E of that; in Taylor's Ware near top of slope 40m W of gateway to Dancing Ledge Ware; **(east)** in ruts on W side of Golter 20m E of E end of wall between Middle Field and Middle Ground; four sites by little-used bendy track halfway down Balston Wear S of Sherwood's Wear; much N of track 25m E of true route of Coast Path (see map 16) 250m W of E wall

of Balston Wear; on N side of track 50m W of E side of Verney Ware 100m N of S fence of ware.
Durlston: along 100m of N edge of Coast Path W of boundary between fields 3A and 6A (much taller than elsewhere); few in SE corner of field 6A; scattered at NE corner of Lighthouse Field both on and by first 40m of path50; about halfway between S-facing escarpment N of lighthouse and Mile Posts; two-thirds way up slope from upper Mile Post to gateway. **Ulwell:** to W and E 10m above water trough which is above Purbeck Way 100m NE of lower lay-by on Ulwell Road.

Does not appear every year at some sites.

Discovery of this species in limestone pastures in this area led to the re-assessment of its status. Earlier, it had been thought to be an introduced arable weed. See photo on back cover.

Harestail Grass *Lagurus ovatus*
Introduction. Rare. Sand. June to July.
Studland Heath: by W-E track between fenced dunes E of N end of Knoll Beach barbeque area.

Early Sand-grass *Mibora minima*
Native or introduced. Rare. Firm open sand. February (when mild), March, early April.
Nationally Rare.
Studland Heath: found by Felicity Woodhead in 1993; site can be shown.

Probably the smallest grass in the world; around 1 cm high here. See Plate 29.

Water Bent *Polypogon viridis*
Introduction. Rare. Casual from birdseed (increasing). June to July.
Swanage: seen both in Taunton Road N and S of Manor Road; in Ulwell Road in N part of one-way section.

Meadow Foxtail *Alopecurus pratensis*
Native. Frequent. Meadows, verges. April to May.
Creech: plentiful in two RSPB fields W of Grange Road. **Steeple:** by path6 W of Hyde Wood. **Church Knowle:** here and there by path17 in fields either side of junction with path18. **Corfe:** SE end of open access hayfield W of UCR just S of West Common. **Corfe Charity's Meadows:** very plentiful in all meadows next to Corfe River (stream). **Harman's Cross:** by path3 just W of bridleway2. **Wares (west)** here and there in N part of Dancing Ledge North Ware; **(east):** 300m N of Belle Vue West Ware in fields on both sides of path46. **Durlston:** in Lighthouse Field SE of Small Copse; in centre of S of Tasker's Meadow. **Swanage:** N of Swan Brook N of Playing Field S of Victoria Avenue.

Marsh Foxtail *Alopecurus geniculatus*
Native. Frequent. By ponds, in wet grassland, in arable fields. June to July.
Holme: on open access part of Battle Plain W of entrance by Doreys Farm. **Stoborough:** E side of path13 100m SE of NW end. **The Moors:** very plentiful indeed – see p.27. **Corfe Charity's Meadows:** much in meadow SW of Sharford Bridge. **Corfe:** deep puddle on Central Ridge of West Common 50m E of path51; where path58 crosses stream between junctions with path61 and 62. **Worth:** towards NW corner of small triangular NE part of Worth Mead. **Knitson:** NW side of path6 275m NE of stile E of New Barn. **Wares (east):** 375m N of Belle Vue West Ware on W side of path46.

Marsh x Bulbous Foxtail – hybrid
Alopecurus x *plettkei*
(*A. geniculatus* x *bulbosus*)
Native. Rare. Wet grassland near sea.
June to July.
The Moors: see p.27.

Bulbous Foxtail *Alopecurus bulbosus*
Native. Rare. Wet grassland near sea.
Late May to June.
Nationally Scarce.
The Moors: see p.27.

Black Grass *Alopecurus myosuroides*
Early Introduction. Occasional.
Arable fields, other disturbed
ground. May to July.
Kingston: sometimes in field edge S
of West Street W of The Plantation.

Timothy, Catstail *Phleum pratense*
Native. Frequent. Grassland. June to
July.
Corfe Charity's Meadows: many by
path80 in Home Mead (W) (Smaller
Catstail is at E side of field); also in
SE of Long Meadow. **Corfe:** 150m
NE of Copper Bridge by path65; N
corner of Middle Common.
Harman's Cross: by path4 in field
just N of A351; by path6 – 150-
250m NE of stile E of New Barn.
Durlston: NW corner of Johnston
Meadow.
    This is best distinguished from the
next species by flowerhead width
(usually over 6mm) and by flower
size (see identification books); not by
length of flowerhead.

Smaller Catstail *Phleum bertolonii*
Native. Frequent. Grassland, if not
acid. June to July.
    Flowerhead usually under 6mm
wide. With experience, it can be distinguished from previous species by
the greyer colour.

Smooth Brome, Meadow Brome
Bromus racemosus
(including *B. commutatus*)
Native. Occasional. Grassland, arable
fields, sometimes with Soft Brome.
Late May to early July (some spikelets
break up in late June).
Kimmeridge: along 10m of N side of
bridleway12 in arable edge 325m W
of E end. **Corfe:** scattered in First
Valley of West Common 100-150m
NW of UCR (may be grazed). **Corfe
Charity's Meadows:** here and there in
Paddle Dock meadow; by path80 in
SW of Bankes Mead; in N of Bankes
Mead; few towards S end of bridle-
way3 in meadow SW of Sharford
Bridge; in same field 30m SE of previ-
ous site for 50m SE-wards; 10m W of
Corfe River (stream) in same field 70-
110m and 170-190m S of Sharford
Bridge. **Durlston:** E side of path56 in
S of Johnston Meadow 10-30m N of
stile into Field 6; on N edge of
Tasker's Meadow 15-35m E of NW
corner (hairy form); E side of path on
W edge of Skipworth Meadow 35m
N of SW corner; very few 20m S of
NE corner of Long Meadow.
    Lemmas are tough, not easily
pierced with needle, with embedded
veins. Spikelets are usually not close
together, somewhat drooping and
hairless. (Compare with next species).

Soft Brome (including **Least,** or **Cliff
Soft Brome, and Lesser Soft Brome**)
Bromus hordeaceus (*B. mollis*)
Native. Abundant. Dry grassland,
verges, cliff-tops. April to June.
Norden: congested form (formerly
regarded as Lesser Soft Brome) on
NE side of A351 325m NW of
roundabout (with Compact Brome
p.259).
    Lemmas are papery, easily pierced
with needle, with embossed veins.

258

Spikelets are usually upright and are hairy. Tall plants may be misidentified as Smooth Brome (p.258). No longer divided into subspecies; also plants formerly recorded as Lesser Soft Brome (*B.* x *pseudothominii*) are now regarded as a congested form of this species (T. Cope, pers. com.)

Hairy Brome
Bromus ramosus (Bromopsis ramosa)
Native. Occasional. Woods, shady verges. June to July.
Creech: here and there on sides of road through Great Wood. **Holme:** S side of Holme Lane 100m W of railway bridge. **Kimmeridge:** on S side of road S of S bay car park. **Kingston:** on NW side of path44 – 250-300m SW of West Street. **Corfe:** S side of Sandy Hill Lane 40m E of railway bridge. **Bushey:** NW side of Meadus' Lane 100m NE of B3351. **Wares (west):** quarter way up S side of Coast Path steps on W side of Seacombe Bottom. **Harman's Cross:** N of track to S platform of railway station 10m W of road. **Langton:** here and there by rides in SE corner of West Wood. **Godlingston:** opposite entrance to brickworks in Brickyard Lane. **Durlston:** by lower half of Zigzag path.

Sometimes confused with Giant Fescue (p.246), with which it may grow. This species has hairy leaves and sheaths.

Upright Brome
Bromus erectus (Bromopsis erecta)
Native. Occasional. Tall calcareous grassland and verges. May to June.
Holme: both sides of B3070 250m SW of Holme Lane for at least 500m SW-wards. **Church Knowle:** N side of road at top of hill NW of Cocknowle. **Hartland Moor:** here

and there on E side of Soldiers Road between track to Isolation Cottages and S cattle grid; here and there on N side of Arne Road E of Soldiers Road. **Corfe:** on N side of bridleway70 75m W of Purbeck Way. **Worth:** by Coast Path E of Coastwatch Station. **Rempstone:** on E side of bridleway9 120m S of N end. **Ulwell:** SW side of road 150m NW of Y-junction. **Durlston:** on E side of Field 14 12m N of gateway from NW corner of South Field. **Studland Heath:** verges of Ferry Road especially N and S of end of bridleway36. **Ballard Down:** plentiful on ungrazed area above S-facing chalk cliffs.

Hairs on edges of leaves point outwards at angle of about 30^0 to the edge.

Great Brome
Bromus diandrus (Anisantha diandra)
Introduction. Occasional. Dunes, sandy cliffs and verges. May to June.
Sandbanks: plentiful here and there around main car park especially on SE side (with Barren Brome). **Canford Cliffs:** cliff-top near SE corner of Cliff Drive. **Branksome Dene Chine:** above promenade 40m NE of chine.

Spikelets are drooping. Lemmas, excluding awn, are 20-36mm long; compare with Barren Brome below.

Barren Brome
Bromus sterilis (Anisantha sterilis)
Early Introduction. Abundant. Arable fields, other disturbed ground, verges. April to June.

Spikelets are drooping. Lemmas, excluding awn, are 13-20mm long.

Compact Brome *Bromus madritensis (Anisantha madritensis)*
Early Introduction. Rare. Verges, gutters. June.

Norden: 325m NW of roundabout on NE side of A351 (with congested form of Soft Brome p.258). **Sandbanks:** back of pavement in places on N side of Panorama Road towards E end (mostly in front of sites awaiting development); casual in gutters nearby.

Spikelets are upright. Lemmas, excluding awn, mostly 12-20mm long.

California Brome *Bromus carinatus* (*Ceratochloa carinata*)
Introduction. Rare. Tracks. June to August.
Norden: in middle of bridleway77 350m from E end of bridleway (gets grazed).

(The brome recorded for **Swanage** allotments in *The Flora of Dorset* (Bowen, 2000) should be Rescue Brome (see below) and not California Brome. Specimens in Bournemouth Natural Science Society herbarium <u>are</u> correctly labelled as Rescue Brome). See drawing.

Rescue Brome *Bromus catharticus* (*B. unioloides*, *B. wildenowii*, *Ceratochloa cathartica*)
Introduction. Rare. Verges. June to November.
Swanage: beside central track through allotments just S of where path from Cauldron Barn Road to Victoria Avenue meets it (may be trimmed).

Tor Grass, Chalk False-brome
Brachypodium rupestre (*B. pinnatum*)
Native. Abundant. Calcareous grassland. June to July.

Leaf-blades shining, light green, usually inrolled even when fresh, 4-6mm wide, with sheaths usually hairless; flowering spike is usually stiffly upright; lemmas are usually hairless.

The division between this species and the next has only been made recently (see below).

Drooping Tor Grass, Heath False-brome *Brachypodium pinnatum*
Native. Occasional. Verges, grassland, open woods, scrub. June to July.
Church Knowle: NE side of road 50-150m NW of bridge at Puddle Mill Farm (next species just E of that); N side of road 375m SE of bridleway39 (with next species). **Knitson:** S side of road 150m W of Knaveswell Farm; S side of road from junction E of that Farm plentiful for 200m E-wards. **Langton:** W side of Crack Lane 20m N of vehicular entrance to cemetery. **Godlingston:** N side of Burnham's Lane 15-60m E of right-angled bend SW of Marsh Copse. **Swanage:** E side of Northbrook Road N of Battlemead along several metres. Almost certainly on **other** roadsides too.

Leaf-blades matt, dull green, flat when fresh, 4-7.5mm wide, with sheaths usually downy with short hairs; flowering spike is usually slightly drooping to one side; lemmas are usually downy with small hairs (Lambinon *et al.*, 1999; Stace *et al.*, 2004). Some botanists in Europe regard them as a species with two subspecies.

Two views of Rescue Brome flowerhead showing flatness, common to it and to Californian Brome

False Brome, Wood False-brome
Brachypodium sylvaticum
Native. Abundant. Woods, verges. July.

Common Couch
Elymus repens subsp. *repens*
(*Elytrigia repens*, *Agropyron repens*)
Native. Frequent. Grassland, verges, wood rides, arable fields, other disturbed ground, shores. June to August. It sometimes has awns (var. *aristate*) and can then be mistaken for Bearded Couch e.g. by ride in SE corner of **Langton** West Wood and above promenade at **Swanage** near N end.

For a species test pull a spikelet off when it is ripe: if it comes away complete, it is Common Couch, if lowest two parts (glumes) remain on the stem, it is Bearded Couch.

Elymus repens subsp. *arenosus*
(*Elytrigia repens* subsp. *arenosa*, *E. campestris* subsp. *maritima*, *Agropyron maritimum*)
Native. Occasional. Top of salt-marshes, clay banks by sea.
Studland Heath: on neck of land at Redhorn Quay; plentiful here and there along SW side of Bramble Bush Bay. **Luscombe Valley:** SW corner. **Sandbanks:** plentiful on wide sandy area opposite W end of Chaddesley Glen; much on bank opposite shops S of roundabout.

Often greyish. It is shorter and most plant parts are smaller than both subspecies *repens* and Sea Couch; it grows with both the latter and the hybrid (see below).

**Common Couch x Sea Couch –
hybrid** *Elymus* x *oliveri* (*E. repens* x *athericus*) (*Elytrigia* x *drucei*, *Agropyron* x *oliveri*)
Native. Occasional. Verges. July to August.

Stoborough Heath: plentiful on both sides of Dismantled Tramway from 70-450m S of Arne Road – discovered by Jonathan Cox (2003), who suggests that it, or Sea Couch, spread from the bank of the River Frome when tramway was in operation. **Studland Heath:** 35, 100 and 130m N of Brand's Bay Hide; 75m W of SE corner of Dyke Bay; halfway along Sandy Point spit; on SW shore of Bramble Bush Bay 25m NW of S corner.

Does not form fertile seed; it is not brittle between spikelets; some flower spikes are still intact in November. It may have awns, like Common Couch, some plants with shorter ones, some with longer. It inherits the tiny hairs on middle and lower leaf-sheaths from Sea Couch. Two edges of the axis between spikelets are rough like those on Sea Couch (lens). Anthers have no pollen so do not split to release it (lens). Seed is small and shrivelled – the easiest way to examine seed is by using a watchmaker's lens, so as to have both hands free, one to hold the flower and other to separate lemma and palea.

**Common Couch x Sand Couch –
hybrid** *Elymus* x *laxus* (*E. repens* x *farctus*) (*Elytrigia* x *laxa*, *Agropyron* x *laxum*)
Native. Rare. Verges. June to July. (**Studland:** record in *The Flora of Dorset* (Bowen, 2000) for S of Redend Point is probably a mistake for Sea Couch x Sand Couch hybrid.) **Sandbanks:** once seen on N side of Panorama Road 75m W of junction with Banks Road.

Spikelets are like a smaller version of Sand Couch; brittle between spikelets in late summer; has no tiny hairs on leaf-sheaths (compare with Sea Couch x Sand Couch p.262).

Anthers have no pollen so do not split to release it (lens).

Sea Couch *Elymus athericus*
(*E. pycanthus*, *Elytrigia atherica*, *Agropyron pungens*)
Native. Occasional. Salt-marshes, clay cliffs, shingle beaches, but not often on dunes.
Studland Heath: on shore near Brand's Bay Hide. **Sandbanks**: fore-dunes opposite end of Haven Road. Probably in other places, but there is not so much around the shores of the E end of Poole Harbour as there is of Common Couch x Sea Couch hybrid.

Common Couch growing by the sea can be greyish like this species, but only Sea Couch and its hybrids have tiny hairs (lens) on the edges of at least the middle and lower leaf-sheaths near their tops, though these hairs are sometimes only visible under a mircroscope and wear off as season progresses. Also, two edges of the axis between spikelets are rough (lens).

Sea Couch x Sand Couch – hybrid
Elymus x *obtusiusculus* (*E. athericus* x *farctus*) (*Elytrigia* x *obtusiuscula*, *Agropyron* x *obtusiusculum*)
Native. Occasional. By the sea. July to August.
Studland Heath: NW side of neck of Sandy Point spit. **Studland:** by Joe's café; here and there NW-wards for 200m. **Sandbanks:** top of beach 425m NE of main car park.

Spikelets like a smaller version of Sand Couch. It inherits the tiny hairs on the middle and lower leaf-sheaths from Sea Couch and brittleness between spikelets in late summer from Sand Couch. Anthers have no pollen so do not split to release it (lens).

Sand Couch *Elymus farctus*
(*Elytrigia juncea*, *Agropyron junceiforme*, *A. junceum*)
Native. Frequent. Fore-dunes. June to July.
Dorset Scarce.
Studland Heath: in seaward edge of fore-dunes 80m N of Knoll Beach Café; then after gap of 375m scattered along 100m N-wards; then after another 50m gap scattered N-wards along further 200m. **Shell Bay:** few W of road N of copse near ferry; few between NE end of boardwalk and ferry. **Sandbanks:** few in front of sea-wall by Haven Hotel (E of ferry); plentiful along seaward side of narrow fenced dunes between houses/flats (not beach chalets) and sea NE of main car park; few by sea wall 600m NE of car park.

Has larger, fatter spikelets than other species and hybrids; stem between spikelets is brittle, so spikelets break off singly when mature.

Lyme Grass *Leymus arenarius*
(*Elymus arenarius*)
Native. Frequent. Fore-dunes, bottom of sandy cliffs. July to August.

Unpleasant brown sooty fungus prevents some stems from flowering.

Six-rowed Barley *Hordeum vulgare*
Cultivated in origin. Occasional. Casual crop remnant. June.
Wall Barley *Hordeum murinum*
Early Introduction. Frequent. Grassland, verges, pavements. May to July.

Meadow Barley
Hordeum secalinum
Native. Frequent. Neutral permanent grassland. June to July.
Kingston: by permissive path 350m SW of Swyre Head; widespread in

W-facing field N of Coast Path with 'Syste' of 'Field System' printed in it on O.S. map. **Corfe:** SE end of open access hayfield W of UCR just S of West Common. **Corfe Charity's Meadows:** plentiful in most fields. **Worth:** in middle of triangular area in NE of Worth Mead. **Wares (west):** plentiful by path25 both in Spyway Meadow and Dancing Ledge North Ware. **Langton:** by path14 in field W of Leeson House. **Durlston:** all meadows.

Bread Wheat *Triticum aestivum*
Cultivated in origin. Frequent. Crop remnant in arable fields, other disturbed ground. June to July.

Heath Grass *Danthonia decumbens* (*Sieglingia decumbens*)
Native. Frequent. Permanent grassland, verges. June to July.
Hartland Moor: S corner of Arne Triangle; both sides of Slepe Road approaching Snag Valley from N and S. **Corfe:** plentiful by tracks on drier areas of West and Middle Commons. **Studland Heath:** here and there on Ferry Road verges in southern 400m of longest straight section; plentiful on track opposite track to Brand's Bay Hide 30-70m E of road. **Branksome Chine:** by tarmac path N of W end of Pinecliff Road 20-30m E of Western Road.

Pampas Grass *Cortaderia selloana*
Introduction. Rare. Planted or self-sown. Mid-August to October.
Studland Heath: SW side of Bramble Bush Bay 200m NW of Ferry Road (known there since 1938). (**Sandbanks:** once grew self-sown beside traffic bollard in middle of Banks Road!) **Canford Cliffs:** foot of sea-cliff 325m NE of Canford Cliffs Chine.

Purple Moor-grass *Molinia caerulea*
Native. Abundant. Wet heaths. June to August.

Common Reed *Phragmites australis*
Native. Abundant. Fens, ditches, watersides. August to September.

Bermuda Grass *Cynodon dactylon*
Perhaps native in one area of Britain; believed to be introduced in this area. Occasional. Verges near the sea. August to September.
Sandbanks: here and there in grass above Poole Harbour sea-wall all the way from Banks Road opposite main car park first NE-wards and then NW-wards to NW end of Evening Hill.

Ligule is a ring of short hairs (compare with Hairy Finger-grass p.264).

Small Cord-grass
Spartina maritima
Native. Top of salt-marshes. July to September.
Appears to have died out in public areas locally, but may still occur somewhere in small amounts. Surviving in one private area, isolated inside a seawall built in the mid-19th century before next hybrid and species existed. Since then they have crowded *S. maritima* out at most other sites.

Ligules are tiny: 0.2-0.6mm long, anthers are 4-7mm long.

Townsend's Cord-grass
Spartina x *townsendii* (*S. maritima* x *alterniflora*)
Native. Abundant. Salt-marshes. July to September.
Arne: area S of RSPB beach noticeboard (with species below).
Godlingston Heath: very plentiful between Mead Point and Brand's

Point; mixed with species below along W side of Brand's Creek. **Studland Heath:** mixed with species below along E side of Brand's Creek; plentiful alone in Redhorn Bay; few mixed with species below along S side of Plateau Bay; many on S side of Dyke Bay; scattered by itself along SW side of Bramble Bush Bay. **Sandbanks:** S of W end of Chaddesley Glen (with species below).

Arose in Southampton Water in second half of 19th century, after arrival of *S. alterniflora* from America, which was presumably accidentally carried by ship.

Ligule usually 1-1.5mm long, anthers usually 5-8mm; compare with next species.

Common Cord-grass
Spartina anglica
Recent species. Abundant. Saltmarshes. July to September.
Arne: in area S of RSPB beach noticeboard (with hybrid above).
Godlingston Heath: few between Mead Point and Brand's Point; mixed with hybrid above along W side of Brand's Creek. **Studland Heath:** mixed with hybrid above along E side of Brand's Creek; many along S side of Plateau Bay; few along S side of Dyke Bay. **Sandbanks:** S of W end of Chaddesley Glen with hybrid above.

Apparently arose naturally in the late 19th century through chromosome duplication of the hybrid above. Ligule usually 2-2.5mm long; however, as they can be damaged by tides, mud or small stones, examine several young shoots. Stigmas, which are feathery, appear before the anthers in this genus. Anthers 8mm or more; they remain attached, in groups, longer than those of the hybrid above.

Common Millet *Panicum miliaceum*
Introduction. Rare. Casual from birdseed. July to September.

Cockspur *Echinochloa crus-galli*
Introduction. Occasional. Maize crops, pavements. July to October.
Church Knowle: 20m W of path2 along N side of road for 25m. **Norden:** W side of S end of Slepe Road in field gateway; in W cattle grid on bridleway77.

Sometimes visible from gateways elsewhere or from paths through maize fields.

Japanese Millet *Echinochloa esculenta*
Introduction. Rare. Casual from birdseed. July to September.

Yellow Bristle-grass *Setaria pumila*
Introduction. Rare. Casual. July to September.

Rough Bristle-grass *Setaria verticillata*
Introduction. Occasional. Arable fields, usually when the crop is Maize, other disturbed ground. July to September.
Kingston: plentiful by path22 near NE corner of Newfoundland (wood).
Ballard Down: NE corner of first field N of Shep's Hollow (view over fence, short range binoculars helpful).

Green Bristle-grass *Setaria viridis*
Introduction. Rare. Casual. July to September.

Hairy Finger-grass
Digitaria sanguinalis
Introduction. Rare. Casual on pavements. July to September.
Swanage: Bay Close pavement.
Sandbanks: pavement in front of flats opposite Shell Bay Ferry hut.
Ligule is short – compare with Bermuda Grass p.263.

BUR-REED FAMILY
Branched Bur-reed
Sparganium erectum
Native. Frequent. Shallow fresh
water. June to August.
Tyneham: by pond E of ruined
Rectory. **Creech Heath:** in small
pond 75m ENE of crossing of path34
by W-E track (best approached from
track to S). **Norden:** NE corner of
Michael's Pond. **Corfe:** N of A351
stream bridge 100m NE of The
Square; by stream near S edge of
Middle Common for 70m E of
Purbeck Way footbridge. **Wares
(west):** by pond S of Priest's Way
250m E of path30. **Swanage:** Swan
Brook at bridge on 18th hole of Pitch
and Putt course (players only; where
you may have to fish your ball out of
the brook); at NE corner of Playing
Field on S side of Victoria Avenue.

Flower spikes are sometimes few
compared with number of leaves. It is
divided into four subspecies on the
basis of seed shape, but records have
not been made of these.

Unbranched Bur-reed
Sparganium emersum
Native. Rare. Flowing water. June to
July.
Holme: plentiful in East Holme
Meadows – see p.23. **Creech Heath:**
many in pond with bed of soft clay at
map reference SY92578346. **The
Moors:** see p.27

Lowest female flower appears to be
on a branch, but that is just a long
flower-stalk.

Least Bur-reed
Sparganium natans (*S. minimum*)
Native. Ditches, ponds. Mid-June to
July.
Dorset Rare.
The Moors: see p.27.

Only one male and 2 or 3 female flowers, just emerging from the water. See
Plate 29.

REEDMACE FAMILY
Reedmace, False Bulrush
Typha latifolia
Native. Frequent. In still water and
ditches. June to July.

Hybrid Reedmace *Typha* x *glauca*
(*T. latifolia* x *angustifolia*)
Native. Occasional. In still water. June
to July.
Bushey: plentiful in opposite corners
of larger pond on Brenscombe South
Heath. **Studland:** village pond.
Studland Heath: few towards S end

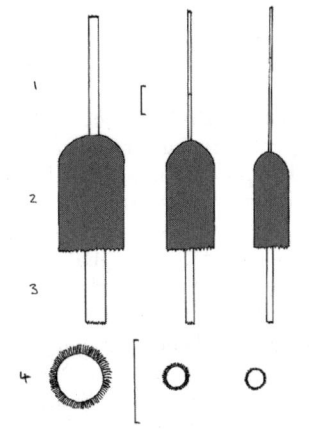

*Sections of Reedmace fruiting stems: Reedmace
(left), Hybrid Reedmace (centre), Lesser
Reedmace (right) showing, from top down, (1)
scar indicating lower end of male flowers
(which have now dropped off)*, (2) part of
female fruiting spike**, (3) stem of latter with
fruit stripped off to reveal flower stalks around
stem, (4) thrice enlarged end-on view of latter,
showing stubby flower-stalks around stem. *No
scar on Reedmace stem because male flowers
abut female. **Width of fruiting spike varies;
Hybrid can be as narrow as Lesser Reedmace.*

of SE side of East Lake; plentiful in NE corner of East Lake (with few of the species below, which see for directions). **Brownsea**: along N and E sides of East Lake (binoculars from gate or hide).

Difficult to tell from the parent below. Gap between male and female flower spikes is usually, <u>but not always</u>, less than 30mm (rarely over 40mm). It forms fewer fruits; do not mistake broad ends of stigmas for ovaries. Best to strip off the female fruits from one end of the flower spike and examine the length of the remaining short stalks – see drawing p265.

Lesser Reedmace
Typha angustifolia
Native. Rare. In still water. June to July.
Studland Heath: NE corner of East Lake (with very much more of the hybrid) – proceed along track from Ferry Road towards nudists' area. After passing through third and last belt of woodland, turn right onto narrow track through heather, which follows the edge of woodland but keeps outside of it, swinging first left, and then right near Scots Pine. Pass two more Scots Pines. Just after the second turn right towards the lake. This route gives you the shortest stretch of wet woodland before the lakeshore. Tall Wellingtons are essential.

Gap between male and female spikes is usually more than 30mm.

PICKERELWEED FAMILY
Pickerelweed *Pontederia cordata*
Introduction. Rare. Planted. June to August.
Bushey: larger pond on Brenscombe South Heath.

LILY FAMILY
Bog Asphodel *Narthecium ossifragum*
Native. Abundant. Wet heaths. June to July.

Orange Day-lily *Hemerocallis fulva*
Introduction. Rare. Escape. June to July.
Hartland Moor: SE side of Soldiers Road 275m SW of S cattle grid.
Corfe: in open area between the two halves of Byle Copse by Byle Brook.
Studland: 10m W of NE corner of Glebeland Estate.

Showing leaves but not flowering at some other sites.

Kaffir Lily *Schizostylis coccinea*
Introduction. Rare. Escape. October to December.
Furzebrook: N side of path13 75m E of Blue Pool ticket booth.

Red Hot Poker *Kniphofia* cv.
Introduction. Rare. Escape. Different cultivars vary in flowering times.
Hartland Moor: SE side of Arne Road opposite Bank Gate Cottages (late July to August). **Ulwell:** E side of Ulwell Road on bend 100m SE of path15 (can begin in July and last to January). **Swanage:** on cliff above three levels of beach chalets 40m N of the end of path from Burlington Road (May to June).

Garden Tulip *Tulipa gesneriana*
Introduction. Rare. Planted. April to May. Short-lived.

Lily-of-the-valley
Convallaria majalis
Native, but introduction here. Rare. Escape. May.
Ridge: N side of Arne Road 300m E of Sunnyside (road).

Poisonous.

Garden Solomon's Seal
Polygonatum x *hybridum*
(*P. multiflorum* x *odoratum*)
Introduction. Rare. Escape. May.
Norden: N side of bridleway77 W of
gate 190m E of A351. **Swanage:** in
copse W of D'Urberville Drive 10m
W of NW entrance.

Spiked Star of Bethlehem
Ornithogalum pyrenaicum
Native, but introduced here. Rare.
Escape.
Durlston: under trees on N side of
large glade in N end of woods N of
large stone seat.

Star of Bethlehem
Ornithogalum angustifolium
Introduction. Occasional. Verges,
grassland. First half of May.
Stoborough: W side of Furzebrook
Road 3m N of kissing gate to short
track leading to path5. **Hartland
Moor:** N side of Arne Road 25m W
of Soldiers Road. **Durlston:** ask at
Visitor Centre – good population.
Townsend Reserve: 30m from NW
corner of Reserve SW of path46.

Sites can be short-lived. Difficult
to find except when they open in
sunshine. All have been checked to
see that they are not the larger
species *Ornithogalum umbellatum*.

Bluebell *Hyacinthoides non-scripta*
Native. Abundant. Woods, verges,
fields with bracken. April to May.
Tyneham: very plentiful for 400m
W of car park on top of Povington
Hill (but Army Range Walks not
open on weekend after May Day
bank holiday weekend). **Steeple:**
either side of path6 where it crosses
stream N of Hyde Wood.
Furzebrook: plentiful in Kilnwood
Reserve in NW part of Reserve and

in open area E of central field.
Church Knowle: in small wood on
N side of road to West Orchard
Farm 200 m E of T-junction.
Kingston: good display in NW of
steep E-facing open access area N of
Coast Path. **Corfe:** very plentiful
along Central Ridge of West
Common (especially near Monkey's
Hump). **Langton:** very plentiful in
Langton West Wood. **Harman's
Cross:** plenty visible from path44 in
S half of The Wilderness.
Kingswood: plentiful in private
conifer plantation S of B3351 visible
to W from N end of bridleway16;
here and there in S side of King's
Wood. **Studland:** very plentiful in
Harmony Farm West Fields in area
on N side of B3351 opposite reser-
voir; plentiful in The Warren Wood.

In open ground at Tyneham and
Studland they are in full flower in
mid-May, about two weeks later than
at the woodland sites. Albinos are
seen at most sites, usually singly. See
Plate 29.

Garden Bluebell
Hyacinthoides x *massartiana*
(*H. non-scripta* x *hispanica*)
Introduction. Frequent. Verges,
woods. March to May.
Leaves can be over 30mm wide.
The introduced parent Spanish
Bluebell is not seen in this area.

Hyacinth *Hyacinthus orientalis*
Introduction. Rare. Planted. March
to April.
Langton: W side of unmade road to
Castle View 25m S of Norman's
Quarry on opposite side (pink and
blue). **Studland:** E side of bridle-
way12 30m S of NE corner of
Glebeland Estate (blue).

Sometimes short-lived in the wild.

Garden Grape Hyacinth
Muscari armeniacum
Introduction. Occasional. Escape on
verges, pavements, woods, dunes.
March to May.
Stoborough: E side of Furzebrook
Road at path24; W side of same road
220m N of railway bridge. **Worth:**
plentiful on bank on N side of road
N of village pond. **Langton:** opposite entrances to Bower's Quarry.
Durlston: in woods at NE of
Country Park 50m E of pedestrian
entrance and N of main glade.
Swanage: W and E ends of copse W
of D'Urberville Drive. **Sandbanks:**
several places by paths between
Grasmere Road and Seacombe Road;
on NE edge of raised dune SW of
main car park. **Canford Cliffs:** cliff-
top near SW end of Cliff Drive;
cliff-top NE of stepped path from
Cliff Drive to beach.

Tassel Hyacinth *Muscari comosum*
Introduction. Rare. Escape. Late May
to early June.
Durlston: one plant – ask at Visitor
Centre.

Chives *Allium schoenoprasum*
Native, but introduced here. Rare.
Escape. May to June.
Langton: road gutter on W side of
Durnford Drove 30m N of turning
circle.

Rosy Garlic *Allium roseum*
Introduction. Occasional. Verges.
June.
Ridge: S side of Arne Road 30m E of
Barnhill Road. **Swanage:** against
hedge on NE side of Northbrook
Road 80m SE of NW corner of Day's
Park. **Ulwell:** NE side of Ulwell
Road 15 and 50m SE of path15.
Studland: E side of Ferry Road 40m

N of village crossroads; NW side of
Beach Road 80m from Ferry Road.

Neopolitan Garlic
Allium neopolitan
Introduction. Rare. Planted or
escaped. April to May.
Durlston: 25m W of NE corner of
Field 10 in hollow N of path50.
Studland: E side of Ferry Road 50m
N of Beach Road.
   White flowers, 5 to 40 in the
head, petals up to 12mm long, no
bulbils; 3-sided stalks up to 50cm
long, with two angles slightly
winged; leaves up to 20mm wide.

Cowan's Garlic *Allium cowanii*
Introduction. Rare. Escape. April to
May.
Swanage: S side Victoria Avenue
20m E of Pitch and Putt entrance.
   White flowers, 15 to 40 in the
head, petals up to13mm long, no
bulbils; 3-sided stalks up to 55cm
long, with two angles conspicuously
winged; leaves up to 30mm wide.
Like previous species but larger.

Hairy Garlic *Allium subhirsutum*
Introduction. Rare. Planted. June.
Swanage: plenty under group of six
Ashes near SW corner of The
Downs 50m S of garden of flats E of
Seymer Road.
   Leaf edges are hairy (lens).

Yellow Garlic *Allium moly*
Introduction. Rare. Verges, though a
perennial it does not seem to persist.

Three-cornered Garlic
Allium triquetrum
Introduction. Frequent. Verges,
woods. March to May.
Kimmeridge: here and there by
road leading down into village plen-

tiful; by road from village to bay; by Coast Path S of Gaulter Cottages. **Corfe:** at S end of N half of Byle Copse. **Durlston:** plentiful in N end of NE woods of Country Park. **Ulwell:** NE side of Ulwell Road 10m SE of path15. **Lilliput:** plentiful by path from Shore Road to Alington Close. **Canford Cliffs:** plentiful at S end of Bessborough Road; at E end of Bodley Road.

Ramsons, Wild Garlic
Allium ursinum
Native. Abundant. Woods, especially N-facing ones, verges. April to May.
Tyneham: plentiful both by Woodland Walk W of village picnic area and from bridge over stream 200m S of village. **East Creech:** plentiful in woods N of Stonehill Down (flowering slightly later than elsewhere). **Kingston:** plentiful on both sides of path44 where it passes through Quarry Wood. **Bushey:** plentiful in Bushey Wood viewed from path13. **King's Wood:** wonderfully plentiful. **Studland Wood:** plentiful. See Plate 29 and 30.

Wild Onion *Allium vineale*
Native. Abundant. Verges, lawns, grassland, arable fields.
Worth: some with flowers as well as bulbils on W side of path13 175m S of junction with path14.

Usually no flowers, only bulbils.

Spring Starflower
Tristagma uniflorum
Introduction. Rare. Planted and spreading. April to May.
Sandbanks: raised lawn of café E of main car park; dunes 200m NE of main car park. **Canford Cliffs:** cliff-top NE of stepped path from Cliff Drive to beach.

Summer Snowflake
Leucojum aestivum subsp. *pulchellum*
Introduction. Occasional. Escape or planted – verges, grassland, wet woods. January to May.
Tyneham: scattered in village. **Stoborough Heath:** by path5 plentiful 65-90m NW of small fenced field. **Ridge:** S side of Arne Road 125-175m W of Dismantled Tramway. **Worth:** on SE side of Purbeck Way 15-20m SW of where Purbeck Way meets UCR from Renscombe Farm; by pond on NE side of Renscombe Road. **Langton:** S of Quarr Farm 10m N of stile on path7. **Swanage:** S side Victoria Avenue 30m W of E end of Prospect Crescent opposite. **Studland Heath:** in wet wood just W of Knoll Beach S car park 150m from N end of car park.

There are several flowers at the top of the stem.

Snowdrop *Galanthus nivalis*
Introduction. Frequent. Verges, near houses or sites of houses. Late January to early March.
Tyneham: best display in this area is around ruined Post Office and preserved School and ruined houses behind them both. **Steeple:** plentiful W of path10 footbridge SW of church one field distant (good view of more while crossing field on path). **East Creech:** where path32 enters N side of woods. **Corfe:** just N of rail viaduct on W bank of Corfe River (stream). **Bushey:** N side of B3351 both 125m E of Thrasher's Lane; just E of Meadus's Lane; E side of Thrasher's Lane 700m from B3351. **Woolgarston:** N side of road 80m W of N end of Tabbit's Hill Lane. **Langton:** S side of B3069 W of Leeson House entrance. **Studland:** both sides of Coast Path from Middle

Beach car park towards Fort Henry.

Sometimes in double form. See Plate 30.

Pleated Snowdrop
Galanthus plicatus subsp. *plicatus*
Introduction. Rare. Escape. January to February.
Swanage: S side Victoria Avenue 20m E of Pitch and Putt entrance.

Leaf wider than Snowdrop, with pale centre and edges folded back for some of length.

Daffodils *Narcissi*
These are the most difficult plants to identify precisely. There is only one native Daffodil in Britain, but there are now over 27,000 cultivated varieties on *The International Daffodil Register and Classified List 1998* (Kington, 1998). These have been bred by creating hybrids from a low number of naturally occurring species. These hybrids are mostly fertile, and so in turn have been bred with other species or hybrids down the centuries, to produce an amazing range of varieties.

The author has four A4 pages of site records of these cultivated Daffodils, escaped or planted in the wild, which he has been able to identify. Anybody interested in these pages, please send a C5 size, stamped and addressed envelope, together with an extra 1st class stamp to pay for copying, to his address (see Appendix).

Wild Daffodil *Narcissus pseudonarcissus* subsp. *pseudonarcissus*
Native, but planted in this area. Occasional. Woods, scrub. March to April.
Godlingston Heath: good display along 125m N-S by stream where bridleway33 enters forest (next to site of former caravan); two areas 20m N of

bridleway27 in wood 450m W of junction of bridleways26 and 27 (some of the double form in W of these two areas); N of old bank 70m E of green-keepers' private depot in small wood (go 80m N from same bridleway); double form in three places by bank 30m and 50m NE and 50m N of previous site (all these six sites now by the golf course are near former buildings). Pale yellow petals, yellow trumpet, smaller than the similar cultivar. See Plate 30.

Asparagus
Asparagus officinalis subsp. *officinalis*
Early Introduction. Rare. Crop relic.
Arne: visible SE-wards from Arne Road some years in abandoned rectangular field SW of triangular field SW of car park.

Butcher's-broom *Ruscus aculeatus*
Native. Frequent. Old woods, hedges. All year.

IRIS FAMILY
Pale Yellow-eyed-grass
Sisyrinchium striatum
Introduction. Rare. Planted or escaped. May to June.
Stoborough Heath: on true (black) route of Purbeck Way at letter 'd' in 'Stock's Wood' on O.S. map; W of Furzebrook Road through gate by paths5 and 37.

Snakeshead Iris
Hermodactylus tuberosus
Introduction. Rare. Escape. March.
Studland: E of bridleway12 – 35-50m S of NE corner of Glebeland Estate.

Bearded Iris *Iris germanica*
Introduction. Rare. Planted and escaped. May to June.
Studland: E of bridleway12 45m S of NE corner of Glebeland Estate.

Lilliput: by path descending NW end of Evening Hill.

Yellow Iris *Iris pseudacorus*
Native. Frequent. By running water or in permanently wet places. May to June.
Ridge: here and there on SW side of Purbeck Way along river to Wareham. **Stoborough Heath:** along 25m by path5 150m NW of small fenced field plentiful. **Corfe:** plentiful in several wet areas on West: Middle and Little East Commons; by Challow Pond. **Hartland Moor:** E and NE sides of White House Wood. **Langton:** S of Quarr Farm by path7 100m SW of bridleway5. **Harman's Cross:** by path26 where it crosses stream from Higher and Lower Grove Woods in third field N of A351. **Wares (west):** pond S of Priest's Way. **Knitson:** N side of next low point on road W of Knaveswell Farm. **Durlston:** W side of pond in Field 3 (flowers late into early July). **Studland:** village pond.

Turkish Iris *Iris orientalis*
Introduction. Rare. Planted or escaped. May to June.
Harman's Cross: near stile on path6 E of New Barn. **Langton:** visible to E from bridleway16 50m S of A351. **Swanage:** NE corner of Playing Field S of Victoria Avenue.

Wild Iris *Iris foetidissima*
Native. Frequent. Woods, verges, permanent grassland. May to July.
   Poisonous.

Spring Crocus *Crocus vernus*
Introduction. Rare. Planted. February to March.
Studland: SE side of Beach Road 150m from Ferry Road (dying out).
   Often only survives a few years – grazed by various animals.

Early Crocus *Crocus tommasinianus*
Introduction. Rare. Escape on verges. February.
Creech: NW side of road 50 and 75m NE of '20%' sign. **Swanage:** near S of two seats on green E of Ballard Estate. **Studland:** by path2 10m W of Beach Road. **Sandbanks:** path S of and parallel to Grasmere Road 20m from E end.
   Often only survives a few years – grazed by various animals.

Yellow Crocus *Crocus* x *stellaris*
(*C. flavus* x *angustifolius*)
Introduction. Rare. Planted. February.
Stoborough: W side of Furzebrook Road 65m S of path37.

Eastern Gladiolus *Gladiolus communis* subsp. *byzantinus*
Introduction. Occasional. Planted or escaped. May to June.
Durlston: plentiful in rough area 20m W of lighthouse enclosure; some by SE corner of same enclosure. **Swanage:** S side of Victoria Avenue W of W end of Prospect Crescent opposite; W side of Northbrook Road 70m N of Walrond Road; 50m N of gate at SW corner of the Downs; S of scrub 100m E of S end of Broad Road car park; on cliff 50m N of path from Burlington Road to beach.

Montbretia *Crocosmia* x *crocosmiiflora* (*C. pottsii* x *aurea*)
Introduction. Frequent. Escape on verges. July to August.

AGAVE FAMILY
Spanish Dagger *Yucca gloriosa*
Introduction. Rare. Planted and escaped. Cliffs, dunes. October.
Sandbanks: dunes 300m NE of main car park. **Branksome Dene Chine:** low on sea cliffs to NE.

Curved-leaved Spanish Dagger
Yucca recurvifolia
Introduction. Rare. Planted and escaped. October.
Tyneham: E end of ponds E of ruined Rectory. **Swanage:** W end of copse W of D'Urberville Drive.

Cabbage Palm *Cordyline australis*
Introduction. Rare. Planted.
Sandbanks: SE end of raised dune SW of main car park.

New Zealand Flax *Phormium tenax*
Introduction. Rare. Planted near sea.
Swanage: on cliff above N end of promenade. **Lilliput:** near SE corner of Evening Hill.

YAM FAMILY
Black Bryony *Tamus communis*
Native. Frequent. Hedges. Late May to June.
　Poisonous.

ORCHID FAMILY
Sadly there are people who dig up orchids, recently Lizard Orchid outside this area, but also others. Therefore sites of those species that are most rare in this area cannot be given here. Digging is not only illegal and selfish, but also foolish, because plants are unlikely to survive for long out of their original habitat.

White Helleborine
Cephalanthera damasonium
Native. Rare. Light areas in woods and verges over calcareous strata. May to June.
Vulnerable.
Only one public site in this area.

Marsh Helleborine *Epipactis palustris*
Native. Rare. Damp places. June to July.

Dorset Scarce.
Hartland Moor. Studland Heath.
Peer into flower to see its full beauty.

Birdsnest Orchid
Neottia nidus-avis
Native. Rare. In shade in the woods. June to July.
Dorset Scarce. Near Threatened.
Langton. (Also **Brownsea** until recently – may reoccur.)

Common Twayblade
Neottia ovata (*Listera ovata*)
Native. Occasional. Woods, by scrub. May to June.
East Creech: few near path32 through woods 35-55m S of N edge (take care not to trample them).
Hartland Moor: S side of Arne Road 100-150m W of Arne Triangle; at NW corner of Triangle itself. **Kingston:** very thinly scattered along NW side of path44 through The Plantation especially 130-170m from West Street and in SW corner of adjacent car park (only some flower at both sites).
Wares (west): few near W edge of Nicholas Down 300m from NW corner 50m from W edge and 380m from same corner 30m from edge.
Bushey: on NW side of bridleway14 – 20-30m SW of junction with bridleway15. **Durlston:** few SW of reservoir fence in copse N of W car park (best entered at NE corner of car park, numbers vary). **Townsend Reserve:** 'Twayblade Bank' (one of the most reliable sites). **Studland:** E side of Ferry Road opposite Knoll House Hotel. **Studland Heath:** 60m E of entrance to Spur Bog.
　Does not appear every year at the same sites. Flower-spikes get eaten off, especially at Durlston and Townsend.

Autumn Lady's-tresses
Spiranthes spiralis
Native. Frequent. Downs, lawns.
Mid-August to mid-September.
Near Threatened.
East Creech: widely and thinly scattered on Stonehill Down especially on middle of S-facing slope. **Church Knowle:** few on 100m length of well-grazed lower slope of down E of Cocknowle. **Worth:** few in places on steep Down NW of Hill Bottom particularly near top at NE end. **Corfe:** few on N side of Purbeck Way 150-325m W of radio mast on Rollington Hill. **Woolgarston:** in short turf along S-facing top of Brenscombe Hill on S of Purbeck Way from junction with bridleway21 SE-wards for 500m (especially at E end). **Wares (west)** and **(east):** best areas of many are: S side of Cliff Middle Field near NW part of Hedbury Ware and areas in N half of Chillmark Ware (many smaller widely scattered colonies elsewhere). **Townsend Reserve:** N half of Orchid Bastion. **Durlston:** especially – near and well below brow of Down at W end of Country Park; W of lighthouse; between Mile Posts. **Swanage:** lawn N of St. Mary's Church; lawn SE of All Saints Church; several house lawns (where it is often mown and to which it may have been transplanted from Durlston before latter became Country Park). **Ulwell:** below reservoir E of stepped path4. **Ballard Down:** plentifully scattered in band 10-70m S of bridleway6 from bridleway14 E-wards for 200m.

Numbers vary from year to year. Any significance of Lady's-tresses presence on Anglican Church lawns in Swanage is left to the surmise of the readers. See Plate 31.

Bog Orchid *Hammarbya paludosa*
Native. Rare. Bogs. Late June to early July.
Dorset Scarce.
Stoborough Heath. Godlingston Heath.
They do not last for many years at any site. These orchids are mostly around 5cm high and it would be easy to step on them accidentally, so recent sites would need to be shown even if they were not otherwise endangered.

Greater Butterfly Orchid
Platanthera chlorantha
Native. Rare. Calcareous verge. Late May to early June.
Near Threatened.
Only one public site in this area.

Lesser Butterfly Orchid
Platanthera bifolia
Native. Rare. Wet heath. Second half of June.
Dorset Rare. Vulnerable.
Hartland Moor: only current site, discovered by David Leadbetter in 2007. (**Kingswood:** one was seen in SE arm of Kingswood Bog in 1981, but not since; plants flower sporadically so it is worth watching out for it. **Studland Heath:** one flowered for some years (3 times in 1990s) and was last seen on Bill Oddie's visit while making a TV programme in 1999.)

Pyramidal Orchid
Anacamptis pyramidalis
Native. Frequent. Calcareous grassland and verges. Late June to July.
Woolgarston: lower slopes of Down between N ends of bridleways22 and 23. **Wares (west** and **east):** plentiful. **Durlston:** very plentiful – over 12,000 at last count. Low numbers elsewhere. See Plate 31.

Green-winged Orchid
Anacamptis (Orchis) morio
Native. Occasional. Undisturbed calcareous or neutral grassland and verges. May.
Near Threatened.
Hartland Moor: E side Soldiers Road 350m N of A351. **Corfe:** few near NE edge of West Common NW of cattle grid. **Wares (west):** few on W-facing slope on E side of Seacombe Bottom towards sea; E part of that area of Hedbury Ware between Coast Path and cliff-top W of Hedbury main quarries (including albinos); **(east)** very plentiful on E side of White Ware; plentiful in Second Hayfield; very plentiful in Sherwood's Wear (2,500 in 2007); N of flush in SW of Belle Vue West Ware. **Durlston:** particularly in SW of Field 10A around 70m from W wall 40m from S fence; near SW corner of South Field 25m NE of entrance from Field 14. **Studland:** few on E side of Ferry Road among planted Daffodils 150m S of bridleway38 on opposite side.

There is usually little if any green in the sepals ('wings') but their veins are always conspicuous. See Plate 31.

Heath Fragrant Orchid
Gymnadenia borealis
(*G. conopsea* subsp. *borealis*)
Native. Rare. Damp heaths. June.
Dorset Rare.
Only one site in this area.

Early Purple Orchid, Soldiers' Jackets *Orchis mascula*
Native. Occasional. Permanent calcareous grassland, calcareous or neutral woods and verges. April to May.
East Creech: few in several places on Stonehill Down Reserve especially on N- and S-facing slopes W of

hairpin road bend. **Corfe:** one quarter to one third up castle mound both at W end of NW side of castle and on N side opposite rail viaduct. **Bushey:** E side of Thrasher's Lane 500 m from B3351. **Woolgarston:** about 700 near foot of Down 20-60m NW of N end of bridleway22; about 300 in NW corner of Higher Grove Wood (view from road). **Langton:** S of bridleway42 75m W of path44; where path44 crosses stream in Langton West Wood; S of stream near old low wall 80m W of previous site. **King's Wood:** near lower gate on bridleway16 at top (S) of wood; in SE corner of wood near bridleway87. **Wares (east):** along old quarry banks near top of Belle Vue East Ware. **Durlston:** especially towards SE corner of Field 3 and towards SW corner of Field 6.
Townsend Reserve: widespread in S end. **Studland:** one of Harmony Farm West Fields near S of height mark '118' on O.S. map. **Ballard Down:** here and there either side of Purbeck Way 50-125m W of path11.

Sepal veins inconspicuous – compare with Green-winged Orchid. Like Pignut, it is at home in both woods and in open grassland.

Spotted and Marsh Orchids
Orchids of this genus frequently hybridise. Their hybrids are fertile, breeding with their parents or interbreeding with themselves, producing puzzling intermediates. The best guide to the parentage of hybrids is to see which true species are nearby, but sometimes one parent may have died out.

Common Spotted Orchid
Dactylorhiza fuchsii
Native. Frequent. Calcareous grassland and verges. Late May to June.

East Creech: few on N-facing slope of Stonehill Down S of wood between path32 and NW corner of Down. **Furzebrook:** S of centre in central field on Kilnwood Reserve (Heath Spotted Orchids N of centre). **Kingston:** both sides of path44 through The Plantation. **Langton:** S of gate on path5 on S side of Talbot's Wood (N not W of cemetery). **Durlston:** N-facing slope on E side of Field 6 25-50m from E wall; many in Paddock (use animal tracks to view); SE corner of Skipworth Meadow. **Townsend Reserve:** N of Fox Hollow on both in Butterfly Hollow and N of it. **Swanage:** by path in copse W of D'Urberville Drive. **Studland:** one or two just S of entrance to Spur Bog.

Common Spotted Orchid x Southern Marsh Orchid – hybrid

Dactylorhiza x grandis
(D. fuchsii x praetermissa)
Native. Occasional. June.
Hartland Moor: 10m W of Slepe Road at top of rise S of junction with old tramway. **Rempstone:** E side of bridleway9 (Oil Road) at junction with bridleway8 (with Southern Marsh Orchid); here and there along 150m of both sides of bridleway34 275m SW of crossing of bridleways31 and 34 (Oil Road) (with both parents).

Inherits lip shape and dark lip markings from Common Spotted Orchid, and has leaves of intermediate width usually with ring spots.

Heath Spotted Orchid

Dactylorhiza maculata
Native. Frequent. Wet pastures and heaths, firmer ground in bogs. June.
Furzebrook: N of centre in central field on Kilnwood Reserve

(Common Spotted Orchids S of centre). **Stoborough Heath:** 75m E of gateway on E side of Dismantled Tramway 625m N of A351 (with hybrids with Southern Marsh Orchid). **Corfe:** widely and plentifully scattered on West and Middle Commons. **Bushey:** NW area of Brenscombe Heath; plentiful along S area N of Bushey Lane (good views from Lane too). **Harman's Cross:** large colony W of path26 in S end of second field N of A351 (between woods) (with Southern Marsh Orchids and hybrids – to preserve the beauty of colony stay on path and do not take dogs). **Kingswood:** 80m N of NE corner of Foxground Plantation W of bridleway29; in SE arm of Kingswood Bog. **Studland Heath:** SE half of Spur Bog (with Early Marsh Orchid and hybrid).

Albinos occasional. See Plate 31.

Heath Spotted Orchid x Early Marsh Orchid – hybrid

Dactylorhiza x carnea
(D. maculata x incarnata)
Native. Occasional. Bogs. June.
Stoborough Heath: one seen at N end of Early Marsh Orchid colony 300m NE of A351 roundabout. **Hartland Moor:** here and there thinly in Upper Fen. **Corfe:** in several wet areas of Common. **Bushey:** on Brenscombe Heath near N edge 250m NE of gates at NW corner. **Kingswood:** SE arm of Kingswood Bog. **Studland Heath:** SE half of Spur Bog.

Heath Spotted Orchid x Southern Marsh Orchid – hybrid

Dactylorhiza x hallii
(D. maculata x praetermissa)
Native. Occasional. Heaths, verges,

wet fields, commons. June.
Stoborough Heath: 75m E of gateway on E side of Dismantled Tramway 625m N of A351 (with Heath Spotted Orchids). **Hartland Moor:** W side of Soldiers Road 450m from N end; S side of Arne Road 250m W of Arne Triangle; here and there on same side from 200m W of Triangle to Triangle itself (with Southern Marsh Orchids). **Corfe:** in several wet areas of Common. **Harman's Cross:** near path41 in N side of first field N of A351; near path26 in S end of next field to N (see note under Heath Spotted Orchid p.275).

Often difficult to tell from Common Spotted x Southern Marsh hybrid p.275. See Plate 32.

Early Marsh Orchid *Dactylorhiza incarnata* subsp. *pulchella*
Native. Occasional. Wet tracks, wet heaths, firmer ground in bogs. June.
Stoborough Heath: colony 300m NE of A351 roundabout; small colony in Rushy Hollow field 50m from NE end; on Dismantled Tramway 250-300m N of A351.
Hartland Moor: widely scattered along N side of Middle Fen E of Jubilee Bridge; 75m WSW of bend in electricity lines near words 'Hartland Moor' on O.S. map; W of Slepe Road 200m S of N cattle grid; near W side of Middlebere Triangle 100m N of S corner; in SW of heath SW of Scotland. **Corfe:** few halfway down South-west Valley of Middle Common; few scattered on Middle Common in area 30m W-E 60m S of Middle Common Pond.
Corfe Charity's Meadows: along N side of Close Next The Barn.
Bushey: on Brenscombe Heath 40m from N edge 250-300m NE of gates

at NW corner. **Kingswood:** midway N-S in SE arm of Kingswood Bog.
Godlingston Heath: small group W side of bog in Western Valley 425m NW of junction of bridleway27 and path32; single ones well spaced out from there N-wards to near SE corner of forest; at map reference SZ01508375; 100m NE of Lily Pond near Black Down; 150m ESE of Agglestone. **Studland Heath:** plentiful in SE half of Spur Bog.

The sides of the lower petal of this subspecies do not fold back until the floret has been out quite some time, and sometimes not even then. The deep petal colour fades with age. See Plate 32.

Early Marsh Orchid x Southern Marsh Orchid – hybrid
Dactylorhiza incarnata subsp. *pulchella* x *D. praetermissa*
Native. Rare. Commons. June.
Corfe: in several wet areas of Common.

Southern Marsh Orchid
Dactylorhiza praetermissa
Native. Occasional. Wet pastures and verges, marshes, dry downland. June.
Stoborough Heath: plentiful 20m S of N edge of Sandlings field 200m W of Dismantled Tramway.
Hartland Moor: W side of Soldiers Road 370m from N end; E side of Soldiers Road 250m SW of S cattle grid; here and there on S side of Arne Road from Soldiers Road to Arne Triangle especially the final 200m W of Arne Triangle (with hybrids with Heath Spotted Orchid); S side of Triangle itself; both sides of Slepe Road where it slopes down to Snag Valley from S.
Corfe Charity's Meadows: E of bri-

dleway3 just N of Close Next The Barn. **Corfe:** plentiful in most wet areas of Common. **Wytch:** by path80 – 25-30m W of Thrasher's Lane; along 200m of both sides of Thrasher's Lane S of bridleway4. **Bushey:** N side of Bushey Lane 550m E of bridleway10. **Rempstone:** large colony by bridleway34 (Oil Road) 350m SW of where bridleway31 crosses it. **Harman's Cross:** near path41 in N side of first field N of A351; near path26 in S end of next field to N (see important note under Heath Spotted Orchid p.275). **Durlston:** dry N-facing slope on E side of Field 6 SW of and above deep quarry; in South Field 15m from W hedge 65m N of Small Copse. **Studland:** S side of bridleway36 from 120-250m NW of Ferry Road; N side of same near Ferry road; S side of E end of bridleway38. **Brownsea:** SW of boardwalk through Orchid Meadow NE of church.

Early Spider Orchid
Ophrys sphegodes
Native. Frequent. Downland. April to early May.
Nationally Scarce.
Worth: S of top of steps by Coast Path on W side of Winspit Quarries. **Wares (west):** (including few with yellow frill to brown petal) many areas – particularly plentiful in Nicholas Down and Scratch Arse Ware (especially W and SE ends); **(east)** many areas – particularly plentiful in White Ware, Middle Ground, the sloping S end of Golter and N of Coast Path in centre of Belle Vue West Ware. **Knitson:** few 35m SW of hairpin corner at middle of zigzag track. **Durlston:** especially on downs and by tracks in

Skipworth Meadow. **Townsend Reserve:** on Orchid Bastion and nearby. **Ballard Down:** first one found by David Leadbetter in 2007.

This is one of the best areas in Britain for this species. At the last count, chiefly by David J. White in 2006, which only covered most areas from Nicholas Down eastwards to Balston Wear, there were over 17,000 flowering. Earlier complete surveys had been done by R. Burt (1988).

Plants are short-lived; half flower only once or twice. They may enter a dormant phase of one, two, three or rarely more years between flowering. About 50% of plants are dormant at any one time, so a population will be about double the number counted flowering. Plants are usually under 10cm high and bear 2 to 4 flowers. Only about 10% of capsules produced ripe seed in a Sussex population studied (compared with 45% on the continent); seed maturation took up to 3 months (Hutchings, 1990). See photo on back cover.

Bee Orchid *Ophrys apifera*
Native. Occasional. Calcareous grassland including lawns, clay cliffs, calcareous-based car parks. Mid-June.
Tyneham: here and there by Coast Path from Arish Mell to and around Flower's Barrow Hill Fort; S of Coast Path along top of Gad Cliff from 500-850m E of Worbarrow Bay (especially 650m from Bay). **Church Knowle:** lower part of down NE of Cocknowle. **Wares (west):** especially in Cliff Field near Coast Path (with aberrant ones). **Durlston:** especially both in NW of Smith Field and S end of The

Finches. **Townsend Reserve:** thin on and near Southern Plateau. **Swanage:** N side of Anglebury Avenue at junction with Wessex Way; private lawns W of N end of Horsecliffe Lane visible from Victoria Avenue (short-range binoculars help). **Studland:** Knoll Beach S car park. Few at other sites. Numbers of flowering plants vary from year to year. Often plants flower only once. See Plate 32.

Wasp Orchid

Ophrys apifera var. *trollii*
Native. Occasional. Calcareous grassland. Mid-June.
Wares: one or few at 15 sites, mostly in **west**, but do not always occur at most of them; however, regularly in large numbers at one site, which can be shown. Should be looked for wherever there are Bee Orchids.

Wasp Orchids have lower petal narrowly V-shaped, with ground colour pale or dark brown, and tip not bending backwards. It is surprising that it is not classed as a subspecies rather than as mere variety, bearing in mind how considerably differt it is from Bee Orchid.

It is good to be able to conclude this Plant List with the fact that The Wares is currently the best area in Britain for Wasp Orchids. See photo on back cover and Plate 32.

Bibliography

Blamey, M., Fitter, R. & Fitter, A. (2003) *Wild Flowers of Britain and Ireland*. A&C Black, London.

Blamey, M. & Grey-Wilson, C. (2003) *Wild Flowers of Britain and Northern Europe*. Cassell, London. (Formerly 1989. *The Illustrated Flora of Britain and Northern Europe*. Hodder and Stoughton.)

Bowen, H.J.M. (2000) *The Flora of Dorset*. Pisces Publications, Newbury, Berks.

Brendell, T. (1985) *Willows of The British Isles*. Shire Publications, UK.

Burt, R. (1988). *A Preliminary Investigation of the Autoecology of the Early Spider Orchid* (Ophrys sphegodes). Dorset County Council.

Chaffey, J. (2006) *Purbeck Landscapes*. Halsgrove (Dorset Books).

Chapman, S.B. (1975) The Distribution and Composition of Hybrid Populations of *Erica ciliaris* L. and *Erica tetralix* L. in Dorset. *Journal of Ecology* **63**, 809-823.

Cheffings, C.M. & Farrell, L. (2005) *The Vascular Plant Red Data List for Great Britain*. Joint Nature Conservation Committee.

Clement, E.J. (2004) What passes as *Leucanthemum* x *superbum*? *BSBI News* **96**.

Cox, J.H.S. (2003) A Sea Couch hybrid *Elytrigia* x *drucei* inland along an old Dorset tramway. *BSBI News* **94**.

Cramb, P. & Cramb, M. (2003) *Wild Flowers of the Dorset Coast Path*. Privately published.

Cramb, P. & Cramb, M. (2006) *Wild Flower Walks in Dorset*. Privately published.

Dudman, A.A. & Richards, A.J. (1997) *Dandelions of Great Britain and Ireland*. BSBI.

Edwards, B. & Pearman, D. (2004) *Dorset Rare Plant Register*. Dorset Environmental Records Centre.

Ensom, P. (1998) *Geology* (Discover Dorset series). Dovecote Press.

Fitter, R., Fitter, A. & Farrer, A. (1984) *Grasses, Sedges, Rushes and Ferns of Britain and Northern Europe*. Collins, London.

Ford, S. (2004) Cut and inject herbicide control of Japanese Knotweed *Fallopia japonica* at Rocky Valley, Cornwall, England. *Conservation Evidence* (2004) **1**, 1-2.

Good, R.D. (1948) *A Geographical Handbook to the Flora of Dorset*. Dorset County Museum.

Good, R.D. (1966) *The Old Roads of Dorset*. HG Commin, Bournemouth.

Good, R.D. (1984) *A Concise Flora of Dorset*. Dorset County Museum.

Graham, G.G. & Primavesi, A.L. (2005) *Roses of Great Britain and Ireland*. BSBI.

Haskins, L. (1978) *The Vegetational History of South-east Dorset*. University of Southampton, UK.

Horsfall, A. (1991) *Names of Wild Flowers in Dorset*. Privately published.

Hubbard, C.E. (1992) *Grasses – A guide to their Structure, Identification, Uses and Distribution in the British Isles*. Third Edition. Penguin, London.

Hutchins, M.J. (1990) The Role of Demographic Studies in Plant Conservation: the case of *Ophrys sphegodes* in Chalk Grassland. In *Calcareous Grassland – Ecology and Conservation* (Hillier, S., Wells, D. and Walton, D.W.H. eds.) Bluntisham Books, Huntingdon, Cambs.

Jenkinson, M.N. (1991) *Wild Orchids of Dorset*. Orchid Sundries Ltd., Stour Provost, Dorset.

Jermy, A.C., Simpson, D.A., Foley, M.J.Y. & Porter, M.S. (2007) *Sedges of the British Isles.* Third Edition. BSBI.

Johnson, O. & More, D. (2004) *Tree Guide.* Collins, London.

Keble Martin – see Martin

Kington, S. (1998) *International Daffodil Register and Classified List 1998.* www.rhs.org.uk/plants/registerpages/intro.asp

Lambinon, J., de Langhe, J.-E., Delvosalle, L & Duvigneaud, J. (1999) *Nouvelle Flore de la Belgique, du Grand-duche de Luxembourg, du Nord de la France et des regions voisines.* Fourth edition. Meise, Belgium.

Lousley, J.E. & Kent, D.H. (1981) Docks and Knotweeds of the British Isles. BSBI.

Mabey, R. (1972) *Food for Free.* Collins, London.

Mansel-Pleydell, J.C. (1874) *The Flora of Dorsetshire.* Whittaker, London & Shipp, Blandford, Dorset.

Mansel-Pleydell, J.C. (1895) *The Flora of Dorsetshire.* Second Edition. Dorchester.

Martin, W. Keble (1965) *The Concise British Flora in Colour.* Ebury Press & Michael Joseph, London.

Meikle, R.D. (1984) *Willows and Poplars of Great Britain and Ireland.* BSBI.

Mitchell, A. (1978) *Field Guide to the Trees of Britain and Northern Europe.* Second Edition. Collins, London.

Mundell, A. (2001) *Conyza bilbaoana* is on its way to you. *BSBI News* 87.

Pearman, D.A. (1994) *Sedges and their Allies in Dorset.* Dorset Environmental Records Centre.

Pearman, D.A & Edwards, B. (2002) *Valerianella eriocarpa* in Dorset, and a reassessment of its status as a presumed introduction in Britain. *Watsonia* 24 Part 1, BSBI.

Pearman, D.A. & Rumsey, F.J. (2004) *Drosera x belezeana* confirmed for the British Isles. *Watsonia* 25 Part 1, BSBI.

Picton, P. (1999) *The Gardener's Guide to Growing Asters.* David and Charles, Newton Abbot, Devon.

Pope, C., Snow, L. & Allen, D. (2003) *The Isle of Wight Flora.* Dovecote Press, Wimborne Minster, Dorset.

Pratt, E.A. (2002) *Valerianella eriocarpa* in Dorset. *BSBI News* 91.

Preston, C.D. (1995) *Pondweeds of Great Britain and Ireland.* BSBI.

Preston, C.D., Pearman, D.A. & Dines, T.D. (2002) *New Atlas of the British and Irish Flora.* Oxford University Press, Oxford.

Rich, T.C.G. (1991) *Crucifers of Great Britain and Ireland.* BSBI.

Rich, T.C.G. & Jermy, A.C. (1998) *Plant Crib 1998.* BSBI.

Rose, F. (1989) *Colour Identification Guide to the Grasses, Sedges, Rushes and Ferns of the British Isles and north-western Europe.* . Viking, London.

Rose, F. & O'Reilly, C. (2006) *The Wild Flower Key – How to identify wild flowers, trees and shrubs in Britain and Ireland.* Revised Expanded Edition. Frederick Warne, London.

Rose, R.J. (2007) The effects of hybridization on the small-scale variation in seed-bank composition of a rare plant species, *Erica ciliaris* L. *Seed Science Research* 17, 201-210.

Rose, R.J., Clarke, R.T. & Chapman, S.B. (1998) Individual variation and the effects of weather, age and flowering history on survival and flowering of the long-lived perennial *Gentiana pneumonanthe.* *Ecography* 21, 317-326.

Ryves, T.B., Clement, E.J. & Foster, M.C. (1996) *Alien Grasses of the British Isles.* BSBI.

Smith, M. (2007) *Galeopsis bifida* and *G. tetrahit*: some interesting observations. *BSBI News* **104**.

Stace, C.A. (1997) *New Flora of the British Isles*. Second Edition. Cambridge University Press, Cambridge.

Stace, C.A. (1999) *Field Flora of The British Isles*. Cambridge University Press.

Stace, C.A., Van der Meijden, R. & De Kort, I. (2004) *Interactive Flora of The British Isles*. (DVD Rom). ETI Information Services.

Tutin, T.G. (1980) *Umbellifers of The British Isles*. BSBI.

Wild Flower Society (1990) *A Guide to Some Difficult Plants*. E. Norman ed. Wild Flower Society, Sawston, Cambs.

Woodhead, F. (1994) *Flora of the Christchurch Area*. Privately published.

Additional reading:

Brewis, A., Bowman, P. & Rose, F. (1996) *The Flora of Hampshire*. Harley Books.

BSBI Species List on BSBI website: www.bsbi.org.com

Clement, E.J. & Foster, M.C. (1994) *Alien Plants of The British Isles*. BSBI.

Haskins, L. (2003) *Heathlands*. Dorset Wildlife Trust, Dovecote Press.

Horsfall, A. (2003) *Woodlands*. Dorset Wildlife Trust, Dovecote Press.

Mahon, A. (1990) *Dorset Wildlife*. Dorset Wildlife Trust, Dovecote Press.

Mahon, A. & Pearman, D.A. (1993) *Endangered Wildlife in Dorset; The County Red Data Book*. Dorset Environmental Records Centre.

White, J. (2003) *Downs, Meadows and Pastures*. Dorset Wildlife Trust, Dovecote Press.

Wright, J. (2003) *Rivers and Streams*. Dorset Wildlife Trust, Dovecote Press.

Appendix

Author's address: 7, Bay Close, Swanage, Dorset, BH19 1RE (send a stamped addressed envelope or your email address if you would like a reply).

Bennett's Water Garden, Chickerell, north of Weymouth, opens April to September, 10am to 5pm, except Mondays and Saturdays (but open on Bank Holidays).

Boatman at Wareham – T: 01929 550688.

Bournemouth Natural Science Society, 39 Christchurch Road, Bournemouth, BH1 3NS, T: 01202 553525. Only open on Tuesday mornings; it is advisable to telephone.

Dorset County Museum, High West Street, Dorchester, DT1 1XA, T: 01305 756821 or 62735. The herbarium may be seen by appointment.

Dorset Flora Group – details from Dorset Environmental Records Centre: derc@dorsetcc.gov.uk or DERC, Library HQ, Colliton Park, Dorchester, DT1 1XJ.

Dorset Wildlife Trust, Brooklands Farm, Forston, Dorchester, DT2 7AA, www.dorsetwildlife.co.uk .

Durlston Country Park, Swanage, BH19 2JL, www.durlston.co.uk .

National Trust, Countryside Office, Middle Beach, Studland, BH19 3AX, T: 01929 450259.

RSPB, Syldata, Arne, Dorset, BH20 5BJ, T: 01929 553360.

Trailwise, Unit R, Mount Pleasant Trading Estate, Mount Pleasant Street, Ashton-under-Lyne, OL6 6HT, T: 0161 343 6166.

Acknowledgements

I am most grateful to those who have taught me to recognise and appreciate flowers, beginning with my late mother Margaret Alice Pratt and late aunts Phyllis Pratt and Kathleen Bland, and also the late County Recorders Kathleen Hollick (Derbyshire), Lady Anne Brewis and Paul Bowman (Hampshire), and also the late Francis Rose.

About one eighth of the plant locations were first discovered by other people, and I am very grateful to others from whom I have learned them, directly or indirectly, including Kathryn Bailey, Naomi Bailey, Katie Black, the late Joyce Bowcott, Ben Bowerman, the late Joan Bowyer, Tim Brodie-James, Dick Burt, Andy Byfield, Ann Cargill, Steve Chapman, Rebecca Charron, Kevin Cook, Ilay Cooper, Jonathan Cox, Rees Cox, Peter Cramb, Tony Dicks, Tricia Earley, Dorothy Evans, David and Melanie Eyles, Julie Floyd, Michael Galliott, Abigail Gibbs, John and Rosemary Gilbert, Phil Grey, Geoff Hann, Tony Hannah, George Hounsome, Anne Horsfall, A.W. (Wilberforce) Jones, Hilarie Lewis, The Rev. David Lloyd, the late Michael Lock, Terence Molloy, Hamish Murray, Steve O'Connell, the late Caroline O'Keeffe, Angela Peters, Bryan Pickess, Robin Plowman, Paul St. Pierre, Chris Preston, Dominic Sheldon, Nick Sturt, P. Symmons, Laurence Taylor, W.G. (Bunny) Teagle, Chris Thain, Jennifer Tiptaft, Scott Titt, Ali Tuckey, Sophie Tweddle, Robin Walls, Margaret Whaley, David White, Jim White, John and Diana Winterbottom, Felicity Woodhead, John F. Wright. I apologise if I have inadvertently omitted anyone. I am also grateful to Carolyn Steele, Alison Stewart and Julia Armstrong of the Dorset Environmental Records Centre, and especially the late Humphry Bowen, and to David Pearman and Bryan Edwards, the past and joint present County Botanical Recorders, who have helped me with details of many sites. I most especially thank David Leadbetter who has also told me of many sites and with whom I have enjoyed hours looking for plants.

I thank Bunny Teagle also for permission to base my sketch map of Townsend Nature Reserve on his, authors of past Reports for The National Trust and other bodies, including Hilary Wallace, Mike Prosser, Charles Flynn and Jonathan Graham. I also thank Anne Cole for finding papers in Natural England's Library, Nigel Webb for access to papers at the Centre of Ecology and Hydrology at Winfrith, Sarah Williams for copies of some Dorset Wildlife Trust road verge surveys, Eric Clement for help with definitions of the words subspecies and variety, also with the Blackthorn virus, William Bond, Peter Bowyer, Geoff and Greta Hann, Treleven Haysom, Colin Nunn, Steve O'Connell, Ann Richards, Guy Ryder, Reg Savile, Trish Sherwood, Phil Stuckey, Doreen White and the staff of the Dorset History Centre for help with place names, Ian MacKenzie, Carol McKay and Steve Kourik for information on public rights of way, Brian Darnton for microscopic identification of Polypodies, Steve Chapman and Rob Rose for copies of their papers on Marsh Gentian and Dorset Heath, Lesley Haskins for a copy of her paper on Dorset Heath, Tony Mundell for information on Marsh Bedstraw leaf-edge prickles, Martin Rand for help with Tor Grasses, John Langmaid for his experience of Mistletoe germination, Ian Killick for information about sheep eating Ivy, Arthur Chater for guidance on Greater Plantain subspecies, Mary Gillham for information on Shoreweed, Arthur Hoare, Tim Rich and David McCosh for help with a Hawkweed, Anita Diaz for advice based on her research on Italian Lords-and-ladies,

Tom Cope for information on the scientific names of species of Brome and Couch Grasses, Clive Stace for help with several species, Nick Viney for agricultural advice on Rye-grasses, Dick Burt for information from his work on Early Spider Orchids, Geoff Hann for advice on deer, John Chaffey and David Pearman for comments on the geology paragraphs, David Haines for information on infectious diseases, Durlston Country Park for the photograph of Early Gentian, my wife Jo who helps me to enjoy the beauty of common flowers as much as rarities and who spots plants I have missed.

I am grateful for help with identification from referees appointed by the Botanical Society of the British Isles, usually for a particular genus, including: P. Acock (Horsetails), the late R.H. Roberts (Polypodies), C.S. Crook (Conifers), M.G. Daker (Fumitories), M. Coleman (Elms), J.R. Akeroyd (Oraches), the late S.M. Walters (Campions), N.K.B. Robson (St. John's Worts), M.C.F. Procter (Rockroses), D.M. Moore (Violets), T.T. Elkington (Whitlowgrasses), E.C. Nelson (Heaths), A. Newton (Brambles), R. Maskew (Roses), J. Poland (Cherries), T.D. Pennington (Willowherbs), P. Benoit (Storksbills), R.M. Harley (Woundworts), V. Johnstone (Mulleins), A.J. Silverside (Eyebrights), C.D. Preston (Pondweeds), T.A. Cope (Rushes and Grasses), A.O. Chater, M.S. Porter and M.J.Y. Foley (Sedges), J.R. Edmondson (Meadow-grasses), R.M. Bateman (Marsh Orchids), M. Cragg-Barber (Aberrations),and for help from A.C. Leslie (Reedmaces), and especially for help on numerous occasions from R.D. Meikle (Willows), A.L. Primavesi (Roses), J. Fryer (Cotoneasters), M.J. Crawley (Daffodils) and E.J. Clement (Aliens).

We should all be grateful to the owners of those areas open to the public, especially the major ones, who manage them, or see that they are managed, with wildlife in mind: The Ministry of Defence (Army Range Walks), Smedmore Estate (Steeple Down), The Royal Society for the Protection of Birds (Grange Heath, parts of Stoborough Heath, The Moors, much of Arne), Holme Estate (part of Battle Plain), Richard Bond (Whiteway Hill), Dorset Wildlife Trust (Stonehill Down, Kilnwood, and Townsend Reserves), Imerys Minerals Ltd. (Creech Heath), Natural England (the rest of Stoborough Heath, half of Hartland Moor), Dennis and Norman Randall (Knowle Hill – west), Simon Edwards (Knowle Hill – central), Rodney Parker (Knowle Hill – east: Buncknowle Hill), Jennifer Barnard (Norden Heath), The National Trust (half of Hartland Moor, West Hill (Corfe), Corfe Castle, Corfe Common, East Man, Purbeck Wares, King's Wood, Godlingston Heath, Ballard Down, Studland Heath, Brownsea, and other smaller areas), Rempstone Estate (East and Challow Hills, Wytch Moor, Brenscombe Heaths, Kingswood Bog), Alan Helfer (down above Knitson), Dorset County Council (Durlston Country Park). We should be grateful to the tenants and managers too; they are too numerous to list.

I am particularly grateful to those who have kindly made comments on this book or parts of it, including David Allen, Jeanette Guinness, Anne Horsfall, David White, John and Diana Winterbottom and my family. John F. Wright made detailed suggestions which considerably improved the writing of the Introduction.

Most especially I thank the two people who read a draft of the book three-quarters of the way through the writing, and who made many suggestions and corrections. One is David Leadbetter, who has lived nearly all his life in Purbeck. He also has a good eye for typing errors. The other is David Pearman, the joint County Botanical Recorder and joint editor of *The New Atlas*, who made several suggestions for improving the layout. He also corrected a number of mistakes, particularly regarding status and habitat. Any errors made since are mine.

I thank Nicola and Hugh Loxdale of Brambleby Books for correcting other mistakes, and noticing inconsistencies, helping me to express myself more clearly and briefly, supplying the name of the lupin aphid and the reference for Japanese Knotweed control and Nicola especially for carefully adding shading to the sketch maps. I also thank botanical artists Sally Pinhey and Delf Smith for guidance in drawing.

The length of these acknowledgements shows that I have endeavoured to thank all who have helped me; if however anyone has been omitted I sincerely apologise to them.

Finally I thank those who made improvements to the Epilogue: my wife Jo, our family – Andrew, Jonathan and Julia – and to Garry Guinness.

Flowers and Faith
- a personal epilogue

In the 19th century most country parishes had their own clergymen. They usually had large gardens, and either walked or rode on horseback when visiting. So it is not surprising that some of them wrote about the flowers of their area. Today a rural Vicar has several parishes and rushes around in a car, being more concerned to take a bend at the safest speed than about knowing what grows on its banks! There are not many parson-naturalists these days. So it seems appropriate to me to conclude with a few things I have learned of how flowers are used in the Bible to illustrate truths about life and death.

Creation
The Bible states that God is creator. As the writer of Psalm 104 states – 'He makes grass grow for the cattle, and plants for man to cultivate - bringing forth food from the earth: wine that gladdens the heart of man, (olive) oil to make his face shine, and bread that sustains his heart.' As I look into a flower, sometimes with a lens, and examine the wonderful and beautiful detail of it, I am often moved to thank God.

The biblical account of creation also teaches that God has put men and women in charge of the Earth. We are to 'rule ... over all the earth ... and subdue it'. From that, it seems, we are called to conserve it. Conservationists have a variety of good motives; obedience to God is a motive for some. In these days of global warming we all need to treat the Earth better.

Later in the Old Testament it says that King Solomon (the first botanist?) gave names to plants, a process which has been continuing ever since: 'Solomon ... described plant life, from the cedar of Lebanon to the hyssop that grows out of walls'.

Learning from flowers
In the Bible, flowers are used to remind us that our life on earth is only temporary. Job reflects: 'Man ... is of few days ... he springs up like a flower and withers away'. Thus, I personally need to be ready to meet God when I die.

Psalm 103 says much the same, but goes on to draw an encouraging contrast with God's love: 'As for man, his days are like grass, he flourishes like a flower of the field; the wind blows over it and it is gone, and its place remembers it no more. But from everlasting to everlasting the Lord's love is with those who fear him ...'.

The Bible also draws a contrast between the short life of humans and flowers and the enduring nature of itself – the word of God. The prophet Isaiah said: 'All people are like grass ... the grass withers and the flowers fall, but the word of our God stands for ever'. I enjoy reading it, and find it as relevant as ever in the twenty-first century.

In childhood, I learned how the wise men brought symbolic gifts of gold, frankincense and myrrh to the child Jesus. In adulthood, I have learned that the latter two of those precious gifts come from the resin of the desert shrubs *Boswellia* and *Commiphora*. In Judaism, only a priest could burn incense, and so that gift indicated that Jesus would have a priestly ministry. Myrrh, however, was a spice used in a burial. That foretold that the death of Jesus would be significant, and in fact his crucifixion was a priestly offering, in which he bore the sins of the world.

Jesus' teaching from flowers

I like the botanical illustrations, so easy to remember, that Jesus used in his teaching ministry. One story was of a sower scattering seed, which fell on different types of ground, but only grew to maturity on good soil. This, Jesus said, was like the message of God's kingdom – it is only fruitful in the lives of some of its hearers.

Another story is of a farmer's enemy sowing weeds – probably poisonous darnel – among the wheat. Farm-workers asked if they could pull the darnel up, but the farmer forbade them to do so until the harvest, in case they pulled up some of the wheat as well. This, Jesus said, was a picture of how God waits until death to separate those going to heaven from those who will not.

Jesus said that just as a small mustard seed grows into a tree, so his kingdom would grow from its small beginnings. How true this has proved to be. Anyone who turns in repentance to follow Jesus Christ enters his kingdom, I believe. His followers now number millions the world over.

As I have sought to follow Jesus, I have experienced his provision in my life, time and again, as Jesus himself taught from flowers in his Sermon on the Mount. He said: 'See how the lilies of the field grow. They do not labour or spin. Yet I tell you that not even Solomon [the richest Old Testament king] in all his splendour was dressed like one of these. If that is how God clothes the grass of the field, which is here today and tomorrow is thrown into the fire, will he not much more clothe you, O ye of little faith?'

Heaven and botany

I realise that my body is gradually wearing out. But I believe that God will give me a new and perfect body in heaven. In his first letter to the Christians at Corinth, the Apostle Paul makes the point by using the illustration of a perishable seed (like our human body) being sown and so disappearing from view in the earth. Then a plant grows from it, a new body. Similarly, after death God gives a Christian a new body, far more splendid, imperishable and fit for heaven.

Before Jesus ascended to heaven he promised to come back to earth. Old Testament writers foresaw this, and sometimes describe it poetically, using imagery involving flowers and trees. The prophet Isaiah wrote: '... the wilderness will rejoice and blossom. Like the crocus it will burst into bloom; it will rejoice greatly and shout for joy ... they will see the glory of the Lord'. In Psalm 96 too: 'Let ... the fields be jubilant and everything in them. Then all the trees of the forest will sing for joy; they will sing before the Lord. For he comes, he comes to judge the earth. He will judge the world in righteousness and the peoples in his truth'.

Index

Backcover:
Early Spider Orchid   Godlingston Heath
Nit Grass   Marsh Gentian
Wasp Orchid   Godlingston Sundew

Front Cover:
Corfe Castle
Inset: Dorset Heath

Primroses on Steeple Down

Common Mallow and Sea Campion in foreground – looking South-East
from Coast Path near Kimmeridge

Plate 1

Purple Loosestrife by River Frome

Icen Barrow Pond on Creech Heath

Plate 2

Hartland Moor from Slepe Road

A Purbeck bridleway (with author's wife)

Plate 3

Common Knapweed in the meadow South-West of Sharford Bridge

Low-lying flower-rich wet area of West Common, Corfe

Plate 4

Looking along The Purbeck Wares in the evening sun

Southern Marsh Orchids by a Rempstone bridleway

Plate 5

Lighthouse Field, Durlston Country Park – home to many notable species

Godlingston Heath looking over Western Valley with Poole Harbour,
Brownsea Island and Sandbanks (on right) in the distance

Plate 6

A scene from Primrose Way, Studland

Stable dunes north of Knoll Beach car park,
where small scarce plants can be found in early summer

Plate 7

Planted trees on Brownsea, left to right:
False Acacia, Sweet Chestnut, young Wellingtonia, English Oak, Horse Chestnut

Ballard Cliffs at the end of May

Sandy grassland at Sandbanks contains some interesting small species

Plate 8

The rare Corn Buttercup's spiky seedcases

Small-flowered Buttercups
– short of petals as usual

Greater Stitchwort brightens banks in spring

Upright Chickweed fully open in sun

Plate 9

Sheep's Sorrel turning a field red

Watercress, Yellow Iris and Hawthorn at Challow Pond

Pale St John's Wort at Corfe

Limonium dodartiforme – the Rock Sea-lavender confined to the Dorset coast

Plate 10

Dorset Heath – the County Flower, an albino of it

Hybrid of Dorset and Cross-leaved Heaths, almost confined to Purbeck

Primrose, normal and umbelled forms

Primrose and False Oxlip (Primrose/Cowslip hybrid)

Plate 11

False Oxlip in its glory

Cowslip field, Acton

Yellow Loosestrife, Corfe Charity's Meadows

Lake Loosestrife – a rare escape

Plate 12

Bog Pimpernel − small is beautiful

Mossy Stonecrop turns scarlet in May

English Stonecrop on Brand's Bay shore

Trailing Tormentil − some flowers
with four petals, some with five.

Plate 13

Rare hybrid of Sweetbriar and Small-flowered Sweetbriar

Sainfoin at Durlston

Hairy Birdsfoot Trefoil
– a species of sandyground.

Plate 14

Narrow-leaved Everlasting-pea, Kimmeridge

Grass Vetchling, Durlston

Yellow Vetchling, Durlston

Zigzag Clover
– note short stalk under flower

Plate 15

South Middlebere looking east, with white Subterranean Clover in foreground and White House Wood on left.

Dyer's Greenweed at Durlston

Petty Whin, scarce near Hartland Moor

Plate 16

The three species of Gorse in flower together on Godlingston Heath – Dwarf Gorse (foreground), Western Gorse (left) & Gorse.

Stars-in-grass, Steeple Down

Allseed, one of Purbeck's smallest species – rabbit droppings give scale!

Whorled Caraway and Vipersgrass at Arne Moors

Plate 17

Meadow Cranesbill, Kingswood roadside

Wild Carrots

Wild Carrot, showing red florets in centre

Plate 18

Tufted Centaury
near Lighthouse at Durlston

Early Gentian, Durlston (photo from
Durlston Country Park collection)

Albino Marsh Gentian

Hybrid of Hedge and Marsh Woundwort
with Small Skipper butterfly

Plate 19

Marjoram, with Grayling and Gatekeeper
butterflies enjoying it

Common Toadflax, a roadside species

Yellow Bartsia, frequent near NE of
Stoborough Heath

Foxgloves near Little Sea

Plate 20

Lousewort on Corfe Common

Toothwort in Stonehill Down Woods

Ivy Broomrape, Durlston

Nordic Bladderwort at Hartland Moor

Plate 21

Townsend Reserve, with blue sheen of Hairy-fruited Cornsalad on anthill

Hairy-fruited Cornsalad

Nettle-leaved Bellflower at East Creech

Hybrid of Hedge and Lady's Bedstraw

Plate 22

Small Scabious in fruit and in flower

Carline Thistle at its golden best

Great Burdock

Woolly Thistle in bud

Plate 23

Musk Thistle

Milk Thistle

Broad-headed form of Common Knapweed,
with Clouded Yellow butterfly

Plate 24

Albino Common Knapweed
in meadow SW of Sharford Bridge

Smooth Catsear, South Middlebere

Golden Samphire in a cliff quarry

Sea Aster with Rock Samphire

Plate 25

Ox-eye Daisies and Rough Hawkbit, Durlston

Hen and Chickens Daisy and normal Daisy

Sneezewort on Corfe Common

Plate 26

Flowering-rush   Lesser Water-plantain, Corfe Common Pond

Leaves of Italian Lords-and-ladies, The Wares   Not a grass but Floating Club-rush

Plate 27

Brown Beak-sedge

Bog Sedge on Hartland Moor

Early Meadow-grass
on right of coin, at Sandbanks

Dotted Sedge on Studland Heath

Plate 28

Bristle Bent in seed on Godlingston Heath

Early Sand-grass at Studland

Least Bur-reed in centre

Red, white and blue –
Red Campion, Ramsons and Bluebells

Plate 29

Ramsons by public path through Quarry Wood, Kingston

Snowdrops at Steeple

Wild Daffodils

Plate 30

Autumn Lady's-tresses
– showing why it is *Spiranthes spiralis*

Pyramidal Orchids

Green-winged Orchid

Heath Spotted Orchids

Plate 31

Early Marsh Orchid subspecies *pulchella*

Hybrid of Heath Spotted and Southern Marsh Orchids

Bee Orchid

Wasp Orchid – dark form

Plate 32

Map 1: The Isle of Purbeck, Brownsea and Sandbanks

BRANKSOME CHINES

LILLIPUT

LUSCOMBE VALLEY

CANFORD CLIFFS

SANDBANKS

22 BROWNSEA

9 ARNE

HOLME

2 WAREHAM (SOUTH), RIDGE, STOBOROUGH, STOBOROUGH HEATH

5 HARTLAND MOOR

13 OWER, REMPSTONE

19 SHELL BAY, STUDLAND HEATH

3 CREECH, CREECH HEATH, EAST CREECH

6 FURZEBROOK, NORDEN

10 WYTCH, BUSHEY

17 GODLINGSTON HEATH

20 STUDLAND, BALLARD DOWN

7 CHURCH KNOWLE

11 CORFE CASTLE AND COMMON

14 WOOL-GARSTON, HARMAN'S CROSS, LANGTON MATRAVERS

KINGSWOOD, KNITSON, ULWELL, GODLINGSTON, HERSTON (NORTH) 18

TYNE-HAM

4 STEEPLE, KIMMERIDGE

8 KINGSTON

SWANAGE

12 WORTH MATRAVERS

15 WARES (WEST)

16 WARES (EAST)

21 DURLSTON

Signs and letters on more than one map:

— — **14** — —	Public path with its number
— **14** —	Public bridleway with its number
• • • • •	Unclassified road (route with public access; UCR)
– – – – –	Other track open to public
– –	Start of private track used as reference point
· · · · · · · · ·	Parish boundary
△	Trig point
→	Entrance point to open access area other than by path
↔	Gateway or stile
+	Church
B	Boardwalk

C	Camp site
F	Field
G	Cattle grid
H	Hide (for birdwatching)
P	Parking: one car or sometimes more
P	Car Park
PB	Permissive bridleway
PP	Permissive path
PW	Purbeck Way
Q	Quarry
R	Restaurant
T	Toilets
V	Viewpoint
X	Tumulus

For other explanations about the sketch maps please see pages 10, 14 and 51.

Map 2: Wareham (south), Stoborough, Stoborough Heath and Ridge

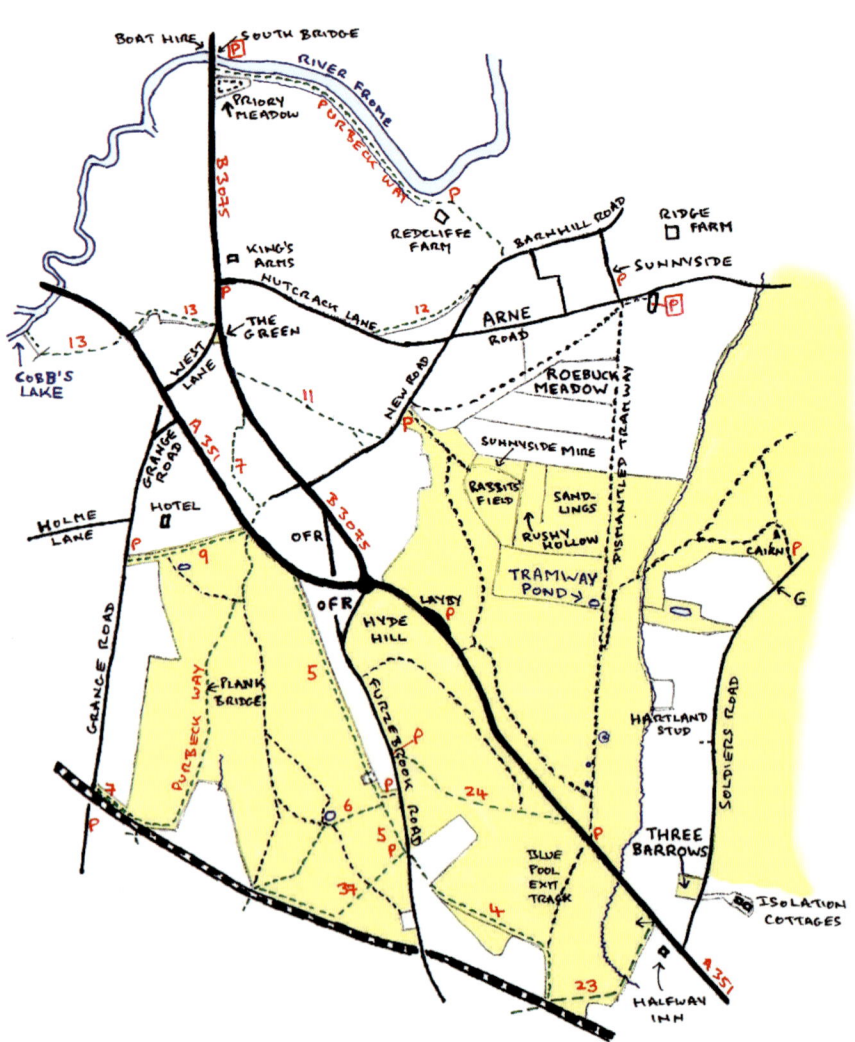

OFR   Old Furzebrook Road

Map 3: Creech, Creech Heath and East Creech

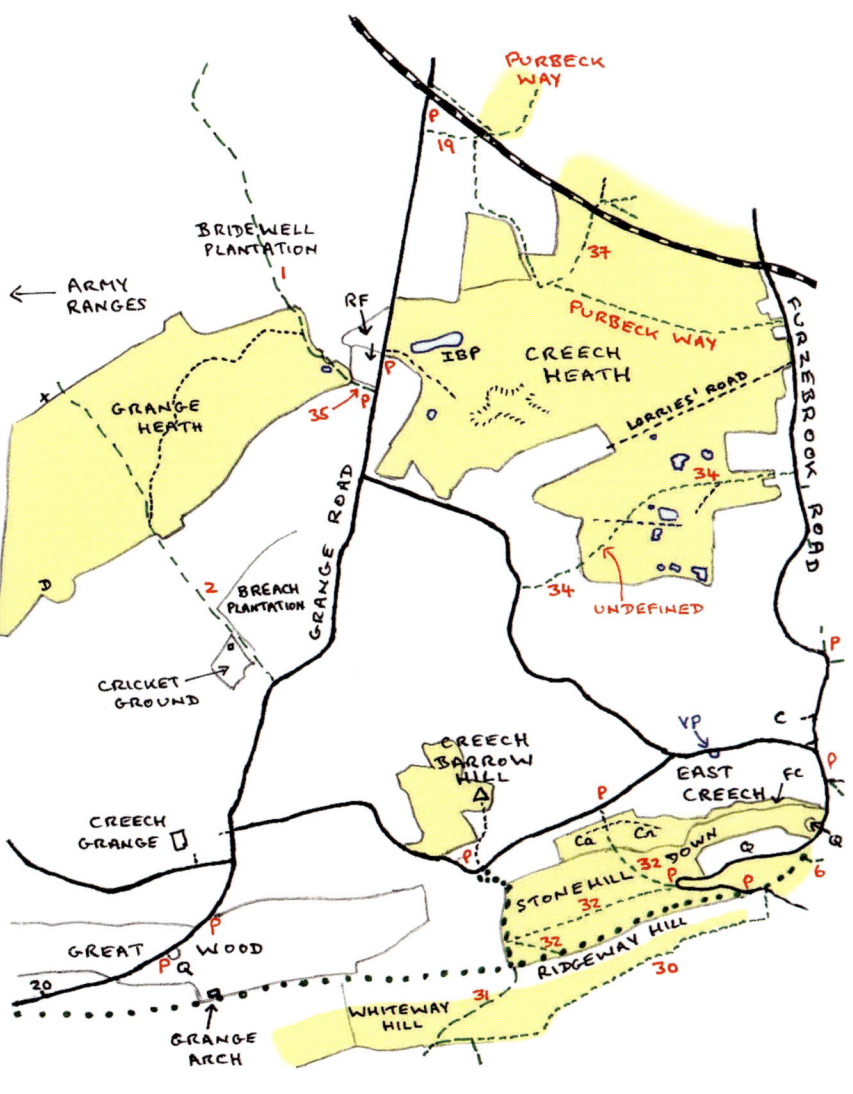

20	'20%' road sign	**FC**	Furlong's Coppice
Ca	Caldecot's Wood	**IB**	Icen Barrow Pond
Cr	Creech Wood	**RF**	RSPB fields
DB	Drinking Barrow	**VP**	Village Pond

Map 4: Kimmeridge and Steeple

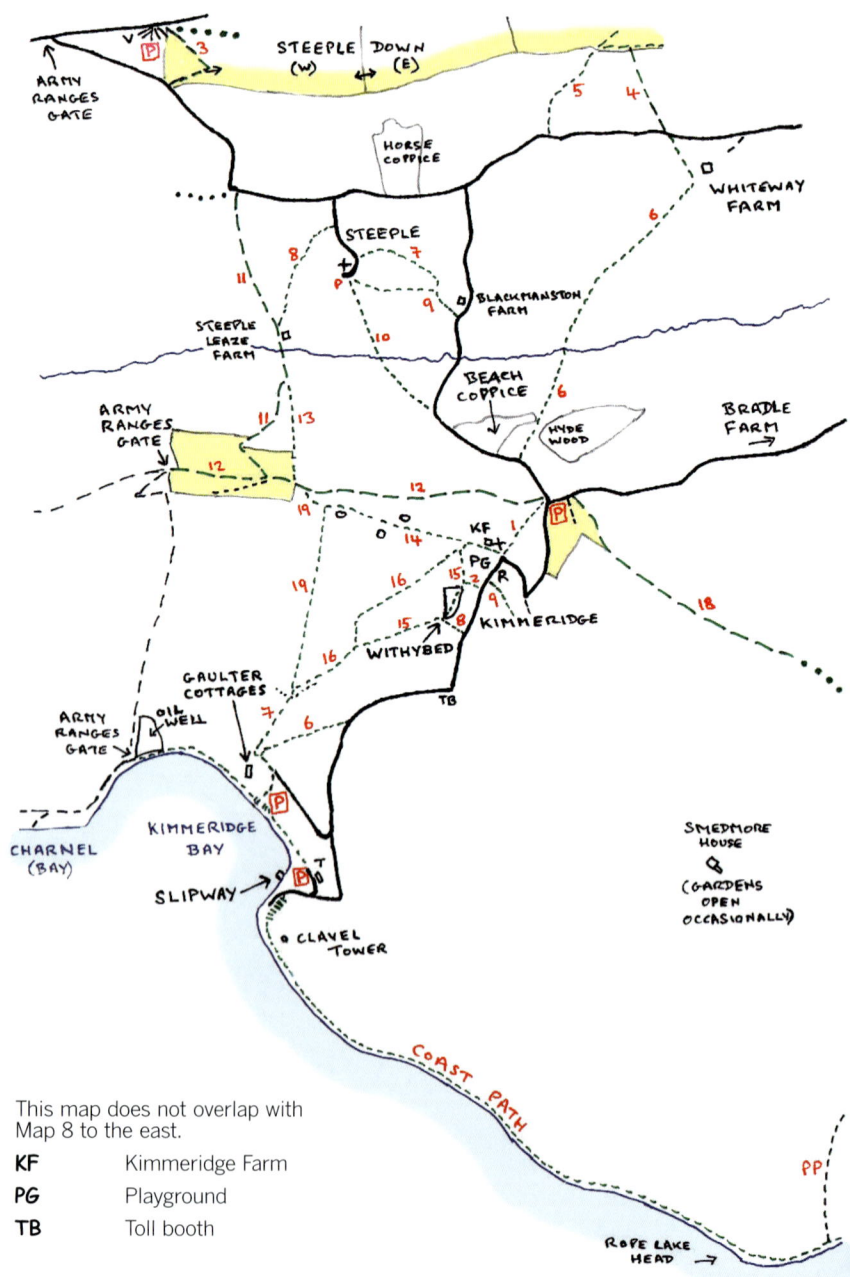

This map does not overlap with Map 8 to the east.

KF — Kimmeridge Farm
PG — Playground
TB — Toll booth

Map 5: Hartland Moor and surrounding area

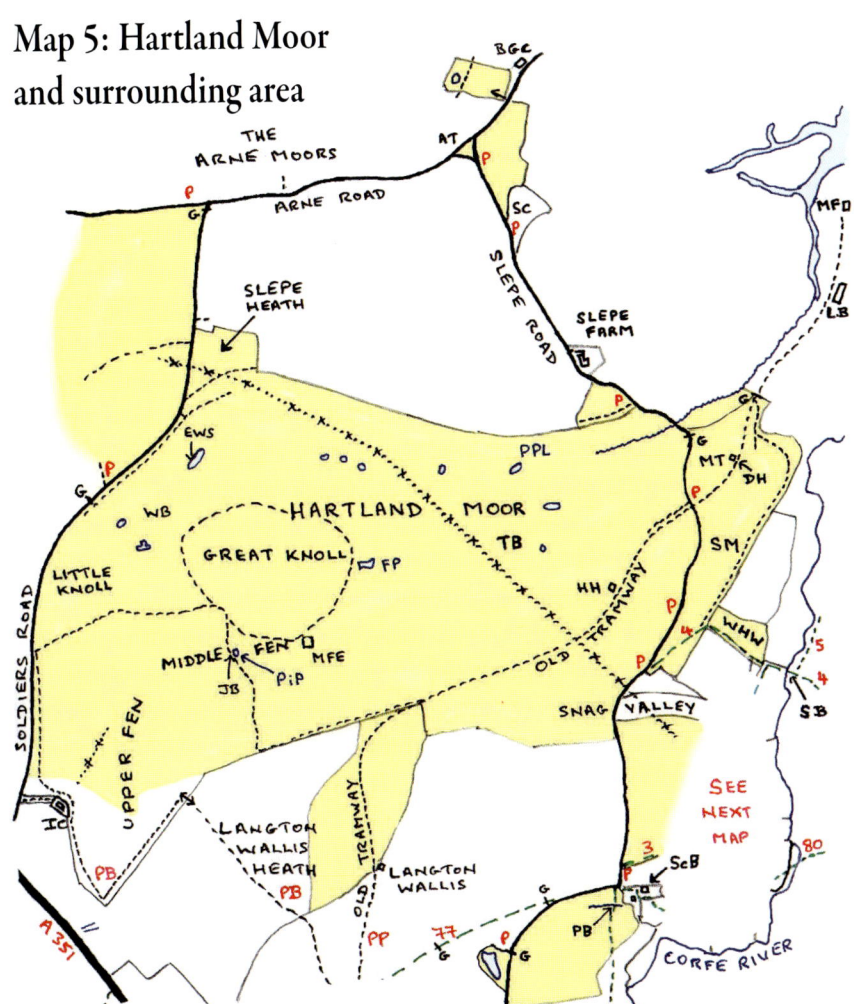

There are other tracks on the heath not shown on this map, so as to avoid congestion.

AT	Arne Triangle		**MT**	Middlebere Triangle
BGC	Bank Gate Cottages		**PiP**	Pillwort Pond
DH	Dartford Hide		**PB**	Plank bridge
EWS	'EWS' sign (Emergency water supply)		**PPL**	Post Pool
			SB	Sharford Bridge
FP	Fen Pool		**ScB**	Scotland Barn
HH	Hart Hide		**SC**	Slepe Copse
IC	Isolation Cottages		**SM**	South Middlebere
JB	Jubilee Bridge		**TB**	Tramway Bog
LB	Large barns		**WB**	West Bog
MFE	Middle Fen Exclosure		**WHW**	White House Wood

Map 5A: Corfe Charity's Meadows area (large scale)

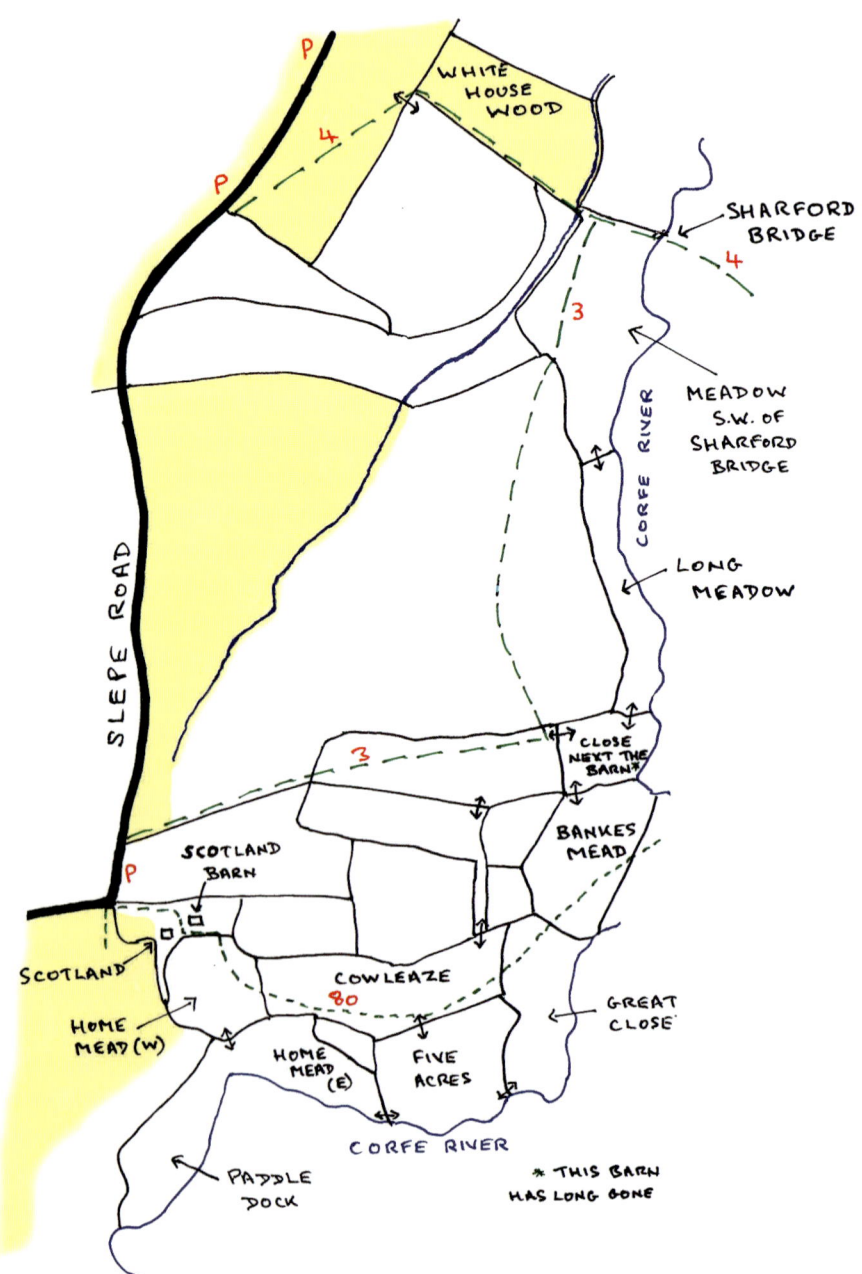

P

WHITE
HOUSE
WOOD

4

P

SHARFORD
BRIDGE

4

3

MEADOW
S.W. OF
SHARFORD
BRIDGE

CORFE RIVER

LONG
MEADOW

SLEPE ROAD

3

CLOSE
NEXT THE
BARN*

BANKES
MEAD

P

SCOTLAND
BARN

SCOTLAND

COWLEAZE
80

GREAT
CLOSE

HOME
MEAD (W)

HOME
MEAD
(E)

FIVE
ACRES

CORFE RIVER

PADDLE
DOCK

* THIS BARN
HAS LONG GONE

Map 6: Furzebrook and Norden

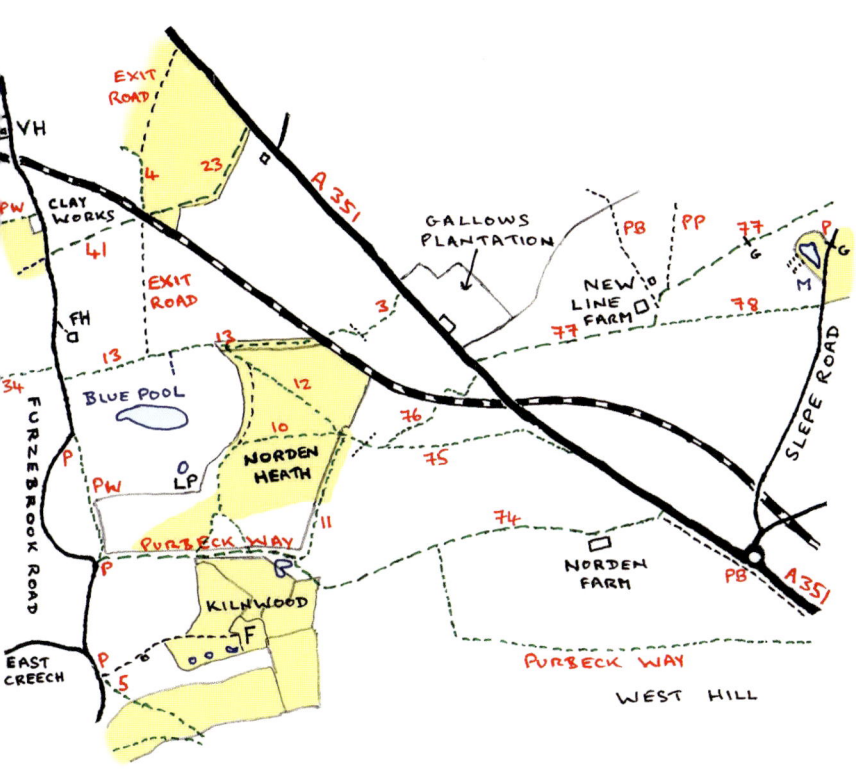

FH	Furzebrook House
LP	Little Pool
MP	Michael's Pond
P&R	Park and ride
VH	Village Hall

Norden Heath is marked in the wrong place on the O.S. map.

Bridleway 41 has been recently designated and so may not appear as a bridleway on the O.S. map.

Map 7: Church Knowle

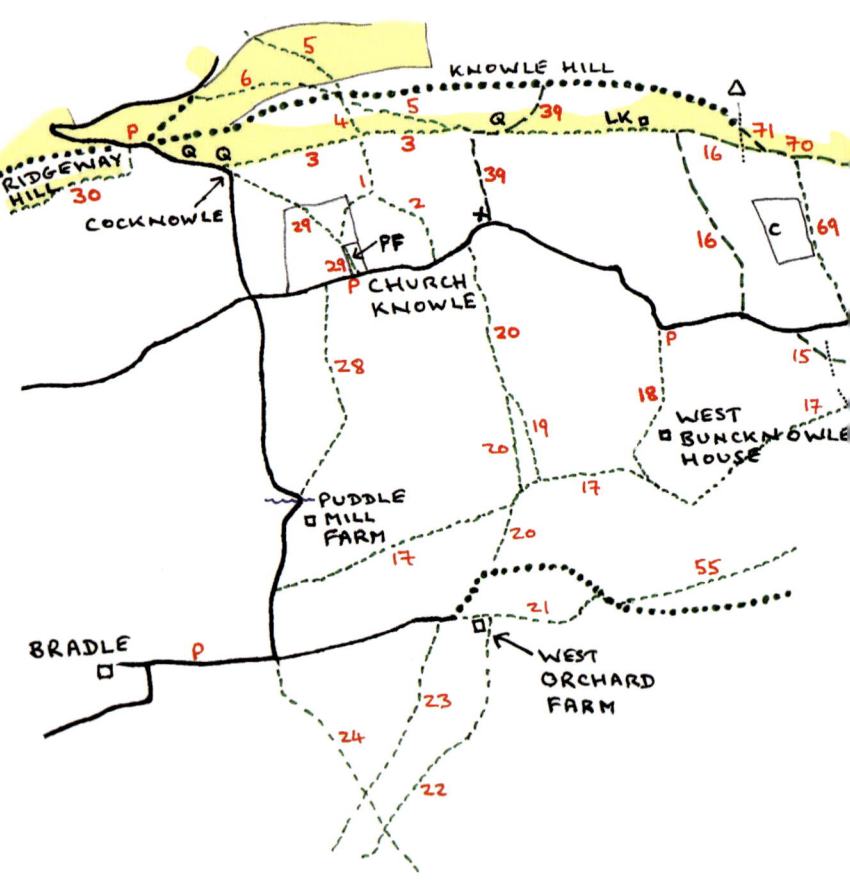

LM   Lime Kiln
PF   Playing field

Map 8: Kingston

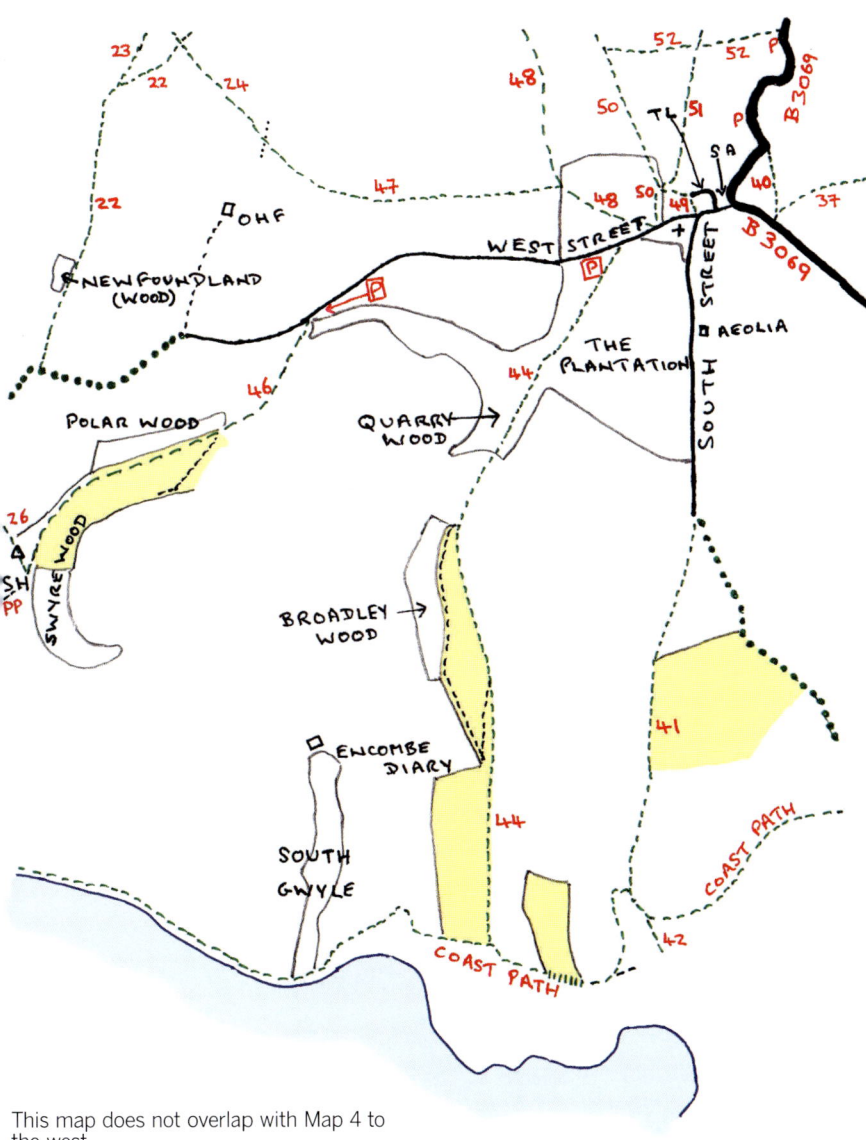

This map does not overlap with Map 4 to the west.

OHF   Orchard Hill Farm
SA   Scott Arms
SH   Swyre Head
TL   The Lane

Map 9: Arne

CRICHTON'S HEATH

BIG WOOD

SP

RN

TC

GRIP HEATH

ARNE ROAD

COOMBE HEATH

BANK GATE COTTAGES

RN   RSPB noticeboard
SP   Shipstal Point
TC   Telegraph cable notice

Map 10: Wytch and Bushey

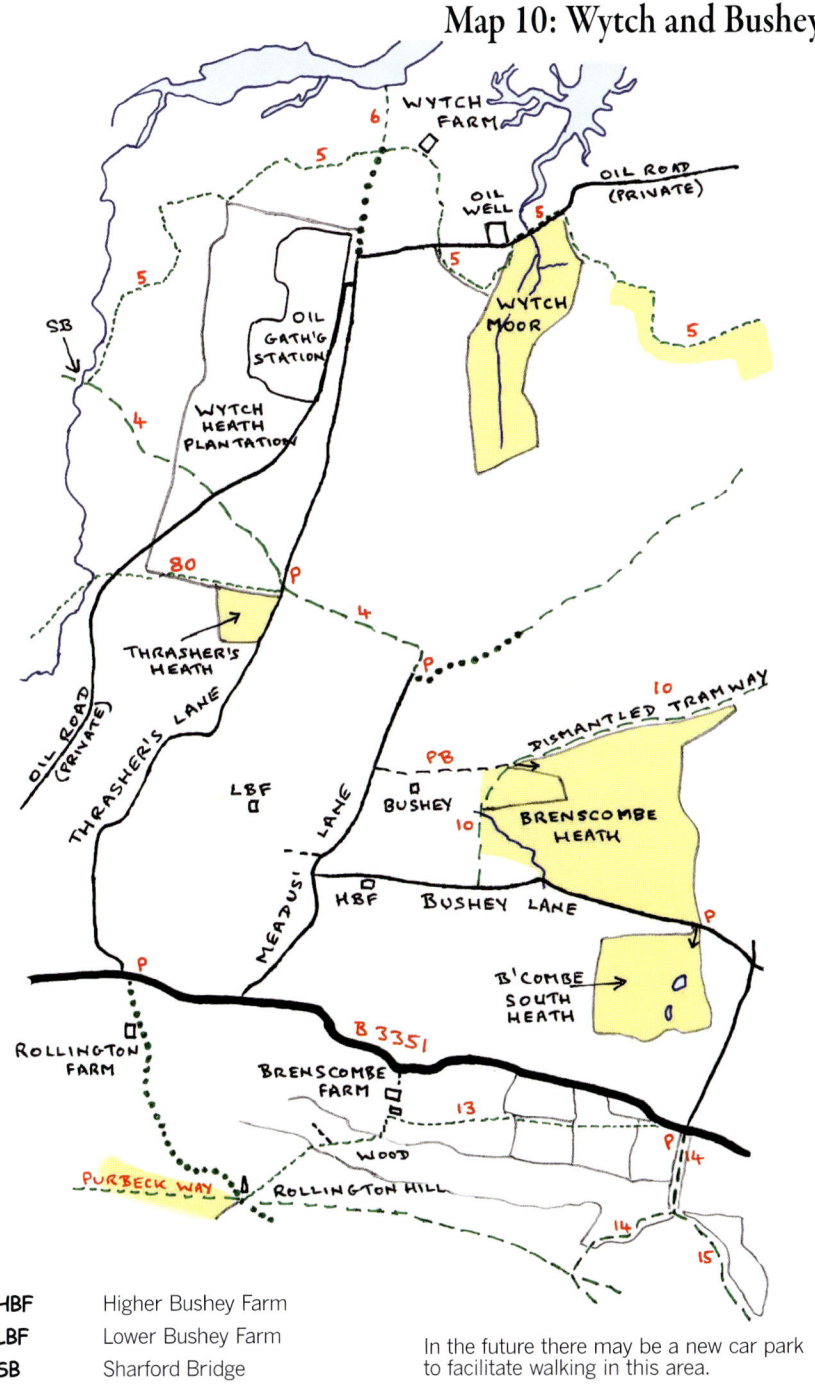

HBF   Higher Bushey Farm
LBF   Lower Bushey Farm
SB   Sharford Bridge

In the future there may be a new car park to facilitate walking in this area.

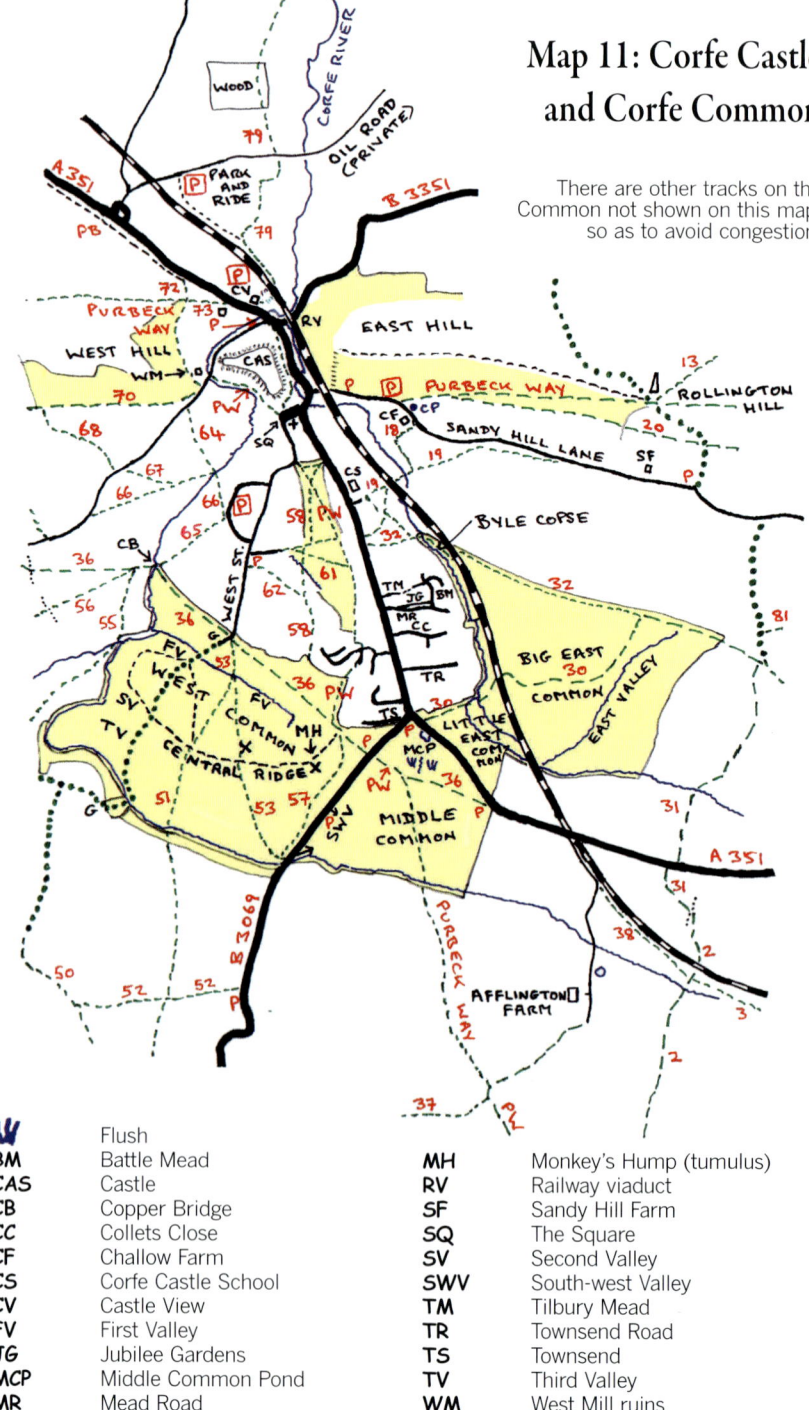

Map 11: Corfe Castle and Corfe Common

There are other tracks on the Common not shown on this map, so as to avoid congestion.

W	Flush	**MH**	Monkey's Hump (tumulus)
BM	Battle Mead	**RV**	Railway viaduct
CAS	Castle	**SF**	Sandy Hill Farm
CB	Copper Bridge	**SQ**	The Square
CC	Collets Close	**SV**	Second Valley
CF	Challow Farm	**SWV**	South-west Valley
CS	Corfe Castle School	**TM**	Tilbury Mead
CV	Castle View	**TR**	Townsend Road
FV	First Valley	**TS**	Townsend
JG	Jubilee Gardens	**TV**	Third Valley
MCP	Middle Common Pond	**WM**	West Mill ruins
MR	Mead Road		

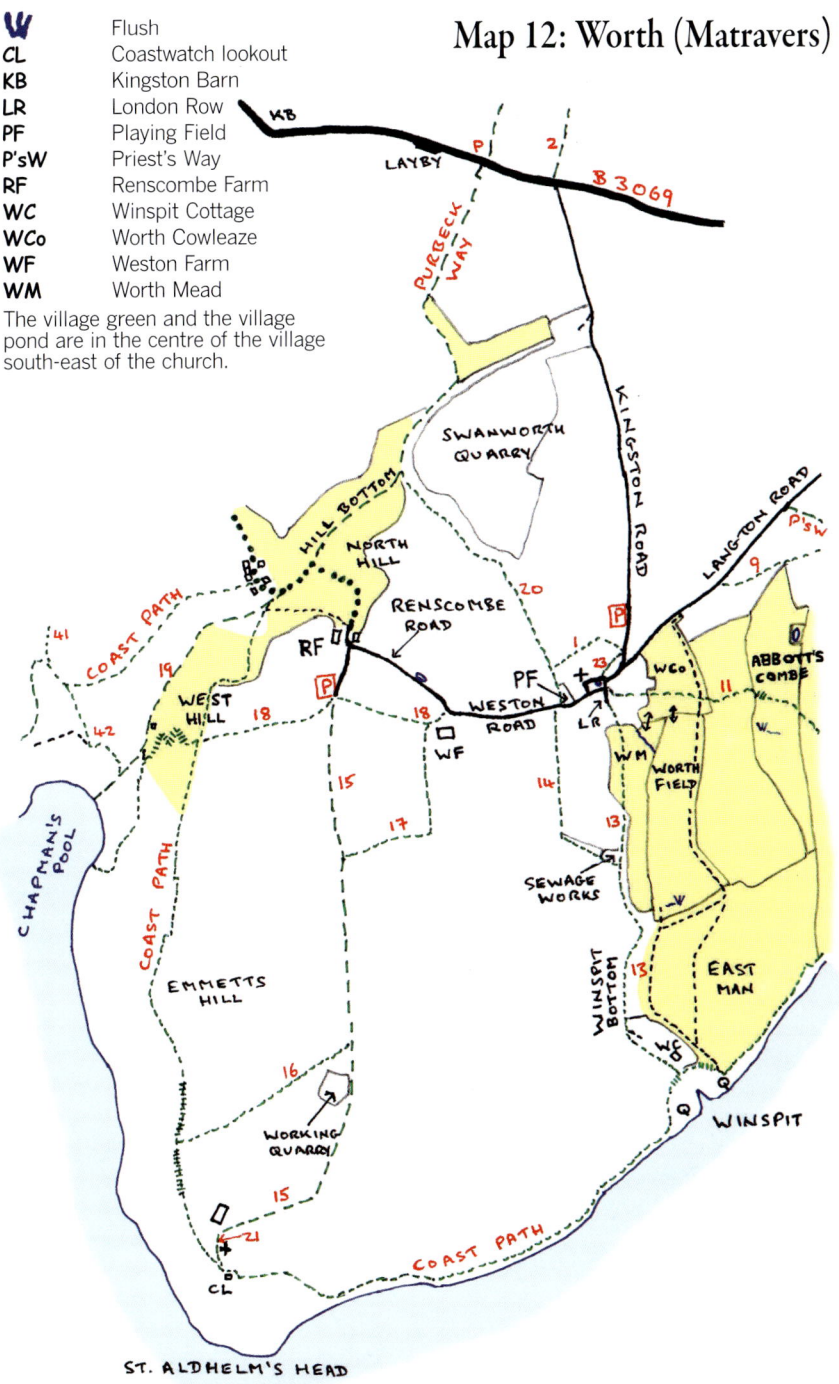

Map 12: Worth (Matravers)

W Flush
CL Coastwatch lookout
KB Kingston Barn
LR London Row
PF Playing Field
P'sW Priest's Way
RF Renscombe Farm
WC Winspit Cottage
WCo Worth Cowleaze
WF Weston Farm
WM Worth Mead

The village green and the village pond are in the centre of the village south-east of the church.

KB

LAYBY

P

2

B 3069

PURBECK WAY

KINGSTON ROAD

LANGTON ROAD

P'sW

SWANWORTH QUARRY

HILL BOTTOM

NORTH HILL

RENSCOMBE ROAD

20

9

COAST PATH

41

19

RF

P

WEST HILL

18

18

WF

WESTON ROAD

PF

LR

WCo

ABBOTT'S COMBE

11

W

WM

WORTH FIELD

42

15

14

17

13

CHAPMAN'S POOL

COAST PATH

SEWAGE WORKS

EMMETTS HILL

16

WINSPIT BOTTOM

13

EAST MAN

WORKING QUARRY

WC

15

21

CL

Q

WINSPIT

COAST PATH

ST. ALDHELM'S HEAD

Map 13: Rempstone and Ower

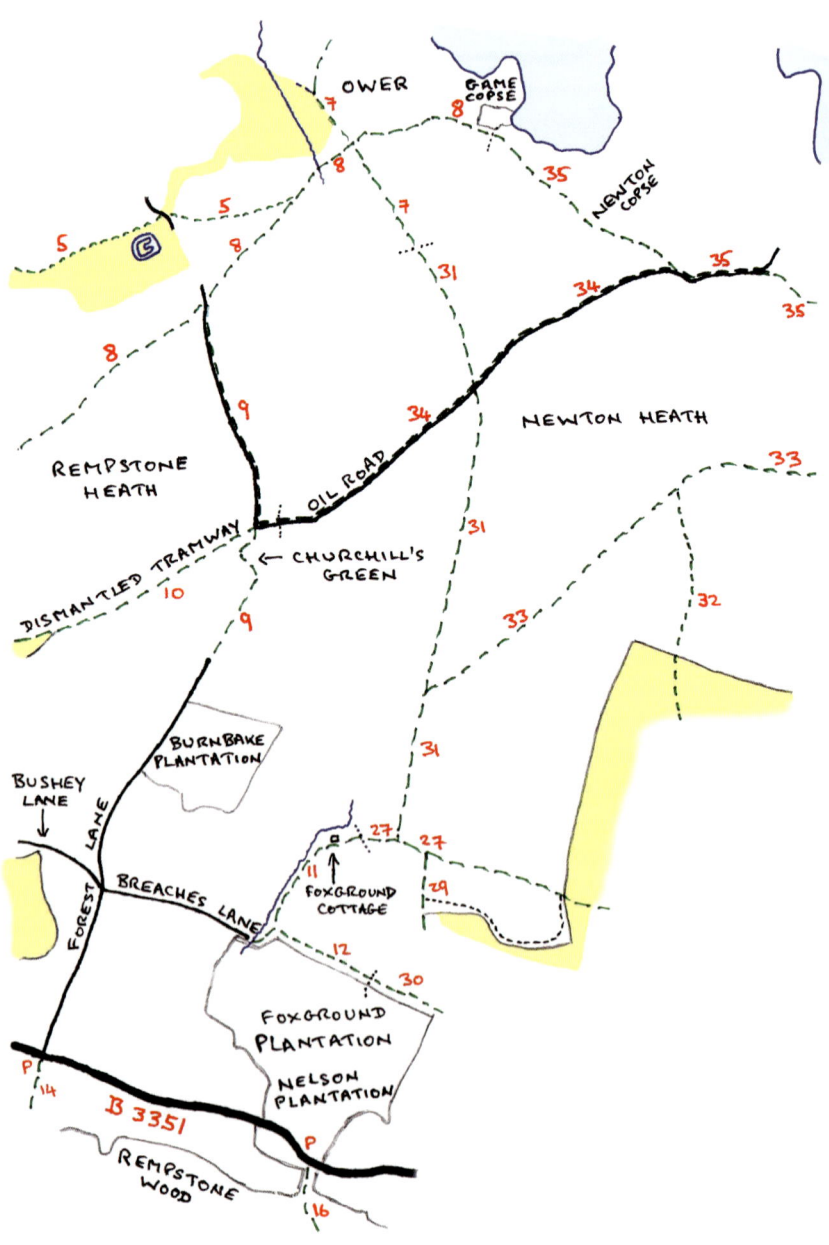

OWER

GAME COPSE

NEWTON COPSE

REMPSTONE HEATH

NEWTON HEATH

OIL ROAD

DISMANTLED TRAMWAY

← CHURCHILL'S GREEN

BURNBAKE PLANTATION

BUSHEY LANE →

FOREST LANE

BREACHES LANE

FOXGROUND COTTAGE

FOXGROUND PLANTATION

NELSON PLANTATION

B 3351

REMPSTONE WOOD

In the future there may be a new car park to facilitate walking in this area.

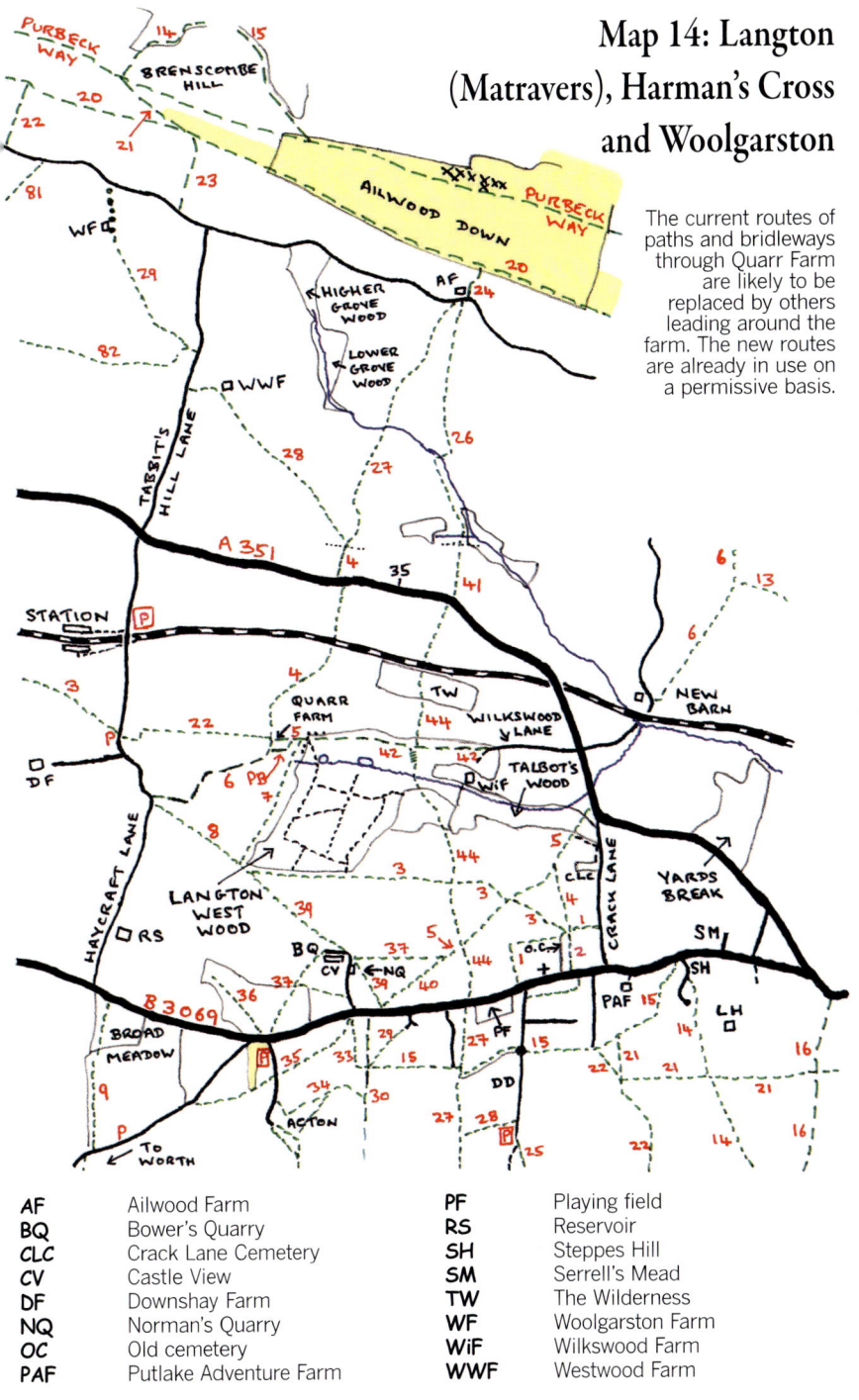

Map 14: Langton (Matravers), Harman's Cross and Woolgarston

The current routes of paths and bridleways through Quarr Farm are likely to be replaced by others leading around the farm. The new routes are already in use on a permissive basis.

AF	Ailwood Farm	**PF**	Playing field
BQ	Bower's Quarry	**RS**	Reservoir
CLC	Crack Lane Cemetery	**SH**	Steppes Hill
CV	Castle View	**SM**	Serrell's Mead
DF	Downshay Farm	**TW**	The Wilderness
NQ	Norman's Quarry	**WF**	Woolgarston Farm
OC	Old cemetery	**WiF**	Wilkswood Farm
PAF	Putlake Adventure Farm	**WWF**	Westwood Farm

Map 15: Wares (west) and area north of them

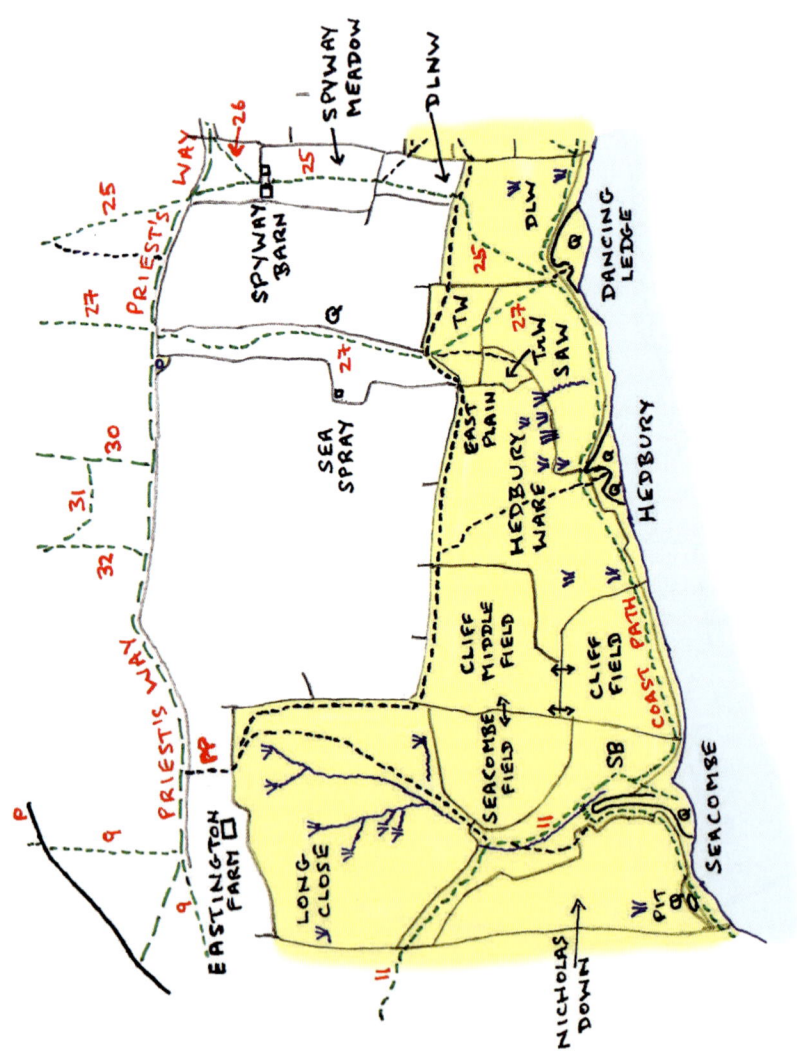

W	Flush
DLNW	Dancing Ledge North Ware
DLW	Dancing Ledge Ware
SAW	Scratch Arse Ware
SB	Seacombe Bottom
TrW	Triangular Ware
TW	Taylor's Ware

Map 16: Wares (east) and area north of them

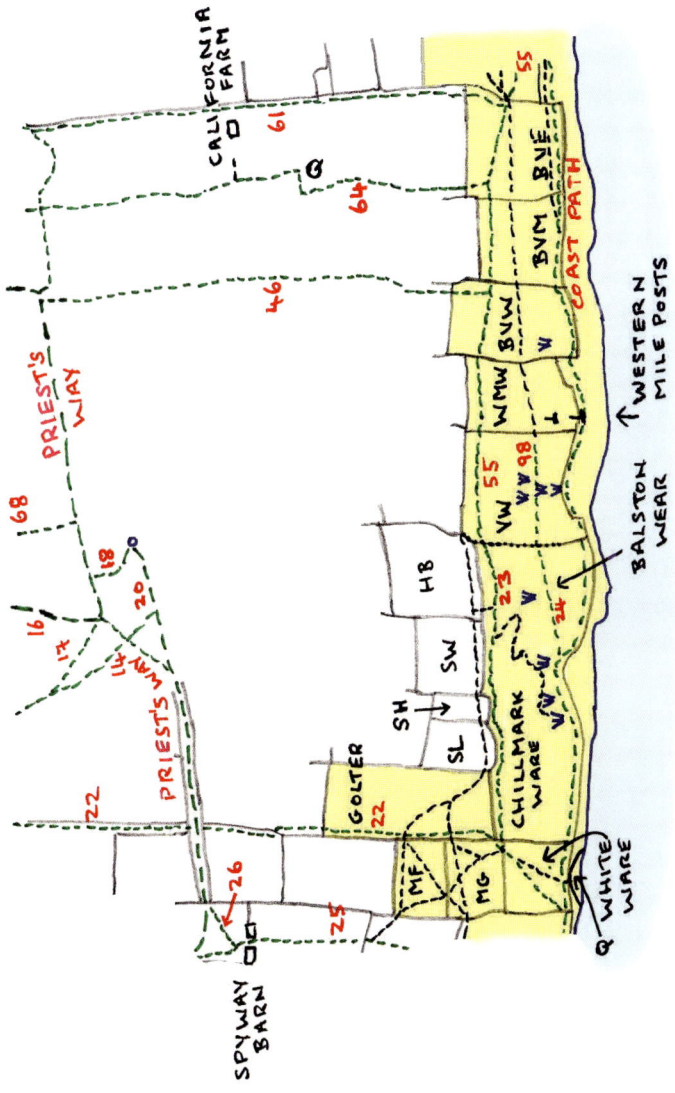

W	Flush	**MG**	Middle Ground
BVE	Belle Vue East Ware	**SH**	Second Hayfield
BVM	Belle Vue Middle Ware	**SL**	Sheep's Leet
BVW	Belle Vue West Ware	**SW**	Sherwood's Wear
HB	Hay Brimble	**VW**	Verney Ware
MF	Middle Field	**WMW**	Western Mile Posts Ware

Map 17: Godlingston Heath

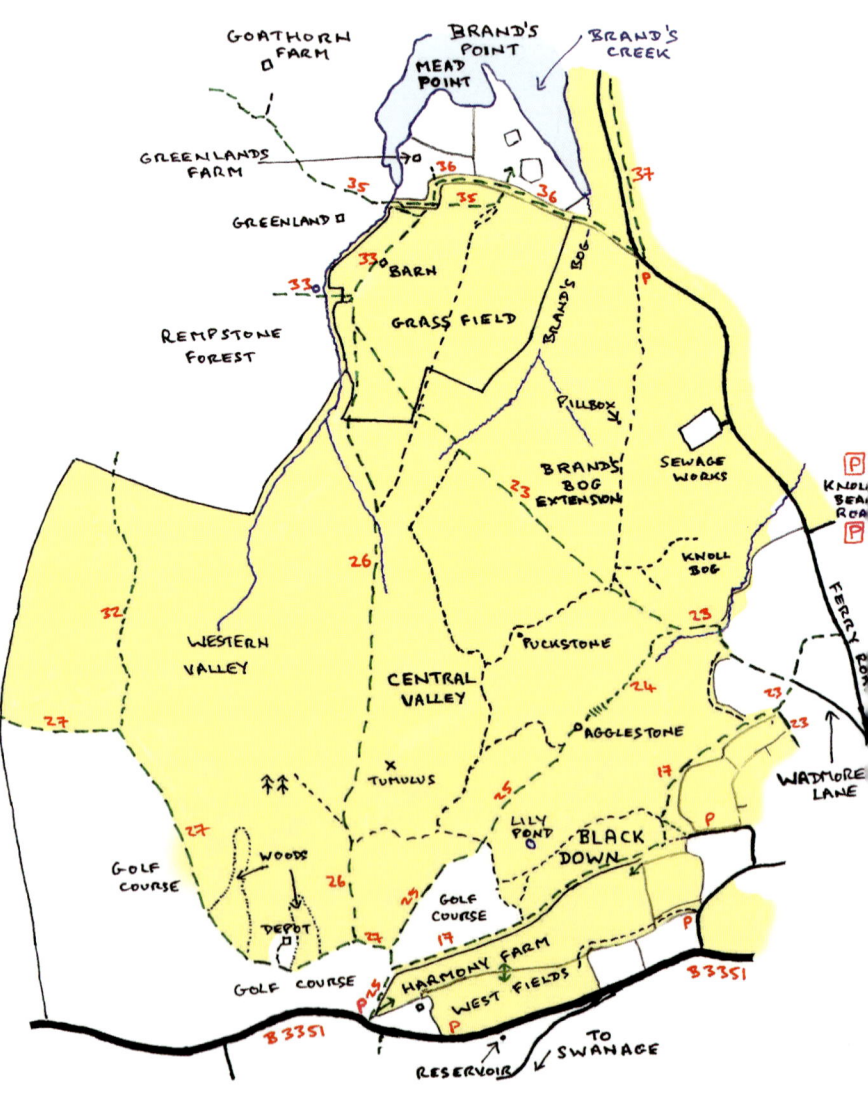

There are other tracks on the heath not shown on this map, so as to avoid congestion.

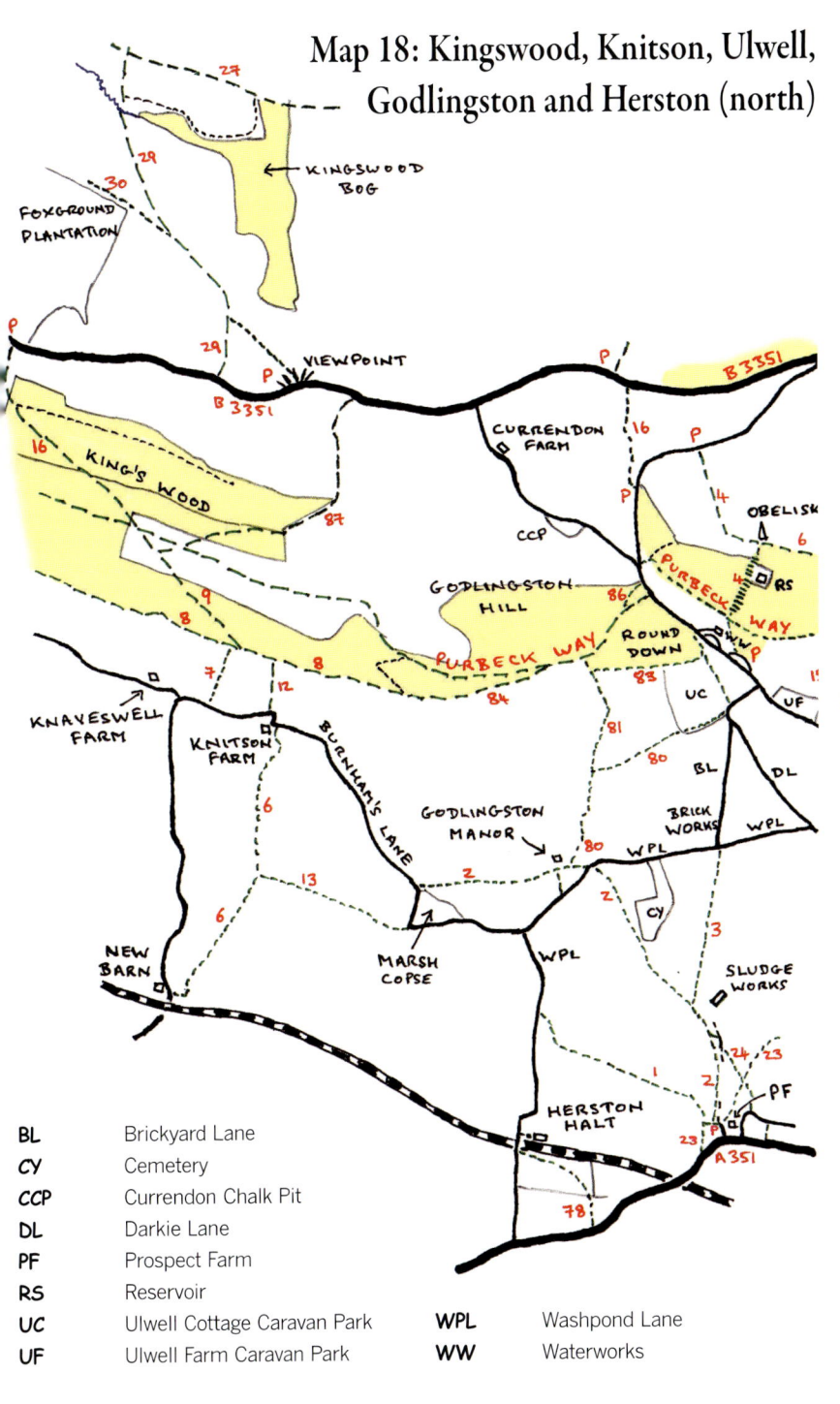

Map 18: Kingswood, Knitson, Ulwell, Godlingston and Herston (north)

27

KINGSWOOD BOG

29

30

FOXGROUND PLANTATION

P

29

VIEWPOINT

P

B 3351

B 3351

16

CURRENDON FARM

P

16

P

4

OBELISK

6

KING'S WOOD

87

CCP

P

4

RS

PURBECK WAY

GODLINGSTON HILL

86

9

8

PURBECK WAY

ROUND DOWN

WW

P

15

7

12

8

84

83

UC

UF

KNAVESWELL FARM

KNITSON FARM

BURNHAM'S LANE

81

80

BL

DL

6

GODLINGSTON MANOR

80

BRICK WORKS

WPL

13

2

WPL

CY

3

6

MARSH COPSE

WPL

SLUDGE WORKS

NEW BARN

24 23

1

2

PF

HERSTON HALT

23

P

A 351

78

BL	Brickyard Lane
CY	Cemetery
CCP	Currendon Chalk Pit
DL	Darkie Lane
PF	Prospect Farm
RS	Reservoir
UC	Ulwell Cottage Caravan Park
UF	Ulwell Farm Caravan Park

WPL	Washpond Lane
WW	Waterworks

Map 19: Studland Heath and Shell Bay

BQ	Barbeque area
CC	Curlew Cottage ruins
CR	Concrete ruins
DP	Dinghy park
EH	Egret Hide
FO	Ferry offices
PW	Primrose Way
RS	Roundabout sign
S+C	Shop and cafe
SC	Study Centre
ST	Sand Dune Nature Trail
TB	Toll booth
WH	Woodland Hide
WT	Woodland Nature Trail

The 'entrance' to Spur Bog is a narrow path opening out 25m east of Ferry Road, from which latter point distances are given in the Plant List. There are other tracks on the heath not shown on this map, so as to avoid congestion. Red dots mark Little Sea Beaches, numbered 1 to 6 in the south-east; there are two more in Western Arm. Parking is possible on verges in many places in the north half of Ferry Road.

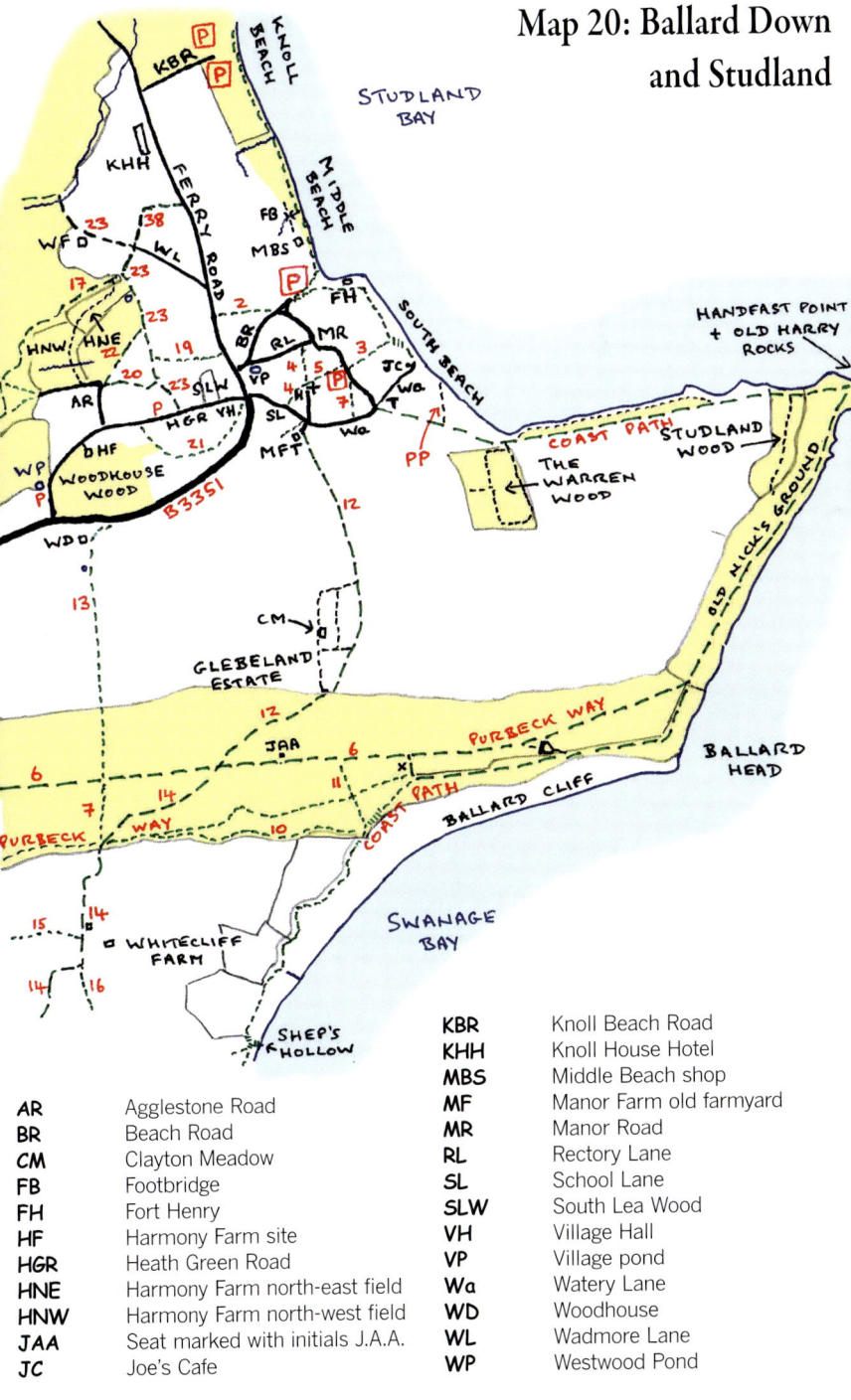

Map 20: Ballard Down and Studland

STUDLAND BAY

KNOLL BEACH

MIDDLE BEACH

STUDLAND BAY

HANDFAST POINT
+ OLD HARRY
ROCKS

COAST PATH

STUDLAND
WOOD

THE
WARREN
WOOD

OLD NICK'S GROUND

SOUTH BEACH

B3351

WOODHOUSE
WOOD

GLEBELAND
ESTATE

PURBECK WAY

BALLARD
HEAD

COAST PATH

BALLARD CLIFF

PURBECK   WAY

SWANAGE
BAY

WHITECLIFF
FARM

SHEP'S
HOLLOW

AR	Agglestone Road	
BR	Beach Road	
CM	Clayton Meadow	
FB	Footbridge	
FH	Fort Henry	
HF	Harmony Farm site	
HGR	Heath Green Road	
HNE	Harmony Farm north-east field	
HNW	Harmony Farm north-west field	
JAA	Seat marked with initials J.A.A.	
JC	Joe's Cafe	

KBR	Knoll Beach Road
KHH	Knoll House Hotel
MBS	Middle Beach shop
MF	Manor Farm old farmyard
MR	Manor Road
RL	Rectory Lane
SL	School Lane
SLW	South Lea Wood
VH	Village Hall
VP	Village pond
Wa	Watery Lane
WD	Woodhouse
WL	Wadmore Lane
WP	Westwood Pond

Map 21: Durlston area

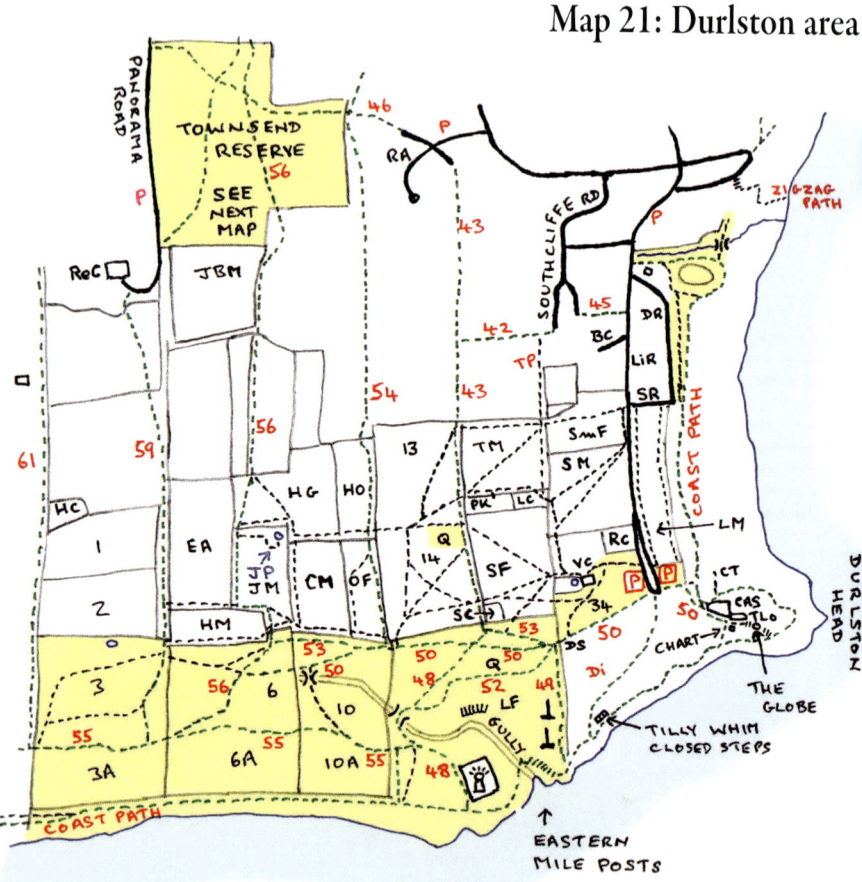

This map is of slightly larger scale than most other maps, so as to accommodate more detail.

BC	Boundary Close	LR	Lighthouse Road
CAS	Castle	OF	Ox-eye Daisy Field
CM	Centenary Meadow	PK	Paddock
CT	Caravan Terrace	RA	Russell Avenue
Di	Diagonal Path	RC	Reservoir Copse
DR	Durlston Road	ReC	Recycling centre
DS	Dry Stone Walling Centre	SC	Small Copse
EA	Eight Acres	SF	South Field
HC	Hingston Copse	SM	Skipworth Meadow
HG	Herren Ground	SmF	Smith Field
HM	Hoggett Mead	SR	Solent Road
HO	Holecombe (field)	TLo	The Lookout
JBM	Jack Baiss Meadow	TM	Tasker's Meadow
JM	Johnston Meadow	TP	Tasker's Path
JP	Johnston Pond	VC	Visitor Centre
LC	Large Copse		
LF	Lighthouse Field		
LM	Long Meadow		

The Durlston Country Park field numbering scheme has been used for fields which do not have individual names.

Map 21A: Townsend Reserve (Swanage)
(large scale)

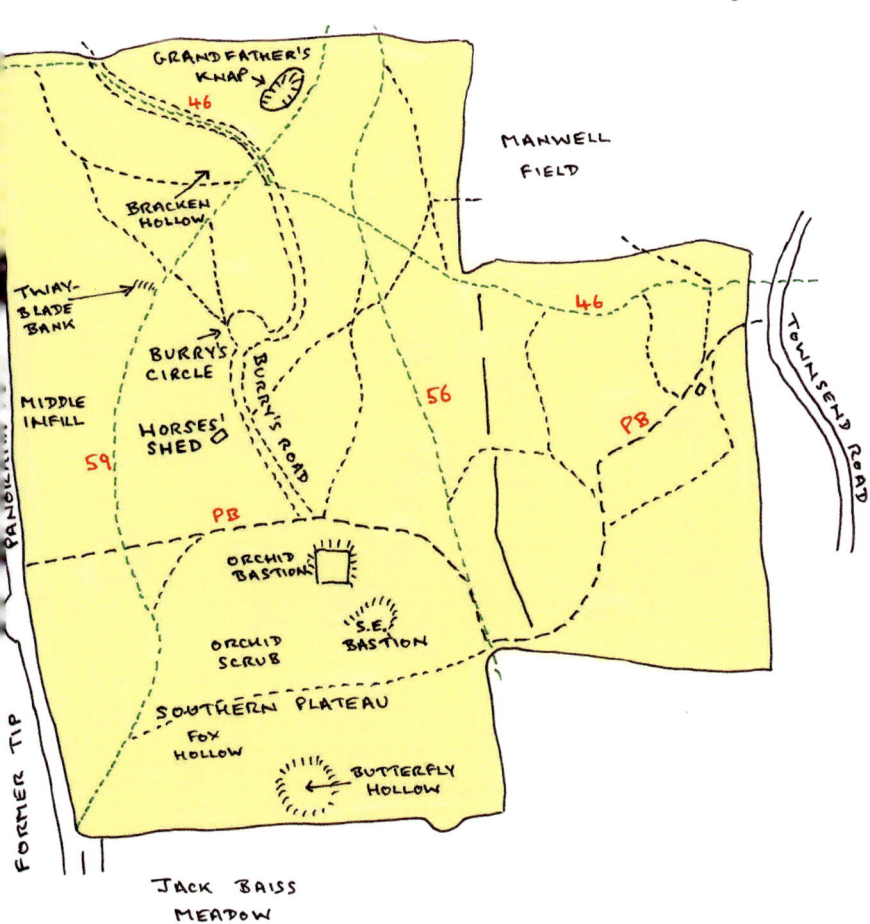

GRANDFATHER'S KNAP
46
MANWELL FIELD
BRACKEN HOLLOW
TWAY-BLADE BANK
46
BURRY'S CIRCLE
BURRY'S ROAD
56
MIDDLE INFILL
HORSES' SHED
59
PB
TOWNSEND ROAD
PB
ORCHID BASTION
S.E. BASTION
ORCHID SCRUB
SOUTHERN PLATEAU
FOX HOLLOW
BUTTERFLY HOLLOW
FORMER TIP
PANORAMA
JACK BAISS MEADOW

Map 22: Brownsea

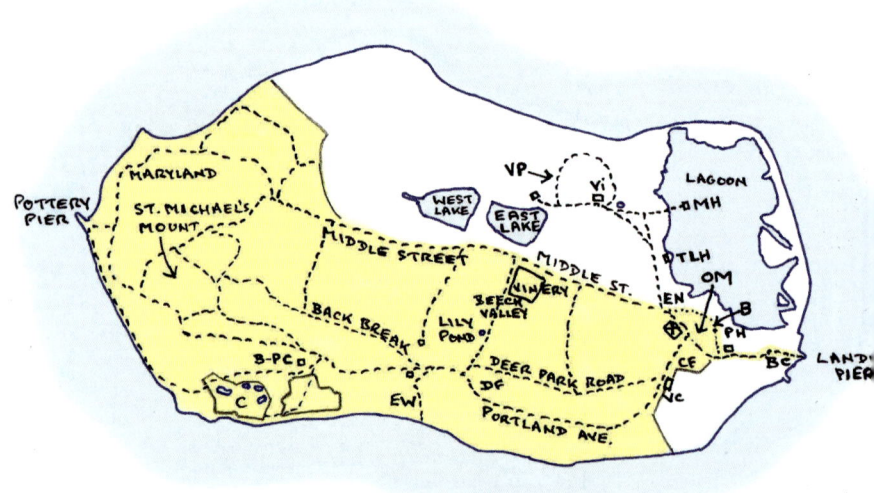

BC	Brownsea Cafe	**OM**	Orchid Meadow
B-PC	Baden-Powell Outdoor Centre	**PH**	Public Hide
CF	Church Field	**TLH**	Two-level Hide
DF	Daffodil Field	**Vi**	The Villa
EN	Entrance to nature reserve	**VC**	Visitor Centre
EW	Easy way down to shore	**VP**	Venetia Park
MH	Macdonald Hide		